T0211707

Lecture Notes in Computer Science 9037

Commenced Publication in 1973
Founding and Former Series Editors:
Gerhard Goos, Juris Hartmanis, and Jan van Leeuwen

More information about this series at http://www.springer.com/series/7408

Tom Holvoet · Mirko Viroli (Eds.)

Coordination Models and Languages

17th IFIP WG 6.1 International Conference, COORDINATION 2015
Held as Part of the 10th International Federated Conference
on Distributed Computing Techniques, DisCoTec 2015
Grenoble, France, June 2–4, 2015
Proceedings

 Springer

Editors
Tom Holvoet
University of Leuven
Heverlee
Belgium

Mirko Viroli
Alma Mater Studiorum–Università di Bologna
Cesena
Italy

ISSN 0302-9743   ISSN 1611-3349   (electronic)
Lecture Notes in Computer Science
ISBN 978-3-319-19281-9   ISBN 978-3-319-19282-6   (eBook)
DOI 10.1007/978-3-319-19282-6

Library of Congress Control Number: 2015939278

LNCS Sublibrary: SL2 – Programming and Software Engineering

Springer Cham Heidelberg New York Dordrecht London
© IFIP International Federation for Information Processing 2015

Printed on acid-free paper

Springer International Publishing AG Switzerland is part of Springer Science+Business Media
(www.springer.com)

Foreword

The 10th International Federated Conference on Distributed Computing Techniques (DisCoTec) took place in Montbonnot, near Grenoble, France, during June 2–5, 2015. It was hosted and organized by Inria, the French National Research Institute in Computer Science and Control. The DisCoTec series is one of the major events sponsored by the International Federation for Information Processing (IFIP). It comprises three conferences:

- COORDINATION, the IFIP WG6.1 International Conference on Coordination Models and Languages.
- DAIS, the IFIP WG6.1 International Conference on Distributed Applications and Interoperable Systems.
- FORTE, the IFIP WG6.1 International Conference on Formal Techniques for Distributed Objects, Components and Systems.

Together, these conferences cover a broad spectrum of distributed computing subjects, ranging from theoretical foundations and formal description techniques to systems research issues.

Each day of the federated event began with a plenary keynote speaker nominated by one of the conferences. The three invited speakers were Alois Ferscha (Johannes Kepler Universität, Linz, Austria), Leslie Lamport (Microsoft Research, USA), and Willy Zwaenepoel (EPFL, Lausanne, Switzerland).

Associated with the federated event were also three satellite workshops, that took place on June 5, 2015:

- The 2nd International Workshop on Formal Reasoning in Distributed Algorithms (FRIDA), with a keynote speech by Leslie Lamport (Microsoft Research, USA).
- The 8th International Workshop on Interaction and Concurrency Experience (ICE), with keynote lectures by Jade Alglave (University College London, UK) and Steve Ross-Talbot (ZDLC, Cognizant Technology Solutions, London, UK).
- The 2nd International Workshop on Meta Models for Process Languages (MeMo).

Sincere thanks go to the chairs and members of the Program and Steering Committees of the involved conferences and workshops for their highly appreciated efforts. Organizing DisCoTec was only possible thanks to the dedicated work of the Organizing Committee from Inria Grenoble-Rhône-Alpes, including Sophie Azzaro, Vanessa Peregrin, Martine Consigney, Alain Kersaudy, Sophie Quinton, Jean-Bernard Stefani, and the excellent support from Catherine Nuel and the people at Insight Outside. Finally, many thanks go to IFIP WG6.1 for sponsoring this event, and to Inria Rhône-Alpes and his director Patrick Gros for their support and sponsorship.

Alain Girault
DisCoTec 2015 General Chair

DisCoTec Steering Committee

Preface

This volume contains the papers presented at COORDINATION 2015: the 17th IFIP WG 6.1 International Conference on Coordination Models and Languages held during June 2–4, 2015 in Grenoble. The conference is the premier forum for publishing research results and experience reports on software technologies for collaboration and coordination in concurrent, distributed, and complex systems. The key focus of the conference is the quest for high-level abstractions that can capture interaction patterns and mechanisms occurring at all levels of the software architecture, up to the end-user domain. COORDINATION called for high-quality contributions on the usage, study, formal analysis, design, and implementation of languages, models, and techniques for coordination in distributed, concurrent, pervasive, multi-agent, and multicore software systems.

The Program Committee (PC) of COORDINATION 2015 consisted of 32 top researchers from 12 different countries. We received 36 submissions out of which the PC selected 14 full papers and 1 short paper for inclusion in the program. All submissions were reviewed by three to four independent referees; papers were selected based on their quality, originality, contribution, clarity of presentation, and relevance to the conference topics. The review process included an in-depth discussion phase, during which the merits of all papers were discussed by the PC. The process culminated in a shepherding phase whereby some of the authors received active guidance by one member of the PC in order to produce a high-quality final version. The selected papers constituted a program covering a varied range of techniques for system coordination: tuple-based coordination, multi-party and logic-based coordination of ensembles, constraints-based coordination, agent-oriented techniques, and finally coordination based on shared spaces. The program was further enhanced by an invited talk by Alois Ferscha from Johannes Kepler Universität Linz (Austria).

The success of COORDINATION 2015 was due to the dedication of many people. We thank the authors for submitting high-quality papers, the PC and their subreviewers, for their careful reviews, and lively discussions during the final selection process, and the Publicity Chair for helping us with advertisement of the CFP. We thank the providers of the EasyChair conference management system, which was used to run the review process and to facilitate the preparation of the proceedings. Finally, we thank the Inria Grenoble—Rhône-Alpes Organizing Committee from Grenoble, led by Alain Girault, for its contribution in making the logistic aspects of COORDINATION 2015 a success.

June 2015

Tom Holvoet
Mirko Viroli

Organization

Program Committee Chairs

Tom Holvoet   University of Leuven, Belgium
Mirko Viroli   Alma Mater Studiorum–Università di Bologna, Italy

Publicity Chair

Giacomo Cabri   University of Modena and Reggio Emilia, Italy

Program Committee

Gul Agha   University of Illinois at Urbana–Champaign, USA
Farhad Arbab   CWI and Leiden University, The Netherlands
Jacob Beal   BBN Technologies, USA
Olivier Boissier   École des Mines de Saint-Etienne, France
Ferruccio Damiani   Università di Torino, Italy
Wolfgang De Meuter   Vrije Universiteit Brussel, Belgium
Rocco De Nicola   IMT - Institute for Advanced Studies Lucca, Italy
Ed Durfee   University of Michigan, USA
Schahram Dustdar   Technische Unversität Wien, Austria
Gianluigi Ferrari   Università degli Studi di Pis a, Italy
José Luiz Fiadeiro   Royal Holloway, University of London, UK
Tom Holvoet   University of Leuven, Belgium
Valerie Issarny   Inria, France
Christine Julien   University of Texas at Austin, USA
Sarit Kraus   Bar-Ilan University, Israel
Eva Kühn   Vienna University of Technology, Austria
Marino Miculan   University of Udine, Italy
Hanne Riis Nielson   Technical University of Denmark, Denmark
Andrea Omicini   Alma Mater Studiorum–Università di Bologna, Italy
Sascha Ossowski   University Rey Juan Carlos, Spain
Paolo Petta   Austrian Research Institute for Artificial Intelligence, Austria

Rosario Pugliese   Università degli Studi di Firenze, Italy
Alessandro Ricci   Alma Mater Studiorum–Università di Bologna,
                            Italy
Juan Antonio Rodriguez   Artificial Intelligence Research Institute (IIIA),
                            Spain
Carles Sierra   Artificial Intelligence Research Institute (IIIA),
                            Spain
Marjan Sirjani   Reykjavík University, Iceland
Carolyn Talcott   SRI International, USA
Emilio Tuosto   University of Leicester, UK
Mirko Viroli   Alma Mater Studiorum–Università di Bologna,
                            Italy
Herbert Wiklicky   Imperial College London, UK
Martin Wirsing   Ludwig-Maximilians-Universität München,
                            Germany
Franco Zambonelli   Università di Modena e Reggio Emilia, Italy

Steering Committee

Gul Agha   University of Illinois at Urbana–Champaign, USA
Farhad Arbab   CWI and Leiden University, The Netherlands
Dave Clarke   Uppsala University, Sweden
Tom Holvoet   University of Leuven, Belgium
Christine Julien   University of Texas at Austin, USA
Eva Kühn   Vienna University of Technology, Austria
Wolfgang De Meuter   Vrije Universiteit Brussel, Belgium
Rocco De Nicola   IMT - Institute for Advanced Studies Lucca, Italy
Rosario Pugliese   Università degli Studi di Firenze, Italy
Marjan Sirjani   Reykjavík University, Iceland
Carolyn Talcott   SRI International, USA
Vasco T. Vasconcelos   University of Lisbon, Portugal
Mirko Viroli   Alma Mater Studiorum–Università di Bologna,
                            Italy
Gianluigi Zavattaro   University of Bologna, Italy

Additional Reviewers

Andric, Marina   DeJonge, Dave
Bocchi, Laura   De Koster, Joeri
Bodei, Chiara   Delzanno, Giorgio
Bruni, Roberto   Dokter, Kasper
Cejka, Stephan   Galletta, Letterio
Chirita, Claudia   Hamboeck, Thomas
Coppieters, Tim   Hildebrandt, Thomas
Crass, Stefan   Hoste, Lode

Jongmans, Sung-Shik T.Q.
Loreti, Michele
Margheri, Andrea
Mariani, Stefano
Mohaqeqi, Morteza
Morales, Javier
Osman, Nardine
Padovani, Luca
Palmskog, Karl

Peressotti, Marco
Proenca, Jose
Renaux, Thierry
Sabahi Kaviani, Zeynab
Sabouri, Hamideh
Sproston, Jeremy
Tiezzi, Francesco
Torquati, Massimo
Varshosaz, Mahsa

Contents

Tuple-Based Coordination

Coordinating Ensembles

Constraints

Agent-Oriented Techniques

Shared Spaces

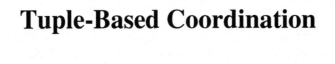

Tuple-Based Coordination

Replica-Based High-Performance Tuple Space Computing

Marina Andrić[1], Rocco De Nicola[1], and Alberto Lluch Lafuente[2(✉)]

[1] IMT Institute for Advanced Studies Lucca, Lucca, Italy
[2] DTU Compute, Technical University of Denmark, Kgs. Lyngby, Denmark
{marina.andric,rocco.denicola}@imtlucca.it, albl@dtu.dk

Abstract. We present the tuple-based coordination language RepliKlaim, which enriches Klaim with primitives for replica-aware coordination. Our overall goal is to offer suitable solutions to the challenging problems of data distribution and locality in large-scale high performance computing. In particular, RepliKlaim allows the programmer to specify and coordinate the replication of shared data items and the desired consistency properties. The programmer can hence exploit such flexible mechanisms to adapt data distribution and locality to the needs of the application, so to improve performance in terms of concurrency and data access. We investigate issues related to replica consistency, provide an operational semantics that guides the implementation of the language, and discuss the main synchronization mechanisms of our prototypical run-time framework. Finally, we provide a performance analysis, which includes scenarios where replica-based specifications and relaxed consistency provide significant performance gains.

1 Introduction

The scale of parallel and distributed computing systems is growing fast to meet the computational needs of our society, ranging from (big) data-driven analyses to massively distributed services. One of the key points in parallel and distributed computing is the division and communication of data between computational entities. Better performances are achieved with increased data locality and minimized data communication. Increasing data locality can be easily achieved by replicating data, but this comes of course at a high price in terms of synchronization if replicated data need to be kept consistent. As a matter of fact the trade-off between consistency and performance is one of the big dilemmas in distributed and parallel computing.

The recent years have seen the advent of technologies that provide software engineers and programmers with flexible mechanisms to conveniently specify data locality, communication and consistency to the benefit of their applications. A pragmatical example for large-scale distributed services is the GOOGLE CLOUD STORAGE[1] service, that allows users to geographically specify data locality (to

---

Research supported by the European projects IP 257414 ASCENS and STReP 600708 QUANTICOL, and the Italian PRIN 2010LHT4KM CINA.
[1] https://cloud.google.com/storage/

© IFIP International Federation for Information Processing 2015
T. Holvoet and M. Viroli (Eds.): COORDINATION 2015, LNCS 9037, pp. 3–18, 2015.
DOI: 10.1007/978-3-319-19282-6_1

reduce cost and speed up access) and provides different consistency levels (e.g. strong and eventual consistency) for different operations (e.g. single data and list operations).

In the realm of parallel computing, one can find several high performance computing languages that offer similar support for designing efficient applications. De-facto standards such as OPENMP[2] (for shared memory multiprocessing) and MPI[3] (for message-passing large-scale distributed computing) are being challenged by new languages and programming models that try to address concerns such as the *memory address to physical location* problem. This is a general concern that needs to be solved when programming scalable systems with a large number of computational nodes. In languages X10[4], UPC[5] and TITANIUM [19], this problem is solved via the *partitioned global address space* (PGAS) model. This model is a middle way approach between shared-memory (OPENMP) and distributed-memory (MPI) programming models, as it combines performance and data locality (partitioning) of distributed-memory and global address space of a shared-memory model. In the PGAS model, variables and arrays are either *shared* or *local*. Each processor has private memory for local data and shared memory for globally shared data.

Summarizing, two key aspects in the design of distributed and parallel systems and software are *data locality* and *data consistency*. A proper design of those aspects can bring significant performance advantages, e.g. in terms of minimization of communication between computational entities.

Contribution. We believe that those two aspects cannot be hidden to the programmer of the high performance applications of the future. Instead, we believe that programmers should be equipped with suitable primitives to deal with those aspects in a natural and flexible way. This paper instantiates such philosophy in the coordination language RepliKlaim, a variant of Klaim [12] with first-class features to deal with data locality and consistency. In particular, the idea is to let the programmer specify and coordinate data replicas and operate on them with different levels of consistency. The programmer can hence exploit such flexible mechanisms to adapt data distribution and locality to the needs of the application, so to improve performance in terms of concurrency and data access. We investigate issues related to replica consistency, provide an operational semantics that guides the implementation of the language, and discuss the main synchronisation mechanisms of our implementation. Finally, we provide a performance evaluation study in our prototype run-time system. Our experiments include scenarios where replica-based specifications and relaxed consistency provide significant performance gains.

Structure of the Paper. This paper is organised as follows. Section 2 presents RepliKlaim and discusses some examples that illustrate its semantics. Section 3

---

[2] www.openmp.org/

[3] http://www.open-mpi.org/

[4] x10-lang.org

[5] upc.lbl.gov

$$
\begin{array}{llll}
N & ::= & \mathbf{0} \mid l :: [K,P] \mid N \parallel N & \text{(networks)} \\
K & ::= & \emptyset \mid \langle et_i, L \rangle \mid K, K & \text{(repositories)} \\
P & ::= & \mathsf{nil} \mid A.P \mid P + P \mid P \mid P & \text{(processes)} \\
A & ::= & \mathsf{out_s}(t_i)@L \mid \mathsf{in_s}(T_\iota)@\ell \mid \mathsf{read}(T_\iota)@\ell & \text{(strong actions)} \\
& & \mathsf{out_w}(t_i)@L \mid \mathsf{in_w}(T_\iota)@\ell \mid & \text{(weak actions)} \\
& & \mathsf{in_u}(T_\iota, L)@\ell \mid \mathsf{out_u}(et_i, L)@\ell & \text{(unsafe actions)} \\
L & ::= & \epsilon \mid \ell \mid \underline{\ell} \mid L \bullet L & \text{(locations)}
\end{array}
$$

Fig. 1. Syntax of RepliKlaim

provides some details about our prototype implementation and presents a set of performance experiments. Section 4 discusses related works. Section 5 concludes the paper and identifies possible future works.

2 RepliKlaim: Klaim with Replicas

We present our language RepliKlaim in this section. We start with the definition of the syntax in Section 2.1 and proceed then with the description of the operational semantics in Section 2.2. Section 2.3 discusses some examples aimed at providing some insights on semantics, implementation and performance aspects, later detailed in Section 3.

2.1 RepliKlaim: Syntax

The syntax of RepliKlaim is based on Klaim [12]. The main differences are the absence of mobility features (i.e. the eval primitive and allocation environments) and the extension of communication primitives to explicitly deal with replicas.

Definition 1 (RepliKlaim Syntax). *The syntax of RepliKlaim is defined by the grammar of Fig. 1, where $\mathcal{L}$ is a set of locations (ranged over by $\ell, \ell', \dots$), $\mathcal{U}$ is a set of values (ranged over by $u, v, \dots$), $\mathcal{V}$ is a set of variables (ranged over by $x, y, \dots$), $!\mathcal{V}$ denotes the set binders over variables in $\mathcal{V}$ (i.e. $!x, !y, \dots$), $\mathcal{I}$ is a set of tuple identifiers (ranged over by i, i', j, j'), $\mathcal{T} \subseteq (\mathcal{U} \cup \mathcal{V})^*$ is a set of $\mathcal{I}$-indexed tuples (ranged over by $t_i, t'_{i'}, \dots$), $\mathcal{ET} \subseteq (\mathcal{U}^*$ is a set of $\mathcal{I}$-indexed evaluated tuples (ranged over by $et_i, et'_{i'}, \dots$), and $\mathcal{TT} \subseteq (\mathcal{U} \cup \mathcal{V} \cup !\mathcal{V})^*$ is a set of templates (ranged over by $T_\iota, T'_{\iota'}, \dots$, with $\iota \in \mathcal{I} \cup !\mathcal{V}$).*

Networks. A RepliKlaim specification is a *network* N, i.e. a possibly empty set of *components* or *nodes*.

Components. A component $\ell :: [K, P]$ has a locality name ℓ which is unique (cf. well-formedness in Def. 2), a *data repository* K, and set of processes P. Components may model a data-coherent unit in a large scale system, where each unit has dedicated memory and computational resources, e.g. an SMP node in a many-core machine.

Repositories. A data repository K is a set of data items, which are pairs of identifier-indexed tuples and their replication information. In particular a data item is a pair $\langle et_i, L \rangle$, where t_i is a tuple, i is a unique identifier of the tuple, and L is a list of localities where the tuple is replicated. For a data item $\langle et_i, L \rangle$ with $|L| > 1$ we say that t_i is *shared* or *replicated*. We use indexed tuples in place of ordinary anonymous tuples to better represent long-living data items such as variables and objects that can be created and updated. We require the replication information to be *consistent* (cf. well-formedness in Def. 2). This property is preserved by our semantics, as we shall see.

It is worth to note that a locality ℓ in L can appear as ℓ or as $\underline{\ell}$. The latter case denotes a sort of *ownership* of the tuple. We require each replicated tuple to have exactly one owner (cf. well-formedness in Def. 2). This is fundamental to avoid inconsistencies due to concurrent *weak* (asynchronous) retrievals or updates of a replicated tuple. This issue will be explained in detail later.

Processes. Processes are the main computational units and can be executed concurrently either at the same locality or at different localities. Each process is created from the nil process, using the constructs for *action prefixing* $(A.P)$, *non-deterministic choice* $(P_1 + P_2)$ and *parallel execution* $(P_1 \mid P_2)$.

Actions and Targets. The actions of RepliKlaim are based on standard primitives for tuple spaces, here extended to suitably enable replica-aware programming. Some actions are exactly as in Klaim. For instance, read$(t_i)@\ell$ is the standard non-destructive read of Klaim.

The standard output operation is enriched here to allow a list of localities L as target. RepliKlaim features two variants of the output operation: a *strong* (i.e. atomic) one and a *weak* (i.e. *asynchronous*) one. In particular, out$_\alpha(t_i)@L$ is used to place the shared tuple t_i at the data repositories located on sites $l \in L$ atomically or asynchronously (resp. for $\alpha = s, w$). In this way the shared tuple is replicated on the set of sites designated with L. In RepliKlaim output operations are blocking: an operation out$_\alpha(t_i)@L$ cannot be enacted if an i-indexed tuple exists at L. This is necessary to avoid inconsistent versions of the same data item in the same location to co-exist. Hence, before placing a new version of a data item, the previous one needs to be removed. However, we will see that weak consistency operations still allow inconsistent versions of the same data item to co-exist but in *different* locations.

As in the case of output operations, RepliKlaim features two variants of the standard destructive operation in: a *strong* input in$_s$ and a *weak* input in$_w$. A strong input in$_s(T_\iota)@\ell$ retrieves a tuple et_i matching T_ι at ℓ and atomically removes all replicas of et_i. A weak input in$_w(T_\iota)@\ell$ tries to asynchronously remove all replicas of a tuple et_i matching T_ι residing in ℓ. This means that replicas are not removed simultaneously. Replicas in the process of being removed are called *ghost* replicas, since they are reminiscent of the *ghost* tuples of [25,14] (cf. the discussion in Section 4).

RepliKlaim features two additional (possibly) *unsafe* operations: out$_u(et_i, L)@\ell$ puts a data item $\langle et_i, L \rangle$ at all locations in L, while in$_u(T_\iota, L)@\ell$ retrieves a tuple

$$P + (Q + R) \equiv (P + Q) + R \qquad\qquad P \mid Q \equiv Q \mid P$$
$$P + \mathsf{nil} \equiv P \qquad\qquad N \parallel (M \parallel W) \equiv (N \parallel M) \parallel W$$
$$P + Q \equiv Q + P \qquad\qquad N \parallel \mathbf{0} \equiv N$$
$$P \mid (Q \mid R) \equiv (P \mid Q) \mid R \qquad\qquad N \parallel M \equiv M \parallel M$$
$$P \mid \mathsf{nil} \equiv P \qquad\qquad \ell :: [K, P] \equiv \ell :: [K, \mathsf{nil}] \parallel \ell :: [\emptyset, P]$$

Fig. 2. Structural congruence for RepliKlaim

et_i matching T_ι at ℓ and does *not* remove the replicas of et_i. These operations are instrumental for the semantics and are not meant to appear in user specifications.

As we have seen, the syntax of RepliKlaim admits some terms that we would like to rule out. We therefore define a simple notion of well-formed network.

Definition 2 (Well-formedness). *Let N be a network. We say that N is well formed if:*

1. *Localities are unique, i.e. no two distinct components $\ell :: [K, P]$, $\ell :: [K', P']$ can occur in N;*
2. *Replication is consistent, i.e. for every occurrence of $\ell :: [(K, \langle et_i, L \rangle), P]$ in a network N it holds that $\ell \in L$ and for all (and only) localities $\ell' \in L$ we have that component ℓ' is of the form $\ell' :: [(K', \langle et'_i, L \rangle), P']$. Note that t' is not required to be t since we allow relaxed consistency of replicas.*
3. *Each replica has exactly one owner, i.e. every occurrence of L has at most one owner location $\underline{\ell}$.*
4. *Tuple identifiers are unique, i.e. there is no K containing two data items $\langle et_i, L \rangle$, $\langle et'_i, L' \rangle$. Note that this guarantees local uniqueness; global uniqueness is implied by condition (2).*

Well-formedness is preserved by the semantics, but as usual we admit some intermediate bad-formed terms which ease the definition of the semantics.

We assume the standard notions of free and bound variables, respectively denoted by $fn(\cdot)$ and $bn(\cdot)$, as well as the existence of a suitable operation for matching tuples against templates, denoted $match(T_\iota, t_i)$ which yields a substitution for the bound variables of T_ι. Note that ι may be a bound variable to record the identifier of the tuple.

2.2 RepliKlaim: Semantics

RepliKlaim terms are to be intended up to the structural congruence induced by the axioms in Fig 2 and closed under reflexivity, transitivity and symmetry.

$$\frac{}{A.P \xrightarrow{A} P} \text{ (ActP)} \qquad \frac{P \xrightarrow{A} P'}{P+Q \xrightarrow{A} P'} \text{ (Choice)} \qquad \frac{P \xrightarrow{A} P'}{P|Q \xrightarrow{A} P'|Q} \text{ (Par)}$$

$$\frac{P \xrightarrow{\mathsf{out_s}(t_i)@L} P' \qquad \forall \ell' \in L. \nexists et', L'. \langle et_i', L' \rangle \in K_{\ell'}}{N \| \ell::[K,P] \| \Pi_{\ell' \in L} \ell'::[K_{\ell'}, P_{\ell'}] \longrightarrow N \| \ell::[K,P'] \| \Pi_{\ell' \in L} \ell'::[(K_{\ell'}, \langle et_i, L \rangle), P_{\ell'}]} \text{ (OutS)}$$

$$\frac{P \xrightarrow{\mathsf{out_w}(t_i)@L} P' \qquad \ell'' \in L \qquad \nexists et', L'. \langle et_i', L' \rangle \in K_{\ell''}}{N \| \ell::[K,P] \| \ell''::[K_{\ell''}, P_{\ell''}] \longrightarrow N \| \ell::[K,P'] \| \ell''::[(K_{\ell''}, \langle et_i, L \rangle), P_{\ell''} | \Pi_{\ell' \in (L \setminus \ell'')} \mathsf{out_u}(et_i, L)@L]} \text{ (OutW)}$$

$$\frac{P \xrightarrow{\mathsf{out_u}(et_i,L)@\ell} P' \qquad \nexists et', L'. \langle et_i', L' \rangle \in K_\ell}{N \| \ell::[K,P] \longrightarrow N \| \ell::[(K, \langle et_i, L \rangle), P']} \text{ (OutU)}$$

$$\frac{P \xrightarrow{\mathsf{in_s}(T_t)@\ell''} P' \qquad \ell'' \in L \qquad \sigma = match(T_t, et_i)}{N \| \ell::[K,P] \| \Pi_{\ell' \in L} \ell'::[(K_{\ell'}, \langle et_i, L \rangle), P_{\ell'}] \longrightarrow N \| \ell::[K,P'\sigma] \| \Pi_{\ell' \in L} \ell'::[K_{\ell'}, P_{\ell'}]} \text{ (InS)}$$

$$\frac{P \xrightarrow{\mathsf{in_w}(T_t)@\ell''} P' \qquad \ell'' \in L \qquad \ell' \in L \qquad \sigma = match(T_t, et_i)}{N \| \ell::[K,P] \| \ell'::[(K_{\ell'}, \langle et_i, L \rangle), P_{\ell'}] \longrightarrow N \| \ell::[K,P'\sigma] \| \ell'::[K_{\ell'}, P_{\ell'} | \Pi_{\ell''' \in (L \setminus \ell')} \mathsf{in_u}(et_i, L)@\ell''']} \text{ (InW)}$$

$$\frac{P \xrightarrow{\mathsf{in_u}(T_t,L)@\ell'} P' \qquad \sigma = match(T_t, et_i)}{N \| \ell::[K,P] \| \ell'::[(K_{\ell'}, \langle et_i, L \rangle), P_{\ell'}] \longrightarrow N \| \ell::[K,P'\sigma] \| \ell'::[K_{\ell'}, P_{\ell'}]} \text{ (InU)}$$

$$\frac{P \xrightarrow{\mathsf{read}(T_t)@\ell'} P' \qquad \sigma = match(T_t, et_i)}{N \| \ell::[K,P] \| \ell'::[(K_{\ell'}, \langle et_i, L \rangle), P_{\ell'}] \longrightarrow N \| \ell::[K,P'\sigma] \| \ell'::[(K_{\ell'}, \langle et_i, L \rangle), P_{\ell'}]} \text{ (Read)}$$

Fig. 3. Operational semantics of RepliKlaim

As usual, besides axiomatising the essential structure of RepliKlaim systems, the structural congruence allows us to provide a more compact and simple semantics. The axioms of the structural congruence are standard. We just remark the presence of a *clone* axiom (bottom right) which is similar to the one used in early works on Klaim. In our case, this clone axiom allows us to avoid cumbersome semantic rules for dealing with multiparty synchronisations where the subject component is also an object of the synchronisation (e.g. when a component ℓ removes a shared tuple t_i that has a replica in ℓ itself). The clone axiom allows a component to participate in those interactions, by separating the processes (the subject) from the repository (the object). It is worth to note that this axiom does not preserve well-formedness (uniqueness of localities is violated).

The operational semantics in Fig. 3 mixes an SOS style for collecting the process actions (cf. rules ActP, Choice and Par) and reductions for the evolution of nets. The standard congruence rules are not included for simplicity.

It is worth to remark that the replicas located at the owner are used in some of the rules as a sort of tokens to avoid undesirable race conditions. The role of such tokens in inputs and outputs is dual: the replica must *not* exist for outputs to be enacted, while the replica *must* exist for inputs to be enacted.

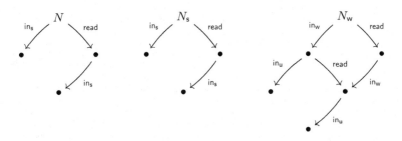

Fig. 4. Concurrent reads and inputs with no replicas (left), replicas and strong input (center) and weak input (right)

Rule OUTS deals with a strong output $\mathsf{out}(et_i)@L$ by putting the tuple et_i in all localities in L. However, the premise of the rule requires a version of data item i (i.e. a tuple et'_i) to *not* exist in the repository of the owner of et_i (ℓ''). Rule OUTW governs weak outputs of the form $\mathsf{out}(et_i)@L$ by requiring the absence of a version of data item i. The difference with respect to the strong output is that the effect of the rule is that of creating a set of processes that will take care of placing the replicas in parallel, through the unsafe output operation. Such operation is handled by rule OUTU which is very much like a standard Klaim rule for ordinary outputs, except that the operation is blocking to avoid overwriting existing data items.

Rule INS deals with actions $\mathsf{in}(T_\iota)@\ell$ by retrieving a tuple et_i matching T_ι from locality ℓ, and from all localities containing a replica of it. Rule INW retrieves a tuple et_i from an owner ℓ' of a tuple that has a replica in the target ℓ. As a result, processes are installed at ℓ' that deal with the removal of the remaining replicas in parallel (thus allowing the interleaving of **read** operations). As in the case of weak outputs, weak inputs resort to unsafe inputs. Those are handled by rule INU, which is like a standard input rule in Klaim.

Finally, rule READ is a standard rule for dealing with non-destructive reads.

2.3 RepliKlaim: Examples

We provide here a couple of illustrative examples aimed at providing insights on semantics, implementation and performance aspects.

Concurrent Reads and Inputs. The following example illustrates three ways of sharing and accessing a tuple and is meant to exemplify the benefit of replicas and weak inputs. The example consists of the networks

$$N \doteq \ell_1 :: [\langle et_i, \ell_1 \rangle, \mathsf{in}_\mathsf{s}(et_j)@\ell_1] \qquad \| \; \ell_2 :: [\emptyset, \mathsf{read}(et_j)@\ell_1]$$
$$N_\alpha \doteq \ell_1 :: [\langle et_i, \{\underline{\ell_1}, \ell_2\} \rangle, \mathsf{in}_\alpha(et_j)@\ell_1] \| \; \ell_2 :: [\langle et_i, \{\underline{\ell_1}, \ell_2\} \rangle, \mathsf{read}(et_j)@\ell_2]$$

with $\alpha \in \{\mathsf{s}, \mathsf{w}\}$. The idea is that in N a tuple has to be accessed by both ℓ_1 and ℓ_2 is shared in the traditional Klaim way: it is only stored in one location

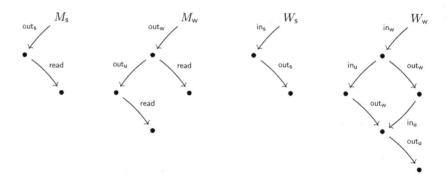

Fig. 5. Transitions for M_s (concurrent read and strong output), M_w (concurrent read and weak output), W_s (concurrent strong input and strong output) and W_w (concurrent weak input and weak output)

(namely, ℓ_1) with no replicas. To the contrary, N_α models the same scenario with explicit replicas. The tuple et_i is replicated at both ℓ_1 and ℓ_2, possibly after some process executed $\mathsf{out}(et_i)@\{\underline{\ell_1}, \ell_2\}$. Networks N_s and N_w differ in the way the tuple et_i is retrieved by ℓ_1: using strong or weak input, respectively. Fig. 4 depicts the transition systems for the three networks, where the actual description of the reachable states is not provided due to lack of space and due to the simplicity of the example. The transition systems of N and N_s are similar but differ in the way the transitions are computed. In N, the input is local to ℓ_1, but the read is remote (from ℓ_2 to ℓ_1), while in N_s the input is global (requires a synchronization of ℓ_1 and ℓ_2 to atomically retrieve all replicas of et_i), and the read is local to ℓ_2. The main point in N_w is that the process in ℓ_2 can keep reading the ghost replicas of et_i even after ℓ_1 started retrieving it.

Concurrent Reads and Outputs. The next example illustrates (see also Fig. 5) the interplay of reads with strong and weak outputs.

$$M_\alpha \doteq \ell_1 :: [\emptyset, \mathsf{out}_\alpha(et_i)@\{\underline{\ell_1}, \ell_2\}] \parallel \ell_2 :: [\emptyset, \mathsf{read}(et_j)@\ell_1]$$

with $\alpha \in \{s, w\}$. The idea is that component ℓ_1 can output a tuple with replicas in ℓ_1 and ℓ_2 in a strong or weak manner, while ℓ_2 is trying to read the tuple from ℓ_1. In the strong case, the read can happen only after all replicas have been created. In the weak case, the read can be interleaved with the unsafe output.

Concurrent inputs and outputs. The last example (see also Fig. 5) illustrates the update of a data item using strong and weak operations.

$$W_\alpha \doteq \ell_1 :: [\emptyset, \mathsf{in}_\alpha(et_i)@\{\underline{\ell_1}, \ell_2\}.\mathsf{out}_\alpha(f(et)_i)@\{\underline{\ell_1}, \ell_2\}] \parallel \ell_2 :: [\emptyset, \mathsf{nil}]$$

with $\alpha \in \{s, w\}$. The idea is that component ℓ_1 retrieves a tuple and then outputs an updated version of it (after applying function f). Relaxing consistency from s to w increases the number of interleavings.

3   Performance Evaluation

We describe in this section our prototype implementation and present a set of experiments aimed at showing that an explicit use of replicas in combination with weakly consistent operations then provide significant performance advantages.

Implementing RepliKlaim in KLAVA. Our prototype run-time framework is based on KLAVA, a Java package used for implementing distributed applications based on Klaim. KLAVA is a suitable framework for testing our hypothesis as it provides a set of process executing engines (nodes) connected in a network via one of the three communication protocols (TCP, UDP, local pipes). The current implementation of RepliKlaim is based on an encoding of RepliKlaim into standard Klaim primitives. We recall the main Klaim primitives we use in the encoding: $in(T)@\ell$ destructively retrieves a tuple matching T in location ℓ. The operation is blocking until a matching tuple is found; $read(T)@\ell$: non-destructive variant of in; $out(t)@\ell$: inserts a tuple t into the tuple space located at ℓ. The actual encoding is based on the operational semantics presented in Fig. 3, which already uses some operations that are close to those of Klaim, namely the unsafe operations in_u and out_u. The rest of the machinery (atomicity, etc.) is based on standard synchronisation techniques.

Experiments: Hypothesis. The main hypothesis of our experiments is that better performances are achieved with improved data locality and data communication minimized through the use of replicated tuples and weak operations. Indeed, minimizing data locality can be easily done by replicating data, however it comes at a cost in terms of synchronization if replicated data need to be kept consistent (e.g. when using strong inputs and outputs). As we shall see, our experimental results show how the ratio between the frequencies of read and update (i.e. sequences of inputs and outputs on the same data item) operations affects the performance of three different versions of a program: a *traditional* one that does not use replicas, and two versions using replicas: one using strong (consistent) operations and another one using weak (weak consistent) operations. We would only like to remark that we had to deviate in one thing from the semantics: while spawning parallel processes in rules INW and OUTW to deal with the asynchronous/parallel actions on replicas seems very appealing, in practice performing such operations in sequence showed to be more efficient. Of course in general the choice between parallel and sequential composition of such actions depends on several aspects, like the number of available processors, the number of processes already running in the system and the size of the data being replicated.

Experiments: Configuration of the Scenario.[6] The general idea of the scenario we have tested is that multiple nodes are concurrently working (i.e. performing

---

[6] The source code and Klava library are available online at http://sysma.imtlucca.it/wp-content/uploads/2015/03/RepliKlaim-test-examples.rar

inputs, reads and outputs) on a list whose elements can be scattered on various nodes. A single element (i.e. the counter) is required to indicate the number of the next element that can be added. In order to add an element to the list, the counter is removed using an input, the value of the counter is increased and the tuple is re-inserted, and then a new list element is inserted. We call such a sequence of input and output operations on the same data item (i.e. the counter) an *update* operation.

Each of the nodes is running processes that perform read or update operations. Both reader and updater processes run in loops. We fix the number of updates to 10, but vary the number of read accesses (20, 30, 50, 100, 150, 200). We consider two variants of the scenario. The first variant has 3 nodes: one node containing just one reader process, another node containing just one updater process and a last one containing both a reader and an updater process. The second variant has 9 nodes, each containing process as in the previous case, i.e. this scenario is just obtained by triplicating the nodes of the previous scenario. The main point for considering these two variants is that we run the experiment in a dual core machine, so that in the first case one would ideally have all processes running in parallel, while this is not the case in the second variant.

Formally, the RepliKlaim nets N we use in our experiments are specified as follows

$$N \doteq \prod_{i=1}^{n} \left\{ \ell_{i,1} :: [\emptyset, \mathsf{P}_1(\ell_{i,1})] \parallel \ell_{i,2} :: [\emptyset, \mathsf{P}_2(\ell_{i,2})] \parallel \ell_{i,3} :: [\emptyset, \mathsf{P}_1(\ell_{i,3}) \mid \mathsf{P}_2(\ell_{i,3})] \right\}$$

where P_1 is an updater process and P_2 is a reader process, both parametric with respect to the locality they reside on. P_1 is responsible for incrementing the counter and adding a new list element, while P_2 only reads the current number of list elements. For the scalability evaluation we compare results for nets obtained when $n = 1$ and $n = 3$, meaning that corresponding nets have 3 and 9 nodes respectively. Our aim is to compare the following three alternative implementations of processes P_1 and P_2 which offer the same functionality, but exhibit different performances:

Program no − replicas: this implementation follows a standard approach that does not make use of replica-based primitives. The idea here is that the shared tuple is stored only in one location, with no replicas. The consistency of such model is obviously strong, as there are no replicas. Local access to the shared tuple is granted only to processes running on the specified location, while other processes access remotely. In the begining we assume that one of the sites has executed $\mathsf{out_s}(counter_a)@\ell_1$ which places the counter tuple $counter_a$ at place ℓ_1, with a being a unique identifier. Then processes P_1 and P_2 can be expressed as follows:

$$\mathsf{P}_1(self) \equiv \mathsf{in_s}(counter_a)@\ell_1.\mathsf{out_s}(f(counter_a))@\ell_1.\mathsf{out_s}(lt_{a_{counter}})@self.\mathsf{P}_1$$
$$\mathsf{P}_2(self) \equiv \mathsf{read}(T_a)@\ell_1.\mathsf{P}_2$$

where $f(\cdot)$ refers to the operation of incrementing the counter and lt refers to the new list element which is added locally after the shared counter had been incremented. Note that we use a as unique identifier for the counter and $a_{counter}$ as unique identifier for the new elements being inserted.

Program strong − replicas: The difference between this model and the non-replicated one is the presence of replicas on each node, while this model also guarantees strong consistency. Concretely, each update of replicated data items is done via operations in_s and out_s. The formalisation is presented below, after the description of the weak variant of this implementation.

Program weak − replicas: In this variant, the replicas are present on each node, but the level of consistency is weak. This means that interleavings of actions over replicas are allowed. However, to make this program closer to the functionality offered by the above ones, we forbid the co-existence of different versions of the same data item. Such co-existence is certainly allowed in sequences of operations like $\text{in}_w(t_i)@\ell.\text{out}_w(t_i')@L$ as we have seen in the examples of Section 2.3. To avoid such co-existence, but still allow concurrent reads we use an additional tuple that the updaters used as sort of lock to ensure that outputs (reps. inputs) are only enacted once inputs (resp. outputs) on the same data item are completed on all replicas. Of course, this makes this program less efficient than it could be but it seems a more fair choice for comparison and still our results show its superiority in terms of performance.

In the above two replication-based implementations we assume that the counter is replicated on all nodes by executing $\text{out}_\alpha(counter_a)@\{\underline{\ell_1}, \ell_2, \ell_3\}$ with $\alpha \in \{\text{s}, \text{w}\}$. In this case the processes are specified as:

$$\text{P}_1(self) \equiv \text{in}_\alpha(counter_a)@self.\text{out}_\alpha(f(counter_a))@\{\ell_1, \ell_2, \ell_3\}.$$
$$\text{out}_s(a_{counter})@self.\text{P}_1$$
$$\text{P}_2(self) \equiv \text{read}(T_a)@self.\text{P}_2$$

where the strong and weak variants are obtained by letting α be s and w, respectively.

Experiments: Data and Interpretation. The results of our experiments are depicted in Fig. 6 and 7. The x axis corresponds to the ratio of reads and updates performed by all processes, while the y axis corresponds to the time needed by the processes to complete their computation. We measure the relation between average running time and the ratio between access frequencies. Time is expressed in seconds and presents the average of 15 executions, while the ratio is a number (2, 3, 5, 10, 15, 20). The results obtained for programs no − replicas, strong − replicas and weak − replicas are respectively depicted in blue, green and red.

It can be easily observed that when increasing the ratio the weak − replicas program is the most efficient. This program improves over program no − replicas only after the ratio of reading operations reaches a certain level that varies from the two variants used (3 and 9 nodes). The variant with 9 nodes requires a higher ratio to show this improvement, mainly due to the fact that the 12 processes of the scenario cannot run in parallel in the dual-core machine we used. Note that strong − replicas offers the worst performance. Indeed, preserving strong

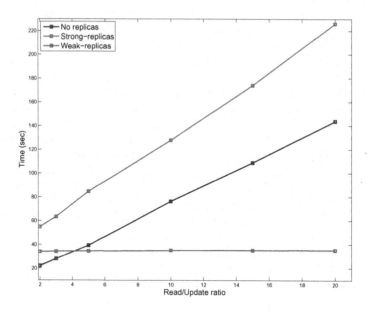

Fig. 6. Comparing three strategies in a scenario with 3 nodes

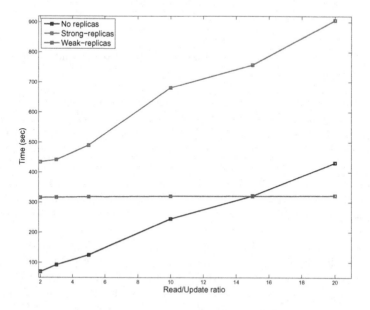

Fig. 7. Comparing three strategies in a scenario with 9 nodes

consistency in presence of replicas is unfeasible in practice because it requires a great deal of synchronization.

4 Related Works

Many authors have investigated issues related to the performance of tuple space implementations and applications of tuple space coordination to large-scale distributed and concurrent systems (cloud computing, high-performance computing, services, etc.). We discuss here some representative approaches that are closely related to our work and, in part, served as inspiration.

One of the first performance improvements for tuple-space implementations was the *ghost* tuple technique, originally presented in [25] and later proven to be correct in [14]. The technique applies to Linda-like languages used in a distributed setting where local tuple replicas are used to improve local operations. Ghost tuple is a local replica of a tuple being destructively read (by a Linda in) operation. The ghost tuple technique allows the non-destructive read of those local replicas (by a Linda read operation). This technique is very similar to our idea of relaxing consistency in tuple space operations. In particular, our local replicas can be seen as ghost tuples as we have mentioned in several occasions in the paper. As a matter of fact, the ghost tuple technique is one of our main sources of inspiration.

Another seminal work considering performance issues in tuple space coordination was the introduction of asynchronous tuple space primitives in Bonita (asynchronous Linda) [24]. This work provided a practical implementation and an illustrative case study to show the performance advantages of asynchronous variants of tuple space primitives for coordinating distributed agents. A thorough theoretical study of possible variants of tuple space operations was later presented in [8]. In particular, the authors study three variants for the output operation: an instantaneous output (where an output can be considered as instantaneous creation of the tuple), and ordered output (where a tuple is placed in the tuple space as one atomic action) and an unordered output (where the tuple is passed to the tuple space handler and the process will continue, the tuple space handler will then place the tuple in the tuple space, not necessarily respecting order of outputs). A clear understanding of (true) concurrency of tuple space operations was developed in [7], where the authors provide a contextual P/T nets semantics of Linda. All these works have inspired the introduction of the asynchronous weak operations in RepliKlaim.

Performance issues have been also considered in tuple space implementations. Besides Klaim implementations [5,4], we mention GigaSpaces [1], a commercial tuple space implementation, Blossom [15], a C++ high performance distributed tuple space implementation, Lime [23], a tuple space implementation tailored for ad-hoc networks, TOTA [22], a middleware for tuple-based coordination in multi-agent systems, and PeerSpace [9] a P2P based tuple space implementation. Moreover, tuple space coordination has been applied and optimised for a large variety of systems where large-scale distribution and concurrency are key aspects. Among other, we mention large-scale infrastructures [10], cluster computing environments [2], cloud computing systems [17], grid computing systems [21], context-aware applications [3], multi-core Java programs [16], and high performance computing systems [18]. As far as we know, none of the above mentioned implementations treats replicas as first-class programming citizens.

Another set of works that are worth considering are recent technologies for high performance computing. Among them we mention *non-uniform cluster computing* systems, which are built out of multi-core SMP chips with non-uniform memory hierarchies, and interconnected in horizontally scalable cluster configurations such as blade servers. The programming language X10, currently under development, is intended as object-oriented language for programing such systems. A recent formalization of some X10 features can be found in [11]. The main concept of X10 is a notion of *place* which is a collection of threads (activities) and data, and it maps to a data-coherent unit of a large system (e.g. SMP node). In X10 the programmer makes the initial distribution of shared data which is not changed throughout the program execution. Each piece of shared data maps to a single place, and all remote accesses are achieved by spawning (asynchronous) activities. In our language, such concept of place would correspond to a single node. We believe that the concept of replicas introduced in RepliKlaim, can be suitable for modeling high-performance programming using X10-like programming languages.

5   Conclusion

We have presented the tuple-based coordination language RepliKlaim, which enriches Klaim with primitives for replica-aware coordination. RepliKlaim allows the programmer to specify and coordinate the replication of shared data items and the desired consistency properties so to obtain better performances in large-scale high performance computing applications. We have provided an operational semantics to formalise our proposal as well as to guide the implementation of the language, which has been encoded into KLAVA [5], a Java-based implementation of Klaim. We have also discussed issues related to replica consistency and the main synchronization mechanisms of our implementation. Finally, we have provided a performance evaluation study in our prototype run-time system. Our experiments include scenarios where replica-based specifications and relaxed consistency provide significant performance gains.

We plan to enrich our performance evaluation to consider large-scale distributed systems since our focus so far has been on local concurrent systems. Moreover, we would like to compare our implementation against existing tuple space implementations (cf. the discussion in Section 4). We may also consider other forms of consistency beyond strong and weak, as advocated e.g. in [26,6], and to understand if there are automatic ways to help the programmer decide when to use which form of consistency as done, e.g. in [20]. Another future work we plan to pursue is to apply our approach to the SCEL language [13]. One characteristic difference between SCEL and Klaim is that the target of tuple operations can be specified by a predicate on the attributes of components.

This provides a great flexibility as it allows to use group-cast operations without explicitly creating groups, called *ensembles* in SCEL. In many applications creating replicas would be a convenient mechanism to share information among groups. However, the dynamicity of ensembles, since components change attributes at run-time and those join and leave ensembles arbitrarily, poses some challenges on the semantics and implementation of shared data items that need to be investigated.

References

1. Gigaspaces technologies ltd, www.gigaspaces.com
2. Atkinson, A.K.: Development and Execution of Array-based Applications in a Cluster Computing Environment. Ph.D. thesis, University of Tasmania (2010)
3. Balzarotti, D., Costa, P., Picco, G.P.: The lights tuple space framework and its customization for context-aware applications. Web Intelligence and Agent Systems 5(2), 215–231 (2007), http://iospress.metapress.com/content/v16153407085177x/
4. Bettini, L., De Nicola, R., Loreti, M.: Implementing mobile and distributed applications in x-klaim. Scalable Computing: Practice and Experience 7(4) (2006), http://www.scpe.org/index.php/scpe/article/view/384
5. Bettini, L., De Nicola, R., Pugliese, R.: Klava: a java package for distributed and mobile applications. Softw., Pract. Exper. 32(14), 1365–1394 (2002), http://dx.doi.org/10.1002/spe.486
6. Brewer, E.: CAP twelve years later: How the "rules" have changed. Computer 45(2), 23–29 (2012)
7. Busi, N., Gorrieri, R., Zavattaro, G.: A truly concurrent view of linda interprocess communication. Tech. rep., University of Bologna (1997)
8. Busi, N., Gorrieri, R., Zavattaro, G.: Comparing three semantics for linda-like languages. Theor. Comput. Sci. 240(1), 49–90 (2000), http://dx.doi.org/10.1016/S0304-3975(99)00227-3
9. Busi, N., Montresor, A., Zavattaro, G.: Data-driven coordination in peer-to-peer information systems. Int. J. Cooperative Inf. Syst. 13(1), 63–89 (2004)
10. Capizzi, S.: A tuple space implementation for large-scale infrastructures. Ph.D. thesis, University of Bologna (2008)
11. Crafa, S., Cunningham, D., Saraswat, V., Shinnar, A., Tardieu, O.: Semantics of (resilient) X10. In: Jones, R. (ed.) ECOOP 2014. LNCS, vol. 8586, pp. 670–696. Springer, Heidelberg (2014)
12. De Nicola, R., Ferrari, G., Pugliese, R.: Klaim: a kernel language for agents interaction and mobility. IEEE Transactions on Software Engineering 24(5), 315–330 (1998)
13. De Nicola, R., Loreti, M., Pugliese, R., Tiezzi, F.: A formal approach to autonomic systems programming: The SCEL language. TAAS 9(2), 7 (2014), http://doi.acm.org/10.1145/2619998
14. De Nicola, R., Pugliese, R., Rowstron, A.: Proving the correctness of optimising destructive and non-destructive reads over tuple spaces. In: Porto, A., Roman, G.-C. (eds.) COORDINATION 2000. LNCS, vol. 1906, pp. 66–80. Springer, Heidelberg (2000)
15. van der Goot, R.: High Performance Linda using a Class Library. Ph.D. thesis, Erasmus University Rotterdam (2001)

16. Gudenkauf, S., Hasselbring, W.: Space-based multi-core programming in java. In: Probst, C.W., Wimmer, C. (eds.) Proceedings of the 9th International Conference on Principles and Practice of Programming in Java, PPPJ 2011, pp. 41–50. ACM (2011), http://doi.acm.org/10.1145/2093157.2093164
17. Hari, H.: Tuple Space in the Cloud. Ph.D. thesis, Uppsala Universitet (2012)
18. Jiang, Y., Xue, G., Li, M., You, J.-y.: Dtupleshpc: Distributed tuple space for desktop high performance computing. In: Jesshope, C., Egan, C. (eds.) ACSAC 2006. LNCS, vol. 4186, pp. 394–400. Springer, Heidelberg (2006)
19. Krishnamurthy, A., Aiken, A., Colella, P., Gay, D., Graham, S.L., Hilfinger, P.N., Liblit, B., Miyamoto, C., Pike, G., Semenzato, L., Yelick, K.A.: Titanium: A high performance java dialect. In: PPSC (1999)
20. Li, C., Porto, D., Clement, A., Gehrke, J., Preguiça, N.M., Rodrigues, R.: Making geo-replicated systems fast as possible, consistent when necessary. In: Thekkath, C., Vahdat, A. (eds.) 10th USENIX Symposium on Operating Systems Design and Implementation (OSDI 2012), pp. 265–278. USENIX Association (2012)
21. Li, Z., Parashar, M.: Comet: a scalable coordination space for decentralized distributed environments. In: Second International Workshop on Hot Topics in Peer-to-Peer Systems, HOT-P2P 2005, pp. 104–111. IEEE Computer Society (2005)
22. Mamei, M., Zambonelli, F.: Programming pervasive and mobile computing applications: The TOTA approach. ACM Trans. Softw. Eng. Methodol. 18(4) (2009)
23. Murphy, A.L., Picco, G.P., Roman, G.: LIME: A coordination model and middleware supporting mobility of hosts and agents. ACM Trans. Softw. Eng. Methodol. 15(3), 279–328 (2006)
24. Rowstron, A.: Using asynchronous tuple-space access primitives (BONITA primitives) for process co-ordination. In: Garlan, D., Le Métayer, D. (eds.) COORDINATION 1997. LNCS, vol. 1282, pp. 426–429. Springer, Heidelberg (1997)
25. Rowstron, A., Wood, A.: An efficient distributed tuple space implementation for networks of workstations. In: Bougé, L., Fraigniaud, P., Mignotte, A., Robert, Y. (eds.) Euro-Par 1996. LNCS, vol. 1123, pp. 510–513. Springer, Heidelberg (1996)
26. Terry, D.: Replicated data consistency explained through baseball. Commun. ACM 56(12), 82–89 (2013), http://doi.acm.org/10.1145/2500500

Investigating Fluid-Flow Semantics of Asynchronous Tuple-Based Process Languages for Collective Adaptive Systems

Diego Latella[1], Michele Loreti[2], and Mieke Massink[1(✉)]

[1] Istituto di Scienza e Tecnologie dell'Informazione 'A. Faedo', CNR, Pisa, Italy
{Diego.Latella,mieke.massink}@isti.cnr.it
[2] Università di Firenze and IMT-Lucca, Lucca, Italy
michele.loreti@unifi.it

Abstract. Recently, there has been growing interest in nature-inspired interaction paradigms for Collective Adaptive Systems, for modelling and implementation of adaptive and context-aware coordination, among which the promising pheromone-based interaction paradigm. System modelling in the context of such a paradigm may be facilitated by the use of languages in which adaptive interaction is decoupled in time and space through asynchronous buffered communication, e.g. asynchronous, repository- or tuple-based languages. In this paper we propose a differential semantics for such languages. In particular, we consider an asynchronous, repository based modelling kernel-language which is a restricted version of LINDA, extended with stochastic information about action duration. We provide stochastic formal semantics for both an agent-based view and a population-based view. We then derive an ordinary differential equation semantics from the latter, which provides a fluid-flow deterministic approximation for the mean behaviour of large populations. We show the application of the language and the ODE analysis on a benchmark example of foraging ants.

Keywords: Asynchronous coordination languages · Stochastic process algebras · Fluid-flow approximation · Continuous time markov chains

1 Introduction and Related Work

Collective Adaptive Systems (CAS) are systems typically composed of a large number of heterogeneous agents with decentralised control and varying degrees of complex autonomous behaviour. Agents may be competing for shared resources and, at the same time, collaborate for reaching common goals. The pervasive nature of CAS, together with the importance of the role they play, for instance in the very core of the ICT support for *smart cities*, implies that a serious *a priori* analysis—and, consequently modelling—of the design of any such a system must be performed and that all critical aspects of its behaviour must be carefully investigated before the system is deployed.

This research has been partially funded by the EU project QUANTICOL (nr. 600708), and the IT MIUR project CINA.

© IFIP International Federation for Information Processing 2015
T. Holvoet and M. Viroli (Eds.): COORDINATION 2015, LNCS 9037, pp. 19–34, 2015.
DOI: 10.1007/978-3-319-19282-6_2

Recently, there has been growing interest in nature-inspired interaction paradigms for CAS, for enforcing adaptive and context-aware coordination. Among these, those based on the metaphor of pheromones seem promising. System modelling in the context of such a paradigm may be facilitated by the use of languages in which adaptive interaction is decoupled in time and space through asynchronous buffered communication, e.g. tuple-based languages, a la LINDA [5]. For systems of limited size, several languages have already been proposed in the literature and have proven useful for modelling—as well as programming—autonomic adaptive coordination. Examples include KLAIM [10], which extends LINDA with, among others, a notion of *space*, the TOTA framework [21], which, additionally, provides for explicit adaptive *tuple propagation* mechanisms and a sort of force field view of tuples, and SCEL [8], where the basic interaction paradigm is enriched with a flexible, *predicate-based* addressing mechanism, with a framework for defining *policies*, and with a notion of tuple-space which is extended to a more general *knowledge*-space. Additionally, quantitative extensions of both KLAIM and SCEL have been developed, namely StoKLAIM [11] and StocS [20], where the quantity of interest is the duration of (the execution of) process actions. Such durations are assumed to be continuous random variables with negative exponential distributions, commonly used in stochastic process algebra [17]. Consequently, each such random variable is fully characterised by its rate, a positive real value that is equal to the inverse of the mean duration of the execution of the action. This choice for action durations gives rise to a Markovian semantics for the languages: the behaviour of each agent of a system is modelled by a continuous time Markov chain (CTMC). The collective behaviour of a system of agents is also modelled by a CTMC, of course obtained as a suitable combination of those of the component agents.

Unfortunately, as soon as the size of the systems under consideration grows, the infamous combinatorial state space explosion problem makes system modelling and analysis essentially unfeasible. On the other hand, one of the key features of CAS is the large size of their component populations. Consequently, *scalability* of modelling—and, most of all, analysis—techniques and tools becomes a *must* in the context of CAS design and development. It is thus essential to develop alternative approaches for modelling systems with *large populations of agents*, possibly based on—and formally linked to—process algebra. In this way, one can try to extend, to such alternative approaches, modelling and analysis techniques which have proven effective for standard stochastic process algebra, such as stochastic model-checking of probabilistic temporal logics. One way to deal with large population systems is the so called *fluid-flow* approach, which consists in computing a deterministic approximation of the mean behaviour of the large population [2]. The first step is to abstract from agent identity and to look only at the *number of agents* in a particular state, for each of the possible states of the agents in the population and at any point in time. Then, a further step is performed by approximating the average values of such numbers by means of a *deterministic, continuous* function of time, which is obtained as the solution of an initial value problem where the set of ordinary differential equations (ODE) is derived from the system model and the initial condition is the initial distribution of the population over the set of local states of the agents. Prominent examples of the fluid-flow approach are the *differential* (i.e. ODE-based) semantics version of the Performance Analysis Process Algebra (PEPA) [23], which we will call ODE-PEPA, Bio-PEPA [7] and, more recently, PALOMA [13]. The advantage of a *fluid-flow* approach is that the transient average behaviour of the system can be analysed orders of magnitude faster than by stochastic simulation, where the mean of a usually large number of simulation traces must be computed. The *fluid-flow* approach is independent of the size of the involved populations, as long as this size is large enough to provide a good deterministic approximation [2].

In this paper we explore the possibility for differential semantics for languages with an asynchronous buffered communication interaction paradigm, e.g. data-repository- /tuple- based ones. We present ODELINDA, a simple experimental language, based on a LINDA-like, asynchronous paradigm, where processes interact only via a data repository by means of **out**, **in** and **read** operations for respectively inserting, withdrawing and reading data values to/from the repository. In particular, we present a *quantitative*, Markovian language; the behaviour of each agent is modelled by a Markov process.

In most stochastic process languages, each action is decorated with its rate, which is typically a constant. In ODELINDA, instead, action rates are allowed to depend on the global state of the complete system; thus they are *functions* from global system states to positive real values, in a similar way as in Bio-PEPA. We provide a formal definition of the Markovian semantics using State-to-Function Labeled Transition Systems (FuTS) [9], an approach that provides for a simple and concise treatment of transition multiplicities—an issue closely related to the CTMC principle of race-condition—and a clean and compact definition of the semantics.

We follow the fluid-flow approach for making the language scalable in order to be able to deal with CAS. We define a population semantics for ODELINDA from which a differential (ODE) semantics is derived, in a similar way as proposed in [13] for PALOMA and in [23] for ODE-PEPA. The interaction paradigm underlying ODELINDA is fundamentally different from those of ODE-PEPA, Bio-PEPA and PALOMA. ODE-PEPA is based on the well-known PEPA process interaction paradigm, with processes synchronising on common, specific activities, Bio-PEPA is based on the chemical-reaction paradigm, whereas PALOMA agents use message multicasting. Additionally, both Bio-PEPA and PALOMA provide some simple means for spatial modelling. Spatial information is currently not incorporated in ODELINDA.

In tuple-based approaches, data repositories are typically *multi-sets* of values and adding/withdrawing a value to/from the repository increases/decreases the multiplicity of that value in the repository. In a "population"-oriented view, this means that the total system population size may change during the computations, i.e. we are dealing with a birth-death type of systems. This is the case for ODELINDA and constitutes another distinguishing feature when compared with e.g. ODE-PEPA. In this respect, our proposal is more similar to sCCP [3], although, from a technical point of view, for the actual definition of the differential semantics we followed the approach used in [23,13] rather than that presented in [3]. Finally, our work is also related to PALPS [1] and MASSPA [15]. PALPS is a language for ecological models. Only an individual-based semantics is available for PALPS. The language is thus usable only in the specific domain of ecological models and, furthermore, seriously suffers of lack of scalability. MASSPA [15] shares some features with PALOMA, e.g. a multicast-like interaction paradigm; it is lacking a Markovian, individual-based semantics.

It is worth noting that the language we present here is a minimal *kernel* language; we intended to address only the basic issues which arise when defining a differential semantics for tuple-based asynchronous languages. For this reason, operations on data, and in particular *templates* and *pattern-matching* are not considered, so that **in** and **read** operations result into pure synchronisation actions (with or without value consumption, respectively). The unconstrained use of templates and pattern-matching, as well as the use of general operations on data types, could result in an unbounded number of *distinct* values in a model, which, in turn, would require an unbounded number of differential equations in the differential semantics. Consequently, only ground terms are allowed in model specifications. It is worth noting that this does *not* imply that we allow only finite computations or that there are bounds on the multiplicity of each piece of data or on the resulting state spaces. In fact, the number of copies of any given value which can be stored in a repository by means of repeated executions of **out** actions in a computation, by one or more processes, is unbounded (and may be infinite for infinite computations). Anyway, one should also keep in mind that ODELINDA is intended to be a process *modelling*, rather than a programming, language and that differently from most process modelling languages, that, typically, do not provide any feature for dealing with data, offers some means, although primitive, for data storage, withdrawal and retrieval. For the sake of simplicity, we also refrain from considering process spawning, although this would not cause particular problems given that the semantic model we use deals with dynamic population sizes in a natural way. The objective of the present paper is to show that the basic notion of ODE semantics for asynchronous, shared-repository based languages is well founded. Additionally, by revisiting the benchmark example of Foraging Ants, we show that even in the restricted form we present in this paper, ODELINDA can be useful for actual system modelling and analysis.

The present paper is organised as follows: the syntax and Markovian, individual-based semantics of ODELINDA are presented in Section 2; the differential semantics of the language are presented in Section 3. An example of model specification as well as ODE analysis is given in Section 4. Finally, some conclusions and considerations for future work are discussed in Section 5.

2   Syntax and Markovian Semantics of OdeLinda

We recall that the main purpose of this paper is to show the basic principles for the definition of a differential semantics of asynchronous repository-based languages rather than the definition of a complete, high-level, ready-to-use process language. Consequently, the language we present here is a very minimal one, although, as we pointed out in Section 1 it can be used for the effective modelling of typical CAS systems like foraging ants, as we will show in Section 4.

2.1   Syntax

Let $\mathcal{D}$ be a denumerable non-empty set of *data* values, ranged over by $d, d', d_1, \ldots$, $\mathcal{A}$ be set of *actions* with $\mathcal{A} = \mathcal{A}_o \cup \mathcal{A}_i \cup \mathcal{A}_r$, where $\mathcal{A}_o = \{\mathbf{out}(d) \mid d \in \mathcal{D}\}, \mathcal{A}_i = \{\mathbf{in}(d) \mid d \in \mathcal{D}\}, \mathcal{A}_r = \{\mathbf{read}(d) \mid d \in \mathcal{D}\}$, ranged over by $\alpha, \alpha', \ldots$, $\mathcal{P}$ be a denumerable non-empty set of *state constants* (or states), ranged over by $C, C', C_1, \ldots$

A system model is the result of the *parallel composition of agents*, i.e. *processes*, which are finite state machines. Thus the language has the following two level grammar for the sets AGENTS of agents and PROC of processes:

$$A ::= (R, \mathbf{out}(d)).C \mid (R, \mathbf{in}(d)).C \mid (R, \mathbf{read}(d)).C \mid A + A \qquad P ::= C \mid P \parallel P$$

where for each used constant C there is a definition of the form $C := A$, which, in the sequel, will be written as $C := \sum_{j \in J}(R_j, \alpha_j).C_j$, for some finite index set J, with obvious meaning. In action prefix, $(R, \alpha)._-$, R is the name of a *rate function* under the scope of a suitable definition $R := E$; E is a numerical expression where the special operator $\#C$ can be used which, for state name C, yields the number of agents which are in state C in the current global system state. We will refrain from giving further details on the syntax of expressions E.

A *process definition* is the collection of definitions for the states of the process. A *system state* is a pair (P, D) where the set REPS of data repositories D is defined according to the following grammar:

$$D ::= \quad \langle \rangle \quad \mid \quad \langle d \rangle \quad \mid \quad D \mid D$$

The language of expressions E for rate function definitions is extended with $\#d$, for values $d \in \mathcal{D}$, with the obvious meaning. A *system* (model) *specification* is composed of the set of definitions for its processes, the set of definitions for the rate functions used therein, and an initial global state (P_0, D_0). It is required that for each state in the system specification there is exactly one definition. For the sake of simplicity, in the present paper we require that for all $i \in I$ and $x \in \{o, i, r\}$, if $\alpha_{ij} \in \mathcal{A}_x$ for some $j \in J_i$, then $\alpha_{ih} \in \mathcal{A}_x$ for all $h \in J_i$ (no mixed choice) and that for $C \neq C'$, if $C := \sum_{j \in J}(R_j, \alpha_j).C_j$ and $C' := \sum_{j \in J'}(R'_j, \alpha'_j).C'_j$ are both state definitions appearing in the system definition then $\{\alpha_j\}_{j \in J} \cap \{\alpha'_j\}_{j \in J'} \neq \emptyset$ implies $\{\alpha_j\}_{j \in J} = \{\alpha'_j\}_{j \in J'}$ (in order not to incur in the possibility of circular definitions in the ODE). In the sequel we let $\mathcal{S}$ denote the set of global system states.

Agents:

Reader	$= (\text{RA}, \mathbf{in}(a)).\text{Comp} + (\text{RB}, \mathbf{in}(b)).\text{Comp}$
Comp	$= (\text{RR}, \mathbf{read}(r)).\text{Reader}$
AWriter	$= (\text{WA}, \mathbf{out}(a)).\text{AWriter}$
BWriter	$= (\text{WB}, \mathbf{out}(b)).\text{AWriter}$

Rate Functions:

RA	$= 10 \cdot \#\text{Reader} \cdot \#a$
RB	$= 5 \cdot \#\text{Reader} \cdot \#b$
RR	$= 10 \cdot \#\text{Comp} \cdot \#r$
WA	$= 9 \cdot \#\text{AWriter}$
WB	$= 4 \cdot \#\text{BWriter}$

Fig. 1. A simple model of Readers and Writers

As a simple running example we consider the specification of a readers/writers model given in Figure 1, where two kinds of writers are considered—those writing messages of type a and those writing messages of type b—and readers perform some computation using some resources r before reading the next item, modelled by synchronisation on r—with the following initial state[1]

$$(Reader[10000] \parallel AWriter[5000] \parallel BWriter[5000], \langle a \rangle[5000] | \langle b \rangle[5000]) | \langle r \rangle[1000]).$$

2.2 Stochastic Semantics

The stochastic semantics are given in Figure 2 using the FuTS framework [9], that is an alternative to the classical approach, based on Labelled Transition Systems (LTS). In LTS, a transition is a triple (s, α, s') where s and α are the source state and the label of the transition, respectively, while s' is the target state reached from s via a transition labeled with α. In FuTS, a transition is a triple of the form $(s, \alpha, \mathscr{F})$. The first and second component are the source state and the label of the transition, as in LTS, while the third component $\mathscr{F}$ is a *continuation function* (or simply a *continuation* in the sequel), which associates a value from an appropriate semiring with each state s'. In the case of Markovian process algebra, the relevant semiring is that of non-negative real numbers. If $\mathscr{F}$ maps s' to 0, then state s' cannot be reached from s via this transition. A positive value for state s' represents the rate for the jump of the system from s to s'. Any FuTS over $\mathbb{R}_{\geq 0}$ uniquely defines a CTMC, which can obviously be built by successive application of the continuations to the set of states. Below we recall the main notions on FuTS. The reader interested in further details is referred to [9].

Given a denumerable non-empty set V, we let $\mathbf{FS}(V, \mathbb{R}_{\geq 0})$ denote the class of finitely supported[2] functions from V to $\mathbb{R}_{\geq 0}$. For $v_1, \ldots, v_n$ in set V and

---

[1] We use the standard notational convention that $P[n]$ means n instances of P in parallel: $P \parallel P \parallel \ldots \parallel P$. We extend it to tuples in the obvious way.

[2] A function $f : V \to \mathbb{R}_{\geq 0}$ has finite support if and only if the set $\{v \in V \mid f\, v \neq 0\}$ is finite. In this paper we often use Currying in function application.

$$\text{PA:} \quad \frac{C := \sum_{j \in J}(R_j, \alpha_j).C_j}{C \overset{R,\alpha}{\rightarrowtail} \sum_{\{h \in J, \alpha_h = \alpha \wedge R_h = R\}}[C_h \mapsto 1]} \qquad \text{DI:} \quad \frac{}{\langle d \rangle \overset{\mathbf{in}(d)}{\rightarrowtail} [\langle \rangle \mapsto 1]}$$

$$\text{DR:} \quad \frac{}{\langle d \rangle \overset{\mathbf{read}(d)}{\rightarrowtail} [\langle d \rangle \mapsto 1]} \qquad \text{DN}_1: \quad \frac{}{\langle \rangle \overset{\alpha}{\rightarrowtail} []} \qquad \text{DN}_2: \quad \frac{\alpha \notin \{\mathbf{in}(d), \mathbf{read}(d)\}}{\langle d \rangle \overset{\alpha}{\rightarrowtail} []}$$

$$\text{PP:} \quad \frac{P_1 \overset{R,\alpha}{\rightarrowtail} \mathscr{P}_1 \quad P_2 \overset{R,\alpha}{\rightarrowtail} \mathscr{P}_2}{P_1|P_2 \overset{R,\alpha}{\rightarrowtail} \mathscr{P}_1|(\mathcal{X} P_2)+(\mathcal{X} P_1)|\mathscr{P}_2} \qquad \text{DP:} \quad \frac{D_1 \overset{\alpha}{\rightarrowtail} \mathscr{D}_1 \quad D_2 \overset{\alpha}{\rightarrowtail} \mathscr{D}_2}{D_1|D_2 \overset{\alpha}{\rightarrowtail} \mathscr{D}_1|(\mathcal{X} D_2)+(\mathcal{X} D_1)|\mathscr{D}_2}$$

$$\text{OUT:} \quad \frac{P \overset{R,\mathbf{out}(d)}{\rightarrowtail} \mathscr{P}}{(P,D) \overset{\mathbf{out}(d)}{\rightarrowtail} \mathcal{R}_o(P,D,\mathscr{P},\mathcal{X}(D|\langle d\rangle),R)}$$

$$\text{IN:} \quad \frac{D \overset{\mathbf{in}(d)}{\rightarrowtail} \mathscr{D} \quad P \overset{R,\mathbf{in}(d)}{\rightarrowtail} \mathscr{P}}{(P,D) \overset{\mathbf{in}(d)}{\rightarrowtail} \mathcal{R}_i(P,D,\mathscr{P},\mathscr{D},R)} \qquad \text{READ:} \quad \frac{D \overset{\mathbf{read}(d)}{\rightarrowtail} \mathscr{D} \quad P \overset{R,\mathbf{read}(d)}{\rightarrowtail} \mathscr{P}}{(P,D) \overset{\mathbf{read}(d)}{\rightarrowtail} \mathcal{R}_r(P,D,\mathscr{P},\mathscr{D},R)}$$

Fig. 2. FuTS semantics of the process language with tuple creation

$r_1, \ldots, r_n \in \mathbb{R}_{\geq 0}$, we let $[v_1 \mapsto r_1, \ldots, v_n \mapsto r_n]$ in $\mathbf{FS}(V, \mathbb{R}_{\geq 0})$ denote the function mapping v_i to r_i, for $i = 1, \ldots n$, and any other $v \in V \setminus \{v_1, \ldots, v_n\}$ to 0; the degenerate case $[]$ denotes the constant function yielding 0 everywhere. For $v \in V$, $\mathcal{X} v$ denotes the function $[v \mapsto 1]$. For functions $\mathscr{F}_1, \mathscr{F}_2 \in \mathbf{FS}(V, \mathbb{R}_{\geq 0})$ we let $(\mathscr{F}_1 + \mathscr{F}_2) \in \mathbf{FS}(V, \mathbb{R}_{\geq 0})$ be defined as $(\mathscr{F}_1 + \mathscr{F}_2) v = (\mathscr{F}_1 v) + (\mathscr{F}_2 v)$ and we extend $(\mathscr{F}_1 + \mathscr{F}_2)$ to the n-ary version $\sum_{j \in J} \mathscr{F}_j$, in the obvious way, for finite index set J. For $r \in \mathbb{R}$ we let $\mathscr{F}/r \in \mathbf{FS}(V, \mathbb{R}_{\geq 0})$ be the defined as $(\mathscr{F}/r) v = (\mathscr{F} v)/r$ if $r \neq 0$ and $(\mathscr{F}/r) v = 0$ otherwise. We let $\oplus \mathscr{F}$ be defined as $\oplus \mathscr{F} = \sum_{v \in V}(\mathscr{F} v)$; note that $\oplus \mathscr{F}$ is finite, and thus well-defined, for $\mathscr{F} \in \mathbf{FS}(V, \mathbb{R}_{\geq 0})$. We recall standard structural congruence $\equiv$ on REPS, with $D|\langle\rangle \equiv D, D_1|D_2 \equiv D_2|D_1, (D_1|D_2)|D_3 \equiv D_1|(D_2|D_3)$. In the sequel, when dealing with data repositories, we will implicitly assume them modulo $\equiv$. For the sake of notational simplicity we will keep $D, D' \ldots$ in the notation (but actually the representatives of their equivalence classes are intended). A similar structural congruence $\equiv$ is assumed for processes, with $P_1 \parallel P_2 \equiv P_2 \parallel P_1, (P_1 \parallel P_2) \parallel P_3 \equiv P_1 \parallel (P_2 \parallel P_3)$, as well as similar conventions concerning notation.

For function $\mathscr{P}$ in $\mathbf{FS}(\text{PROC}_{/\equiv}, \mathbb{R}_{\geq 0})$ and $\mathscr{D}$ in $\mathbf{FS}(\text{REPS}_{/\equiv}, \mathbb{R}_{\geq 0})$ the notation $(\mathscr{P}, \mathscr{D})$ defines a function in $\mathbf{FS}(\mathcal{S}_{/\equiv}, \mathbb{R}_{\geq 0})$ as follows: for system state $(P, D) \in \mathcal{S}_{/\equiv}$, we have $(\mathscr{P}, \mathscr{D})(P, D) = (\mathscr{P} P) \cdot (\mathscr{D} D)$, where $\cdot$ denotes product in $\mathbb{R}_{\geq 0}$. For each rate function definition $R = E$, we consider the function $R : \mathcal{S}_{/\equiv} \to \mathbb{R}_{\geq 0}$ defined in the following. For all $(P, D) \in \mathcal{S}_{/\equiv} \ R(P, D) = [\![E]\!]_{(P,D)}$, where $[\![E]\!]_{(P,D)}$ denotes the value of expression E in the current global state (P, D). Obviously $[\![\#C]\!]_{(C,D)} = 1$ and $[\![\#C]\!]_{(P_1 \parallel P_2, D)} = [\![\#C]\!]_{(P_1, D)} + [\![\#C]\!]_{(P_2, D)}$. The definition for $[\![\#d]\!]_{(P,D)}$ is similar.

The continuation summation in Rule (PA) takes care of multiple alternatives with the same action and rate function. Different choices for functions

$\mathcal{R}_o$, $\mathcal{R}_i$, $\mathcal{R}_r$ in rules (IN), (OUT) and (READ) give rise to different interaction policies. For instance, for a TIPP-like synchronisation policy, assuming each rate function definition be of the form $R := k_R$, for $k_R \in \mathbb{R}_{>0}$, one can let $\mathcal{R}_o(P, D, \mathscr{P}, \mathscr{D}, R) = \mathcal{R}_i(P, D, \mathscr{P}, \mathscr{D}, R) = \mathcal{R}_r(P, D, \mathscr{P}, \mathscr{D}, R) = R(P, D) \cdot (\mathscr{P}, \mathscr{D})$. Similarly, for a PEPA-like interaction paradigm, assuming again each rate function be a constant, we get $\mathcal{R}_o(P, D, \mathscr{P}, \mathscr{D}, R) = R(P, D) \cdot (\mathscr{P}, \mathscr{D})$, and $\mathcal{R}_i(P, D, \mathscr{P}, \mathscr{D}, R) = \mathcal{R}_r(P, D, \mathscr{P}, \mathscr{D}, R) = R(P, D) \cdot \frac{\min\{\oplus\mathscr{P}, \oplus\mathscr{D}\}}{\oplus\mathscr{P}\cdot\oplus\mathscr{D}}(\mathscr{P}, \mathscr{D})$. In this paper we choose $\mathcal{R}_o = \mathcal{R}_i = \mathcal{R}_r = \mathcal{R}$ where

$$\mathcal{R}(P, D, \mathscr{P}, \mathscr{D}, R) = R(P, D) \cdot (\frac{\mathscr{P}}{\oplus\mathscr{P}}, \frac{\mathscr{D}}{\oplus\mathscr{D}}).$$

The idea is that the rate of the action is the full responsibility of the modeller, being equal to $R(P, D)$; in fact $(\frac{\mathscr{P}}{\oplus\mathscr{P}}, \frac{\mathscr{D}}{\oplus\mathscr{D}})(P', D')$ is equal to 1 if (P', D') is reachable in one transition from (P, D) and 0, if it is not.

3   Differential Semantics of OdeLinda

In this section we define the differential semantics for the language introduced in Sect. 2. We follow a similar approach as in [13,23]: we first define a population semantics for the language and then we define the differential semantics by means of deriving, from the population semantics, suitable ODEs for the mean-field model.

3.1   Population Semantics

Assume we are given a system specification where $\{C_1, \dots C_s\}$ is the set of all states of all processes and $\{d_1, \dots d_t\}$ is the set of all data values textually occurring in the specification. Given a global system state (P, D) we consider the corresponding vector $\mathbf{X} = (x_1, \dots, x_m)$ of counting variables such that, for $i = 1, \dots, s$, x_i records the number of agents in P which are in (local) state C_i, and for $i = s + 1, \dots, m = s + t$, x_i records the number of instances of d_{i-s} in D. Clearly, every transition at the single agent level corresponds to a change in the value of $\mathbf{X}$, i.e. a *population-based* transition. In order to formalise how single agent transitions induce population-based transitions, let (P', D') and (P'', D'') be two global system states with $P' = C'_1 \parallel \dots \parallel C'_{s'}$, $P'' = C''_1 \parallel \dots \parallel C''_{s''}$, $D' = d'_1|\dots|d'_{t'}$, and $D'' = d''_1|\dots|d''_{t''}$ and, with reference to the given system specification, define the *update vector* $\boldsymbol{\delta}$ in the usual way[3]: $\boldsymbol{\delta}((P'', D''), (P', D')) = (\delta_1, \dots, \delta_m)$ with

$$\delta_i = \begin{cases} \sum_{j=1}^{s''} \mathbf{1}\{C''_j = C_i\} - \sum_{j=1}^{s'} \mathbf{1}\{C'_j = C_i\}, & \text{for } i = 1, \dots, s \\[2mm] \sum_{j=1}^{t''} \mathbf{1}\{d''_j = d_i\} - \sum_{j=1}^{t'} \mathbf{1}\{d'_j = d_i\}, & \text{for } i = s + 1, \dots, m \end{cases}$$

---

[3] $\mathbf{1}\{C = C'\}$ is equal to 1 if $C = C'$ and to 0 otherwise.

With the definition of the update vector in place we can easily define the population-based transitions using the following rule:

$$\frac{(P,D) \overset{\alpha}{\rightarrowtail} (\mathscr{P}, \mathscr{D}) \quad r(P,D) = (\mathscr{P}, \mathscr{D})(P', D') > 0}{\mathbf{X} \overset{\alpha, r(P,D)}{\rightarrow} \mathbf{X} + \boldsymbol{\delta}((P', D'), (P, D))}$$

Using the above procedure, for any system specification we can derive a population-based CTMC (PCTMC) [2]. Such a PCTMC is defined as the tuple $(\mathbf{X}, \mathbb{Z}^m, \mathcal{T}, \mathbf{x}_0)$, where, :

- $\mathbf{X} = (x_1, \ldots, x_m)$ is the state vector, where, for $i = 1, \ldots, s$ element x_i is the count of agents in state C_i and, for $i = s+1, \ldots, m = s+t$ it counts the number of instances of d_{i-s};
- $\mathcal{T}(\mathbf{X}) = \{\tau_1, \ldots, \tau_h\}$ is the set of population-based transitions enabled in state $\mathbf{X}$. Each transition τ is associated with a update vector $\boldsymbol{\delta}_\tau$ and a rate $r_\tau(\mathbf{X}) = \sum\{r \mid \mathbf{X} \overset{\alpha, r}{\rightarrow} \mathbf{X} + \boldsymbol{\delta}_\tau \text{ for some } \alpha\}$;
- $\mathbf{x}_0 \in \mathbb{Z}^m$ is the initial state of the PCTMC.

3.2 Mean-Field Model

The dynamics of the above PCTMC is as follows: if the PCTMC is currently in state $\mathbf{X}$, then, every $1/r_\tau(\mathbf{X})$ time units, on average, a change in the population level of some agents and data items $\boldsymbol{\delta}_\tau$ occurs. We can approximate such a discrete change in a continuous way so that for small finite time interval Δt the change in the population level is

$$\mathbf{X}(t + \Delta t) = \mathbf{X}(t) + r_\tau(\mathbf{X}(t)) \cdot \Delta t \cdot \boldsymbol{\delta}_\tau$$

from which, for $\Delta t \to 0$, we get the ODE $\frac{d\mathbf{X}(t)}{dt} = r_\tau(\mathbf{X}(t)) \cdot \boldsymbol{\delta}_\tau$. Taking all enabled transitions into account the ODE describing the approximated transient evolution of the complete population-level system dynamics is given by the initial value problem:

$$\frac{d\mathbf{X}(t)}{dt} = \sum_{k=1}^{h} r_{\tau_k}(\mathbf{X}(t)) \cdot \boldsymbol{\delta}_{\tau_k} \qquad \text{with } \mathbf{X}(0) = \mathbf{x}_0$$

for large populations and under suitable scalability assumptions (on the rate functions); the interested reader is referred to [2] for the technical details.

With reference to our running example of Figure 1 we get the equations of Figure 3. Note that there is no dynamics for the writer processes in this example, since each of these agents has just a single state (and a self-loop). Similarly for the resource r.

$$\frac{d\,\mathrm{Reader}(t)}{dt} = 10 \cdot \mathrm{r}(t) \cdot \mathrm{Comp}(t) - (10 \cdot \mathrm{a}(t) + 5 \cdot \mathrm{b}(t)) \cdot \mathrm{Reader}(t)$$

$$\frac{d\,\mathrm{Comp}(t)}{dt} = (10 \cdot \mathrm{a}(t) + 5 \cdot \mathrm{b}(t)) \cdot \mathrm{Reader}(t) - 10 \cdot \mathrm{r}(t) \cdot \mathrm{Comp}(t)$$

$$\frac{d\,\mathrm{a}(t)}{dt} = 9 \cdot \mathrm{AWriter}(t) - 10 \cdot \mathrm{a}(t) \cdot \mathrm{Reader}(t)$$

$$\frac{d\,\mathrm{b}(t)}{dt} = 4 \cdot \mathrm{BWriter}(t) - 5 \cdot \mathrm{a}(t) \cdot \mathrm{Reader}(t)$$

Fig. 3. ODE for the simple model of Readers and Writers of Figure 1

4   Example - Foraging Ants

As an example, we revisit a somewhat simplified model of a colony of foraging ants inspired by earlier work in the literature [14,12,22]. The ants initially reside at a *Nest* and will move between the *Nest* and a *Food* site. There are two, bidirectional, paths connecting the *Nest* to the *Food* site (and vice-versa), the *Fast* path and the *Slow* path. Each path is composed by a finite sequence of (path) stages: the number ℓ_F of stages of the *Fast* path is smaller than the number ℓ_S of stages of the *Slow* path. The average time it takes an ant to traverse a stage is the same for each stage, regardless of whether it is situated on the *Slow* or the *Fast* path; such traversal times are modelled by exponentially distributed random variables. The situation is depicted in Fig. 4 where FP_j stands for the j-th of the ℓ_F stages of the *Fast* path and SP_j stands for the j-th of the ℓ_S stages of the *Slow* path, for $\ell_F < \ell_S$. A model for foraging ants is specified in Fig. 5. The set of data values occurring in the model specification is the finite set $(\bigcup_{j=1}^{\ell_F}\{\mathrm{Phe@FP}_j\}) \cup (\bigcup_{j=1}^{\ell_S}\{\mathrm{Phe@SP}_j\})$ where tuple $\langle\mathrm{Phe@FP}_j\rangle$ ($\langle\mathrm{Phe@SP}_j\rangle$, respectively) represents a unit of pheromone in stage j of the *Fast* path (*Slow* path, respectively). There are two process types, one modelling an ant and one modelling the expiration, i.e. decay, of pheromones; the (finite) set of states is as follows:

$\{\mathrm{Ant@Nest, Ant@Food}\} \cup$
$(\bigcup_{j=1}^{\ell_F}\{\mathrm{AntToFood@FP}_j\}) \cup (\bigcup_{j=1}^{\ell_S}\{\mathrm{AntToFood@SP}_j\}) \cup$
$(\bigcup_{j=1}^{\ell_F}\{\mathrm{AntToNest@FP}_j\}) \cup (\bigcup_{j=1}^{\ell_S}\{\mathrm{AntToNest@SP}_j\}) \cup$
$(\bigcup_{j=1}^{\ell_F}\{\mathrm{ExpPhe@FP}_j\}) \cup (\bigcup_{j=1}^{\ell_S}\{\mathrm{ExpPhe@SP}_j\}).$

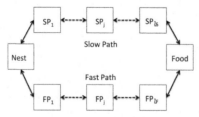

Fig. 4. Schematic of a *Fast* Path and a *Slow* Path for ants; FP_j represents stage j of the Fast Path and SP_j represents stage j of the Slow Path; $\ell_F < \ell_S$ is assumed

$$\text{Ant@Nest} = (\text{NFF}, \textbf{read}(\text{Phe@FP}_1)).\text{AntToFood@FP}_1 +$$
$$(\text{NFS}, \textbf{read}(\text{Phe@SP}_1)).\text{AntToFood@SP}_1$$

$$\text{AntToFood@FP}_j = (\text{NFF}_j, \textbf{out}(\text{Phe@FP}_j)).\text{AntToFood@FP}_{j+1} \qquad j = 1 \ldots \ell_F - 1$$
$$\vdots$$
$$\text{AntToFood@FP}_{\ell_F} = (\text{NFF}_{\ell_F}, \textbf{out}(\text{Phe@FP}_{\ell_F})).\text{Ant@Food}$$
$$\text{AntToFood@SP}_j = (\text{NFS}_j, \textbf{out}(\text{Phe@SP}_j)).\text{AntToFood@SP}_{j+1} \qquad j = 1 \ldots \ell_S - 1$$
$$\vdots$$
$$\text{AntToFood@SP}_{\ell_S} = (\text{NFS}_{\ell_F}, \textbf{out}(\text{Phe@SP}_{\ell_S})).\text{Ant@Food}$$
$$\text{Ant@Food} = (\text{FNF}_{\ell_F}, \textbf{read}(\text{Phe@FP}_{\ell_F})).\text{AntToNest@FP}_{\ell_F} +$$
$$(\text{FNS}_{\ell_S}, \textbf{read}(\text{Phe@SP}_{\ell_S})).\text{AntToNest@SP}_{\ell_S}$$
$$\text{AntToNest@FP}_{\ell_F - j} = (\text{FNF}_{\ell_F - j}, \textbf{out}(\text{Phe@FP}_{\ell_F - j})).\text{AntToNest@FP}_{\ell_F - (j+1)} \quad j = 1 \ldots \ell_F - 1$$
$$\vdots$$
$$\text{AntToNest@FP}_1 = (\text{FNF}_1, \textbf{out}(\text{Phe@FP}_1)).\text{Ant@Nest}$$
$$\text{AntToNest@SP}_{\ell_S - j} = (\text{FNS}_{\ell_S - j}, \textbf{out}(\text{Phe@SP}_{\ell_F - j})).\text{AntToNest@SP}_{\ell_F - (j+1)}$$
$$j = 1 \ldots \ell_S - 1$$
$$\vdots$$
$$\text{AntToNest@SP}_1 = (\text{FNS}_1, \textbf{out}(\text{Phe@SP}_1)).\text{Ant@Nest}$$
$$\text{ExpPhe@FP}_j = (\text{PHF}, \textbf{in}(\text{Phe@FP}_j)).\text{ExpPhe@FP}_j \qquad j = 1 \ldots \ell_F$$
$$\text{ExpPhe@SP}_j = (\text{PHS}, \textbf{in}(\text{Phe@SP}_j)).\text{ExpPhe@SP}_j \qquad j = 1 \ldots \ell_S$$

Fig. 5. ODELINDA model for foraging ants

State Ant@Nest (Ant@Food, respectively) represents an ant at the *Nest* (at the *Food* site, respectively). State AntToFood@FP$_j$ (AntToFood@SP$_j$, respectively) represents an ant in stage j of the *Fast* (*Slow*, respectively) path, when travelling from the *Nest* to the *Food*. State AntToNest@FP$_j$ (AntToNest@SP$_j$, respectively) represents an ant in stage j of the *Fast* (*Slow*, respectively) path, when travelling from the *Food* to the *Nest*. For the sake of simplicity, in this model, once an ant leaves the *Nest*, it can only proceed to the *Food* and then come back to the *Nest* (i.e. an ant cannot change its mind half-way a path or get stuck there). This is common in foraging ants models (see [22] and references therein). Finally, processes ExpPhe@FP$_j$ and ExpPhe@SP$_j$ are used for modelling pheromone decay. The definitions of rate functions NFF, NFS, NFF$_j$, NFS$_j$, PHF, and PHS are given below, where parameters k, m and p will be discussed later on in this section:

$$\text{NFF} = \frac{(k + \#\text{Phe@FP}_1)^2}{(k + \#\text{Phe@FP}_1)^2 + (k + \#\text{Phe@SP}_1)^2} \cdot \#\text{Ant@Nest}$$

$$\text{NFS} = \frac{(k + \#\text{Phe@SP}_1)^2}{(k + \#\text{Phe@FP}_1)^2 + (k + \#\text{Phe@SP}_1)^2} \cdot \#\text{Ant@Nest}$$

$$\text{NFF}_j = m \cdot \#\text{AntToFood@FP}_j$$

$$\text{NFS}_j = m \cdot \#\text{AntToFood@SP}_j$$

$$\text{PHF} = p \cdot \#\text{ExpPhe@FP}_j$$

$$\text{PHS} = p \cdot \#\text{ExpPhe@SP}_j$$

The expressions for the definitions of NFF and NFS are written in accordance with results from experimental studies on colonies of Argentine ants, as discussed in [14,12,22]. The definition of functions $\mathrm{FNF}, \mathrm{FNS}, \mathrm{FNF}_j$, and FNS_j are similar to those of $\mathrm{NFF}, \mathrm{NFS}, \mathrm{NFF}_j$ and NFS_j due to the symmetry of the model.

In the following we present some analysis results for two specific instantiations of the model and its parameters. We consider a model where the *Fast* path is composed of two stages while the *Slow* path is seven stages long, i.e. $\ell_F = 2$ and $\ell_S = 7$.

We first assume that pheromones do not decay: they accumulate in the path stages so that their total amount grows larger and larger. This is achieved by setting the decay rate p to zero. The value chosen for k is 10, while the ants rate of movement m from one path stage to the next one is set to 0.1. Fig. 6 shows the solution of the equations for the first 500 time units for an initial number of 1000 ants in the *Nest*, while no ants are assumed present in any other path stage, neither at the *Food* site, initially. One unit of pheromone is assumed to be present at time 0 at the stages of the *Slow* and the *Fast* paths closest to the *Nest*. Fig. 6 (left) shows that there is a quick drop in the number of ants at the *Nest* and that for a brief time frame of about 50 time units the cumulative number of ants on the *Slow* path is actually higher than that on the *Fast* path. This situation changes rapidly when ants start to return from the *Food* to the *Nest* providing implicitly feedback to the system by reinforcing the pheromone trace on the *Fast* path. This leads to a rather quick convergence of ants on the *Fast* path. The cumulative amount of pheromones on the *Fast* and the *Slow* path is shown in Fig. 6 (right).

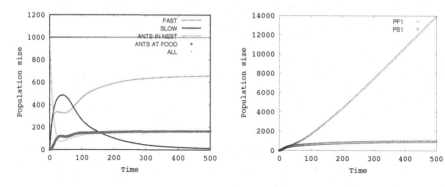

Fig. 6. Evolution over the first 500 time units of the number of ants in the *Nest*, at the *Food* and on the *Fast* and the *Slow* path (left) and the amounts of pheromones on the start of the short (PF1) and long (PS1) path (right)

Fig. 7 shows the results for a variant of the model where pheromone decays with constant rate $p = 0.03$. The evolution of both the cumulative number of ants in various locations and the amount of pheromone on the paths is shown over a time interval of 500 time units. Also in this case the ants converge on the *Fast* path and they are doing so in shorter time than in the case without decay of pheromones. Fig. 7 (left) has been obtained using Octave[4] for solving

---

[4] See for information on Octave http://www.octave.org. Version 3.4.0 was used.

the ODE for the model specification. Fig. 7 (right) shows the results obtained via stochastic simulation for the same model with 1000 ants taking the average over 100 runs[5].

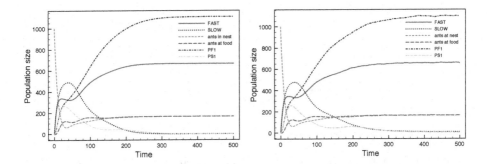

Fig. 7. Evolution over the first 500 time units of the system allowing decay of pheromones with rate 0.03. Solution of the differential equations (left) and stochastic simulation average over 100 runs for a model with 1000 ants (right)

We close this section showing the application of the mean field model-checker FlyFast [19] on the foraging ants example. Fluid model-checking techniques have recently been proposed as scalable techniques for the verification of properties of one (or a few) agents in the context of large populations [4]. These techniques are based on differential semantics, or on difference equations, when considering their discrete time counterparts, as is the case for FlyFast. The input language of the model-checker does not support the specification of models with dynamic population size, but if we can assume sufficiently large upper bounds on the sizes of the data sub-populations for the time horizon of interest[6], it is rather straightforward to translate the model of foraging ants shown in Fig. 5 into such a language, modelling data by two-state (i.e. "present" and "absent") processes and using an appropriate scaling of rates to turn the stochastic model into an equivalent probabilistic one [18]. We briefly illustrate the results for two properties for the ants model in Fig. 8. Property A shows how the probability of an ant in the nest to move to the short path within 30 time units changes over time due to the pheromones left behind by other ants. Property B shows the probability to reach a system state within t time units, where t ranges from 0 to 500, in which an ant in the nest moves to the short path within 30 time units with a probability of more than 0.95. Both properties can be expressed using the standard PCTL logic, a probabilistic extension of CTL [16]. Model-checking times for property A is 10 ms, whereas that of property B is 41,047 ms.

The purpose of the foraging ants example is to illustrate the ODELINDA language and mean field analysis approach for asynchronous, tuple based languages.

---

[5] Experiments were conducted with a 1.8 GHz Core i7 Intel processor and 4 GB RAM running Mac OS X 10.7.5.

[6] This can be checked using the result of an ODE analysis or simulation.

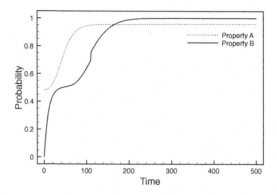

Fig. 8. Mean field model-checking results for properties A and B

Results better matching those of the original experiments in [14,12] can be obtained by a somewhat more complicated model in which ants leave the nest at a constant rate and in which the length of the paths and the constant traversal times are more accurately modelled by adding further path stages on each path implicitly using an Erlang distribution with more stages to approximate the constant traversal times. We omitted this here for the sake of simplicity.

5   Conclusions and Future Work

In this paper we have provided a differential semantics for languages with an asynchronous buffered communication interaction paradigm, e.g. data-repository-/ tuple-based ones. In particular, we have defined an individual-based Markovian as well as population based differential semantics for ODELINDA, a simple data-repository-based language. As example of use of the language we have shown a benchmark model of Foraging Ants and some results of its ODE-based analysis. There are several lines of research we plan to follow for moving from a simple experimental kernel language like ODELINDA to a complete, full fledged population modelling language. One line of research focuses of the introduction of an appropriate notion of *space*. One possibility is to take StoKLAIM [11] as a starting point, thus using a simple, locality based approach. Another, perhaps more interesting possibility, instead, is to use a richer, predicate based, addressing mechanism, like (a possibly restricted version of) the addressing mechanism of StocS [20], where the location is just one of the agents' attributes and its values are instances of an appropriate data type, namely *space*. This can take different forms, from topological spaces—including bi- or tri-dimensional continuous space—to more general closure spaces—including generic graphs—as in [6]. Another issue is the inclusion of richer data and operations including templates and pattern-matching. This implies the definition of syntactical restrictions, or static analysis techniques, for guaranteeing that in all computations of a model specification the set of *distinct* data values is bounded, while the multiplicity of each item can of course be unbounded. This also holds for the inclusion of process spawning and processes to be stored/retrieved to/from repositories. Finally, we plan to adapt fluid model-checking techniques to tuple-based languages.

References

1. Antonaki, M., Philippou, A.: A process calculus for spatially-explicit ecological models. In: Ciobanu, G. (ed.) Proceedings 6th Workshop on Membrane Computing and Biologically Inspired Process Calculi, MeCBIC 2012, Newcastle, UK, vol. 100, pp. 14–28. EPTCS (September 8, 2012), http://dx.doi.org/10.4204/EPTCS.100.2

2. Bortolussi, L., Hillston, J., Latella, D., Massink, M.: Continuous approximation of collective systems behaviour: A Tutorial. Performance Evaluation - An International Journal 70, 317–349 (2013), doi:10.1016/j.peva.2013.01.001

3. Bortolussi, L., Policriti, A.: Dynamical systems and stochastic programming: To ordinary differential equations and back. T. Comp. Sys. Biology 11, 216–267 (2009), doi:10.1007/978-3-642-04186-0_11

4. Bortolussi, L., Hillston, J.: Fluid model checking. In: Koutny, M., Ulidowski, I. (eds.) CONCUR 2012. LNCS, vol. 7454, pp. 333–347. Springer, Heidelberg (2012), http://dx.doi.org/10.1007/978-3-642-32940-1_24

5. Carriero, N., Gelernter, D., Mattson, T.G., Sherman, A.H.: The linda® alternative to message-passing systems. Parallel Computing 20(4), 633–655 (1994), http://dx.doi.org/10.1016/0167-8191(94)90032-9

6. Ciancia, V., Latella, D., Loreti, M., Massink, M.: Specifying and verifying properties of space. In: Diaz, J., Lanese, I., Sangiorgi, D. (eds.) TCS 2014. LNCS, vol. 8705, pp. 222–235. Springer, Heidelberg (2014), http://dx.doi.org/10.1007/978-3-662-44602-7_18

7. Ciocchetta, F., Hillston, J.: Bio-pepa: A framework for the modelling and analysis of biological systems. Theor. Comput. Sci. 410(33-34), 3065–3084 (2009), http://dx.doi.org/10.1016/j.tcs.2009.02.037

8. De Nicola, R., et al.: The SCEL Language: Design, Implementation, Verification. In: Wirsing, M., Hölzl, M., Koch, N., Mayer, P. (eds.) Collective Autonomic Systems. LNCS, vol. 8998, pp. 3–71. Springer, Heidelberg (2015)

9. De Nicola, R., Latella, D., Loreti, M., Massink, M.: A Uniform Definition of Stochastic Process Calculi. ACM Computing Surveys 46(1), 5:1–5:35 (2013), doi:10.1145/2522968.2522973

10. De Nicola, R., Ferrari, G.L., Pugliese, R.: KLAIM: A kernel language for agents interaction and mobility. IEEE Trans. Software Eng. 24(5), 315–330 (1998), http://doi.ieeecomputersociety.org/10.1109/32.685256

11. De Nicola, R., Katoen, J., Latella, D., Loreti, M., Massink, M.: Model checking mobile stochastic logic. Theor. Comput. Sci. 382(1), 42–70 (2007), http://dx.doi.org/10.1016/j.tcs.2007.05.008

12. Deneubourg, J.L., Aron, S., Goss, S., Pasteels, J.M.: The self-organizing exploratory pattern of the argentine ant. Journal of Insects Behaviour 3(2) (1990)

13. Feng, C., Hillston, J.: PALOMA: A Process Algebra for Located Markovian Agents. In: Norman, G., Sanders, W. (eds.) QEST 2014. LNCS, vol. 8657, pp. 265–280. Springer, Heidelberg (2014)

14. Goss, S., Aron, S., Deneubourg, J.L., Pasteels, J.M.: Self-organized shortcuts in the Argentine Ant. Naturwissenschaften 76, 579–581 (1989)

15. Guenther, M.C., Bradley, J.T.: Higher moment analysis of a spatial stochastic process algebra. In: Thomas, N. (ed.) EPEW 2011. LNCS, vol. 6977, pp. 87–101. Springer, Heidelberg (2011), http://dx.doi.org/10.1007/978-3-642-24749-1_8

16. Hansson, H., Jonsson, B.: A logic for reasoning about time and reliability. Formal Aspects of Computing. The International Journal of Formal Methods 6(5), 512–535 (1994)
17. Hermanns, H., Herzog, U., Katoen, J.: Process algebra for performance evaluation. Theor. Comput. Sci. 274(1-2), 43–87 (2002), http://dx.doi.org/10.1016/S0304-3975(00)00305-4
18. Latella, D., Loreti, M., Massink, M.: On-the-fly Fluid Model Checking via Discrete Time Population Models. Extended Version. Technical Report TR-QC-08-2014, QUANTICOL (2014)
19. Latella, D., Loreti, M., Massink, M.: On-the-fly fast mean-field model-checking. In: Abadi, M., Lluch Lafuente, A. (eds.) TGC 2013. LNCS, vol. 8358, pp. 297–314. Springer, Heidelberg (2014), http://dx.doi.org/10.1007/978-3-319-05119-2_17
20. Latella, D., Loreti, M., Massink, M., Senni, V.: Stochastically timed predicate-based communication primitives for autonomic computing. In: Bertrand, N., Bortolussi, L. (eds.) Proceedings Twelfth International Workshop on Quantitative Aspects of Programming Languages and Systems, QAPL 2014, Grenoble, France, April 12-13, vol. 154, pp. 1–16. EPTCS (2014), http://dx.doi.org/10.4204/EPTCS.154.1
21. Mamei, M., Zambonelli, F.: Programming pervasive and mobile computing applications: The TOTA approach. ACM Trans. Softw. Eng. Methodol. 18(4) (2009), http://doi.acm.org/10.1145/1538942.1538945
22. Massink, M., Latella, D.: Fluid analysis of foraging ants. In: Sirjani, M. (ed.) CO-ORDINATION 2012. LNCS, vol. 7274, pp. 152–165. Springer, Heidelberg (2012), http://dx.doi.org/10.1007/978-3-642-30829-1_11
23. Tribastone, M., Gilmore, S., Hillston, J.: Scalable differential analysis of process algebra models. IEEE Transactions on Software Engineering. IEEE CS 38(1), 205–219 (2012)

Logic Fragments: A Coordination Model Based on Logic Inference

Francesco Luca De Angelis[✉] and Giovanna Di Marzo Serugendo

Institute of Information Services Science, University of Geneva, Switzerland
{francesco.deangelis,giovanna.dimarzo}@unige.ch

Abstract. Chemical-based coordination models have proven useful to engineer self-organising and self-adaptive systems. Formal assessment of emergent global behaviours in self-organising systems is still an issue, most of the time emergent properties are being analysed through extensive simulations. This paper aims at integrating logic programs into a chemical-based coordination model in order to engineer self-organising systems as well as assess their emergent properties. Our model is generic and accommodates various logics. By tuning the internal logic language we can tackle and solve coordination problems in a rigorous way, without renouncing to important engineering properties such as compactness, modularity and reusability of code. This paper discusses our logic-based coordination model and shows how to engineer and verify a simple pattern detection example and a gradient-chemotaxis example.

1 Introduction

Coordination models have been proven useful for designing and implementing distributed systems. They are particularly appealing for developing self-organising systems, since the shared tuple space on which they are based is a powerful paradigm to implement self-organising mechanisms, particularly those requiring indirect communication (e.g. stigmergy) [16]. Chemical-based coordination models are a category of coordination models that use the chemical reaction metaphor and have proven useful to implement several types of self-organising mechanisms [18]. A well-known difficulty in the design of self-organising systems stems from the analysis, validation and verification (at design-time or run-time) of so-called emergent properties - i.e. properties that can be observed at a global level but that none of the interacting entities exhibit on its own. Few coordination models integrate features supporting the validation of emergent properties, none of them relying on the chemical metaphor.

In this paper, we propose to enrich a chemical-based coordination model with the notion of Logic Fragments (i.e. a combination of logic programs). Our logic-based coordination model allows agents to inject Logic Fragments into the shared space. Those fragments actually define on-the-fly ad hoc chemical reactions that apply on matching data tuples present in the system, removing tuples and producing new tuples, possibly producing also new Logic Fragments. Our model is defined independently of the logic language used to define the syntax of the

© IFIP International Federation for Information Processing 2015
T. Holvoet and M. Viroli (Eds.): COORDINATION 2015, LNCS 9037, pp. 35–48, 2015.
DOI: 10.1007/978-3-319-19282-6_3

Logic Fragment, an actual instantiation and implementation of the model can use its own logic(s). The advent of new families of logic languages (e.g. [17]) has enriched the paradigm of logic programming, allowing, among other things, practical formalisation and manipulation of data inconsistency, knowledge representation of partial information and constraints satisfaction. By combining those logics with a chemical-based coordination model, we argue that global properties can be verified at design time.

Section 2 discusses related works, section 3 presents our logic-based coordination model. Section 4 shows two case studies: a simple pattern recognition example and another one with the gradient and chemotaxis patterns. Finally, section 5 concludes the paper.

2   Related Works

2.1   Chemical-Based Coordination Models

An important class of coordination models is represented by so-called chemical-based coordination models, where "chemical" stands for the process of imitating the behaviours of chemical compounds in chemical systems.

Gamma (General Abstract Model for Multiset mAnipulation) [2] and its evolutions historically represents an important chemical-inspired coordination model. The core of the model is based on the concept of virtual chemical reactions expressed through *condition-action* rewriting pairs. Virtual chemical reactions are applied on input multisets which satisfy a *condition* statement and they produce as output multisets where elements are modified according to the corresponding *action* (like for chemical compounds); the execution of virtual chemical reactions satisfying a *condition* pair is nondeterministic. Gamma presents two remarkable properties: (i) the constructs of the model implicitly support the definition of parallel programs; (ii) the language was proposed in the context of systematic program derivation and correctness as well as termination of programs is easy to prove ([8]). Its major drawback is represented by the complexity of modeling real large applications.

The SAPERE model [4] (Figure 1a) is a coordination model for multiagent pervasive systems inspired by chemical reactions. It is based on four main concepts: *Live Semantic Annotations* (LSAs), *LSA Tuple Space*, *agents* and *eco-laws*. LSAs are tuples of types (*name, value*) used to store applications data. For example, a tuple of type (*date*, 04/04/1988) can be used to define a hypothetical date. LSAs belonging to a computing node are stored in a shared container named LSA Tuple Space. Each LSA is associated with an agent, an external entity that implements some domain-specific logic program. For example, agents can represent sensors, services or general applications that want to interact with the LSA space - injecting or retrieving LSAs from the LSA space. Inside the shared container, tuples react in a virtual chemical way by using a predefined set of coordination rules named *eco-laws*, which can: (i) instantiate relationships among LSAs (*Bonding* eco-law); (ii) aggregate them (*Aggregate* eco-law); (iii) delete them (*Decay* eco-law) and (iv) spread them across remote

LSA Tuples Spaces (*Spreading* eco-law). Spontaneous executions of *eco-laws* can be fired when specific commands (named *operators*) are present in tuple values. When a tuple is modified by an *eco-law*, its corresponding agent is notified: in this way, agents react to virtual chemical reactions according to the program they implement. The implementation of the SAPERE model, named SAPERE middleware, has been proven to be powerful enough and robust to permit the development of several kinds of real distributed self-adaptive and self-organising applications, as reported in [18]. Nevertheless, the model does not aim at proving correctness or emergence of global properties programs built on it: this means that proving correctness of applications may turn to be a complex task.

2.2 Formal Approaches for Tuple Based Coordination Models

Coordination models based on tuple spaces are amenable to several kinds of analytical formalisation.

PoliS [5] is a coordination model based on multiset rewriting in which co-ordination rules consume and produce multisets of tuples; rules are expressed in a Chemical Abstract Machine style [3]. In PoliS, properties can be proved by using the PoliS Temporal Logic and the PoliMC model checker.

Tuples centres [15] allow the use of a specification language (named RespecT) to define computations performed in the tuple space. Computations are associated with events triggered internally because of reactions previously fired or during the execution of traditional input/output operations by agents. RespecT is based on first-order logic and unification of unitary clauses (tuple templates) and ground atoms (tuples) represent the basic tuple matching mechanism.

In the ACLT model [7], the tuple space is treated as a container of logic theories, which can be accessed by logic agents to perform deduction processes. Again, the first-order logic and unification of unitary clauses and ground atoms is used as matching mechanism; the model offers specific input-output primitives tailored to provide different meaning for unification by allowing a certain control in selecting the set of unitary clauses to be treated as facts in case of backtracks or temporary missing information in the deduction process.

In our model we do not express coordination in terms of rewriting rules; moreover, the logic layer is enhanced by considering several types of logic languages.

3 Logic- and Chemical-Based Coordination Model

3.1 Definition of the Model

The chemical-based coordination model we present in this paper is designed to exploit several important features of the models cited above in the context of self-organising and self-adaptive applications; our goal is to define a coordination model with the following characteristics: (i) coordination algorithms can be described in an sufficiently abstract way starting from high-level specifications; (ii) the constructs used to express coordination algorithms are amenable to formal analysis of their correctness, they incentivize the decoupling of logic from implementation and they meet software engineering properties such as modularity, reusability and compactness. The rationale leading the definition of our coordination model can be synthesized as the adoption of Kowalski's terminology [12]: algorithm = logic + control. This formulation promotes the dichotomy of algorithms in: (i) logic components (formulae) that determine the meaning of the algorithm, the knowledge used to solve a problem (i.e. what has to be done) and (ii) control components, which specify the manner the knowledge is used (i.e. how it has to be done).

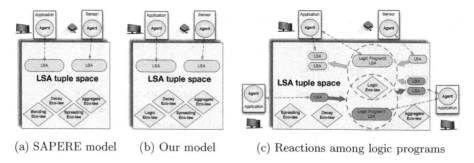

(a) SAPERE model   (b) Our model   (c) Reactions among logic programs

Fig. 1. The generalization of the SAPERE Model

The coordination model we define (Figure 1b) is a generalization of the SAPERE model with two additional features: (i) LSAs can store not only data tuples but actual logic programs (Section 3.2); (ii) the bonding eco-law is replaced by a new one named Logic eco-law, which is in charge of executing logic programs and performing the bonding actions. The remaining components of the model are exactly the same as the ones of the SAPERE model. The virtual chemical reactions among tuples taking place in the shared container are now driven by logic inferences processes, which produce either data tuples or new logic programs during the "execution" of logic programs (Figure 1c). This process brings the idea promulgated by [12] in the context of chemical-based coordination models: the logic components of an algorithm are expressed in terms of logic programs, here embedded in LSAs, which can react among each other in a chemical fashion. Similarly, agents implement the control components (written in a programming language such as Java), and they perform computations according to the knowledge inferred by logic programs. This approach to separation and mapping of concepts helps designing coordination algorithms from an abstract point of view. On the one hand, algorithms are thought as interactions of atomic logic entities which define the meaning (in Kowalski's terminology) of subparts of the original algorithm. On the other hand, once logic entities have been defined, a specific problem-solving strategy can be chosen to be implemented for each subpart of the original problem. The intuition of using logic programs is twofold: (i) tuples exchanges represent the basic mechanism to carry out indirect communication among agents, thus the state and the evolution of a coordination process can be defined by analysing the set of tuples in the containers; (ii) tuples are used as inputs (facts) and produced as outputs of logic programs (models and formulae obtained by resolution rules). By considering points (i) and (ii), logic programs provide a natural formal tool to express coordination, allowing for inferred formulae to state relationships among entities of the system, depicting the evolution of coordination processes and proving system properties.

3.2   Logic Programs

Logic programs [14] are sets of logic formulae and are expressed in a logic language (e.g. first-order logic). Executing a logic program means either: (i) providing queries to the program and testing whether they logically follow from the program by using a proof engine (*logic inference*) or (ii) inferring all sentences that logically follow from the program (*logic semantics*). An interpretation of a formal language is an interpretation (see [14]) of constants, predicate and functions of the language over a given domain. The truth-value of a logic sentence is determined by the interpretation of the logic connectives. Given a logic program P, a model is an interpretation M such that every formula in P is true (depicted as $M \models P$). Here we are interested in Herbrand interpretations ([14]): (i) the implicit domain is the Herbrand Universe, the closure of the set of constants under all the functions symbols of the language; (ii) constants are interpreted as themselves and every function symbol as the function it refers to. In classical 2-valued logic programs, Herbrand interpretation can be defined through sets of atoms implicitly interpreted as *true*.

Example: $P = (C(x) \leftarrow A(x), B(x); \quad A(c) \leftarrow \Box; B(c) \leftarrow \Box;)$ is a *definite* logic program [14]. Clauses are implicitly universally quantified. This is a definite logic program (i.e. containing Horn clauses): x is a variable, c is a constant and here they range over an (implicitly) defined domain. The first rule is composed of the head $C(X)$ and the body $A(X), B(X)$ and it can be read as "$C(X)$ is true if both $A(X)$ and $B(X)$ are true". Rules with empty bodies ($\Box$) are named *facts* and they state sentences whose heads must be considered satisfied; in this case $A(c)$ and $B(c)$ hold. $M = \{A(c), B(c), C(c)\}$ is a model for the program in the example, because it satisfies all the rules.

3.3   Logic Languages

In our model, logic programs are executed by the Logic eco-law. An important point in our approach is the generality of the coordination model w.r.t. the logic. We consider only logic languages that support Herbrand's interpretations, whereas we do not put any constraint on the inference methods or the semantics. Both inference methods and semantics are treated as parameters associated with logic programs. From the practical point of view, for each logic language we require the implementation of a dedicated Logic eco-law that executes the corresponding logic programs. This feature makes possible to use, possibly simultaneously: (i) several types of logic programs (e.g. *definite, general logic programs*, several types *DATALOG* or *DATALOG-inspired* programs) associated with *two-valued, multi-valued* (e.g. *Belnap's logic*) or *paraconsistent* logics; (ii) several inference procedures (e.g. *SLD, SLDNF*) and semantics (e.g. *Apt-van Emden-Kowalski, Kripke-Kleen, stable,well-founded* model semantics) [11,13,1,9,17].

3.4 Logic Fragments

In our model, logic programs are embedded in logic units named Logic Fragments. The following set of definitions will be used to clarify the concept. We assume that *Prop, Const* and *Var* are finite mutually disjoint sets of relation symbols, constants and variables respectively. We will identify variables with letters $x, y, \ldots$ and constants with letters $a, b, \ldots$.

Definition 1 (Literals, Ground Literals). A *literal* $\hat{P}$ is an expression of type $P(X_1, \ldots, X_n)$ or $\neg P(X_1, \ldots, X_n)$ where $P \in Prop$ and $X_i \in (Const \cup Var)$ for $i = 1, \ldots, n$. A *ground literal* is a literal without variables. The set of all ground literals w.r.t. a set $Const$ is denoted $G(Const)$. The power set of $G(Const)$ is depicted $\mathcal{P}(G)$.

Definition 2 (Valuations). A *valuation* w is a function from Var to $Const$ that assigns a constant c_i to each variable x_i. The set of all possible valuations is depicted as $\mathcal{W} = \{w | w : Var \to Const\}$.

Definition 3 (Instances of Literal). If $\hat{P}$ is a literal and w is a valuation, with $\hat{P}_w$ we identify the ground literal where every variable of $\hat{P}$ has been replaced by a constant according to the definition of w. $\hat{P}_w$ is named an *instance* of $\hat{P}$. We denote $I_{\hat{P}} = \{\hat{P}_w | w \in \mathcal{W}\} \subseteq G(Const)$.

Definition 4 (Logic Programs). A logic program is a set of logic formulae written in a logic language using: (i) literals $\hat{P}_1, \ldots, \hat{P}_n$ defined over $Prop, Const, Var$ and (ii) logic operators.

Definition 5 (A-generator). Given a literal $P(X_1, \ldots, X_n)$, an A-generator w.r.t. a function $U : Const^n \to \{T, F\}$ is the finite set:
$$P^U(X_1, \ldots, X_n) = \{P(c_1, \ldots, c_n) \in I_{P(X_1, \ldots, X_n)} | U(c_1, \ldots, c_n) = T\}.$$

Example: $A^U(X) = \{A(X) | X \in \{a, b, c\}\} = \{A(a), A(b), A(c)\}$, with $U(a) = U(b) = U(c) = T$.

Definition 6 (I-generator). Given a literal $P(X_1, \ldots, X_n)$, an I-generator w.r.t a function $V : \mathcal{P}(G) \to \mathcal{P}(G)$ and a finite set $H \subseteq \mathcal{P}(G)$ is the set:
$$P^{H,V}(X_1, \ldots, X_n) = \{P(c_1, \ldots, c_n) \in I_{P(X_1, \ldots, X_n)} \cap V(H)\}$$
If V is omitted, we assume that $V(H) = H$ (identity function).

Example: if $N = \{2, 3, 4\}$ and $V(N) = \{Even(x) | x \in N \wedge x \text{ is even}\}$, then $Even^{N,V}(X) = \{Even(2), Even(4)\}$.

The rationale of such definitions is to provide the program with a set of facts built from conditions holding on tuples stored in the container. The unfolding of these generators produces new facts for the interpretation of the logic program.

By $\mathcal{LF}$ we identify the algebraic structure of Logic Fragments, recursively defined as follows:

Definition 7. (Logic Fragments $\mathcal{LF}$)

(I) $\triangle \in \mathcal{LF}$

(II) *(Grouping)* If $e \in \mathcal{LF}$ then $(e) \in \mathcal{LF}$

(III) *(Parallel-and)* If $e_1, e_2 \in \mathcal{LF}$ then $e_1 \sqcap e_2 \in \mathcal{LF}$

(IV) *(Parallel-or)* If $e_1, e_2 \in \mathcal{LF}$ then $e_1 \sqcup e_2 \in \mathcal{LF}$

(V) *(Composition)* If P is a logic program, $\mathcal{M}$ an execution modality, S a set of A,I-generators, $\varphi : \mathcal{P}(G) \to \{T, F\}$ and $e_p \in \mathcal{LF}$ then $(P, \mathcal{M}, e_P, S, \varphi) \in \mathcal{LF}$.

$\triangle$ is a special symbol used only in Logic Fragments to depict *all* the tuples in the container (both LSAs and Logic Fragments). $\mathcal{M}$ is the identifier of the way P is "executed" (we will use $\mathcal{M} = \mathcal{A}$ for the Apt-van Emden-Kowalski and $\mathcal{M} = \mathcal{K}$ for the Kripke-Kleen semantics). e_P is named *constituent* of the Logic Fragment and it is interpreted as a set of tuples used as support to generate the facts for the program. S is a set of A,I-generators used to derive new facts from P. The function $\varphi : \mathcal{P}(G) \to \{T, F\}$ returns T if the tuples represented by the constituent e_p satisfy some constraints; the logic program is executed if and only if $\varphi(e_P) = T$ (Def. 8). φ_T is constant and equal to T. For style reason, we will write $P^{\mathcal{M}}(e_P, S, \varphi)$ instead of $(P, \mathcal{M}, e_P, S, \varphi)$.

Every Logic Fragment is executed by the Logic eco-law; its semantics is defined by using the function v_L.

Definition 8 (Semantic function). $v_L : \mathcal{LF} \to \mathcal{P}(G) \cup \{\bowtie\}$ associates the fragment with the set of tuples inferred by the logic program (*consequent*) or with $\bowtie$, which stands for *undefined interpretation*. L denotes the set of actual tuples in the container before executing a Logic Fragment. Operators are ordered w.r.t. these priorities: grouping (highest priority), composition, $\sqcap$ and $\sqcup$ (lowest priority). v_L is recursively defined as follows:

I) $v_L(\triangle) \triangleq L$

II) $v_L((e)) \triangleq v_L(e)$

III) $v_L(e_1 \sqcap ... \sqcap e_n)_{n \geq 2} \triangleq \begin{cases} \bowtie & \text{if } \exists i \in \{1, ..., n\}.v_L(e_i) = \bowtie \\ \bigcup_{i=1}^{n} v_L(e_i) & \text{otherwise} \end{cases}$

IV) $v_L(e_1 \sqcup ... \sqcup e_n)_{n \geq 2} \triangleq \begin{cases} \bigcup_{i \in \mathcal{I}} v_L(e_i) & \text{if } \mathcal{I} = \{e_i | v_L(e_i) \neq \bowtie, 0 \leq i \leq n\} \neq \emptyset \\ \bowtie & \text{otherwise} \end{cases}$

V) $v_L(P^{\mathcal{M}}(e_P, S, \varphi)) \triangleq Q$

Q is the *consequent* of $P^{\mathcal{M}}$ and it is defined as follows: if $\mathcal{M}$ is not compatible with the logic program P or if $v_L(e_p) = \bowtie$ or if $\varphi(v_L(e_p)) = F$ then $Q = \bowtie$. φ "blocks" the execution of the program as long as a certain condition over e_p is not satisfied. Otherwise, based on $S = \{P_0^{H_0, V_0}(X_{01}, ..., X_{0t_0}), ..., P_n^{H_n, V_n}(X_{n1}, ..., X_{nt_n}), P_0(Y_{01}, ..., Y_{0z_0}), ... P_m(Y_{m1}, ..., Y_{mz_m})\}$, the Logic eco-law produces the set of facts $Fs =$

$\bigcup_{i=0}^{n} P_i^{v_L(H_i),V_i}(X_{i1},\ldots,X_{it_i}) \cup \bigcup_{i=0}^{m} P_i(Y_{i1},\ldots,Y_{iz_i})$. A,I-generators are then used to define sets of ground literals for the logic program which satisfy specific constraints; during the evaluation, for every set H_i we have either $H_i = e_p$ or $H_i = \triangle$. Q is finally defined as the set of atoms inferred by applying $\mathcal{M}$ on the new logic program $P' = P \cup \{l \leftarrow \Box | l \in Fs\}$, enriched by all the facts contained in Fs. Note that there may be no need to explicitly calculate all the literals of A,I-generators beforehand: the membership of literals to generators sets may be tested one literal at a time or skipped because of the short-circuit evaluation.

Lemma 1 (Properties of Operators). Given $a, b \in \mathcal{LF}$ with $a \equiv b$ we state that $v_L(a) = v_L(b)$ for every set of literals L. Then for any $a, b, c \in \mathcal{LF}$:

I)	$a \sqcup a \equiv a$	(Idempotence of $\sqcup$)
II)	$a \sqcup b \equiv b \sqcup a$	(Commutativity of $\sqcup$)
III)	$a \sqcup (b \sqcup c) \equiv (a \sqcup b) \sqcup c$	(Associativity of $\sqcup$)
IV)	$a \sqcap a \equiv a$	(Idempotence of $\sqcap$)
V)	$a \sqcap b \equiv b \sqcap a$	(Commutativity of $\sqcap$)
VI)	$a \sqcap (b \sqcap c) \equiv (a \sqcap b) \sqcap c$	(Associativity of $\sqcap$)
VII)	$a \sqcap (b \sqcup c) \equiv (a \sqcap b) \sqcup (a \sqcap c) \equiv (b \sqcup c) \sqcap a$	(Distrib. of $\sqcap$ over $\sqcup$)

Intuitively, composing two Logic Fragments means calculating the inner one first and considering it as constituent for the computation of the second one. *Parallel-and* ($\sqcap$) means executing all the Logic Fragments them in a row or none, whereas *Parallel-or* ($\sqcup$) means executing only those ones that can be executed at a given time.

3.5 Update of the Container

In our model, all the Logic Fragments are carried on a snapshot image of the container, i.e. given a Logic Fragment e in the container, if $v_L(e) \neq \bowtie$, then it is evaluated as an atomic operation (every symbol $\triangle$ in the sub Logic Fragments which composes e is always translated with the same set of actual tuples). Multiple Logic Fragments ready to be evaluated are computed in a non-deterministic order. The tuples inferred by the logic programs (with all used facts) are inserted in the container only when the evaluation of the whole logic program terminates. At that point, the Logic eco-law injects the inferred tuples in the container and notifies the end of inference process to the agent. The Logic Fragment is subject to a new evaluation process as soon as the set Fs changes due to updates of the shared container, but there are no concurrent parallel evaluations of the same Logic Fragment at a given time (unless it appears twice); this aspect can potentially hide tuples updates in the evaluation process (Section 5). The representation of the functions associated with A,I-generators depends on the implementation.

4   Case Studies

By using Logic Fragments we can easily tackle interesting coordination problems and properties. Additional examples are reported in [6].

4.1 Palindrome Recognition

As a first example we show an easy pattern recognition scenario. Assuming that an agent A inserts positive integers into the container, we want to discover which ones are palindromic numbers (i.e. numbers that can be read in the same way from left to right and from right to left). We assume that these integers are represented by tuples of type $N(a)$, where a is a number, e.g. $N(3)$ represents the number 3. Agent A inserts the Logic Fragment $LF_p : P_p^A(\triangle, \{N^\triangle, TestPalin\}, \varphi_p)$.

$$\varphi_p(\triangle) = T \Leftrightarrow \exists w : N(X)_w \in \triangle$$
$$TestPalin(x) = \{TestPalin(a)|a \text{ is a positive palindromic number less than } d_{max}\}$$

Logic code 1.1 Definite logic program P_p

$Palin(x) \leftarrow N(x), TestPalin(x)$

P_p is the logic program in Code 1.1, evaluated with the Apt-van Embden Kowalski semantics ($\mathcal{A}$). The set S of A,I-generators is composed of two elements: $N^\triangle$ contains all literals $N(a)$ (numbers) existing in the container ($\triangle$); $TestPalin(x)$ contains all the literals of type $TestPalin(a)$, where a is a positive palindromic number less then d_{max}. These two sets of literals are treated as facts for P_p. According to φ, P_p is executed as soon as a number $N(a)$ is inserted into the container. The rule of the logic program P_p states that a number a is a palindromic number $(Palin(a))$ if a is a number $(N(a))$ and a passes the test for being palindromic $(TestPalin(a))$. We consider the tuple space shown in Figure 2a and 2b. At the beginning, agent A injects LF_p (Figure 2a). At a later stage A injects $N(22)$ and the Logic Fragment is then executed. In this case, $N^\triangle$ is evaluated as $\{N(22)\}$. Moreover, $TestPalin(a)$ will contain $TestPalin(22)$, because it is palindromic. This means the consequent Q of LF_p contains $Palin(22)$, along with all the facts generated by the A,I-generators used in the logic program. If now agent A injects $N(12)$, the Logic Fragment is re-executed and $N^\triangle$ is evaluated as $\{N(22), N(12)\}$. This second number does not satisfy the palindromic test $(N(12) \notin TestPalin(x))$, so the 12 will not be considered as palindromic. Finally A injects $N(414)$ and during the re-execution of LF_p we obtain: $N^\triangle = \{N(22), N(12), N(414)\}$ and $N(414) \in TestPalin(x)$, so the consequent Q will contain $Palin(22)$ and $Palin(414)$ (Figure 2b). Note that if numbers were injected by agents different from A (like a sensor), the same reactions would take place.

Property 1. A palindromic integer $a \geq 0$ exists in the container if and only if $Palin(a)$ exists in the least Herbrand model of P_p' (the extension of P_p with all the facts created by A,I-generators).

Proof Sketch. *The property above states that by using the Logic Fragment LF_p we are able to correctly find out all the palindromic integers. Thanks to the logic programs and the semantic of Logic Fragments, we can easily verify that if such integers exist in the container then their literals are inferred in Herbrand model*

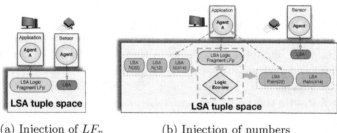

(a) Injection of LF_p (b) Injection of numbers

Fig. 2. Evolution of the container for the example of Section 4.1

of P'_p. Moreover, given that such literals are only generated by LF_p, if such literals exist in the model then there must be the associated palindromic integers in the shared space.

4.2 Gradient and Chemotaxis Patterns - General Programs

In this second example we use Logic Fragments to implement the gradient and chemotaxis design patterns ([10]), which are two bio-inspired mechanisms used to build and follow shortest paths among nodes in a network. The chemotaxis is based on the gradient pattern. A gradient is a message spread from one source to all the nodes in the network, carrying a notion of distance from the source (hop-counter). Gradient messages can also carry user-information. Once a node receives a gradient from a known source whose hop-counter is less than the local one (i.e. a new local shortest-path has been found), the node updates its local copy of the hop-counter (aggregation) and spreads it towards the remaining neighbours with a hop-counter incremented by one unit. In these terms, the gradient algorithm is similar to the distance-vector algorithm. The chemotaxis pattern resorts to gradient shortest-paths to route messages towards the source of the gradient. We can implement the gradient and chemotaxis patterns by using an agent A_{gc} associated with the Logic Fragment:

$$LF_{gc} : P_g^{\mathcal{A}}\left(P_a^{\mathcal{A}}(\triangle \sqcap P_n^{\mathcal{K}}(\triangle, S_n, \varphi_n), S_a, \varphi_T), S_g, \varphi_T\right) \sqcup P_{ch}^{\mathcal{A}}(\triangle, S_{ch}, \varphi_{ch})$$

Logic code 1.2 Program P_n - Next hop initialization

GPath(x,d_{max},*null*) $\leftarrow$ ¬existsGPath(x)

Logic code 1.3 Program P_a - Aggregation

cmpGradient(x_1, x_2, y_1, y_2, z) $\leftarrow$ Gmsg(x_1, x_2, y_1, z), GPath(x_1, y_2, w)
updateGPath(x_1, y_1, x_2, z) $\leftarrow$ cmpGradient(x_1, x_2, y_1, y_2, z), less(y_1, y_2)

Logic code 1.4 Program P_g - Spreading

spreadGradient$(x_1, local, z, y, x_2) \leftarrow$ updateGPath(x_1, y, x_2, z)

Logic code 1.5 Program P_{ch} - Chemotaxis

sendChemo$(m, x, w) \leftarrow$ Cmsg(m, x), GPath(x, y, w)

$\varphi_n(\triangle) = T \Leftrightarrow \exists w : Gmsg(x_1, x_2, y, z)_w \in \triangle, \quad \varphi_{ch}(\triangle) = T \Leftrightarrow \exists w : Cmsg(x, y)_w \in \triangle$

$S_{ch} = \{Cmsg^{\triangle}, GPath^{\triangle}\} \quad S_g = \{updateGPath^{e P_g}\} \quad S_n = \{existsGPath^{\triangle, V}, Gmsg^{\triangle}\}$

$S_a = \{Gmsg^{e P_a}, GPath^{e P_a}, less\} \quad less(x, y) = \{less(a, b) | a < b, \ a, b \in \{1, ..., d_{max}\}\}$

$existsGPath(x)^{\triangle, V} = \{\neg existsGPath(a) \in I_{\neg existsGPath(x)} \cap V(\triangle)\}$

$V(\triangle) = \{\neg existsGPath(a) | \exists w : Gmsg(a, x, y, z)_w \in \triangle \wedge \neg \exists GPath(a, y, w)_w \in \triangle\}$

Gradients are represented by tuples $Gmsg(a, b, c, d)$ where a is the ID of the source, b is the ID of the last sender of the gradient, c is the hop-counter and d is the content of the message. Values $null$, d_{max} and $local$ are considered constants. Local hop-counter are stored in tuples of type $GPath(a, c, e)$, where a and c are as above and e is the previous node in the path, this will be used to route the chemotaxis message downhill towards the source. LF_{gc} is composed of several Logic Fragments; the *parallel-or* operator makes the agent A_{gc} to react simultaneously to chemotaxis and gradients messages. The innermost fragment $e_{P_a} = \triangle \sqcap P_n^{\mathcal{K}}(\triangle, S_n, \varphi_n)$ is executed when a gradient message is received from a neighbour ($\triangle$ can be executed directly but the *parallel-and* operator blocks the execution of outer fragments until $P_n^{\mathcal{K}}(\triangle, S_n, \varphi_n)$ finishes); it initializes the $GPath$ tuple for the source of the gradient. By using the composition operator, the literals inferred in the model of P_n', along with all the tuples in the container (fragment $\triangle$) are then treated as constituent for the fragment $e_{P_a} = P_a^{\mathcal{A}}(e_{P_e}, S_a, \varphi_T)$, i.e. they are used to generate facts for the program P_a'. This one is used to aggregate the hop-counter for the source with the one stored in the local container. e_{P_a} is finally treated as constituent for the fragment $e_{P_g} = P_g^{\mathcal{A}}(e_{P_a}, S_g, \varphi_T)$. Note that aggregation happens before spreading, imposing an order on the reactions. $P_g^{\mathcal{A}}$ is used to verify whether the gradient message must be spread to the neighbours. If so, a literal $spreadGradient(a, local, d, c, b)$ is inferred during the computation of its semantics, where $local$ is translated with the name of the current node. Simultaneously, the Logic Fragment $P_{ch}^{\mathcal{A}}(\triangle, S_{ch}, \varphi_{ch})$ is executed as soon as a chemotaxis message is received (described as $Cmsg(f, g)$, with f content of the message and g ID of the receiver). That Logic Fragment uses the local copy of the hop-counter to infer which is the next hop to which the chemotaxis message must be sent to (relay node). If the local hop-counter exists, a literal $sendChemo(f, g, h)$ is generated in the model of P_{ch}', with h representing the ID of the next receiver of the chemotaxis message. Otherwise, the message remains in the container until such a literal is finally inferred. All the literals contained in the consequent Q of LF_{gc} are used by the agent A_{gc} to manage the control part of the algorithm, described in the following code.

Control code 1.6 Behaviour of agent A_{gc}

> **if** $spreadGradient(a, local, d, c, b) \in Q$ **then**
>   **send** $Gmsg(a, local, c + 1, d)$ **to all neighbours but** b
>   **remove** $container.Gmsg(a, x, y, z)_w$ for any w
> **if** $updateGPath(a, c, b, d) \in Q$ **then**
>   **update** $container.GPath(a, x, y)_w = GPath(a, c, b)$ for any w
> **if** $sendChemo(f, g, h) \in Q$ **then**
>   **send** $Cmsg(f, g)$ **to node** h
>   **remove** $container.Cmsg(f, g)$

We consider the network of Figure 3; the Logic Fragment can be used to provide the gradient and chemotaxis functionalities as services to other agents running on the same nodes. Assuming that agent A_{Gm} on node A wants to send a query message m_1 to all the nodes of the network, it creates and injects the gradient message $Gmsg(A, A, 0, m_1)$. At this point a reaction with LF_{gc} takes place, generating in the consequent Q of LF_{gc} literals $GPath(A, 0, A)$ (semantics of P'_n) and $spreadGradient(A, A, m_1, 0, A)$ (semantics of P'_g). The second literal causes the spreading of the gradient message to nodes B and C. Similar reactions take place in the remaining nodes. If we assume that the gradient passed by node D is the first one to reach E then $GPath(A, 3, D)$ is inferred in the consequent Q on node E. When the gradient message coming from B reaches E, $updateGPath(A, 1, B, m_1)$ is inferred in the semantics of program P'_a, so the hop-counter tuple is updated in $GPath(A, 2, B)$. Now assuming that agent A_{Cm} on node E wants to send a reply-message m_2 to node A, it creates and injects a chemotaxis message $Cmsg(m_2, A)$. On the basis of the tuple $GPath(A, 2, C)$, the literal $sendChemo(m_2, A, C)$ is inferred in the model of P'_g, so the message is sent to node B. Similar reactions take place on node B, which finally sends the chemotaxis message to node A.

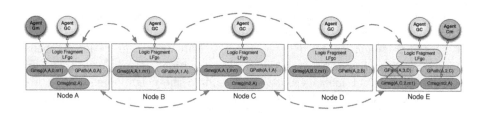

Fig. 3. Network of 5 nodes

Property 2. Let $\mathcal{N}$ be a network with no disconnected hosts. If we assume that: (i) nodes do not move; (ii) every node has a Logic Fragment of type LF_{gc}; (iii) every information sent from one node to another one arrives at destination in a finite time (eventually due to multiple spreading); (iv) a gradient message is created by an agent A_{Gm} on one node S of $\mathcal{N}$, then there exists a finite time t^* for which the following statement holds: if an agent A_{Cm} on node R creates a chemotaxis message for A at time $t > t^*$, then the chemotaxis message reaches the destination S following a shortest-path between R and S.

Proof Sketch. *The rationale behind the proof consists in proving two categories of properties: (i) a local property which states that the number of gradient messages sent by each node is finite, due to the decrements of the hop-counter caused by the applications of the aggregation-function; (ii) global properties, based on the local property holding in each node (e.g. we prove the creation of the shortest-path). The details are reported in [6]. Additional studies focusing on the integration of spatial-temporal logics in Logic Fragment are needed to prove the analogous statement when considering mobile nodes.*

5   Conclusion and Future Works

In this paper we have presented a chemical-based coordination model based on a logic framework. Virtual chemical reactions are lead by logic deductions, implemented in terms of combination of logic programs. This approach combines the benefits of using a chemical-based coordination model along with the expressiveness of several distinct types of logic languages to formalise coordination logically. Intuitively, even though no formal verification or validation methods were presented, the rationale behind the proof of the correctness of coordination algorithm follows from a formalisation of the system properties to be proved in terms of logical formulae. This paves the way for at least two formal analysis: (i) *what-if* assessment - coordination events can be modeled in terms of injected/removed tuples and deducted literals can be used to test the satisfaction of the system properties formulae. This first kind of verification can be done at design time, to assess properties of the whole system under certain conditions (events) and partially at run-time, to infer how the system will evolve assuming a knowledge restricted to a certain subset of locally perceived events; (ii) the second type of design time analysis starts from the literals that satisfy the properties formulae and proceeds backwards, to derive what are the events that lead the system to that given state. Future works will focus on such aspects, to derive formal procedures for correctness verification of algorithm built on top of Logic Fragments.

Several kinds of logics present interesting features to model and validate coordination primitives: (i) paraconsistent logics (e.g. [17]) and (ii) spatial-temporal logics, to assert properties depending on location and time parameters of system components. We plan also to realise an implementation of the model, including several semantics for Logic Fragments taking inspiration from the coordination primitives presented in [7].

References

1. Apt, K.R., van Emden, M.H.: Contributions to the theory of logic programming. J. ACM 29(3), 841–862 (1982)
2. Banâtre, J.P., Le Métayer, D.: The gamma model and its discipline of programming. Sci. Comput. Program. 15(1), 55–77 (1990)
3. Berry, G., Boudol, G.: The chemical abstract machine. In: Proceedings of the 17th ACM SIGPLAN-SIGACT Symposium on Principles of Programming Languages, POPL 1990, pp. 81–94. ACM (1990)

4. Castelli, G., Mamei, M., Rosi, A., Zambonelli, F.: Pervasive middleware goes social: The sapere approach. In: Proceedings of the 2011 Fifth IEEE Conference on Self-Adaptive and Self-Organizing Systems Workshops, SASOW 2011, pp. 9–14 (2011)
5. Ciancarini, P., Franzè, F., Mascolo, C.: A coordination model to specify systems including mobile agents. In: Proceedings of the 9th International Workshop on Software Specification and Design, IWSSD 1998, IEEE Computer Society, Washington, DC (1998)
6. De Angelis, F.L., Di Marzo Serugendo, G.: Towards a logic and chemical based coordination model (2015), https://archive-ouverte.unige.ch/
7. Denti, E., Natali, A., Omicini, A., Venuti, M.: Logic tuple spaces for the coordination of heterogeneous agents. In: Baader, F., Schulz, K.U. (eds.) Proceedings of 1st International Workshop (FroCoS 1996) Frontiers of Combining Systems, Applied Logic Series, Munich, Germany, March 26–29, vol. 3, pp. 147–160. Kluwer Academic Publishers (1996)
8. Dershowitz, N., Manna, Z.: Proving termination with multiset orderings. Commun. ACM 22(8) (1979)
9. Emden, M.H.V., Kowalski, R.A.: The semantics of predicate logic as a programming language. Journal of the ACM 23, 569–574 (1976)
10. Fernandez-Marquez, J.L., Di Marzo Serugendo, G., Montagna, S., Viroli, M., Arcos, J.L.: Description and composition of bio-inspired design patterns: a complete overview. Natural Computing 12(1), 43–67 (2013)
11. Fitting, M.: Fixpoint semantics for logic programming a survey. Theoretical Computer Science 278(1-2), 25–51 (2002), Mathematical Foundations of Programming Semantics 1996
12. Kowalski, R.: Algorithm = logic + control. Commun. ACM 22(7), 424–436 (1979)
13. Kowalski, R., Kuehner, D.: Linear Resolution with Selection Function. Artificial Intelligence 2(3-4), 227–260 (1971)
14. Nilsson, U., Maluszynski, J.: Logic, Programming, and PROLOG, 2nd edn. John Wiley & Sons, Inc., New York (1995)
15. Omicini, A., Denti, E.: From tuple spaces to tuple centres. Science of Computer Programming 41(3), 277–294 (2001)
16. Viroli, M., Casadei, M., Omicini, A.: A framework for modelling and implementing self-organising coordination. In: Shin, S.Y., Ossowski, S., Menezes, R., Viroli, M. (eds.) 24th Annual ACM Symposium on Applied Computing (SAC 2009), March 8-12, vol. III, pp. 1353–1360. ACM, Honolulu (2009)
17. Vitória, A., Maluszyński, J., Szałas, A.: Modeling and reasoning in paraconsistent rough sets. Fundamenta Informaticae 97(4), 405–438 (2009)
18. Zambonelli, F., Omicini, A., Anzengruber, B., Castelli, G., Angelis, F.L.D., Serugendo, G.D.M., Dobson, S., Fernandez-Marquez, J.L., Ferscha, A., Mamei, M., Mariani, S., Molesini, A., Montagna, S., Nieminen, J., Pianini, D., Risoldi, M., Rosi, A., Stevenson, G., Viroli, M., Ye, J.: Developing pervasive multi-agent systems with nature-inspired coordination. Pervasive and Mobile Computing 17, 236–252 (2015); Special Issue 10 years of Pervasive Computing In Honor of Chatschik Bisdikian

Coordinating Ensembles

Comingle: Distributed Logic Programming
for Decentralized Mobile Ensembles

Edmund Soon Lee Lam[✉], Iliano Cervesato, and Nabeeha Fatima

Carnegie Mellon University, University in Pittsburgh, Pennsylvania, Pittsburgh, PA, USA
{sllam,nhaque}@andrew.cmu.edu, iliano@cmu.edu

Abstract. Comingle is a logic programming framework aimed at simplifying the development of applications distributed over multiple mobile devices. Applications are written as a single declarative program (in a system-centric way) rather than in the traditional node-centric manner, where separate communicating code is written for each participating node. Comingle is based on committed-choice multiset rewriting and is founded on linear logic. We describe a prototype targeting the Android operating system and illustrate how Comingle is used to program distributed mobile applications. As a proof of concept, we discuss several such applications orchestrated using Comingle.

1 Introduction

Distributed computing, the coordination of independent computations to achieve a desired objective, has become one of the defining technologies of modern society. We rely on it every time we use a search engine like Google, every time we make a purchase on Amazon, in fact every time we use the Internet. In recent years, *mobile* distributed computing has taken off thanks to advances in mobile technologies, from inexpensive sensors and low-energy wireless links to the very smartphones we carry around: apps talk to each other both within a phone and across phones, connected devices work together to make our homes safer and more comfortable, and personal health monitors combine sensor data into a picture of our well-being. Each such system constitutes a decentralized mobile application which orchestrates the computations of its various constituent nodes. As such applications gain in sophistication, it becomes harder to ensure that they correctly and reliably deliver the desired behavior using traditional programming models. Specifically, writing separate communicating programs for each participating node becomes more costly and error-prone as the need for node-to-node coordination grows.

In this paper, we introduce Comingle, a framework aimed at simplifying the development of distributed applications over a decentralized ensemble of mobile devices. Comingle supports a system-centric style of programming, where the distributed behavior of an application is expressed as a single program, rather than the traditional

This work was made possible by grant JSREP 4-003-2-001, *Effective Parallel and Distributed Programming via Join Pattern with Guards, Propagation and More*, from the Qatar National Research Fund (a member of the Qatar Foundation). The statements made herein are solely the responsibility of the authors.

© IFIP International Federation for Information Processing 2015
T. Holvoet and M. Viroli (Eds.): COORDINATION 2015, LNCS 9037, pp. 51–66, 2015.
DOI: 10.1007/978-3-319-19282-6_4

node-centric style mentioned above. This system-centric view underlies popular frameworks such as Google Web Toolkit [7] (for client-server web development) and Map Reduce [4] (for parallel distributed algorithms on large-scale computing clusters). In earlier work [9,10], we generalized this approach to a much broader class of distributed computations by relying on a form of logic programming to orchestrate interactive distributed computations [9,10]. Comingle specializes this work to distributed applications running on mobile devices. Comingle is based on committed-choice multiset rewriting extended with explicit locality [9] and multiset comprehension patterns [10]. This provides declarative and concise means of implementing distributed computations, thus allowing the programmer to focus on *what* computations to synchronize rather than *how* to synchronize them. The present work extends [9] by introducing *triggers* and *actuators* to integrate the Comingle multiset rewriting runtime with traditional code from mainstream mobile development frameworks (specifically Java and the Android SDK). This allows a developer to marry the best of both programming paradigms, using Comingle to orchestrate distributed computations among devices and traditional native code for computations within a device (e.g., user interface functionalities, local computations). The main contributions of this paper are as follows:

– We detail the semantics of Comingle, in particular the use of triggers and actuators as an abstract interface between Comingle and a device's application runtime.
– We describe a prototype implementation of Comingle, a runtime system implemented in Java and integrated with the Android SDK.
– As a proof of concept, we show three case-studies of distributed applications orchestrated by Comingle on the Android SDK.

The rest of the paper is organized as follows: we illustrate Comingle by means of an example in Section 2. In Section 3, we introduce its abstract syntax and its semantics, while Section 4 outlines our compiler and runtime system for the Android SDK. In Section 5, we examine three case-study applications implemented in Comingle. We discuss related works in Section 6 and make some concluding remarks in Section 7. Further details can be found in a companion technical report [12].

2   A Motivating Example

Figure 1 shows a simple Comingle program that lets two generic devices swap data that they each possess on the basis of a pivot value P and displays on each of them the number of items swapped, all in one atomic step. This program gives a bird eye's view of the exchanges that need to take place — it is system-centric. Our prototype will then compile it into the node-centric code that needs to run at each device to realize this behavior. The high-level Comingle program in Figure 1 relies on a few functionalities expressed using the devices' native programming support (Java and the Android SDK in our case). Specifically, these functionalities are the two local functions, `size` and `format`, imported in lines 1-4, and the code associated with triggers and actuators (see below). This low-level code (not shown) implements purely local computations.

In Comingle, devices are identified by means of a *location* and a piece of information held at location ℓ is represented as a *located fact* of the form $[\ell]\,p(\vec{t})$ where p is

```
1   module comingle.lib.ExtLib import {
2           size   :: A -> int,
3           format :: (string,A) -> string
4   }
5
6   predicate swap    :: (loc,int) -> trigger.
7   predicate item    :: int -> fact.
8   predicate display :: string -> actuator.
9
10  rule pSwap :: [X]swap(Y,P),
11             { [X]item(I) | I -> Is. I <= P },
12             { [Y]item(J) | J -> Js. J >= P }
13      --o [X]display( format("Received %s items from %s", (size(Js),Y)) ),
14          [Y]display( format("Received %s items from %s", (size(Is),X)) ),
15          { [X]item(J) | J <- Js }, { [Y]item(I) | I <- Is }.
```

Fig. 1. Pivot Swap, orchestrated by Comingle

a predicate name and $\vec{t}$ are terms. The program in Figure 1 mentions two generic locations, X and Y, and uses the three predicates declared on lines 6-8. A located fact of the form $[\ell]\,\text{swap}(\ell',P)$ represents ℓ's intent to swap data with device ℓ' based on the pivot value P, fact $[\ell]\,\text{item}(I)$ indicates that value I is held at location ℓ, while $[\ell]\text{display}(S)$ represents a message S to be shown on ℓ's screen. From a system-centric perspective, the set of all located facts defines the *rewriting state* of the system. The rewriting state evolves through the application of Comingle rules and indirectly by the effect of the local computation of each device.

Lines 10-15 in Figure 1 define a Comingle rule called pSwap. We call the comma-separated expressions before "--o" the rule *heads*, while the expressions after it are collectively called its *body*. Informally, applying a Comingle rule to the current state rewrites an instance of its head into the corresponding instance of its body. Rule heads and body can contain parametric facts such as [X]swap(Y,P), where X, Y and P are variables, and *comprehension patterns* which stand for a multiset of facts in the rewriting state. In our example, the comprehension pattern {[X]item(I) | I -> Is. I <= P} identifies all of X's items I such that I <= P. Similarly, all of Y's items J such that J >= P are identified by {[Y]item(J) | J -> Js. J >= P}. The instances of I and J matched by each comprehension pattern are accumulated in the variables Is and Js, respectively. Finally, these collected bindings are used in the rule body to complete the rewriting by redistributing all of X's selected data to Y and vice versa, as well as invoking the appropriate display messages on X's and Y's screen.

Facts such as $\text{item}(I)$ are meaningful only at the rewriting level. Facts are also used as an interface to a device's local computations. Specifically, facts like $[\ell]\,\text{swap}(\ell',P)$ are entered into the rewriting state by a local program running at ℓ and used to trigger rule applications. These *trigger facts*, which we underline as $[\ell]\,\underline{\text{swap}}(\ell',P)$ for emphasis, are only allowed in the heads of a rule. Dually, facts like $[\ell]\text{display}(S)$ are generated by the rewriting process for the purpose of starting a local computation at ℓ, here displaying a message on ℓ's screen. This is an *actuator fact*, which we underline with a dashed line, as in $[\ell]\,\underline{\text{display}}(S)$, for clarity. Each actuator predicate is associated with a local function which is invoked when the rewriting engine deposits an instance in the state (actuators can appear only in a rule body). For example, actuators

Locations: ℓ Terms: t Guards: g Standard / trigger / actuator predicates: p_s, p_t, p_a

Standard facts $F_s ::= [\ell]\, p_s(\vec{t})$ Triggers $F_t ::= [\ell]\, p_t(\vec{t})$ Actuators $F_a ::= [\ell]\, p_a(\vec{t})$

Facts $f, F ::= F_s \mid F_t \mid F_a$

Head atoms	$h ::= F_s \mid F_t$	Body atoms	$b ::= F_s \mid F_a$
Head expressions $H ::= h \mid \langle h \mid g \rangle_{\vec{x} \in t}$		Body expressions $B ::= b \mid \langle b \mid g \rangle_{\vec{x} \in t}$	
Comingle rule	$R ::= \overline{H} \setminus \overline{H} \mid g \multimap B$	Comingle program $\mathcal{P} ::= \overline{R}$	

Local state: $[\ell]\psi$

Rewriting state $St ::= \overline{F}$ Application state $\Psi ::= \overline{[\ell]\psi}$ Comingle state $\Theta ::= \langle St; \Psi \rangle$

Fig. 2. Abstract Syntax and Runtime Artifacts of Comingle

of the form $[\ell]\,\underline{\mathtt{display}}(S)$ are concretely implemented using a Java callback operation (not shown here) that calls the Android SDK's $\mathtt{toast}$ pop-up notification library to display the message S on ℓ's screen. This callback is invoked at ℓ every time the Comingle runtime produces an instance $[\ell]\,\underline{\mathtt{display}}(S)$.

By being system-centric, the code in Figure 1 lets the developer think in terms of overall behavior rather than reason from the point of view of each device, delegating to the compiler to deal with communication and synchronization, two particularly error-prone aspects of distributed computing. This also enable global type-checking and other forms of static validation, which are harder to achieve when writing separate programs. This code is also declarative, which simplifies reasoning about its correctness and security. Finally, this code is concise: just 15 lines. A native implementation of this example, while not difficult, is much longer.

3   Abstract Syntax and Semantics

In this section, we describe the abstract semantics of Comingle. We begin by first introducing the notations used throughout this section. We write $\bar{o}$ for a multiset of syntactic objects o. We denote the extension of a multiset $\bar{o}$ with an object o as "$\bar{o}, o$", with $\varnothing$ indicating the empty multiset. We also write "$\bar{o}_1, \bar{o}_2$" for the union of multisets $\bar{o}_1$ and $\bar{o}_2$. We write $\vec{o}$ for a tuple of o's and $[\vec{t}/\vec{x}]o$ for the simultaneous replacement within object o of all occurrences of variable x_i in $\vec{x}$ with the corresponding term t_i in $\vec{t}$. When traversing a binding construct (e.g., a comprehension pattern), substitution implicitly α-renames variables as needed to avoid capture. It will be convenient to assume that terms get normalized during substitution.

3.1   Abstract Syntax

The top part of Figure 2 defines the abstract syntax of Comingle. The concrete syntax used in the various examples in this paper maps to this abstract syntax. *Locations* ℓ are names that uniquely identify computing nodes, and the set of all nodes participating in a Comingle computation is called an *ensemble*. At the Comingle level, computation happens by rewriting *located facts* F of the form $[\ell]\, p(\vec{t})$. We categorize predicate names

p into *standard, trigger* and *actuator*, indicating them with p_s, p_r and p_a, respectively. This induces a classification of facts into standard, trigger and actuator facts, denoted F_s, F_t and F_a, respectively. Facts also carry a tuple $\vec{t}$ of *terms*. The abstract semantics of Comingle is largely agnostic to the specific language of terms.

Computation in Comingle happens by applying *rules* of the form $\overline{H}_p \setminus \overline{H}_s \mid g \multimap \overline{B}$. We refer to $\overline{H}_p$ and $\overline{H}_s$ as the *preserved* and the *consumed head* of the rule, to g as its *guard* and to $\overline{B}$ as its *body*. The heads and the body of a rule consist of *atoms* f and of *comprehension patterns* of the form $\wr f \mid g\int_{\vec{x}\in t}$. An atom f is a located fact $[\ell] p(\vec{t})$ that may contain variables in the terms $\vec{t}$ or even as the location ℓ. Atoms in rule heads are either standard or trigger facts (F_s or F_t), while atoms in a rule body are standard or actuator facts (F_s or F_t). Guards in rules and comprehensions are Boolean-valued expressions constructed from terms and are used to constrain the values that the variables in a rule can assume. Just like for terms we keep guards abstract, writing $\models g$ to express that ground guard g is satisfiable. A comprehension pattern $\wr f \mid g\int_{\vec{x}\in t}$ represents a multiset of facts that match the atom f and satisfy guard g under the bindings of variables $\vec{x}$ that range over t, a multiset of tuples called the *comprehension range*. The scope of $\vec{x}$ is the atom f and the guard g. We implicitly α-rename bound variables to avoid capture. Abstractly, a Comingle *program* is a collection of rules.

The concrete syntax of Comingle is significantly more liberal than what we just described. In particular, components $\overline{H}_p$ and g can be omitted if empty. We concretely write a comprehension pattern $\wr f \mid g\int_{\vec{x}\in t}$ as $\{f \mid \vec{x} \rightarrow t. \; g\}$ in rule heads and $\{f \mid \vec{x} \leftarrow t. \; g\}$ in a rule body, where the direction of the arrow acts as a reminder of the flow of information. Terms in the current prototype include standard base types such as integers and strings, locations, term-level multisets, and lists. Its guards are relations over such terms (e.g., equality and $x < y$) and can contain effect-free operations imported from the local application (e.g., `size` and `format` in Figure 1).

3.2 Abstract Semantics

We will describe the computation of a Comingle system by means of a small-step transition semantics. Its basic judgment will have the form $\mathcal{P} \triangleright \Theta \mapsto \Theta'$ where $\mathcal{P}$ is a program, Θ is a *state* and Θ' is a state that can be reached in one (abstract) step of computation. A state Θ has the form $\langle St; \Psi \rangle$. The first component St is a collection of ground located facts $[\ell] p(\vec{t})$ and is called the *rewriting state* of the system. Comingle rules operate exclusively on the rewriting state. The second component, the *application state* Ψ, is the collection of the *local states* $[\ell]\psi$ of each computing node ℓ and captures the notion of state of the underlying computation model (the Java virtual machine in our Android-based prototype) — it typically has nothing to do with facts. As we will see, a local computation step transforms the application state Ψ but can also consume triggers from the rewriting state and add actuators into it. These run-time artifacts are formally defined at the bottom of Figure 2.

We will now describe the two types of state transitions $\mathcal{P} \triangleright \Theta \mapsto \Theta'$ in Comingle: the application of a rule and a local step — see Figure 5 for a preview.

Rewriting Steps. The application of a Comingle rule $\overline{H}_p \setminus \overline{H}_s \mid g \multimap \overline{B}$ involves two main operations: identifying fragments of the rewriting state St that match the

Matching: $\overline{H} \triangleq_{\text{lhs}} St$ $H \triangleq_{\text{lhs}} St$

$$\dfrac{\overline{H} \triangleq_{\text{lhs}} St \quad H \triangleq_{\text{lhs}} St'}{\overline{H}, H \triangleq_{\text{lhs}} St, St'}\,(\mathsf{I}_{mset\text{-}1}) \qquad \dfrac{}{\varnothing \triangleq_{\text{lhs}} \varnothing}\,(\mathsf{I}_{mset\text{-}2}) \qquad \dfrac{}{F \triangleq_{\text{lhs}} F}\,(\mathsf{I}_{fact})$$

$$\dfrac{[\vec{t}/\vec{x}]f \triangleq_{\text{lhs}} F \quad \models [\vec{t}/\vec{x}]g \quad \textstyle\wr f \mid g \wr_{\vec{x} \in \overline{ts}} \triangleq_{\text{lhs}} St}{\textstyle\wr f \mid g \wr_{\vec{x} \in \vec{t}, \overline{ts}} \triangleq_{\text{lhs}} St, F}\,(\mathsf{I}_{comp\text{-}1}) \qquad \dfrac{}{\textstyle\wr f \mid g \wr_{\vec{x} \in \varnothing} \triangleq_{\text{lhs}} \varnothing}\,(\mathsf{I}_{comp\text{-}2})$$

Residual Non-matching: $\overline{H} \triangleq^{\neg}_{\text{lhs}} St$ $H \triangleq^{\neg}_{\text{lhs}} St$

$$\dfrac{\overline{H} \triangleq^{\neg}_{\text{lhs}} St \quad H \triangleq^{\neg}_{\text{lhs}} St}{\overline{H}, H \triangleq^{\neg}_{\text{lhs}} St}\,(\mathsf{I}^{\neg}_{mset\text{-}1}) \qquad \dfrac{}{\varnothing \triangleq^{\neg}_{\text{lhs}} St}\,(\mathsf{I}^{\neg}_{mset\text{-}2}) \qquad \dfrac{}{F \triangleq^{\neg}_{\text{lhs}} St}\,(\mathsf{I}^{\neg}_{fact})$$

$$\dfrac{F \not\sqsubseteq_{\text{lhs}} \textstyle\wr f \mid g \wr_{\vec{x} \in ts} \quad \textstyle\wr f \mid g \wr_{\vec{x} \in ts} \triangleq^{\neg}_{\text{lhs}} St}{\textstyle\wr f \mid g \wr_{\vec{x} \in ts} \triangleq^{\neg}_{\text{lhs}} St, F}\,(\mathsf{I}^{\neg}_{comp\text{-}1}) \qquad \dfrac{}{\textstyle\wr f \mid g \wr_{\vec{x} \in ts} \triangleq^{\neg}_{\text{lhs}} \varnothing}\,(\mathsf{I}^{\neg}_{comp\text{-}2})$$

Subsumption: $F \sqsubseteq_{\text{lhs}} \textstyle\wr f \mid g \wr_{\vec{x} \in ts}$ iff $F = \theta f$ and $\models \theta g$ for some $\theta = [\vec{t}/\vec{x}]$

Fig. 3. Matching a Rule Head

rule heads $\overline{H}_p$ and $\overline{H}_s$, and replacing $\overline{H}_s$ in the rewriting state with the corresponding instance of the body $\overline{B}$. We now review how these operations are formalized in the presence of comprehension patterns and then describe how they are combined during a rewriting step (taking the guard g into account). Further details can be found in [10].

Matching Rule Heads. Let $\overline{H}$ be a (preserved or consumed) rule head without free variables — we will deal with the more general case momentarily. Intuitively, matching $\overline{H}$ against a store St means splitting St into two parts, St^+ and St^-, and checking that $\overline{H}$ matches St^+ completely. The latter is achieved by the judgment $\overline{H} \triangleq_{\text{lhs}} St^+$ defined in the top part of Figure 3. Rules $\mathsf{I}_{mset\text{-}*}$ partition St^+ into fragments to be matched by each atom in $\overline{H}$: plain facts F must occur identically (rule I_{fact}) while for comprehension atoms $\wr f \mid g \wr_{\vec{x} \in \overline{ts}}$ the state fragment must contain a distinct instance of f for every element of the comprehension range $\overline{ts}$ that satisfies the comprehension guard g (rules $\mathsf{I}_{comp\text{-}*}$).

In Comingle, comprehension patterns must match *maximal* fragments of the rewriting state. Therefore, no comprehension pattern should match any fact in St^-. This check is captured by the judgment $\overline{H} \triangleq^{\neg}_{\text{lhs}} St^-$ in the bottom part of Figure 3. Rules $\mathsf{I}^{\neg}_{mset\text{-}*}$ tests each individual atom and rule $\mathsf{I}^{\neg}_{fact}$ ignore facts. Rules $\mathsf{I}^{\neg}_{comp\text{-}*}$ deal with comprehensions $\wr f \mid g \wr_{\vec{x} \in \overline{ts}}$: they check that no fact in St^- matches any instance of f while satisfying g — note that the comprehension range $\overline{ts}$ is not taken into account.

Processing Rule Bodies. Applying a Comingle rule involves extending the rewriting state with the facts corresponding to its body. This operation is specified in Figure 4 for a closed body $\overline{B}$. Rules $\mathsf{r}_{mset\text{-}*}$ go through $\overline{B}$. Atomic facts F are added immediately (rule r_{fact}). Instead, comprehension atoms $\wr f \mid g \wr_{\vec{x} \in \overline{ts}}$ need to be *unfolded* (rules $\mathsf{r}_{comp\text{-}*}$):

Unfolding Rule Body: $\overline{B} \ggg_{\mathbf{rhs}} St$ $B \ggg_{\mathbf{rhs}} St$

$$\dfrac{\overline{B} \ggg_{\mathbf{rhs}} St \quad B \ggg_{\mathbf{rhs}} St'}{\overline{B}, B \ggg_{\mathbf{rhs}} St, St'}\ (r_{mset\text{-}1}) \qquad \dfrac{}{\varnothing \ggg_{\mathbf{rhs}} \varnothing}\ (r_{mset\text{-}2}) \qquad \dfrac{}{F \ggg_{\mathbf{rhs}} F}\ (r_{fact})$$

$$\dfrac{\models [\vec{t}/\vec{x}]g \quad [t/\vec{x}]b \ggg_{\mathbf{rhs}} F \quad \{b \mid g\}_{\vec{x}\in ts} \ggg_{\mathbf{rhs}} St}{\{b \mid g\}_{\vec{x}\in \vec{t}, ts} \ggg_{\mathbf{rhs}} F, St}\ (r_{comp\text{-}1})$$

$$\dfrac{\not\models [\vec{t}/\vec{x}]g \quad \{b \mid g\}_{\vec{x}\in ts} \ggg_{\mathbf{rhs}} St}{\{b \mid g\}_{\vec{x}\in \vec{t}, ts} \ggg_{\mathbf{rhs}} St}\ (r_{comp\text{-}2}) \qquad \dfrac{}{\{b \mid g\}_{\vec{x}\in \varnothing} \ggg_{\mathbf{rhs}} \varnothing}\ (r_{comp\text{-}3})$$

Fig. 4. Processing a Rule Body

for every item $\vec{t}$ in $\overline{ts}$ that satisfies the guard g, the corresponding instance $[\vec{t}/\vec{x}]f$ is added to the rewriting state; instances that do not satisfy g are discarded.

Rule Application.   Rule rw_ens in Figure 5 brings these ingredients together and describes a step of computation that applies a rule $\overline{H}_p \setminus \overline{H}_s \mid g \multimap \overline{B}$. This involves identifying a closed instance of the rule obtained by means of a substitution θ. The instantiated guard must be satisfiable ($\models \theta g$) and we must be able to partition the rewriting state into three parts St_p, St_s and St. The instances of the preserved and consumed heads must match fragments St_p and St_s respectively ($\theta\overline{H}_p \triangleq_{\mathbf{lhs}} St_p$ and $\theta\overline{H}_s \triangleq_{\mathbf{lhs}} St_s$), while the remaining fragment St must be free of residual matchings ($\theta(\overline{H}_p, \overline{H}_s) \triangleq_{\mathbf{lhs}}^{\neg} St$). The rule body instance $\theta\overline{B}$ is then unfolded ($\theta\overline{B} \ggg_{\mathbf{rhs}} St_b$) into St_b which replaces $\overline{St}_s$ in the rewriting state.

Rule rw_ens embodies a system-centric abstraction of the rewriting semantics of Comingle as it atomically accesses facts at arbitrary locations. Indeed, it views the facts of all participating locations in the ensemble as one virtual collection. Our prototype, discussed in Section 4, is instead based on a concurrent, node-centric model of computation, where each node manipulates its local facts and exchanges message with other nodes. We achieve this by compiling Comingle rules into the code that runs at each participating node [9].

Local Steps.   Global rewriting steps can be interleaved by local computations at any node ℓ. From the point of view of Comingle, such local computations are viewed as an abstract transition $\langle \mathcal{A}; \psi \rangle \mapsto_l \langle \psi'; \mathcal{T} \rangle$ that consumes some actuators $\mathcal{A}$ located at ℓ, modifies ℓ's internal application state ψ into ψ', and produces some triggers $\mathcal{T}$. Note that an abstract transition of this kind can (and generally will) correspond to a large number of steps of the underlying model of computation of node ℓ. Rule rw_loc in Figure 5 incorporate local computation into the abstract semantics of Comingle. Here, we write $[\ell]\mathcal{A}$ for a portion of the actuators located at ℓ in the current rewriting state — there may be others. We similarly write $[\ell]\mathcal{T}$ for the action of locating each trigger in $\mathcal{T}$ at ℓ.

Rule rw_loc enforces locality by drawing actuators strictly from ℓ and putting back triggers at ℓ. In particular, local computations at a node cannot interact with other nodes.

Local transitions: $\langle \mathcal{A}; \psi \rangle \mapsto_l \langle \mathcal{T}; \psi' \rangle$

Comingle transitions: $\mathcal{P} \rhd \langle St; \Psi \rangle \mapsto \langle St; \Psi \rangle$

$$\frac{(\overline{H}_p \setminus \overline{H}_s \mid g \multimap \overline{B}) \in \mathcal{P} \qquad \models \theta g}{\theta \overline{H}_p \triangleq_{\mathrm{lhs}} St_p \quad \theta \overline{H}_s \triangleq_{\mathrm{lhs}} St_s \quad \theta(\overline{H}_p, \overline{H}_s) \triangleq_{\mathrm{lhs}}^{\neg} St \quad \theta \overline{B} \ggg_{\mathrm{rhs}} St_b \over \mathcal{P} \rhd \langle St_p, St_s, St; \Psi \rangle \mapsto \langle St_p, St_b, St; \Psi \rangle} \text{(rw\_ens)}$$

$$\frac{\langle \mathcal{A}; \psi \rangle \mapsto_l \langle \mathcal{T}; \psi' \rangle}{\mathcal{P} \rhd \langle St, [l]\mathcal{A}; \Psi, [l]\psi \rangle \mapsto \langle St, [l]\mathcal{T}; \Psi, [l]\psi' \rangle} \text{(rw\_loc)}$$

Fig. 5. Abstract Semantics of Comingle

Hence, communication and orchestration can only occur through rewriting steps, defined by rule rw_ens. Note also that, since local transitions are kept abstract and are parametrized by a location, rule rw_loc accommodates ensembles that comprise devices based on different underlying models of computation.

4   Implementation

We now describe our Comingle prototype. In Section 4.1, we highlight the compilation phase, while Section 4.2 discusses the runtime system. Source code and examples are available for download at https://github.com/sllam/comingle.

4.1   Compilation

The Comingle front-end compiler consists of a typical lexer and parser, type-checker, an intermediate language preprocessor and a code generator, all implemented in Python. The type-checker enforces basic static typing of Comingle programs via a constraint solving approach adapted from [14] that allows for concise syntax highlight of type error sites. This is achieved by having the type-checker generate typing constraints with additional bookkeeping data to pinpoint the syntax fragments responsible for each error. Satisfiability of these typing constraints are determined by an SMT solver library built on top of Microsoft's Z3 [3]. Our SMT solver library includes an extension to reason about set comprehensions [11] which we use for optimizations involving comprehension patterns. An example is the selection of the indexing structures used by the Comingle runtime to carry out multiset matching with the best possible asymptotic time complexity [10]. Once a program has been statically checked, the compiler first applies a high-level source-to-source transformation [9] that converts a class of system-centric Comingle programs into node-centric rules. In addition to preserving soundness, the resulting node-centric program explicitly implements the communications and synchronizations that are required to correctly orchestrate the distributed execution of multi-party Comingle rules among a group of participating devices. Details of this choreographic transformation are out of the scope of this paper, but can be found in [9]. Finally, the code generator produces Java code that implements multiset matching as specified by the node-centric encodings. This generated matching code uses a

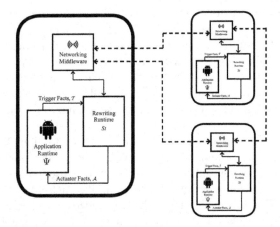

Fig. 6. Runtime System of a Distributed Comingle Mobile Application

compilation scheme formalized in [10] that first compiles node-centric code into a sequence of procedural operations, each of which implements a part of the matching and unfolding operations described in Section 3.2.

4.2 Runtime System

Figure 6 illustrates the organization of a running Comingle ensemble. Within each mobile device, the Comingle runtime has three components: a *rewriting runtime* that executes compiled rewrite rules, an *application runtime* that performs all local operations on the mobile device, and a *network middleware* that provides the basic communication primitives between the mobile devices. In the rest of this section, we highlight the important features of each of these components.

Rewriting Runtime. The rewriting runtime implements an operational semantics [10] which is sound with respect to the abstract semantics highlighted in Section 3. This operational semantics implements rule rw_ens on the node-centric rewriting rules resulting from the compilation process. In particular, it performs matching by incrementally processing atoms in a rule head on the basis of *newly added* facts. This execution model is highly compatible with our setup, where multiset rewriting is driven by external triggers generated by the local application runtime. Facts are matched to rule heads in top-down, left-to-right order, while facts in a rule body are processed left to right. The actions associated with actuators are executed in order of rule application. Each instance of the rewriting runtime is single-threaded, which entails that actuations invoked on the same device are guaranteed to be sequentially consistent with respect to the local ordering of rule application.

The rewriting runtime is implemented as a set of Java libraries. During compilation, the code generator produces Java code sprinkled with calls to functions from these libraries. Matching, for instance, is realized through various library functions that manipulate the data structures that implement the rewriting state St, supporting multi-index storage for efficiently querying facts. Communication is realized by other library calls that interface with the network middleware to send and receive facts to and from other participating instances of Comingle. Other library functions allows the rewriting runtime to call actuators that affects the local application runtime. Furthermore, the rewriting runtime exposes interface functions to the local application to carry out administrative commands (e.g., start or stop rewriting) as well as interfaces to add user-defined triggering facts to the rewriting runtime. These interface functions, called by the rewriting runtime, are engineered to be abstract and they make no assumptions about the local application calling them, and hence can be customized for various platforms.

Application Runtime. The application runtime is the Android application that implements rule rw_loc, performing all the local operations on the mobile device, from screen rendering to managing callback routines invoked by user input (e.g., keystrokes, taps on the display). It is implemented in Java with the Android SDK, but also uses a library (distributed as part of Comingle) that concretizes the interface functions that the rewriting runtime invokes. Its purpose is to allow the application developer to integrate locally-defined functions into Comingle rewriting rules (as shown in Figure 1). Specifically, it includes a set of predefined actuation callback methods for the Android SDK. The current prototype only supports three built-in primitive actuators (display a toast message, cause a delay in milliseconds, play a note), but interfaces to the Comingle runtime allow the application developer to implement his/her own domain-specific actuators. The application runtime also include libraries that implement boilerplate routines that help the developer integrate the Comingle rewriting runtime to an `Activity` of the Android SDK.

Network Middleware. As shown in Figure 6, the network middleware provides the underlying communication support between devices running Comingle. We have implemented a concrete instance that utilizes Android's WiFi-direct network protocol to establish connections and send and receive facts between mobile devices. It includes libraries that implement an asynchronous first-in-first-out message sending and receiving service on top of basic network sockets, and libraries that maintains, on each participating location, an active IP address directory of the local ad-hoc network. This allows a group of mobile devices to setup an ad-hoc WiFi-direct network, and supports peer-to-peer communication between any two devices of the group.

5   Case Studies

In this section, we describe three mobile applications we have implemented using the Comingle framework on the Android SDK. Two are multi-player games and one is a networking service. In all three, the overall distributed behavior is orchestrated by the Comingle runtime, while the user interfaces are implemented locally using traditional Android SDK libraries. For brevity, we omit all predicate declarations. These declarations, the code implementing local operations, and the details of the integration with Java and the Android SDK are discussed at length in [12].

Drag Racing. *Drag Racing* is a simple multi-player game inspired by a Google Chrome experiment called Chrome Racer [6]. A number of players compete to reach the finish

```
1   rule init :: [I]initRace(Ls)
2     --o {[A]next(B)|(A,B)<-Cs}, [E]last(),
3         {[I]has(P), [P]all(Ps), [P]at(I), [P]renderTrack(Ls) | P<-Ps}
4       where (Cs,E) = makeChain(I,Ls), Ps = list2mset(Ls).
5
6   rule start :: [X]all(Ps) \ [X]startRace() --o {[P]release()|P<-Ps}.
7
8   rule tap :: [X]at(Y) \ [X]sendTap() --o [Y]recvTap(X).
9
10  rule trans :: [X]next(Z) \ [X]exiting(Y),[Y]at(X) --o [Z]has(Y),[Y]at(Z).
11
12  rule win :: [X]last()\[X]all(Ps),[X]exiting(Y) --o {[P]decWinner(Y)|P<-Ps}.
```

Fig. 7. Drag Racing, a racing game inspired by Chrome Racer

line of a linear racing track. The device of each player shows a distinct segment of the track, and the players advance their car by tapping on their screen. The initial configuration for a three-player instance is shown in Figure 7.[1] In Chrome Racer, the devices interact via a dedicated server. By contrast, the devices in our Drag Racing game communicate with each other directly, without the need of a third party to manage coordination.

An initial configuration such as the one in Figure 7 is generated when rule init is executed. Its head is the trigger fact [I]initRace(Ls), where node I will hold the initial segment of the track and Ls lists all locations participating in the game (including I). Several actions need to take place at initialization time, all implemented by the body of init. First, the participating locations need to be arranged into a linear chain starting at I. This is achieved by the local function *makeChain* in the guard (Cs,E) = *makeChain*(I,Ls) where Cs is instantiated to a multiset of logically adjacent pairs of locations and E to the end of the chain. The guard Ps = *list2mset*(Ls) converts the list Ls into a multiset Ps. Second, each node other than E needs to be informed of which location holds the segment of the track after it, while E needs to be told that it has the finishing segment: this is achieved by the atoms {[A]next(B) | (A,B) <- Cs} and [E]last(), respectively. Third, each location (P<-Ps) needs to be informed of who the players are ([P]all(Ps)) and of the fact that its car is currently at I ([P]at(I)), and it needs to be instructed to render the lane of all players ([P]renderTrack(Ls)). Fourth, location I needs to be instructed to draw the car of all the players ([I]has(P)). The facts renderTrack and has are actuators

---

[1] In Chrome Racer, the track loops around so that each device shows two segments. While we could easily achieve this effect, our linear "drag" racing variant suffices to demonstrate Comingle's ability to orchestrate distributed computations.

```
1   rule init :: [I]initGame(Ships,Ps)
2       --o [I]turn(), [I]notifyTurn(), {[A]next(B) | (A,B)<-Cs},
3       {[P]all(Ps), [P]randomFleet(Ships) | P <- Ps}
4           where Cs = makeRRchain(Ps).
5
6   rule shoot :: [A]next(B) \ [A]turn(), [A]fireAt(D,X,Y)
7       --o [D]blastAt(A,X,Y), [B]turn(), [B]notifyTurn().
8   rule miss :: [D]empty(X,Y) \ [D]blastAt(A,X,Y)
9       --o [D]missed(A,D,X,Y), [A]missed(A,D,X,Y).
10  rule goodHit :: [D]blastAt(A,X,Y), [D]hull(S,X,Y)
11      --o [D]damaged(S,X,Y), [D]hit(A,D,X,Y), [A]hit(A,D,X,Y).
12  rule dmgHit :: [D]damaged(S,X,Y) \ [D]blastAt(A,X,Y)
13      --o [D]hit(A,D,X,Y), [A]hit(A,D,X,Y).
14
15  rule sunk :: [D]all(Ps) \
16      [D]damaged(S,X,Y), {[D]damaged(S,X',Y')|(X',Y')->Ds'}
17      {[D]hull(S,W,V)|(W,V)->Hs} | size(Hs)=0
18      --o {[P]sunk(D,S,Ds)|P<-Ps}, [D]checkFleet()
19          where Ds = insert((X,Y),Ds').
20
21  rule deadFleet :: [D]all(Ps), [D]checkFleet(), {[D]checkFleet()},
22      {[D]hull(S,W,V)|(S,W,V)->Hs} | size(Hs)=0
23      --o {[P]notifyDead(D), [P]dead(D) | P<-Ps}.
24
25  rule winner :: [D]all(Ps), {[D]dead(O) | O->Os}
26      | Ps=insert(D,Os) --o {[P]notifyWinner(D) | P<-Ps}.
```

Fig. 8. Multi-way Battleship

since they cause a local computation in the form of screen display. Because the instances of the last four predicate forms are determined by the same multiset (Ps), Comingle allows combining them into a single comprehension pattern.

At this point the game has been initialized, but it has not started yet. The race starts the first time a player X taps his/her screen. This has the effect of depositing the trigger [X]startRace() in the rewriting state, which enables rule start. Its body broadcasts the actuator [P]release() to every node P, which has the effect of informing P's local runtime that subsequent taps will cause its car to move forward. This behavior is achieved by rule tap, which is triggered at any node X by the fact [X]sendTap(), generated by the application runtime every time X's player taps his/her screen. The trigger [X]exiting(Y) is generated when the car of player Y reaches the right-hand side of the track segment on X's device. If the track continues on player Z's screen ([X]next(Z)), rule trans hands Y's car over to Z by ordering Z to draw it on his/her screen ([Z]has(Y)) and by informing X of the new location of his/her car ([Y]at(Z)). Notice that, because fact [Y]at(X) is in the simplified head of the rule, it gets consumed. If instead X holds the final segment of the track ([X]last()) when the trigger [X]exiting(Y) materializes, Y's victory is broadcast to all participating locations ({[P]decWinner(Y) | P <- Ps}). Besides displaying a banner, it disables moving one's car by tapping the screen.

Multi-way Battleship. Multi-way Battleship extends the classic battleship game with support for more than just two players. Each player begins with an equal assortment of battleships of varying sizes, randomly placed on a two-dimensional grid of cells. The players then take turns selecting an opponent's cell and firing at it. A battleship is sunk when each cell it resides in is hit at least once. The winner of the game is the last player with at least one unsunk ship.

Figure 8 shows a Comingle program that orchestrates this game. Rule `init` initializes an instance of the game. Its head is the trigger `[I]`<u>`initGame`</u>`(Ships,Ps)`, where node `I` is the player who will fire the first shot, `Ships` lists the number of ships of each kind, and `Ps` is the multiset of device locations playing the game. Its body informs `I` that it is its turn to play by means of the fact `[I]turn()` and inserts the actuator `[I]`<u>`notifyTurn`</u>`()` which posts a notification on `I`'s display and enables touchscreen input. The body of `init` also constructs a round robin sequence of facts `[A]next(B)`, distributes the location of all participants (`[P]all(Ps)`), and deposits the actuator `[P]`<u>`randomFleet`</u>`(Ships)` at each node `P`. The application layer of `P` will service this actuator by generating a random placement of the fleet in `Ships` at node `P` and by installing triggers `[P]`<u>`empty`</u>`(X,Y)` and `[P]`<u>`hull`</u>`(S,X,Y)` to indicate that cell `(X,Y)` is empty or contains a portion of ship `S`, respectively.

The trigger `[A]`<u>`fireAt`</u>`(D,X,Y)` is added to the rewriting state when player `A` fires at cell `(X,Y)` of player `D`. It enables rule `shoot`, but only if it is `A`'s turn. This results in the fact `[D]blast(A,X,Y)` added at `D`'s. This rule also passes the turn to the next player (`[A]next(B)`) by asserting the fact `[B]turn()` and causing a notification on `B`'s display (`[B]`<u>`notifyTurn`</u>`()`).

The next three rules implement the possible outcomes of such a shot. Specifically, if cell `(X,Y)` is empty, rule `miss` renders an appropriate animation on `A`'s and `B`'s display via the actuator <u>`missed`</u>`(A,D,X,Y)`. If ship `S` is (partially) in cell `(X,Y)`, rule `goodHit` replaces the fact `[D]hull(S,X,Y))` with `[D]damage(S,X,Y)` and informs `A` and `D` of this event via the actuator <u>`hit`</u>`(A,D,X,Y)`. If a damaged hull is hit again, rule `dmgHit` generates the <u>`hit`</u>`(A,D,X,Y)` actuators once more.

Rule `sunk` handles the sinking of a ship `S`. It is enabled if there is at least one fact `[D]damaged(S,X,Y)` in the rewriting state. It then checks that `S` has no intact fragment (`{[D]`<u>`hull(S,W,V)`</u>` | (W,V)->Hs}` | `size(Hs)=0`), collects the coordinates of the other hit fragments (`{[D]damaged(S,X',Y') | (X',Y')->Ds'}`), notifies each player that `S` has sunk (`{[P]`<u>`sunk`</u>`(D,S,Ds) | P<-Ps}`), and issues the fact `[D]checkFleet()` to check if the game is over for `D`. The function `insert` inserts an element in a multiset.

If at least one `[D]checkFleet()` fact is present, rule `deadFleat` similarly checks that no ship fragment is intact (`{[D]`<u>`hull(S,W,V)`</u>` | (S,W,V)->Hs}` | `size(Hs)=0`) and if this is the case it informs all players of `D`'s annihilation with `{[P]`<u>`notifyDead`</u>`(D), [P]dead(D) | P<-Ps}`. Finally, rule `winner` is executed by the winning player `D` when it can ascertain that all other players are dead (`[D]all(Ps) {[D]dead(O) | O->Os} where Ps=insert(D,Os)`).

WiFi-Direct Directory. WiFi-Direct Directory is an implementation of a networking service built on top of the Android SDK WiFi-direct library. In the WiFi-direct protocol, one device is designated as the *owner* of a newly established group. The owner can

```
 1   rule owner   :: [O]startOwner(C)  --o [O]owner(C), [O]joined(O).
 2   rule member  :: [M]startMember(C) --o [M]member(C).
 3   rule connect :: [M]member(C) \ [M]connect(N)
 4        --o [O]joinRequest(C,N,M) where O = ownerLoc().
 5
 6   rule join :: [O]owner(C), {[O]joined(M')|M'->Ms},
 7           \ [O]joinRequest(C,N,M) | notIn(M,Ms)
 8        --o {[M']added(D)|M'<-Ms}, {[M]added(D')|D'<-Ds},
 9            [M]added(D), [O]joined(M), [M]connected()
10        where IP = lookupIP(M), D = (M,IP,N), Ds = retrieveDir().
11
12   rule quitO :: [O]owner(C), [O]quit(), {[O]joined(M)|M->Ms}
13        --o {[M]ownerQuit()|M<-Ms} .
14
15   rule quitM :: {[O]joined(M')|M'->Ms.not(M' = M)}
16           \ [M]member(C), [M]quit(), [O]joined(M)
17        --o {[M']removed(M)|M'<-Ms}, [M]deleteDir().
```

Fig. 9. WiFi-Direct Directory

obtain the IP address of each device in the group from its network middleware, but the other members only know the owner's IP address and location. This means that, initially, the group owner can communicate with all members but the members can only communicate with the owner. WiFi-Direct Directory disseminates and maintains an IP address table on each node of the group in order to enable peer-to-peer IP socket communication.

Figure 9 shows the Comingle program that orchestrates this service. Once the group has been established, the triggers [O]startOwner(C) and [M]startMember(C) are entered in the rewriting state of the owner and of each other member M, respectively. The argument C identifies the application this group is for (e.g., one of the two games seen earlier) — the WiFi-direct protocols allows a node to be part of at most one group at any time. Rule owner initializes the owner by adding the facts [O]owner(C) that sets O's role as the owner of the group for application C and [O]joined(O) that identifies it as having joined the group. Rule member simply sets M's role as a group member ([M]member(C)).

The runtime of a member M also periodically generates triggers [M]connect(N) where N is the device's screen name — this is to protect against message losses while the group owner bootstraps. Rule connect turn this trigger into the request [O]join-Request(C,N,M) to be sent to the owner O — the library function *ownerLoc* retrieves the owner of the current group, which is initially available to all members. This request is processed in rule join: the owner O checks that a join request by the same member has not been serviced already ([O]joinRequest(C,N,M) | *notIn*(M,Ms)), it then records M as having joined the group ([O]joined(M)), sends its location, IP address and screen name (D = (M,IP,N)) to the active members ({[M']added(D)|M'<-Ms}). This same data is sent to M ([M]added(D)) as well as information about each active member ({[M]added(D')|D'<-Ds}). The actuator [X]added(D) updates node X's internal routing table with entry D and the actuator [M]connected() stops the issuance of the triggers [M]connect(N).

The last two rules handle a member M leaving the group, which is initiated by trigger [M] quit(). If this member is the owner, rule quitO dismantles the group and send the actuator ownerQuit() to each active member. If M is a regular member, rule quitM consumes M's [O]joined(M) fact, notifies all other members to remove M's entry from their local directory ({[M']removed(M)|M'<-Ms}) and instructs M's runtime to delete its entire local directory ([M]deleteDir()).

6   Related Work

To the best of our knowledge, Comingle is the first framework to introduce the logic programming paradigm to the development of applications on modern mobile devices. However, it draws from work on distributed and parallel programming languages for decentralized micro-systems, which we now review.

Comingle is greatly influenced by Meld [1], a logic programming language initially designed for programming distributed ensembles of communicating robots. It used the Blinky Blocks platform [8] as a proof of concept to demonstrate simple ensemble programming behaviors. Meld was based on a variant of Datalog extended with sensing and action facts. Recent refinements [2] extended Meld with comprehension patterns and linearity, but refocused it on distributed programming of multicore architectures.

Sifteo [13] is an interactive system that runs an array of puzzle games on Lego-like cubes. Each cube is equipped with a small LCD screen and various means of interaction with the user (e.g., tilting, shaking) and is capable of sensing alignments with neighboring cubes. Developers can implement new games in C/C++ via the Sifteo SDK. Sifteo's decentralized and interactive setup makes it a suitable target platform for Comingle.

The Comingle language is a descendant of CHR [5], a logic programming language targeting traditional constraint solving problems. Comingle extends it with multiset comprehension, explicit locations, triggers and actuators.

7   Future Developments and Conclusions

In this paper, we introduced Comingle, a distributed logic programming language for orchestrating decentralized ensembles. It is designed to simplify the development of interactive applications and to provide a high-level programming abstraction for coordinating distributed computations. As proof of concept, we described three distributed applications orchestrated by Comingle and running on Android mobile devices — two are multi-player games and one is a networking service. By segregating all communication and coordination events in a few rules, it promotes a system-centric, declarative style of programming a distributed application, which simplifies detecting errors and ensuring correctness.

In the immediate future, we intend to expand the language capabilities to capture recurrent synchronization patterns and enrich the programming primitives available at the Comingle level. We will also extend the library support for developing applications that integrate with the Comingle rewriting runtime.

References

1. Ashley-Rollman, M.P., Lee, P., Goldstein, S.C., Pillai, P., Campbell, J.D.: A Language for Large Ensembles of Independently Executing Nodes. In: Hill, P.M., Warren, D.S. (eds.) ICLP 2009. LNCS, vol. 5649, pp. 265–280. Springer, Heidelberg (2009)
2. Cruz, F., Rocha, R., Goldstein, S.C., Pfenning, F.: A linear logic programming language for concurrent programming over graph structures. In: ICLP 2014, Vienna, Austria (2014)
3. de Moura, L., Bjørner, N.S.: Z3: An Efficient SMT Solver. In: Ramakrishnan, C.R., Rehof, J. (eds.) TACAS 2008. LNCS, vol. 4963, pp. 337–340. Springer, Heidelberg (2008)
4. Dean, J., Ghemawat, S.: Mapreduce: simplified data processing on large clusters. In: OSDI 2004. USENIX Association (2004)
5. Frühwirth, T., Raiser, F.: Constraint Handling Rules: Compilation, Execution and Analysis (2011), BOD ISBN 9783839115916
6. New York Google. Chrome Racer, A Chrome Experiment (2013), http://www.chrome.com/racer
7. Google Inc. Google Web Toolkit, http://code.google.com/webtoolkit/
8. Kirby, B.T., Ashley-Rollman, M., Goldstein, S.C.: Blinky blocks: A physical ensemble programming platform. In: CHI 2011, pp. 1111–1116. ACM, New York (2011)
9. Lam, E.S.L., Cervesato, I.: Decentralized Execution of Constraint Handling Rules for Ensembles. In: PPDP 2013, Madrid, Spain, pp. 205–216 (2013)
10. Lam, E.S.L., Cervesato, I.: Optimized Compilation of Multiset Rewriting with Comprehensions. In: Garrigue, J. (ed.) APLAS 2014. LNCS, vol. 8858, pp. 19–38. Springer, Heidelberg (2014)
11. Lam, E.S.L., Cervesato, I.: Reasoning about Set Comprehension. In: SMT 2014 (2014)
12. Lam, E.S.L., Cervesato, I.: Comingle: Distributed Logic Programming for Decentralized Android Applications. Technical Report CMU-CS-15-101, Carnegie Mellon University (March 2015)
13. Merrill, D., Kalanithi, J.: Sifteo, Interactive Game Cubes (2009), https://www.sifteo.com/cubes cubes
14. Stuckey, P.J., Sulzmann, M., Wazny, J.: Interactive Type Debugging in Haskell. In: Haskell 2003, pp. 72–83. ACM, New York (2003)

Dynamic Choreographies

Safe Runtime Updates of Distributed Applications

Mila Dalla Preda[1], Maurizio Gabbrielli[2], Saverio Giallorenzo[2],
Ivan Lanese[2], and Jacopo Mauro[2(✉)]

[1] Department of Computer Science, University of Verona, Verona, Italy
`mila.dallapreda@univr.it`
[2] Department of Computer Science and Engineering,
University of Bologna / INRIA, Bologna, Italy
{`sgiallor,gabbri,lanese,jmauro`}`@cs.unibo.it`

Abstract. Programming distributed applications free from communication deadlocks and races is complex. Preserving these properties when applications are updated at runtime is even harder.

We present DIOC, a language for programming distributed applications that are free from deadlocks and races by construction. A DIOC program describes a whole distributed application as a unique entity (choreography). DIOC allows the programmer to specify which parts of the application can be updated. At runtime, these parts may be replaced by new DIOC fragments from outside the application. DIOC programs are compiled, generating code for each site, in a lower-level language called DPOC. We formalise both DIOC and DPOC semantics as labelled transition systems and prove the correctness of the compilation as a trace equivalence result. As corollaries, DPOC applications are free from communication deadlocks and races, even in presence of runtime updates.

1 Introduction

Programming distributed applications is an error-prone activity. Participants send and receive messages and, if the application is badly programmed, participants may get stuck waiting for messages that never arrive (communication deadlock), or they may receive messages in an unexpected order, depending on the speed of the other participants and of the network (races).

Recently, language-based approaches have been proposed to tackle the complexity of programming concurrent and distributed applications. Languages such as Rust [21] or SCOOP [19] provide higher-level primitives to program concurrent applications which avoid by construction some of the risks of concurrent programming. Indeed, in these settings most of the work needed to ensure a correct behaviour is done by the language compiler and runtime support. Using these languages requires a conceptual shift from traditional ones, but reduces

This work is partly supported by the MIUR FIRB project FACE (Formal Avenue for Chasing malwarE) RBFR13AJFT and by the Italian MIUR PRIN Project CINA Prot. 2010LHT4KM.

© IFIP International Federation for Information Processing 2015
T. Holvoet and M. Viroli (Eds.): COORDINATION 2015, LNCS 9037, pp. 67–82, 2015.
DOI: 10.1007/978-3-319-19282-6_5

times and costs of development, testing, and maintenance by avoiding some of the most common programming errors.

Here, we propose an approach based on *choreographic programming* [4,5,15,22] following a similar philosophy, tailored for distributed applications. In choreographic programming, a whole distributed application is described as a unique entity, by specifying the expected interactions and their order. For instance, a price request from a buyer to a seller is written as `priceReq: buyer( b_prod )` → `seller( s_prod )`. It specifies that the `buyer` sends along channel `priceReq` the name of the desired product `b_prod` to the `seller`, which stores it in its local variable `s_prod`. Since in choreographic languages sends and receives are always paired, the coupling of exactly one receive with each send and vice versa makes communication deadlocks or races impossible to write. Given a choreography, a main challenge is to produce low-level distributed code which correctly implements the desired behaviour.

We take this challenge one step forward: we consider *updatable* applications, whose code can change while the application is running, dynamically integrating code from the outside. Such a feature, tricky in a sequential setting and even more in a distributed one, has countless uses: deal with emergency requirements, cope with rules and requirements which depend on contextual properties, improve and specialize the application to user preferences, and so on. We propose a general mechanism, which consists in delimiting inside the application blocks of code, called *scopes*, that may be dynamically replaced with new code, called *update*. The details of the behaviour of the updates do not need to be foreseen, updates may even be written while the application is running.

Runtime code replacement performed using languages not providing dedicated support is extremely error-prone. For instance, considering the price request example above, assume that we want to update the system allowing the buyer to send to the seller also its fidelity card ID to get access to some special offer. If the buyer is updated first and it starts the interaction before the seller has been updated, the seller is not expecting the card ID, which may be sent and lost, or received later on, when some different message is expected, thus breaking the correctness of the application. Vice versa, if the seller is updated first, (s)he will wait for the card ID, which the buyer will not send, leading the application to a deadlock. In our setting, the available updates may change at any time, posing an additional challenge. Extra precautions are needed to ensure that all the participants agree on which code is used for a given update. For instance, in the example above, suppose that the buyer finds the update that allows the sending of the card ID, and applies this update before the seller does. If the update is no more available when the seller looks for it, then the application ends up in an inconsistent state, where the update is only partially applied, and the seller will receive an unexpected message containing the card ID.

If both the original application and the updates are programmed using a choreographic language, these problems cannot arise. In fact, at the choreographic level, the update is applied atomically to all the involved participants. Again, the tricky part is to compile the choreographic code to low-level distributed code ensuring correct behaviour. In particular, at low-level, the different participants have to coordinate their updates avoiding inconsistencies. The present paper proposes a solution to this problem. In particular:

- we define a choreographic language, called DIOC, to program distributed applications and supporting code update (§ 2);
- we define a low-level language, called DPOC, based on standard send and receive primitives (§ 3);
- we define a behaviour-preserving projection function compiling DIOCs into DPOCs (§ 3.1);
- we give a formal proof of the correctness of the projection function (§ 4). Correctness is guaranteed even in a scenario where the new code used for updates dynamically changes at any moment and without notice.

The contribution outlined above is essentially theoretical, but it has already been applied in practice, resulting in AIOCJ, an adaptation framework described in [9]. The theoretical underpinning of AIOCJ is a specific instantiation of the results presented here. Indeed, AIOCJ further specifies how to manage the updates, e.g., how to decide when updates should be applied and which ones to choose if many of them apply. For more details on the implementation and more examples we refer the interested reader to the website [1]. Note that the user of AIOCJ does not need to master all the technicalities we discuss here, since they are embedded within AIOCJ. In particular, DPOCs and the projection are automatically handled and hidden from the user.

Proofs, additional details, and examples are available in the companion technical report [8].

2 Dynamic Interaction-Oriented Choreography (DIOC)

This section defines the syntax and semantics of the DIOC language.

The languages that we propose rely on a set *Roles*, ranged over by $r, s, \ldots$, whose elements identify the participants in the choreography. Roles exchange messages over channels, also called *operations*: *public operations*, ranged over by o, and *private operations*, ranged over by o^*. We use $o^?$ to range over both public and private operations. Public operations represent relevant communications inside the application. We ensure that both the DIOC and the corresponding DPOC perform the same public operations, in the same order. Vice versa, private communications are used when moving from the DIOC level to the DPOC level, for synchronisation purposes. We denote with *Expr* the set of expressions, ranged over by e. We deliberately do not give a formal definition of expressions and of their typing, since our results do not depend on it. We only require that expressions include at least values, belonging to a set *Val* ranged over by v, and variables, belonging to a set *Var* ranged over by $x, y, \ldots$. We also assume a set of boolean expressions ranged over by b.

The syntax of DIOC *processes*, ranged over by $\mathcal{I}, \mathcal{I}', \ldots$, is defined as follows:

$$\mathcal{I} ::= o^? : r_1(e) \rightarrow r_2(x) \mid \mathcal{I}; \mathcal{I}' \mid \mathcal{I}|\mathcal{I}' \mid x@r = e \mid \mathbf{1} \mid \mathbf{0} \mid$$
$$\text{if } b@r \; \{\mathcal{I}\} \text{ else } \{\mathcal{I}'\} \mid \text{while } b@r \; \{\mathcal{I}\} \mid \text{scope } @r \; \{\mathcal{I}\}$$

Interaction $o^? : r_1(e) \rightarrow r_2(x)$ means that role r_1 sends a message on operation $o^?$ to role r_2 (we require $r_1 \neq r_2$). The sent value is obtained by evaluating expression e in the local state of r_1 and it is then stored in variable x in r_2. Processes $\mathcal{I}; \mathcal{I}'$ and $\mathcal{I}|\mathcal{I}'$ denote sequential and parallel composition. Assignment $x@r = e$ assigns the evaluation of expression e in the local state of r to its local variable x. The empty process $\mathbf{1}$ defines a DIOC that can only terminate. $\mathbf{0}$ represents a terminated DIOC. It is needed for the definition of the operational semantics and it is not intended to be used by the programmer. We call *initial* a DIOC process where $\mathbf{0}$ never occurs. Conditional if $b@r \; \{\mathcal{I}\}$ else $\{\mathcal{I}'\}$ and iteration while $b@r \; \{\mathcal{I}\}$ are guarded by the evaluation of boolean expression b in the local state of r. The construct scope $@r \; \{\mathcal{I}\}$ delimits a subterm $\mathcal{I}$ of the DIOC process that may be updated in the future. In scope $@r \; \{\mathcal{I}\}$, role r coordinates the updating procedure by interacting with the other roles involved in the scope.

DIOC processes do not execute in isolation: they are equipped with a *global state* Σ and a set of (available) updates $\mathbf{I}$. A global state Σ is a map that defines the value v of each variable x in a given role r, namely $\Sigma : Roles \times Var \rightarrow Val$. The local state of role r is $\Sigma_r : Var \rightarrow Val$ and it verifies $\forall x \in Var : \Sigma(r, x) = \Sigma_r(x)$. Expressions are always evaluated by a given role r: we denote the evaluation of expression e in local state Σ_r as $[\![e]\!]_{\Sigma_r}$. We assume $[\![e]\!]_{\Sigma_r}$ is always defined (e.g., an error value is given as a result if evaluation is not possible) and that for each boolean expression b, $[\![b]\!]_{\Sigma_r}$ is either true or false. $\mathbf{I}$ denotes a set of updates, i.e., DIOCs that may replace a scope. $\mathbf{I}$ may change at runtime.

Listing 1.1 gives a realistic example of DIOC process where a buyer orders a product from a seller, paying via a bank.

```
1   price_ok@buyer = false; continue@buyer = true;
2   while ( !price_ok and continue )@buyer {
3     b_prod@buyer = getInput();
4     priceReq : buyer( b_prod ) → seller( s_prod );
5     scope @seller {
6       s_price@seller = getPrice( s_prod );
7       offer : seller( s_price ) → buyer( b_price )
8     };
9     price_ok@buyer = getInput();
10    if ( !price_ok )@buyer {
11      continue@buyer = getInput()} };
12  if ( price_ok )@buyer {
13    payReq : seller( payDesc( s_price ) ) → bank( desc );
14    scope @bank {
15      payment_ok@bank = true;
16      pay : buyer( payAuth( b_price ) ) → bank( auth );
17      ... // code for the payment
18    };
```

```
19   if ( payment_ok )@bank {
20     confirm : bank( null ) → seller( _ ) |
21     confirm : bank( null ) → buyer( _ )
22   } else { abort : bank( null ) → buyer( _ ) } }
```

Listing 1.1. DIOC process for Buying Scenario

Before starting the application by iteratively asking the price of some goods to the `seller`, the `buyer` at Line 1 initializes its local variables `price_ok` and `continue`. Then, by using function `getInput` (Line 3) (s)he reads from the local console the name of the product to buy and, at Line 4, engages in a communication via operation `priceReq` with the `seller`. The `seller` computes the price of the product calling the function `getPrice` (Line 6) and, via operation `offer`, it sends the price to the `buyer` (Line 7), that stores it in a local variable `b_price`. These last two operations are performed within a scope, allowing this code to be updated in the future to deal with changing business rules. If the offer is accepted, the `seller` sends to the `bank` the payment details (Line 13). The `buyer` then authorises the payment via operation `pay`. We omit the details of the local execution of the payment at the `bank`. Since the payment may be critical for security reasons, the related communication is enclosed in a scope (Lines 14-18), thus allowing the introduction of a more refined procedure later on. After the scope successfully terminates, the application ends with the `bank` acknowledging the payment to the `seller` and the `buyer` in parallel (Lines 20-21). If the payment is not successful, the failure is notified to the `buyer` only. Note that at Line 1, the annotation `@buyer` means that the variables belong to the `buyer`. Similarly, at Line 2, the annotation `@buyer` means that the guard of the while is evaluated by `buyer`. The term `@seller` in Line 5 instead, being part of the scope construct, indicates the participant that coordinates the code update.

Assume now that the seller direction decides to define new business rules. For instance, the seller may distribute a fidelity card to buyers, allowing them to get a 10% discount on their purchases. This business need can be faced by adding the DIOC below to the set of available updates, so that it can be used to replace the scope at Lines 5-8 in Listing 1.1.

```
1   cardReq : seller( null ) → buyer( _ );
2   card_id@buyer = getInput();
3   cardRes : buyer( card_id ) → seller( buyer_id );
4   if isValid( buyer_id )@seller {
5     s_price@seller = getPrice( s_prod ) * 0.9
6   } else { s_price@seller = getPrice( s_prod ) };
7   offer : seller( s_price ) → buyer( b_price )
```

Listing 1.2. Fidelity Card Update

When this code executes, the `seller` asks the card ID to the `buyer`. The `buyer` inputs the ID, stores it into the variable `card_id` and sends this information to the `seller`. If the card ID is valid then the discount is applied, otherwise the standard price is computed.

Table 1. Auxiliary functions transl and transF

$\mathsf{transl}(o^? : r_1(e) \to r_2(x)) = \mathsf{transF}(o^? : r_1(e) \to r_2(x)) = \{r_1 \to r_2\}$
$\mathsf{transl}(x@r = e) = \mathsf{transF}(x@r = e) = \{r \to r\}$
$\mathsf{transl}(\mathbf{1}) = \mathsf{transl}(\mathbf{0}) = \mathsf{transF}(\mathbf{1}) = \mathsf{transF}(\mathbf{0}) = \emptyset$
$\mathsf{transl}(\mathcal{I}|\mathcal{I}') = \mathsf{transl}(\mathcal{I}) \cup \mathsf{transl}(\mathcal{I}') \qquad\qquad \mathsf{transF}(\mathcal{I}|\mathcal{I}') = \mathsf{transF}(\mathcal{I}) \cup \mathsf{transF}(\mathcal{I}')$
$\mathsf{transl}(\mathcal{I};\mathcal{I}') = \begin{cases} \mathsf{transl}(\mathcal{I}') & \text{if } \mathsf{transl}(\mathcal{I}) = \emptyset \\ \mathsf{transl}(\mathcal{I}) & \text{otherwise} \end{cases} \quad \mathsf{transF}(\mathcal{I};\mathcal{I}') = \begin{cases} \mathsf{transF}(\mathcal{I}) & \text{if } \mathsf{transF}(\mathcal{I}') = \emptyset \\ \mathsf{transF}(\mathcal{I}') & \text{otherwise} \end{cases}$
$\mathsf{transl}(\mathtt{if}\ b@r\ \{\mathcal{I}\}\ \mathtt{else}\ \{\mathcal{I}'\}) = \mathsf{transl}(\mathtt{while}\ b@r\ \{\mathcal{I}\}) = \{r \to r\}$
$\mathsf{transF}(\mathtt{if}\ b@r\ \{\mathcal{I}\}\ \mathtt{else}\ \{\mathcal{I}'\}) = \begin{cases} \{r \to r\} & \text{if } \mathsf{transF}(\mathcal{I}) \cup \mathsf{transF}(\mathcal{I}') = \emptyset \\ \mathsf{transF}(\mathcal{I}) \cup \mathsf{transF}(\mathcal{I}') & \text{otherwise} \end{cases}$
$\mathsf{transF}(\mathtt{while}\ b@r\ \{\mathcal{I}\}) = \begin{cases} \{r \to r\} & \text{if } \mathsf{transF}(\mathcal{I}) = \emptyset \\ \mathsf{transF}(\mathcal{I}) & \text{otherwise} \end{cases}$
$\mathsf{transl}(\mathtt{scope}\ @r\ \{\mathcal{I}\}) = \{r \to r\}$
$\mathsf{transF}(\mathtt{scope}\ @r\ \{\mathcal{I}\}) = \begin{cases} \{r \to r\} & \text{if } \mathsf{roles}(\mathcal{I}) \subseteq \{r\} \\ \bigcup_{r' \in \mathsf{roles}(\mathcal{I}) \smallsetminus \{r\}} \{r' \to r\} & \text{otherwise} \end{cases}$

2.1   Connectedness

In order to prove our main result, we require the DIOC code of the updates and of the starting programs to satisfy a well-formedness syntactic condition called *connectedness*. This condition is composed by *connectedness for sequence* and *connectedness for parallel*. Intuitively, connectedness for sequence ensures that the DPOC network obtained by projecting a sequence $\mathcal{I};\mathcal{I}'$ executes first the actions in $\mathcal{I}$ and then those in $\mathcal{I}'$, thus respecting the intended semantics of sequential composition. Connectedness for parallel prevents interferences between parallel interactions. To formally define connectedness we introduce, in Table 1, the auxiliary functions transl and transF that, given a DIOC process, compute sets of pairs representing senders and receivers of possible initial and final interactions in its execution. We represent one such pair as $r_1 \to r_2$. Actions located at r are represented as $r \to r$. For instance, given an interaction $o^? : r_1(e) \to r_2(x)$ both its transl and transF are $\{r_1 \to r_2\}$. For conditional, $\mathsf{transl}(\mathtt{if}\ b@r\ \{\mathcal{I}\}\ \mathtt{else}\ \{\mathcal{I}'\}) = \{r \to r\}$ since the first action executed is the evaluation of the guard by role r. The set $\mathsf{transF}(\mathtt{if}\ b@r\ \{\mathcal{I}\}\ \mathtt{else}\ \{\mathcal{I}'\})$ is normally $\mathsf{transF}(\mathcal{I}) \cup \mathsf{transF}(\mathcal{I}')$, since the execution terminates with an action from one of the branches. If instead the branches are both empty then transF is $\{r \to r\}$, representing guard evaluation.

We assume a function $\mathsf{roles}(\mathcal{I})$ that computes the roles of a DIOC process $\mathcal{I}$. We also assume a function sig that given a DIOC process returns the set of signatures of its interactions, where the signature of interaction $o^? : r_1(e) \to r_2(x)$ is $o^? : r_1 \to r_2$. For a formal definition of the functions roles and sig we refer the reader to the companion technical report [8].

Definition 1 (Connectedness). *A DIOC process $\mathcal{I}$ is connected if it satisfies:*

- **connectedness for sequence:** *each subterm of the form $\mathcal{I}';\mathcal{I}''$ satisfies* $\forall r_1 \to r_2 \in \mathsf{transF}(\mathcal{I}'), \forall s_1 \to s_2 \in \mathsf{transl}(\mathcal{I}'') . \{r_1, r_2\} \cap \{s_1, s_2\} \neq \emptyset$;
- **connectedness for parallel:** *each subterm of the form $\mathcal{I}'|\mathcal{I}''$ satisfies* $\mathsf{sig}(\mathcal{I}') \cap \mathsf{sig}(\mathcal{I}'') = \emptyset$.

Requiring connectedness does not hamper programmability, since it naturally holds in most of the cases (see, e.g., [1, 9]), and it can always be enforced automatically restructuring the DIOC while preserving its behaviour, following the lines of [16]. Also, connectedness can be checked efficiently.

Theorem 1 (Connectedness-check Complexity)
The connectedness of a DIOC process $\mathcal{I}$ can be checked in time $O(n^2 \log(n))$, where n is the number of nodes in the abstract syntax tree of $\mathcal{I}$.

Note that we allow only connected updates. Indeed, replacing a scope with a connected update always results in a deadlock- and race-free DIOC. Thus, there is no need to perform expensive runtime checks to ensure connectedness of the application after an arbitrary sequence of updates has been applied.

2.2 DIOC Semantics

We can now define DIOC systems and their semantics.

Definition 2 (DIOC Systems). *A DIOC system is a triple $\langle \Sigma, \mathbf{I}, \mathcal{I} \rangle$ denoting a DIOC process $\mathcal{I}$ equipped with a global state Σ and a set of updates $\mathbf{I}$.*

Definition 3 (DIOC Systems Semantics). *The semantics of DIOC systems is defined as the smallest labelled transition system (LTS) closed under the rules in Table 6 in the companion technical report [8] (excerpt in Table 2), where symmetric rules for parallel composition have been omitted.*

The rules in Table 2 describe the behaviour of a DIOC system by induction on the structure of its DIOC process. We use μ to range over labels. Also, we use A as an abbreviation for $\Sigma, \mathbf{I}$. We comment below on the main rules.

Rule [INTERACTION] executes a communication from r_1 to r_2 on operation $o^?$, where r_1 sends to r_2 the value v of an expression e. The value v is then stored

Table 2. DIOC system semantics (excerpt)

[INTERACTION]
$$\frac{[\![e]\!]_{\Sigma_{r_1}} = v}{\left\langle A, o^? : r_1(e) \to r_2(x) \right\rangle \xrightarrow{o^?:r_1(v)\to r_2(x)} \langle A, x@r_2 = v \rangle}$$

[SEQUENCE]
$$\frac{\langle A, \mathcal{I} \rangle \xrightarrow{\mu} \langle A', \mathcal{I}' \rangle \; \mu \neq \surd}{\langle A, \mathcal{I}; \mathcal{J} \rangle \xrightarrow{\mu} \langle A', \mathcal{I}'; \mathcal{J} \rangle}$$

[ASSIGN]
$$\frac{[\![e]\!]_{\Sigma_r} = v}{\langle \Sigma, \mathbf{I}, x@r = e \rangle \xrightarrow{\tau} \langle \Sigma[v/x, r], \mathbf{I}, \mathbf{1} \rangle}$$

[SEQ-END]
$$\frac{\langle A, \mathcal{I} \rangle \xrightarrow{\surd} \langle A, \mathcal{I}' \rangle \; \langle A, \mathcal{J} \rangle \xrightarrow{\mu} \langle A, \mathcal{J}' \rangle}{\langle A, \mathcal{I}; \mathcal{J} \rangle \xrightarrow{\mu} \langle A, \mathcal{J}' \rangle}$$

[UP]
$$\frac{\mathsf{roles}(\mathcal{I}') \subseteq \mathsf{roles}(\mathcal{I}) \quad \mathcal{I}' \in \mathbf{I} \quad \mathcal{I}' \text{ connected}}{\langle A, \mathbf{scope} \; @r \; \{\mathcal{I}\} \rangle \xrightarrow{\mathcal{I}'} \langle A, \mathcal{I}' \rangle}$$

[NOUP]
$$\langle A, \mathbf{scope} \; @r \; \{\mathcal{I}\} \rangle \xrightarrow{\text{no-up}} \langle A, \mathcal{I} \rangle$$

[END]
$$\langle A, \mathbf{1} \rangle \xrightarrow{\surd} \langle A, \mathbf{0} \rangle$$

[CHANGE-UPDATES]
$$\langle \Sigma, \mathbf{I}, \mathcal{I} \rangle \xrightarrow{\mathbf{I}'} \langle \Sigma, \mathbf{I}', \mathcal{I} \rangle$$

in x by r_2. Rule [ASSIGN] evaluates the expression e in the local state Σ_r and stores the resulting value v in the local variable x in role r ($[v/x, r]$ represents the substitution). The rules [UP] and [NOUP] deal with the code replacement and thus the application of an update. Rule [UP] models the application of the update $\mathcal{I}'$ to the scope `scope @r` $\{\mathcal{I}\}$ which, as a result, is replaced by the DIOC process $\mathcal{I}'$. This rule requires the update to be connected. Rule [NOUP] removes the scope boundaries and starts the execution of the body of the scope. Rule [CHANGE-UPDATES] allows the set $\mathbf{I}$ of available updates to change. This rule is always enabled since its execution can happen at any time and the application cannot forbid it.

In our theory, whether to update a scope or not, and which update to apply if many are available, is completely non-deterministic. We have adopted this view to maximize generality. However, for practical applications, one needs rules and conditions which define when an update has to be performed. Refining the semantics to introduce rules for decreasing (or eliminating) the non-determinism would not affect the correctness of our approach. One such refinement has been explored in [9].

We define DIOC *traces*, where all the performed actions are observed, and *weak* DIOC *traces*, where interactions on private operations and silent actions τ are not visible.

Definition 4 (DIOC Traces). *A (strong) trace of a DIOC system $\langle \Sigma_1, \mathbf{I}_1, \mathcal{I}_1 \rangle$ is a sequence (finite or infinite) of labels $\mu_1, \mu_2, \ldots$ such that there is a sequence of DIOC system transitions $\langle \Sigma_1, \mathbf{I}_1, \mathcal{I}_1 \rangle \xrightarrow{\mu_1} \langle \Sigma_2, \mathbf{I}_2, \mathcal{I}_2 \rangle \xrightarrow{\mu_2} \ldots$.*
A weak trace of a DIOC system $\langle \Sigma_1, \mathbf{I}_1, \mathcal{I}_1 \rangle$ is a sequence of labels $\mu_1, \mu_2, \ldots$ obtained by removing all the labels corresponding to private communications, i.e., of the form $o^* : r_1(v) \to r_2(x)$, and the silent labels τ from a trace of $\langle \Sigma_1, \mathbf{I}_1, \mathcal{I}_1 \rangle$.

3   Dynamic Process-Oriented Choreography (DPOC)

This section describes the syntax and operational semantics of DPOCs. DPOCs include *processes*, ranged over by P, P', ..., describing the behaviour of participants. $(P, \Gamma)_r$ denotes a DPOC *role* named r, executing process P in a local state Γ. *Networks*, ranged over by $\mathcal{N}$, $\mathcal{N}'$, ..., are parallel compositions of DPOC roles with different names. DPOC systems, ranged over by $\mathcal{S}$, are DPOC networks equipped with a set of updates $\mathbf{I}$, namely pairs $\langle \mathbf{I}, \mathcal{N} \rangle$.

$$P ::= o^? : x \text{ from } r \mid o^? : e \text{ to } r \mid o^* : X \text{ to } r \mid P; P' \mid P|P' \mid x = e \mid \text{while } b \{P\}$$
$$\mid \text{if } b \{P\} \text{ else } \{P'\} \mid n : \text{scope @r } \{P\} \text{ roles } \{S\} \mid n : \text{scope @r } \{P\} \mid \mathbf{1} \mid \mathbf{0}$$

$$X ::= \text{no} \mid P \qquad\qquad \mathcal{N} ::= (P, \Gamma)_r \mid \mathcal{N} \parallel \mathcal{N}' \qquad\qquad \mathcal{S} ::= \langle \mathbf{I}, \mathcal{N} \rangle$$

Processes include receive action $o^? : x$ `from` r on a specific operation $o^?$ (either public or private) of a message from role r to be stored in variable x, send action $o^? : e$ `to` r of an expression e to be sent to role r, and higher-order send action $o^* : X$ to r of the higher-order argument X to be sent to role r. Here X may be either a DPOC process P, which is the new code for a scope in r, or a token no, notifying that no update is needed. $P; P'$ and $P|P'$ denote the sequential and parallel composition of P and P', respectively. Processes also feature assignment $x = e$ of expression e to variable x, the process $\mathbf{1}$, that can only successfully terminate, and the terminated process $\mathbf{0}$. We also have conditionals if b $\{P\}$ else $\{P'\}$ and loops while b $\{P\}$. Finally, we have two constructs for scopes. Scope $n :$ scope $@r$ $\{P\}$ roles $\{S\}$ may occur only inside role r and acts as coordinator to apply (or not apply) the update. The shorter version $n :$ scope $@r$ $\{P\}$ is used instead when the role is not the coordinator of the scope. In fact, only the coordinator needs to know the set S of involved roles to communicate which update to apply. Note that scopes are prefixed by an index n. Indexes are unique in each role and are used to avoid interference between different scopes in the same role.

3.1 Projection

Before defining the semantics of DPOCs, we define the projection of a DIOC process onto DPOC processes. This is needed to define the semantics of updates at the DPOC level. The projection exploits auxiliary communications to coordinate the different roles, e.g., ensuring that in a conditional they all select the same branch. To define these auxiliary communications and avoid interference, it is convenient to annotate DIOC main constructs with unique indexes.

Definition 5 (Well-annotated DIOC). *Annotated DIOC processes are obtained by indexing every interaction, assignment, scope, and if and while constructs in a DIOC process with a natural number $n \in \mathbb{N}$, resulting in the following grammar:*

$$\mathcal{I} ::= n : o^? : r_1(e) \to r_2(x) \mid \mathcal{I}; \mathcal{I}' \mid \mathcal{I}|\mathcal{I}' \mid \mathbf{1} \mid \mathbf{0} \mid n : x@r = e$$
$$\mid n : \text{while } b@r \ \{\mathcal{I}\} \mid n : \text{if } b@r \ \{\mathcal{I}\} \text{ else } \{\mathcal{I}'\} \mid n : \text{scope } @r \ \{\mathcal{I}\}$$

A DIOC process is well-annotated if all its indexes are distinct.

Note that we can always annotate a DIOC process to make it well-annotated.

We now define the *process-projection function* that derives DPOC processes from DIOC processes. Given an annotated DIOC process $\mathcal{I}$ and a role s, the projected DPOC process $\pi(\mathcal{I}, s)$ is defined by structural induction on $\mathcal{I}$ in Table 3. Here, with a little abuse of notation, we write roles$(\mathcal{I}, \mathcal{I}')$ for roles$(\mathcal{I}) \cup$ roles$(\mathcal{I}')$. We assume that operations o_n^* and variables x_n are never used in the projected DIOC and we use them for auxiliary synchronisations. In most of the cases the projection is trivial. For instance, the projection of an interaction is an output on the sender role, an input on the receiver, and $\mathbf{1}$ on any other role. For a conditional $n :$ if $b@r$ $\{\mathcal{I}\}$ else $\{\mathcal{I}'\}$, role r locally evaluates the guard and then sends its value to the other roles using auxiliary communications. Similarly, in a loop $n :$ while $b@r$ $\{\mathcal{I}\}$ role r communicates the evaluation of the guard to the other roles. Also, after an iteration has terminated, role r waits for the other roles to terminate and then starts a new iteration. In both the conditional and

Table 3. Process-projection function π

$$\boxed{\pi(1,s)} = 1 \qquad \boxed{\pi(0,s)} = 0$$

$$\boxed{\pi(\mathcal{I};\mathcal{I}',s)} = \pi(\mathcal{I},s); \pi(\mathcal{I}',s) \qquad \boxed{\pi(n : x@r = e, s)} = \begin{cases} x = e & \text{if } s = r \\ 1 & \text{otherwise} \end{cases}$$

$$\boxed{\pi(\mathcal{I}|\mathcal{I}',s)} = \pi(\mathcal{I},s) \mid \pi(\mathcal{I}',s)$$

$$\boxed{\pi(n : o^? : r_1(e) \to r_2(x), s)} = \begin{cases} o^? : e \text{ to } r_2 & \text{if } s = r_1 \\ o^? : x \text{ from } r_1 & \text{if } s = r_2 \\ 1 & \text{otherwise} \end{cases}$$

$$\boxed{\pi(n : \text{if } b@r \ \{\mathcal{I}\} \text{ else } \{\mathcal{I}'\}, s)} =$$
$$\begin{cases} \text{if } b \ \{(\Pi_{r' \in \text{roles}(\mathcal{I},\mathcal{I}')\setminus\{r\}} \ o_n^* : \text{true to } r'); \ \pi(\mathcal{I},s)\} \\ \quad \text{else } \{(\Pi_{r' \in \text{roles}(\mathcal{I},\mathcal{I}')\setminus\{r\}} \ o_n^* : \text{false to } r'); \ \pi(\mathcal{I}',s)\} & \text{if } s = r \\ o_n^* : x_n \text{ from } r; \text{ if } x_n \ \{\pi(\mathcal{I},s)\} \text{ else } \{\pi(\mathcal{I}',s)\} & \text{if } r \in \text{roles}(\mathcal{I},\mathcal{I}') \setminus \{s\} \\ 1 & \text{otherwise} \end{cases}$$

$$\boxed{\pi(n : \text{while } b@r \ \{\mathcal{I}\}, s)} =$$
$$\begin{cases} \text{while } b \ \{(\Pi_{r' \in \text{roles}(\mathcal{I})\setminus\{r\}} o_n^* : \text{true to } r'); \pi(\mathcal{I},s); \\ \quad \Pi_{r' \in \text{roles}(\mathcal{I})\setminus\{r\}} \ o_n^* : \_ \text{ from } r'\}; & \text{if } s = r \\ \quad \Pi_{r' \in \text{roles}(\mathcal{I})\setminus\{r\}} \ o_n^* : \text{false to } r' \\ o_n^* : x_n \text{ from } r; \\ \quad \text{while } x_n \ \{\pi(\mathcal{I},s); o_n^* : \text{ok to } r; o_n^* : x_n \text{ from } r\} & \text{if } s \in \text{roles}(\mathcal{I}) \setminus \{r\} \\ 1 & \text{otherwise} \end{cases}$$

$$\boxed{\pi(n : \text{scope } @r \ \{\mathcal{I}\}, s)} = \begin{cases} n : \text{scope } @r \ \{\pi(\mathcal{I},s)\} \text{ roles } \{\text{roles}(\mathcal{I})\} & \text{if } s = r \\ n : \text{scope } @r \ \{\pi(\mathcal{I},s)\} & \text{if } s \in \text{roles}(\mathcal{I})\setminus\{r\} \\ 1 & \text{otherwise} \end{cases}$$

the loop, indexes are used to choose names for auxiliary operations: the choice is coherent among the different roles and interference between different loops or conditionals is avoided.

There is a trade-off between efficiency and ease of programming that concerns how to ensure that all the roles are aware of the evolution of the computation. Indeed, this can be done in three ways: by using auxiliary communications generated either *i*) by the projection (e.g., as for if and while constructs above) or *ii*) by the semantics (as we will show for scopes) or *iii*) by restricting the class of allowed DIOCs (as done for sequential composition using connectedness for sequence). For instance, auxiliary communications for the if $b@r \ \{\mathcal{I}\}$ else $\{\mathcal{I}'\}$ construct are needed unless one requires that $r \in \{r_1, r_2\}$ for each $r_1 \to r_2 \in \text{transl}(\mathcal{I}) \cup \text{transl}(\mathcal{I}')$. The use of auxiliary communications is possibly less efficient, while stricter connectedness conditions leave more burden on the shoulders of the programmer.

We now define the projection $\text{proj}(\mathcal{I}, \Sigma)$, based on the process-projection π, to derive a DPOC network from a DIOC process $\mathcal{I}$ and a global state Σ. We denote with $\|_{i \in I} \mathcal{N}_i$ the parallel composition of networks $\mathcal{N}_i$ for each $i \in I$.

Table 4. DPOC role semantics (excerpt)

[One]
$$(1, \Gamma)_r \xrightarrow{\sqrt{}} (0, \Gamma)_r$$

[Assign]
$$\frac{[\![e]\!]\Gamma = v}{(x = e, \Gamma)_r \xrightarrow{\tau} (1, \Gamma[v/x])_r}$$

[Out-Up]
$$(o^? : X \text{ to } r', \Gamma)_r \xrightarrow{\overline{o^?}\langle X \rangle @r':r} (1, \Gamma)_r$$

[In]
$$(o^? : x \text{ from } r', \Gamma)_r \xrightarrow{o^?(x \leftarrow v)@r':r} (x = v, \Gamma)_r$$

[Out]
$$\frac{[\![e]\!]\Gamma = v}{(o^? : e \text{ to } r', \Gamma)_r \xrightarrow{\overline{o^?}\langle v \rangle @r':r} (1, \Gamma)_r}$$

[Sequence]
$$\frac{(P, \Gamma)_r \xrightarrow{\delta} (P', \Gamma')_r \quad \delta \neq \sqrt{}}{(P; Q, \Gamma)_r \xrightarrow{\delta} (P'; Q, \Gamma')_r}$$

[Seq-end]
$$\frac{(P, \Gamma)_r \xrightarrow{\sqrt{}} (P', \Gamma)_r \quad (Q, \Gamma)_r \xrightarrow{\delta} (Q', \Gamma')_r}{(P; Q, \Gamma)_r \xrightarrow{\delta} (Q', \Gamma')_r}$$

[Lead-Up]
$$\frac{\mathcal{I}' = \text{freshIndex}(\mathcal{I}, n) \quad \text{roles}(\mathcal{I}') \subseteq S}{(n : \text{scope } @r \ \{P\} \text{ roles } \{S\}, \Gamma)_r \xrightarrow{\mathcal{I}} (\Pi_{r_i \in S \setminus \{r\}} o_n^* : \pi(\mathcal{I}', r_i) \text{ to } r_i; \pi(\mathcal{I}', r); \Pi_{r_i \in S \setminus \{r\}} o_n^* : \_ \text{ from } r_i, \Gamma)_r}$$

[Lead-NoUp]
$$(n : \text{scope } @r \ \{P\} \text{ roles } \{S\}, \Gamma)_r \xrightarrow{\text{no-up}} (\Pi_{r_i \in S \setminus \{r\}} o_n^* : \text{no to } r_i; P; \Pi_{r_i \in S \setminus \{r\}} o_n^* : \_ \text{ from } r_i, \Gamma)_r$$

[Up]
$$(n : \text{scope } @r' \ \{P\}, \Gamma)_r \xrightarrow{o_n^*(\leftarrow P')@r'} (P'; o_n^* : \text{ok to } r', \Gamma)_r$$

[NoUp]
$$(n : \text{scope } @r' \ \{P\}, \Gamma)_r \xrightarrow{o_n^*(\leftarrow \text{no})@r'} (P; o_n^* : \text{ok to } r', \Gamma)_r$$

Definition 6 (Projection). *The projection of a* DIOC *process* $\mathcal{I}$ *with global state* Σ *is the* DPOC *network defined by* $\text{proj}(\mathcal{I}, \Sigma) = \|_{s \in \text{roles}(\mathcal{I})} (\pi(\mathcal{I}, s), \Sigma_s)_s$

The technical report [8] shows the DPOC processes obtained by projecting the DIOC for the Buying scenario in Listing 1.1 on `buyer`, `seller`, and `bank`.

3.2 DPOC Semantics

Definition 7 (DPOC Systems Semantics). *The semantics of* DPOC *systems is defined as the smallest LTS closed under the rules in Table 5 here and Table 7 in the companion technical report [8] (excerpt in Table 4). Symmetric rules for parallel composition have been omitted.*

We use δ to range over labels. The semantics in the early style. We comment below on the main rules.

Rule [In] receives a value v from role r' and assigns it to local variable x of r. Rules [Out] and [Out-Up] execute send and higher-order send actions, respectively. The send evaluates expression e in the local state Γ. In rule [Assign], $[v/x]$ represents the substitution of value v for variable x.

Table 5. DPOC system Semantics

[LIFT]

$$\frac{\mathcal{N} \xrightarrow{\delta} \mathcal{N}' \quad \delta \neq \mathcal{I}}{\langle \mathbf{I}, \mathcal{N} \rangle \xrightarrow{\delta} \langle \mathbf{I}, \mathcal{N}' \rangle}$$

[LIFT-UP]

$$\frac{\mathcal{N} \xrightarrow{\mathcal{I}} \mathcal{N}' \quad \mathcal{I} \text{ connected} \quad \mathcal{I} \in \mathbf{I}}{\langle \mathbf{I}, \mathcal{N} \rangle \xrightarrow{\mathcal{I}} \langle \mathbf{I}, \mathcal{N}' \rangle}$$

[CHANGE-UPDATES]

$$\langle \mathbf{I}, \mathcal{N} \rangle \xrightarrow{\mathbf{I}'} \langle \mathbf{I}', \mathcal{N} \rangle$$

[SYNCH]

$$\frac{\langle \mathbf{I}, \mathcal{N} \rangle \xrightarrow{\overline{o^?}\langle v \rangle @r_2:r_1} \langle \mathbf{I}, \mathcal{N}' \rangle \quad \langle \mathbf{I}, \mathcal{N}'' \rangle \xrightarrow{o^?(x \leftarrow v)@r_1:r_2} \langle \mathbf{I}, \mathcal{N}''' \rangle}{\langle \mathbf{I}, \mathcal{N} \parallel \mathcal{N}'' \rangle \xrightarrow{o^?:r_1(v) \rightarrow r_2(x)} \langle \mathbf{I}, \mathcal{N}' \parallel \mathcal{N}''' \rangle}$$

[SYNCH-UP]

$$\frac{\langle \mathbf{I}, \mathcal{N} \rangle \xrightarrow{\overline{o^?}\langle X \rangle @r_2:r_1} \langle \mathbf{I}, \mathcal{N}' \rangle \quad \langle \mathbf{I}, \mathcal{N}'' \rangle \xrightarrow{o^?(\leftarrow X)@r_1:r_2} \langle \mathbf{I}, \mathcal{N}''' \rangle}{\langle \mathbf{I}, \mathcal{N} \parallel \mathcal{N}'' \rangle \xrightarrow{o^?:r_1(X) \rightarrow r_2()} \langle \mathbf{I}, \mathcal{N}' \parallel \mathcal{N}''' \rangle}$$

[EXT-PARALLEL]

$$\frac{\langle \mathbf{I}, \mathcal{N} \rangle \xrightarrow{\eta} \langle \mathbf{I}, \mathcal{N}' \rangle \quad \eta \neq \checkmark}{\langle \mathbf{I}, \mathcal{N} \parallel \mathcal{N}'' \rangle \xrightarrow{\eta} \langle \mathbf{I}, \mathcal{N}' \parallel \mathcal{N}'' \rangle}$$

[EXT-PAR-END]

$$\frac{\langle \mathbf{I}, \mathcal{N} \rangle \xrightarrow{\checkmark} \langle \mathbf{I}, \mathcal{N}' \rangle \quad \langle \mathbf{I}, \mathcal{N}'' \rangle \xrightarrow{\checkmark} \langle \mathbf{I}, \mathcal{N}''' \rangle}{\langle \mathbf{I}, \mathcal{N} \parallel \mathcal{N}'' \rangle \xrightarrow{\checkmark} \langle \mathbf{I}, \mathcal{N}' \parallel \mathcal{N}''' \rangle}$$

Rule [LEAD-UP] concerns the role r coordinating the update of a scope. Role r decides which update to use. It is important that this decision is taken by the unique coordinator r for two reasons. First, r ensures that all involved roles agree on whether to update or not. Second, since the set of updates may change at any time, the choice of the update inside **I** needs to be atomic, and this is guaranteed using a unique coordinator. Role r transforms the DIOC $\mathcal{I}$ into $\mathcal{I}'$ using function freshIndex($\mathcal{I}, n$), which produces a copy $\mathcal{I}'$ of $\mathcal{I}$. In $\mathcal{I}'$ the indexes of scopes are fresh, which avoids clashes with indexes already present in the target DPOC. Moreover, to avoid that interactions in the update interfere with (parallel) interactions in the context, freshIndex($\mathcal{I}, n$) renames all the operations inside $\mathcal{I}$ by adding to them the index n. To this end we extend the set of operations without changing the semantics. For each operation $o^?$ we define extended operations of the form $n \cdot o^?$. The coordinator r also generates the processes to be executed by the roles in S using the process-projection function π. The processes are sent via higher-order communications only to the roles that have to execute them. Then, r starts its own updated code $\pi(\mathcal{I}', r)$. Finally, auxiliary communications are used to synchronise the end of the execution of the replaced process (here _ denotes a fresh variable to store the synchronisation message ok). The auxiliary communications are needed to ensure that the update is performed in a coordinated way, i.e., the roles agree on when the scope starts and terminates and on whether the update is performed or not.

Rule [LEAD-NOUP] instead defines the behaviour when the coordinator r decides to not update. In this case, r sends a token no to each other involved role, notifying them that no update is applied. End of scope synchronisation is as above. Rules [UP] and [NOUP] define the behaviour of the scopes for the other roles involved in the update. The scope waits for a message from the coordinator. If the content of the message is no, the body of the scope is executed. Otherwise, it is a process P' which is executed instead of the body of the scope.

Table 5 defines the semantics of DPOC systems. We use η to range over DPOC systems labels. Rule [LIFT] and [LIFT-UP] lift roles transitions to the system level. [LIFT-UP] also checks that the update $\mathcal{I}$ is connected and in the set of currently available updates $\mathbf{I}$. Rule [SYNCH] synchronises a send with the corresponding receive, producing an interaction. Rule [SYNCH-UP] is similar, but it deals with higher-order interactions. The labels of these transitions store the information on the occurred communication: label $o^? : r_1(v) \to r_2(x)$ denotes an interaction on operation $o^?$ from role r_1 to role r_2 where the value v is sent by r_1 and then stored by r_2 in variable x. Label $o^? : r_1(X) \to r_2()$ denotes a similar interaction, but concerning a higher-order value X. No receiver variable is specified, since the received value becomes part of the code of the receiving process. Rule [EXT-PARALLEL] allows a network inside a parallel composition to compute. Rule [EXT-PAR-END] synchronises the termination of parallel networks. Finally, rule [CHANGE-UPDATES] allows the set of updates to change arbitrarily.

We can now define DPOC traces.

Definition 8 (DPOC Traces). *A (strong) trace of a DPOC system $\langle \mathbf{I}_1, \mathcal{N}_1 \rangle$ is a sequence (finite or infinite) of labels $\eta_1, \eta_2, \ldots$ with $\eta_i \in \{\tau, o^? : r_1(v) \to r_2(x), o^* : r_1(X) \to r_2(), \sqrt{}, \mathcal{I}, \mathsf{no\text{-}up}, \mathbf{I}\}$ such that there is a sequence of transitions $\langle \mathbf{I}_1, \mathcal{N}_1 \rangle \xrightarrow{\eta_1} \langle \mathbf{I}_2, \mathcal{N}_2 \rangle \xrightarrow{\eta_2} \ldots$.*
A weak trace of a DPOC system $\langle \mathbf{I}_1, \mathcal{N}_1 \rangle$ is a sequence of labels $\eta_1, \eta_2, \ldots$ obtained by removing all the labels corresponding to private communications, i.e. of the form $o^* : r_1(v) \to r_2(x)$ or $o^* : r_1(X) \to r_2()$, and the silent labels τ, from a trace of $\langle \mathbf{I}_1, \mathcal{N}_1 \rangle$. Furthermore, all the extended operations of the form $n \cdot o^?$ are replaced by $o^?$.

Note that DPOC traces do not include send and receive actions. We do this since these actions have no correspondence at the DIOC level, where only whole interactions are allowed.

In the companion technical report [8] one can find a sample execution of the DPOC obtained by projecting the DIOC for the Buying scenario in Listing 1.1.

4 Correctness

In the previous sections we have presented DIOCs, DPOCs, and described how to derive a DPOC from a given DIOC. This section presents the main technical result of the paper, namely the correctness of the projection. Correctness here means that the weak traces of a connected DIOC coincide with the weak traces of the projected DPOC.

Definition 9 (Trace Equivalence). *A DIOC system $\langle \Sigma, \mathbf{I}, \mathcal{I} \rangle$ and a DPOC system $\langle \mathbf{I}, \mathcal{N} \rangle$ are (weak) trace equivalent iff their sets of (weak) traces coincide.*

Theorem 2 (Correctness). *For each initial, connected DIOC process $\mathcal{I}$, each state Σ, each set of updates $\mathbf{I}$, the DIOC system $\langle \Sigma, \mathbf{I}, \mathcal{I} \rangle$ and the DPOC system $\langle \mathbf{I}, \mathsf{proj}(\mathcal{I}, \Sigma) \rangle$ are weak trace equivalent.*

Trace-based properties of the DIOC are inherited by the DPOC. Examples include termination (see the technical report [8]) and deadlock-freedom.

Definition 10 (Deadlock-freedom). *An internal* DIOC *(resp.* DPOC*) trace is obtained by removing transitions labelled* **I** *from a* DIOC *(resp.* DPOC*) trace. A* DIOC *(resp.* DPOC*) system is deadlock-free if all its maximal finite internal traces have* $\sqrt{}$ *as label of the last transition.*

Intuitively, internal traces are needed since labels **I** do not correspond to activities of the application and may be executed also after application termination.

By construction initial DIOCs are deadlock-free. Hence:

Corollary 1 (Deadlock-freedom). *For each initial, connected* DIOC $\mathcal{I}$, *state* Σ, *and set of updates* **I** *the* DPOC *system* $\langle \mathbf{I}, \mathsf{proj}(\mathcal{I}, \Sigma) \rangle$ *is deadlock-free.*

Moreover, our DIOCs and DPOCs are free from races and orphan messages. A race occurs when the same receive (resp. send) may interact with different sends (resp. receives). In our setting, an orphan message is an enabled send that is never consumed by a receive. Orphan messages are more relevant in asynchronous systems, where a message may be sent, and stay forever in the network, since the corresponding receive operation may never become enabled. However, even in synchronous systems orphan messages should be avoided: the message is not communicated since the receive is not available, hence a desired behaviour of the application never takes place due to synchronization problems.

Trivially, DIOCs avoid races and orphan messages since send and receive are bound together in the same construct. Differently, at the DPOC level, since all receive of the form $o^? : x$ **from** r_1 in role r_2 may interact with the sends of the form $o^? : e$ **to** r_2 in role r_1, races may happen. However, thanks to the correctness of the projection, race-freedom holds also for the projected DPOCs.

Corollary 2 (Race-freedom). *For each initial, connected* DIOC $\mathcal{I}$, *state* Σ, *and set of updates* **I**, *if* $\langle \mathbf{I}, \mathsf{proj}(\mathcal{I}, \Sigma) \rangle \xrightarrow{\mu_1} \cdots \xrightarrow{\mu_n} \langle \mathbf{I}', \mathcal{N} \rangle$, *then in* $\mathcal{N}$ *two sends (resp. receives) cannot interact with the same receive (resp. send).*

As far as orphan messages are concerned, they may appear in infinite DPOC computations since a receive may not become enabled due to an infinite loop. However, as a corollary of trace equivalence, we have that terminating DPOCs are orphan message-free.

Corollary 3 (Orphan Message-freedom). *For each initial, connected* DIOC $\mathcal{I}$, *state* Σ, *and set of updates* **I**, *if* $\langle \mathbf{I}, \mathsf{proj}(\mathcal{I}, \Sigma) \rangle \xrightarrow{\mu_1} \cdots \xrightarrow{\sqrt{}} \langle \mathbf{I}', \mathcal{N} \rangle$, *then* $\mathcal{N}$ *contains no sends.*

5   Related Works and Discussion

This paper presents an approach for the dynamic update of distributed applications. It guarantees the absence of communication deadlocks and races by construction for the running distributed application, even in presence of updates that were unknown when the application was started. More generally, the DPOC is compliant with the DIOC description, and inherits its properties.

The two approaches closest to ours we are aware of are in the area of multiparty session types [4–6, 13], and deal with dynamic software updates [2] and with monitoring of self-adaptive systems [7]. The main difference between [2] and our approach is that [2] targets concurrent applications which are not distributed. Indeed, it relies on a check on the global state of the application to ensure that the update is safe. Such a check cannot be done by a single role, thus is impractical in a distributed setting. Furthermore, the language in [2] is much more constrained than ours, e.g., requiring each pair of participants to interact on a dedicated pair of channels, and assuming that all the roles not involved in a choice behave the same in the two branches. The approach in [7] is very different from ours, too. In particular, in [7] all the possible behaviours are available since the very beginning, both at the level of types and of processes, and a fixed adaptation function is used to switch between them. This difference derives from the distinction between self-adaptive applications, as they discuss, and applications updated from the outside, as in our case.

We also recall [10], which uses types to ensure safe adaptation. However, [10] allows updates only when no session is active, while we change the behaviour of running DIOCs. Our work shares with [18] the interest in choreographies composition. However, [18] uses multiparty session types and only allows static parallel composition, while we replace a term inside an arbitrary context at runtime.

In principle, our update mechanism can be used to inject guarantees of freedom from deadlocks and races into existing approaches to adaptation, e.g., the ones in the surveys [11, 17]. However, this task is cumbersome, due to the huge number and heterogeneity of those approaches, and since for each of them the integration with our techniques is far from trivial. Nevertheless, we already started it. Indeed, in [9], we apply our technique to the adaptation mechanism described in [14]. While applications in [14] are not distributed and there are no guarantees on the correctness of the application after adaptation, applications in [9], based on the same adaptation mechanisms, are distributed and free from deadlocks and races by construction.

Furthermore, on the website [1], we give examples of how to integrate our approach with distributed [20] and dynamic [23] Aspect-Oriented Programming (AOP) and with Context-Oriented Programming (COP) [12]. In general, we can deal with cross-cutting concerns like logging and authentication, typical of AOP, viewing pointcuts as empty scopes and advices as updates. Layers, typical of COP, can instead be defined by updates which can fire according to contextual conditions. We are also planning to apply our techniques to multiparty session types [4–6, 13]. The main challenge here is to deal with multiple interleaved sessions. An initial analysis of the problem is presented in [3].

References

1. AIOCJ website, http://www.cs.unibo.it/projects/jolie/aiocj.html
2. Anderson, G., Rathke, J.: Dynamic software update for message passing programs. In: Jhala, R., Igarashi, A. (eds.) APLAS 2012. LNCS, vol. 7705, pp. 207–222. Springer, Heidelberg (2012)

3. Bravetti, M., Carbone, M., Hildebrandt, T., Lanese, I., Mauro, J., Pérez, J.A., Zavattaro, G.: Towards global and local types for adaptation. In: Counsell, S., Núñez, M. (eds.) SEFM 2013. LNCS, vol. 8368, pp. 3–14. Springer, Heidelberg (2014)
4. Carbone, M., Honda, K., Yoshida, N.: Structured communication-centered programming for web services. ACM Trans. Program. Lang. Syst. 34(2), 8 (2012)
5. Carbone, M., Montesi, F.: Deadlock-Freedom-by-Design: Multiparty Asynchronous Global Programming. In: POPL, pp. 263–274. ACM (2013)
6. Castagna, G., Dezani-Ciancaglini, M., Padovani, L.: On global types and multiparty session. Logical Methods in Computer Science 8(1) (2012)
7. Coppo, M., Dezani-Ciancaglini, M., Venneri, B.: Self-adaptive multiparty sessions. In: Service Oriented Computing and Applications, pp. 1–20 (2014)
8. Dalla Preda, M., Gabbrielli, M., Giallorenzo, S., Lanese, I., Mauro, J.: Dynamic Choreographies - Safe Runtime Updates of Distributed Applications. Technical report (2014), http://arxiv.org/abs/1407.0970
9. Dalla Preda, M., Giallorenzo, S., Lanese, I., Mauro, J., Gabbrielli, M.: AIOCJ: A choreographic framework for safe adaptive distributed applications. In: Combemale, B., Pearce, D.J., Barais, O., Vinju, J.J. (eds.) SLE 2014. LNCS, vol. 8706, pp. 161–170. Springer, Heidelberg (2014)
10. Di Giusto, C., Pérez, J.A.: Disciplined structured communications with consistent runtime adaptation. In: SAC, pp. 1913–1918. ACM (2013)
11. Ghezzi, C., Pradella, M., Salvaneschi, G.: An evaluation of the adaptation capabilities in programming languages. In: SEAMS, pp. 50–59. ACM (2011)
12. Hirschfeld, R., Costanza, P., Nierstrasz, O.: Context-oriented Programming. Journal of Object Technology 7(3), 125–151 (2008)
13. Honda, K., Yoshida, N., Carbone, M.: Multiparty Asynchronous Session Types. In: POPL, pp. 273–284. ACM (2008)
14. Lanese, I., Bucchiarone, A., Montesi, F.: A Framework for Rule-Based Dynamic Adaptation. In: Wirsing, M., Hofmann, M., Rauschmayer, A. (eds.) TGC 2010, LNCS, vol. 6084, pp. 284–300. Springer, Heidelberg (2010)
15. Lanese, I., Guidi, C., Montesi, F., Zavattaro, G.: Bridging the Gap between Interaction- and Process-Oriented Choreographies. In: SEFM, pp. 323–332. IEEE (2008)
16. Lanese, I., Montesi, F., Zavattaro, G.: Amending choreographies. In: WWV. EPTCS, vol. 123, pp. 34–48 (2013)
17. Leite, L.A.F., et al.: A systematic literature review of service choreography adaptation. Service Oriented Computing and Applications 7(3), 199–216 (2013)
18. Montesi, F., Yoshida, N.: Compositional choreographies. In: D'Argenio, P.R., Melgratti, H. (eds.) CONCUR 2013. LNCS, vol. 8052, pp. 425–439. Springer, Heidelberg (2013)
19. Nienaltowski, P.: Practical framework for contract-based concurrent object-oriented programming. PhD thesis, ETH Zurich (2007)
20. Pawlak, R., et al.: JAC: an aspect-based distributed dynamic framework. Softw., Pract. Exper. 34(12), 1119–1148 (2004)
21. Rust website, http://www.rust-lang.org/
22. Scribble website, http://www.jboss.org/scribble
23. Yang, Z., Cheng, B.H.C., Stirewalt, R.E.K., Sowell, J., Sadjadi, S.M., McKinley, P.K.: An aspect-oriented approach to dynamic adaptation. In: WOSS, pp. 85–92. ACM (2002)

Type Reconstruction Algorithms
for Deadlock-Free and Lock-Free Linear π-Calculi

Luca Padovani[1($\boxtimes$)], Tzu-Chun Chen[1,2], and Andrea Tosatto[1]

[1] Università di Torino, Torino, Italy
[2] Technische Universität Darmstadt, Germany
luca.padovani@di.unito.it

Abstract. We define complete type reconstruction algorithms for two type systems ensuring deadlock and lock freedom of linear π-calculus processes. Our work automates the verification of deadlock/lock freedom for a non-trivial class of processes that includes interleaved binary sessions and, to great extent, multiparty sessions as well. A Haskell implementation of the algorithms is available.

1 Introduction

Type systems help finding potential errors during the early phases of software development. In the context of communicating processes, typical errors are: making invalid assumptions about the nature of a received message; using a communication channel beyond its nominal capabilities. Some type systems are able to warn against subtler errors, and sometimes can even guarantee liveness properties as well. For instance, the type systems presented in [18] for the linear π-calculus [14] ensure well-typed processes to be deadlock and lock free. Such stronger guarantees come at the cost of a richer type structure, hence of a greater programming effort, when programmers are supposed to explicitly annotate programs with types. In this respect, *type reconstruction* becomes a most wanted tool in the programmer's toolkit: type reconstruction is the procedure that automatically synthesizes, whenever possible, the types of the entities used by a program; in particular, the types of the channels used by a communicating process. In the present work, we describe type reconstruction algorithms for the type systems presented in [18], thereby automating the static deadlock and lock freedom analysis for a non-trivial class of communicating processes.

A *deadlock* is a configuration with pending communications that cannot complete. A paradigmatic example of deadlock modeled in the π-calculus is illustrated below

$$(\nu a,b)(\,a?(x).b!x \mid b?(y).a!y\,) \tag{1.1}$$

where the input on a blocks the output on b, and the input on b blocks the output on a. The key idea used in [18] for detecting deadlocks, which is related to earlier works by Kobayashi [11,13], is to associate each channel with a number – called *level* – specifying the relative order in which different channels should be used. In (1.1), this mechanism requires a to have smaller level than b in the left subprocess, and greater level than b in the right one. Since no level assignment can simultaneously satisfy both requirements, (1.1) is flagged as ill typed. This mechanism does not prevent *locks*, namely

© IFIP International Federation for Information Processing 2015
T. Holvoet and M. Viroli (Eds.): COORDINATION 2015, LNCS 9037, pp. 83–98, 2015.
DOI: 10.1007/978-3-319-19282-6_6

configurations where some communication remains pending although the process as a whole can make progress. A deadlock-free configuration that is not lock free is

$$(va)(*c?(x).c!x \mid c!a \mid a!42)   \tag{1.2}$$

where the communication pending on a cannot complete. There are no interleaved communications on different channels in (1.2), therefore the level-based mechanism spots no apparent issue. The idea put forward in [18] to reject (1.2) is to also associate each channel with another number – called *ticket* – specifying the maximum number of times the channel can travel in a message. With this mechanism in place, (1.2) is ill typed because a would need an infinite number of tickets to travel infinitely many times on c.

Finding appropriate level and tickets for the channels used by a process can be difficult. We remedy to such difficulty with three contributions. First, we develop complete type reconstruction algorithms for the type systems in [18] so that appropriate level and tickets are synthesized automatically, whenever possible. The linear π-calculus [14], for which the type systems are defined, can model a variety of communicating systems with both static and dynamic network topologies. In particular, binary sessions [5] and, to a large extent, also multiparty sessions [18, technical report], can be encoded in it. Second, we purposely use a variant of the linear π-calculus with pairs instead of a polyadic calculus. While this choice has a cost in terms of technical machinery, it allows us to discuss how to deal with structured data types, which are of primary importance in concrete languages but whose integration in linear type systems requires some care [19]. We give evidence that our algorithms scale easily to other data types, including disjoint sums and polymorphic variants. Third, we present the algorithms *assuming* the existence of type reconstruction for the linear π-calculus [9,19]. This approach has two positive upshots: (1) we focus on the aspects of the algorithms concerning deadlock and lock freedom, thereby simplifying their presentation and the formal study of their properties; (2) we show how to combine in a modular way increasingly refined type reconstruction stages and how to address some of the issues that may arise in doing so.

In what follows we review the linear π-calculus with pairs (Section 2) and the type systems for deadlock and lock freedom of [18] (Section 3). Such type systems are unsuitable to be used as the basis for type reconstruction algorithms. So, we reformulate them to obtain reconstruction algorithms that are both correct and complete (Section 4). Then, we sketch an algorithm for solving the constraints generated by the reconstruction algorithms (Section 5) We conclude presenting a few benchmarks, further connections with related work, and directions of future research (Section 6).

The algorithms have been implemented and integrated in a tool for the static analysis of π-calculus processes. The archive with the source code of the tool, available at the page http://di.unito.it/hypha, includes a wide range of examples, of which we can discuss only one in the paper because of space constraints.

2   The Simply-Typed Linear π-calculus with Pairs

The process language we work with is the asynchronous π-calculus extended in two ways: (1) we generalize names to *expressions* to account for pairs and other data types; (2) we assume that names are explicitly annotated with *simple types* possibly inferred in a previous reconstruction phase ("simple" means without level/ticket decorations). We annotate free names instead of bound names because, in a behavioral type system, each occurrence of a name may be used according to a different type. Typically, two distinct occurrences of the same linear channel are used for complementary I/O actions. We use $m, n, \ldots$ to range over integer numbers; we use sets of *variables* $x, y, \ldots$ and *channels* $a, b, \ldots$; names $u, v, \ldots$ are either channels or variables; we let *polarities* $p, q, \ldots$ range over subsets of $\{?, !\}$; we abbreviate $\{?\}$ with ?, $\{!\}$ with !, and $\{?, !\}$ with #. *Processes* $P, Q, \ldots$, *expressions* e, f, $\ldots$, and *simple types* $t, s, \ldots$ are defined below:

Process	P, Q	$::=$	$\mathbf{0} \mid \mathrm{e?}(x).P \mid \mathrm{e!f} \mid P \mid Q \mid (va)P \mid *P$
Expression	e, f	$::=$	$n \mid u^t \mid (\mathrm{e,f}) \mid \mathrm{fst}(\mathrm{e}) \mid \mathrm{snd}(\mathrm{e})$
Simple type	t, s	$::=$	$\mathrm{int} \mid p[t] \mid p[t]^* \mid t \times s$

Expressions include integer constants, names, pairs, and the two pair projection operators $\mathtt{fst}$ and $\mathtt{snd}$. Simple types are the regular, possibly infinite terms built using the rightmost productions in grammar above and include the type $\mathtt{int}$ of integers, the type $p[t]$ of linear channels to be used according to the polarity p and carrying messages of type t, the type $p[t]^*$ of unlimited channels to be used according to the polarity p and carrying messages of type t, and the type $t \times s$ of pairs whose components have respectively type t and s. Recall that linear channels are meant to be used for *one* communication, whereas unlimited channels can be used any number of communications. We require every infinite branch of a type to contain infinitely many occurrences of channel constructors. For example, the term t satisfying the equation $t = ?[t]$ is a valid type while the one satisfying the equation $t = t \times \mathtt{int}$ is not. We impose this requirement to simplify the formal development, but it can be lifted (for example, the implementation supports ordinary recursive types such as lists and trees).

Since we are only concerned with type reconstruction, we do not give an operational semantics of the calculus. The interested reader may refer to [14,19] for generic properties of the linear π-calculus and to [18] for the formalization of (dead)lock freedom. We conclude this section with a comprehensive example that is representative of a class of processes for which our type systems are able to prove deadlock and lock freedom.

Example 2.1 (full duplex communication). The term

$$*c?(x).(va)(\ \mathrm{fst}(x)!a \ \mid \ \mathrm{snd}(x)?(y).c!(a,y)\ ) \ \mid \ c!(e,f) \ \mid \ c!(f,e)$$

(where we have omitted simple type annotations) models a system composed of two neighbor processes connected by channels e and f. The process spawned by $c!(e,f)$ uses e for sending a message to the neighbor. Simultaneously, it waits on f for a message from the neighbor. The process spawned by $c!(f,e)$ does the opposite. Each exchanged message consists of a payload (omitted) and a *continuation channel* on which subsequent messages are exchanged. Above, each process sends and receives a fresh continuation a. Once the two communications have been performed, each process iterates with a new pair of corresponding continuations.   ∎

3   Type Systems for Deadlock and Lock Freedom

In this section we review the type systems ensuring deadlock and lock freedom [18] for which we want to define corresponding reconstruction algorithms. Both type systems rely on refined linear channel types of the form $p\,[t]_m^n$ where the decorations n and m are respectively the *level* and the *tickets* of a channel with this type. Intuitively, levels are used for imposing an ordering on the input/output operations performed on channels: channels with lower level must be used *before* channels with higher level; tickets limit the number of "travels" for channels: a channel with m tickets can be sent at most m times in a message. From now on, we use T, S, ... to range over *types*, which have the same structure and constructors as simple types, but where linear channel types are decorated with levels and tickets. We write $\lfloor T \rfloor$ for the *stripping* of T, namely for the simple type obtained by removing all level and ticket decorations from T. For example, $\lfloor ?\,[\text{int} \times \,!\,[\text{int}]_m^n]^* \rfloor = ?\,[\text{int} \times \,!\,[\text{int}]]^*$. Note that $\lfloor \cdot \rfloor$ is a non-injective function.

We need some auxiliary operators. First, we extend the notion of level from channel types to arbitrary types. The level of a type T, written $|T|$, is an element of the set $\mathbb{Z} \cup \{\bot, \top\}$ ordered in the obvious way and formally defined thus:

$$|T| \overset{\text{def}}{=} \begin{cases} \bot & \text{if } T = p\,[S]^* \text{ and } ? \in p \\ n & \text{if } T = p\,[S]_m^n \text{ and } p \neq \emptyset \\ \min\{|T_1|, |T_2|\} & \text{if } T = T_1 \times T_2 \\ \top & \text{otherwise} \end{cases} \tag{3.1}$$

As an example, we have $|\text{int} \times ?\,[!\,[\text{int}]_0^1]_0^1| = \min\{|\text{int}|, |?\,[!\,[\text{int}]_0^1]_0^1|\} = \min\{\top, 0\} = 0$. Intuitively, the level of T measures the inverse urgency for using values of type T in order to ensure (dead)lock freedom: the lowest level (and highest urgency) $\bot$ is given to unlimited channels with input polarity, for which we want to guarantee input receptiveness; finite levels are reserved for linear channels; the highest level (and lowest urgency) $\top$ is given to values such as numbers or channels with empty polarity whose use is not critical as far as (dead)lock is concerned. Note that $|T|$ is well defined because every infinite branch of T has infinitely many channel constructors.

We also need an operator to *shift* the topmost levels and tickets in types. We define

$$\$_m^n T \overset{\text{def}}{=} \begin{cases} p\,[S]_{m+k}^{n+h} & \text{if } T = p\,[S]_k^h \\ (\$_m^n T_1) \times (\$_m^n T_2) & \text{if } T = T_1 \times T_2 \\ T & \text{otherwise} \end{cases} \tag{3.2}$$

so that, for example, we have $\$_1^2(\text{int} \times ?\,[!\,[\text{int}]_0^1]_0^0) = \text{int} \times ?\,[!\,[\text{int}]_0^1]_1^2$.

Next, we define an operator for *combining* the types of different occurrences of the same object. If an object is used according to type T in one part of a process and according to type S in another part, then it is used according to the type $T + S$ overall, where $T + S$ is inductively defined thus:

$$T + S \overset{\text{def}}{=} \begin{cases} \text{int} & \text{if } T = S = \text{int} \\ (T_1 + S_1) \times (T_2 + S_2) & \text{if } T = T_1 \times T_2 \text{ and } S = S_1 \times S_2 \\ (p \cup q)\,[T]_{h+k}^n & \text{if } T = p\,[T]_h^n \text{ and } S = q\,[T]_k^n \text{ and } p \cap q = \emptyset \\ (p \cup q)\,[T]^* & \text{if } T = p\,[T]^* \text{ and } S = q\,[T]^* \\ \text{undefined} & \text{otherwise} \end{cases}$$

Table 1. Typing rules for the deadlock-free ($k = 0$) and lock-free ($k = 1$) linear π-calculus

---

Typing rules for expressions $\boxed{\Gamma \vdash e : t}$

$$[\text{T-INT}] \quad \frac{}{\Gamma \vdash n : \texttt{int}} \; \text{un}(\Gamma) \qquad\qquad [\text{T-NAME}] \quad \frac{}{\Gamma, u : T \vdash u^{\lfloor T \rfloor} : T} \; \text{un}(\Gamma)$$

$$[\text{T-PAIR}] \quad \frac{\Gamma_i \vdash e_i : T_i \;\; (i=1,2)}{\Gamma_1 + \Gamma_2 \vdash (e_1, e_2) : T_1 \times T_2} \qquad [\text{T-FST}] \quad \frac{\Gamma \vdash e : T \times S}{\Gamma \vdash \texttt{fst}(e) : T} \; \text{un}(S) \qquad [\text{T-SND}] \quad \frac{\Gamma \vdash e : T \times S}{\Gamma \vdash \texttt{snd}(e) : S} \; \text{un}(T)$$

Typing rules for processes $\boxed{\Gamma \vdash_k P}$

$$[\text{T-IN}] \quad \frac{\Gamma_1 \vdash e : ?[T]^n_m \qquad \Gamma_2, x : \$^n_0 T \vdash_k P}{\Gamma_1 + \Gamma_2 \vdash_k e?(x).P} \; n < |\Gamma_2| \qquad\qquad [\text{T-OUT}] \quad \frac{\Gamma_1 \vdash e : ![T]^n_m \qquad \Gamma_2 \vdash f : \$^n_k T}{\Gamma_1 + \Gamma_2 \vdash_k e!f} \; n < |\Gamma_2|$$

$$[\text{T-IN*}] \quad \frac{\Gamma_1 \vdash e : ?[T]^* \qquad \Gamma_2, x : T \vdash_k P}{\Gamma_1 + \Gamma_2 \vdash_k *e?(x).P} \; \overline{\text{un}}(\Gamma_2) \qquad\qquad [\text{T-OUT*}] \quad \frac{\Gamma_1 \vdash e : ![T]^* \qquad \Gamma_2 \vdash f : \$^n_k T}{\Gamma_1 + \Gamma_2 \vdash_k e!f} \; \perp < |\Gamma_2|$$

$$[\text{T-IDLE}] \quad \frac{}{\Gamma \vdash_k \mathbf{0}} \; \text{un}(\Gamma) \qquad [\text{T-PAR}] \quad \frac{\Gamma_1 \vdash_k P \qquad \Gamma_2 \vdash_k Q}{\Gamma_1 + \Gamma_2 \vdash_k P \mid Q} \qquad [\text{T-NEW}] \quad \frac{\Gamma, a : \#[T]^m_n \vdash_k P}{\Gamma \vdash_k (va)P} \qquad [\text{T-NEW*}] \quad \frac{\Gamma, a : \#[T]^* \vdash_k P}{\Gamma \vdash_k (va)P}$$

Type combination is partial and is only defined when the combined types have the same structure. In particular, channel types can be combined only if they have equal message types; linear channel types can be combined only if they have disjoint polarities and equal level. Also, the combination of two channel types has the union of their polarities and, in the case of linear channels, the sum of their tickets. For example, a channel that is used both with type $?[\texttt{int}]^0_1$ and with type $![\texttt{int}]^0_2$ is used overall according to the type $?[\texttt{int}]^0_1 + ![\texttt{int}]^0_2 = \#[\texttt{int}]^0_3$.

Lastly, we define *type environments* $\Gamma, \ldots$ as finite maps from names to types written $u_1 : T_1, \ldots, u_n : T_n$. As usual, $\text{dom}(\Gamma)$ is the domain of Γ and Γ_1, Γ_2 is the union of Γ_1 and Γ_2 when $\text{dom}(\Gamma_1) \cap \text{dom}(\Gamma_2) = \emptyset$. We extend type combination to type environments:

$$\Gamma_1 + \Gamma_2 \stackrel{\text{def}}{=} \Gamma_1, \Gamma_2 \qquad\qquad \text{if } \text{dom}(\Gamma_1) \cap \text{dom}(\Gamma_2) = \emptyset$$
$$(\Gamma_1, u : T) + (\Gamma_2, u : S) \stackrel{\text{def}}{=} (\Gamma_1 + \Gamma_2), u : T + S$$

We let $|\Gamma| \stackrel{\text{def}}{=} \min\{|\Gamma(u)| \mid u \in \text{dom}(\Gamma)\}$ be the level of a type environment, we write $\text{un}(\Gamma)$ if $|\Gamma| = \top$ and $\overline{\text{un}}(\Gamma)$ if $\text{un}(\Gamma)$ and Γ has no top-level linear channel types. Note that $\overline{\text{un}}(\Gamma)$ is strictly stronger than $\text{un}(\Gamma)$. For example, if $\Gamma \stackrel{\text{def}}{=} x : \texttt{int} \times \emptyset[\texttt{int}]^0_0$ we have $\text{un}(\Gamma)$ but not $\overline{\text{un}}(\Gamma)$ because $\Gamma(x)$ has a top-level linear channel type.

The type systems for deadlock and lock freedom are defined by the rules in Table 1 deriving judgments $\Gamma \vdash e : T$ for expressions and $\Gamma \vdash_k P$ for processes. The type system for deadlock freedom is obtained by taking $k = 0$, whereas the type system for lock freedom is obtained by taking $k = 1$ and restricting all levels in linear channel types to be non negative. We illustrate the typing rules as we work through the typing derivation of the replicated process in Example 2.1. The interested reader may refer to the implementation or [18] for more examples and detailed descriptions of the rules.

Let T and S be the types defined by the equations $T = \; ! [S]_0^0 \times \; ? [S]_0^0$ and $S = \; ? [S]_1^1$. We build the derivation bottom up, from the judgment stating that the whole process is well typed. Since the process is a replicated input, we apply [T-IN*] thus:

$$\frac{c : ? [T]^* \vdash c : ? [T]^* \quad c : \; ! [T]^*, x : T \vdash_1 (va)(\texttt{fst}(x) \, ! a \mid \texttt{snd}(x) ? (y).c! (a,y))}{c : \# [T]^* \vdash_1 *c?(x).(va)(\texttt{fst}(x) \, ! a \mid \texttt{snd}(x) ? (y).c! (a,y))}$$

In applying this rule we have $\Gamma_2 = c : \; ! [T]^*$ so the side condition $\overline{\mathsf{un}}(\Gamma_2)$ of [T-IN*] is satisfied: since a replicated input process is permanently available, its body cannot contain any free linear channel except those possibly received through the unlimited channel. The side condition $\overline{\mathsf{un}}(\Gamma_2)$, which is stronger than simply $\mathsf{un}(\Gamma_2)$, makes sure that a replicated input process does not contain linear channels and therefore is level polymorphic. We will see a use of this feature at the very end of the derivation. The continuation of the process gains visibility of the message x with type T and is a restriction of a linear channel a. Hence, the next step is an obvious application of [T-NEW]:

$$\frac{c : \; ! [T]^*, x : T, a : \# [S]_3^1 \vdash_1 \texttt{fst}(x) \, ! a \mid \texttt{snd}(x) ? (y).c! (a,y)}{c : \; ! [T]^*, x : T \vdash_1 (va)(\texttt{fst}(x) \, ! a \mid \texttt{snd}(x) ? (y).c! (a,y))} \tag{3.3}$$

We guess level 1 and 3 tickets for a. The rationale is that a is a continuation channel that will be used *after* the channels in x, which have level 0, so a must have strictly positive level. Also, in Example 2.1 the channel a travels three times. At this point the typing derivation forks, for we deal with the parallel composition of two processes. This means that we have to split the type environment in two parts, each describing the resources used by the corresponding subprocess in (3.3). We have $\Gamma = \Gamma_1 + \Gamma_2$ where

$$\Gamma \stackrel{\text{def}}{=} c : \; ! [T]^*, x : T, a : \# [S]_3^1 \qquad \Gamma_1 \stackrel{\text{def}}{=} \qquad x : \; ! [S]_0^0 \times \emptyset [S]_0^0, a : \; ? [S]_2^1$$
$$\Gamma_2 \stackrel{\text{def}}{=} c : \; ! [T]^*, x : \emptyset [S]_0^0 \times \; ? [S]_0^0, a : \; ! [S]_1^1$$

Observe that Γ is split in such a way that: c only occurs in Γ_2, because it is only used in the right subprocess in (3.3); in each subprocess, the unused linear channel in the pair x is given empty polarity; the type of the continuation a has input polarity (and 2 tickets) in Γ_1 and output polarity (and 1 ticket) in Γ_2. The type of a in Γ_1 is the same as $\$_1^0 S$, and we use the latter form from now on. We complete the typing derivation for the left subprocess in (3.3) using Γ_1 and applying [T-OUT]:

$$\frac{x : \; ! [S]_0^0 \times \emptyset [S]_0^0 \vdash \texttt{fst}(x) : \; ! [S]_0^0 \qquad a : \$_1^0 S \vdash a : \$_1^0 S}{x : \; ! [S]_0^0 \times \emptyset [S]_0^0, a : \$_1^0 S \vdash_1 \texttt{fst}(x) \, ! a} \quad 0 < |\$_1^0 S| = 1$$

The side condition $0 < 1$ ensures that the message has higher level than the channel on which it travels, according to the intuition that the message can only be used *after* the communication has occurred and the message has been received. In this case, the level of $\texttt{fst}(x)$ is 0 that is smaller than the level of a, which is 1. Shifting the tickets from the type of a consumes one of its tickets, meaning that after this communication a gets closer to the point where it must be the subject of a communication.

Concerning the right subprocess in (3.3), we use Γ_2 above and apply [T-IN] to obtain

$$\frac{x : \emptyset [S]_0^0 \times \, ? [S]_0^0 \vdash \mathsf{snd}(x) : \, ? [S]_0^0 \qquad c : \, ! [T]^*, a : \, ! [S]_1^1, y : S \vdash_1 c! (a,y)}{c : \, ! [T]^*, x : \emptyset [S]_0^0 \times \, ? [S]_0^0, a : \, ! [S]_1^1 \vdash_1 \mathsf{snd}(x)?(y).c! (a,y)} \; 0 < 1$$

The side condition $0 < 1$ checks that the level of the linear channel used for input is smaller than the level of any other channel occurring free in the continuation of the process. In this case, c has level $\top$ because it is an unlimited channel with output polarity, whereas a has level 1. To close the derivation we must type the recursive invocation of c. We do so with an application of [T-OUT*]:

$$\frac{c : \, ! [T]^* \vdash c : \, ! [T]^* \qquad a : \, ! [S]_1^1, y : S \vdash (a,y) : \$_1^1 T}{c : \, ! [T]^*, a : \, ! [S]_1^1, y : S \vdash_1 c! (a,y)} \; \bot < 1$$

The side condition $\bot < 1$ ensures that no unlimited channel with input polarity is sent in the message. This is necessary to guarantee input receptiveness on unlimited channels. There is a mismatch between the actual type $\$_1^1 T$ and the expected type T of the message. The shifting on the tickets is due, once again, to the fact that 1 ticket is required and consumed for the channels to travel. The shifting on the levels realizes a form of *level polymorphism* whereby we are allowed to send on c a pair of channels with level 1 even if c expects a pair of channels with level 0. This is safe because we know, from the side condition of [T-IN*], that the receiver of the message does not own any linear channel except those possibly contained in the message itself. Therefore, the exact level of the channels in the message is irrelevant, as long as it is obtained by shifting of the expected message type. Level polymorphism is a key distinguishing feature of our type systems that makes it possible to deal with non-trivial recursive processes.

4 Type Reconstruction

We now face the problem of defining a type reconstruction algorithm for the type system presented in the previous section. The input of the algorithm is a process P where names are explicitly annotated with simple types, possibly resulting from a previous reconstruction stage [9,19]. Notwithstanding such explicit annotations, the typing rules in Table 1 rely on guesses concerning (i) the splitting of type environments, (ii) levels and tickets that decorate linear channel types, and (iii) how tickets are distributed in combined types. We address these issues using standard strategies. Concerning (i), we synthesize type environments for expressions and processes by looking at the free names occurring in them. Concerning (ii) and (iii), we proceed in two steps: first, we transform each simple type t in P into a *type expression* T that has the same structure as t, but where we use fresh level and ticket *variables* in every slot where a level or a ticket is expected; we call this transformation *dressing*. Then, we accumulate (rather than check) the constraints that these level and ticket variables should satisfy, as by the side conditions of the typing rules (Table 1). Finally, we look for a solution of these constraints. It turns out that the accumulated constraints can always be expressed as an integer programming problem for which there exist dedicated solvers.

There is still a subtle source of ambiguity in the procedure outlined so far. We have remarked that stripping is a non-injective function, meaning that different types may be stripped to the same simple type. For example, if we take $T = ? [T]_1^1$ and $S = ? [T]_1^0$ we have $\lfloor T \rfloor = \lfloor S \rfloor = s$ where $s = ? [s]$. Now, if we were to reconstruct either T or S from s, we would have to dress s with level and ticket variables in every slot where a level or a ticket is expected. But since s is infinite, such dressing is not unique. For example, $T = ? [T]_{\theta_1}^{\eta_1}$ and $S = ? [T]_{\theta_2}^{\eta_2}$ are just two of the infinitely many possible dressings of s with level and ticket variables: in T we have used two distinct variables η_1 and θ_1, one for each slot; in S we have used four. The problem is that from the dressing T we can only reconstruct T, by taking $\eta_1 = \theta_1 = 1$, whereas from the dressing S we can reconstruct both T (by assigning all variables to 1) as well as S, by taking $\eta_1 = \theta_1 = 1$ and $\eta_2 = \theta_2 = 0$. This means that the choice of the number of integer variables we use in dressing (infinite) simple types constrains the types that we can reconstruct from them, which is a risk for the completeness of the type reconstruction algorithms. To cope with this issue, we dress simple types *lazily*, only to their topmost linear channel constructors, and we put fresh type variables in place of message types, leaving them undressed. It is only when the message is used that we (lazily) dress its type as well. The introduction of fresh type variables for message types means that we redo part of the work already carried out for reconstructing simple types [19]. This appears to be an inevitable price to pay to have completeness of the type reconstruction algorithms, when they build on top of (instead of being performed together with) previous stages.

To formalize the algorithms, we introduce countable sets of *type variables* α, β and of *integer variables* η, θ; *type expressions* and *integer expressions* are defined below:

Type expression	T, S	$::=$	$\texttt{int} \mid \alpha \mid p[T]_\tau^\lambda \mid p[T]^* \mid T \times S$
Integer expression	$\lambda, \varepsilon, \tau$	$::=$	$n \mid \eta \mid \varepsilon + \varepsilon \mid \varepsilon - \varepsilon$

Type expressions differ from types in three ways: they are always finite, they have integer expressions in place of levels and tickets, and they include type variables α denoting unknown types awaiting to be lazily dressed. Integer expressions are linear polynomials of integer variables.

We say that T is *proper*, written $\text{prop}(T)$, if all the type variables in T are guarded by a channel constructor. For example, both $\texttt{int}$ and $p[\alpha]^*$ are proper (all type variables occur within channel types), but α and $\texttt{int} \times \alpha$ are not. Since the level and tickets of a type expression are solely determined by its top-level linear channel constructors, properness characterizes those type expressions that are "sufficiently dressed" so that it is possible to extract their level and to combine them with other type expressions, even if these type expressions contain type variables.

We now revisit and adapt all the auxiliary operators and notions defined for types to type expressions. Recall that the level of T is the minimum level of any topmost linear channel type in T, or $\perp$ if T has a topmost unlimited channel type with input polarity. Since a type expression T may contain unevaluated level expressions, we cannot compute a minimum level in general. However, a quick inspection of Table 1 reveals that minima of levels always occur on the right hand side of inequalities, and an inequality like $n < \min\{m_i \mid i \in I\}$ can equivalently be expressed as a set of inequalities

$\{n < m_i \mid i \in I\}$. Following this observation, we define the *level* $|\mathsf{T}|$ of a proper type expression T as the *set* of level expressions that decorate the topmost linear channel types in T, and possibly the element $\bot$. Formally:

$$|\mathsf{T}| \stackrel{\text{def}}{=} \begin{cases} \{\bot\} & \text{if } \mathsf{T} = p[\mathsf{S}]^* \text{ and } ? \in p \\ \{\lambda\} & \text{if } \mathsf{T} = p[\mathsf{S}]_\tau^\lambda \text{ and } p \neq \emptyset \\ |\mathsf{T}_1| \cup |\mathsf{T}_2| & \text{if } \mathsf{T} = \mathsf{T}_1 \times \mathsf{T}_2 \\ \emptyset & \text{otherwise} \end{cases} \tag{4.1}$$

We write $\mathsf{un}(\mathsf{T})$ if $|\mathsf{T}| = \emptyset$, in which case T denotes an unlimited type. *Shifting* for proper type expressions is defined just like for types, except that we symbolically record the sum of level/ticket expressions instead of computing it:

$$\$_\tau^\lambda\, \mathsf{T} \stackrel{\text{def}}{=} \begin{cases} p[\mathsf{S}]_{\tau+\tau'}^{\lambda+\lambda'} & \text{if } \mathsf{T} = p[\mathsf{S}]_{\tau'}^{\lambda'} \\ (\$_\tau^\lambda\, \mathsf{T}_1) \times (\$_\tau^\lambda\, \mathsf{T}_2) & \text{if } \mathsf{T} = \mathsf{T}_1 \times \mathsf{T}_2 \\ \mathsf{T} & \text{otherwise} \end{cases} \tag{4.2}$$

Because type expressions may contain type and integer variables, we cannot determine *a priori* whether the combination of two type expressions is possible. For instance, the combination of $?[\mathsf{T}]_{\tau_1}^{\lambda_1}$ and $![\mathsf{S}]_{\tau_2}^{\lambda_2}$ is possible only if T and S denote the same type and if λ_1 and λ_2 evaluate to the same level. We cannot check these conditions right away, when T, S and the level expressions contain variables. Instead, we record these conditions into a *constraint*. Constraints φ, ... are conjunctions of *type constraints* $\mathsf{T} = \mathsf{S}$ (equality relations between type expressions) and *integer constraints* $\varepsilon \leq \varepsilon'$ (inequality relations between integer expressions). Formally, their syntax is defined by

Constraint φ ::= true $\mid$ $\mathsf{T} = \mathsf{T}$ $\mid$ $\varepsilon \leq \varepsilon$ $\mid$ $\varphi \wedge \varphi$

We write $\varepsilon < \varepsilon'$ in place of $\varepsilon + 1 \leq \varepsilon'$ and $\varepsilon = \varepsilon'$ in place of $\varepsilon \leq \varepsilon' \wedge \varepsilon' \leq \varepsilon$; if $\mathscr{E} = \{\varepsilon_i\}_{i \in I}$ is a finite set of integer expressions, we write $\varepsilon < \mathscr{E}$ for the constraint $\bigwedge_{i \in I} \varepsilon < \varepsilon_i$; finally, we write $\mathsf{dom}(\varphi)$ for the set of type expressions occurring in φ.

The *combination* operator $\mathsf{T} \sqcup \mathsf{S}$ for type expressions returns a pair $\mathsf{R}; \varphi$ made of the resulting type expression R and the constraint φ that must be satisfied for the combination to be possible. The definition of $\sqcup$ mimics exactly that of $+$ in Section 3, except that all non-checkable conditions accumulate in constraints:

$$\mathsf{T} \sqcup \mathsf{S} \stackrel{\text{def}}{=} \begin{cases} \mathsf{int} & ; \mathsf{true} & \text{if } \mathsf{T} = \mathsf{int} \text{ and } \mathsf{S} = \mathsf{int} \\ (p \cup q)[\mathsf{T}']_{\tau+\tau'}^\lambda & ; \mathsf{T}' = \mathsf{S}' \wedge \lambda = \lambda' & \text{if } \mathsf{T} = p[\mathsf{T}']_\tau^\lambda \text{ and } \mathsf{S} = q[\mathsf{S}']_{\tau'}^{\lambda'} \\ & & \text{and } p \cap q = \emptyset \\ (p \cup q)[\mathsf{T}']^* & ; \mathsf{T}' = \mathsf{S}' & \text{if } \mathsf{T} = p[\mathsf{T}']^* \text{ and } \mathsf{S} = q[\mathsf{S}']^* \\ \mathsf{R}_1 \times \mathsf{R}_2 & ; \varphi_1 \wedge \varphi_2 & \text{if } \mathsf{T} = \mathsf{T}_1 \times \mathsf{T}_2 \text{ and } \mathsf{S} = \mathsf{S}_1 \times \mathsf{S}_2 \\ & & \text{and } \mathsf{T}_i \sqcup \mathsf{S}_i = \mathsf{R}_i; \varphi_i \\ \mathsf{undefined} & & \text{otherwise} \end{cases}$$

Like type combination, also $\sqcup$ is a partial operator: $\mathsf{T} \sqcup \mathsf{S}$ is undefined if T and S are structurally incompatible (*e.g.*, if $\mathsf{T} = \mathsf{int}$ and $\mathsf{S} = p[\mathsf{int}]^*$) or if T and S are not proper. When $\mathsf{T} \sqcup \mathsf{S}$ is defined, though, the resulting type expression is always proper.

We use $\Delta, \ldots$ to range over *type expression environments* (or just environments, for short), namely finite maps from names to type expressions, and we inherit all the notation introduced for type environments. We let $|\Delta| \stackrel{\text{def}}{=} \bigcup_{u \in \text{dom}(\Delta)} |\Delta(u)|$ and write $\overline{\text{un}}(\Delta)$ if $|\Delta| = \emptyset$ and Δ has no top-level linear channel type in its range. By now, the extension of $\sqcup$ to environments is easy to imagine: when defined, $\Delta_1 \sqcup \Delta_2$ is a pair $\Delta; \varphi$ made of the resulting environment Δ and of a constraint φ that results from the combination of the type expressions in Δ_1 and Δ_2. More precisely:

$$\Delta_1 \sqcup \Delta_2 \stackrel{\text{def}}{=} \Delta_1, \Delta_2 \ ; \text{true} \qquad \text{if } \text{dom}(\Delta_1) \cap \text{dom}(\Delta_2) = \emptyset$$
$$(\Delta_1, u : \mathsf{T}) \sqcup (\Delta_2, u : \mathsf{S}) \stackrel{\text{def}}{=} \Delta, u : \mathsf{R} \ ; \ \varphi \wedge \varphi' \qquad \text{if } \Delta_1 \sqcup \Delta_2 = \Delta; \varphi \text{ and } \mathsf{T} \sqcup \mathsf{S} = \mathsf{R}; \varphi'$$

The last notion we need to formalize, before introducing the reconstruction algorithms, is that of *dressing*. Dressing a simple type t means placing fresh integer variables in the level/ticket slots of t. Formally, we say that T is a *dressing* of t if $t \uparrow \mathsf{T}$ is inductively derivable by the following rules which pick globally fresh variables:

$$\text{int} \uparrow \text{int} \qquad \frac{\alpha \text{ fresh}}{p[t]^* \uparrow p[\alpha]^*} \qquad \frac{\alpha, \eta, \theta \text{ fresh}}{p[t] \uparrow p[\alpha]_\theta^\eta} \qquad \frac{t_i \uparrow \mathsf{T}_i \ ^{(i=1,2)}}{t_1 \times t_2 \uparrow \mathsf{T}_1 \times \mathsf{T}_2}$$

Note that the decoration of t with fresh integer variables stops at the topmost channel types in t and that message types are left undecorated. By definition, the dressing of a simple type is always a proper type expression.

We can now present the type reconstruction algorithms, defined by the rules in Table 2. The rules in the upper part of the table derive judgments of the form e : $\mathsf{T} \blacktriangleright \Delta; \varphi$, stating that e has type T in the environment Δ if the constraint φ is satisfied. The expression e is the only "input" of the judgment, while T, Δ, and φ are synthesized from it. There is a close correspondence between these rules and those for expressions in Table 1. Observe the use of $\sqcup$ where $+$ was used in Table 1, the accumulation of constraints from the premises to the conclusion of each rule and, most notably, the dressing of the simple type that annotates u in [I-NAME]. Type expressions synthesized by the rules are always proper, so the side conditions in [I-FST] and [I-SND] can be safely checked.

The rules in the lower part of the table derive judgments of the form $P \blacktriangleright_k \Delta; \varphi$, stating that P is well typed in the environment Δ if the constraint φ is satisfied. The parameter k plays the same role as in the type system (Table 1). The process P and the parameter k are the only "inputs" of the judgments, and Δ and φ are synthesized from them. All rules except [I-WEAK] have a corresponding one in Table 1. Like for expressions, environments are combined through $\sqcup$ and constraints accumulate from premises to conclusions. We focus on the differences with respect to the typing rules.

In rule [T-IN], the side condition verifies that the level of the channel e on which an input is performed is smaller than the level of any channel used for typing the continuation process P. This condition can be decomposed in two parts: (1) no unlimited channel with input polarity must be in P; this condition is necessary to ensure input receptiveness on unlimited channels in the original type system [18] and is expressed in [I-IN] as the side condition $\perp \notin |\Delta_2|$, which can be checked on type expressions environments directly; (2) the level of e must satisfy the ordering with respect to all the linear channels in P; this is expressed in [I-IN] as the constraint $\lambda < |\Delta_2|$, where λ is the level of e. The same side condition and constraint are found in [I-OUT].

Table 2. Type reconstruction rules for expressions and processes

---

Reconstruction rules for expressions $\qquad\qquad\qquad\qquad\qquad\qquad$ $\boxed{e : \mathsf{T} \blacktriangleright \Delta; \varphi}$

[I-INT]

$$n : \mathtt{int} \blacktriangleright \emptyset; \mathtt{true}$$

[I-PAIR]

$$\frac{e_i : \mathsf{T}_i \blacktriangleright \Delta_i; \varphi_i \ {}^{(i=1,2)}}{(e_1, e_2) : \mathsf{T}_1 \times \mathsf{T}_2 \blacktriangleright \Delta; \bigwedge_{1 \leq i \leq 3} \varphi_i} \ \Delta_1 \sqcup \Delta_2 = \Delta; \varphi_3$$

[I-NAME]

$$\frac{}{u^t : \mathsf{T} \blacktriangleright u : \mathsf{T}; \mathtt{true}} \ t \uparrow \mathsf{T}$$

[I-FST]

$$\frac{e : \mathsf{T} \times \mathsf{S} \blacktriangleright \Delta; \varphi}{\mathtt{fst}(e) : \mathsf{T} \blacktriangleright \Delta; \varphi} \ \mathtt{un}(\mathsf{S})$$

[I-SND]

$$\frac{e : \mathsf{T} \times \mathsf{S} \blacktriangleright \Delta; \varphi}{\mathtt{snd}(e) : \mathsf{S} \blacktriangleright \Delta; \varphi} \ \mathtt{un}(\mathsf{T})$$

Reconstruction rules for processes $\qquad\qquad\qquad\qquad\qquad\qquad$ $\boxed{P \blacktriangleright_k \Delta; \varphi}$

[I-WEAK]

$$\frac{P \blacktriangleright_k \Delta; \varphi \quad \mathtt{un}(\mathsf{T})}{P \blacktriangleright_k \Delta, u : \mathsf{T}; \varphi \ \mathtt{prop}(\mathsf{T})}$$

[I-IDLE]

$$\frac{}{\mathbf{0} \blacktriangleright_k \emptyset; \mathtt{true}}$$

[I-PAR]

$$\frac{P_i \blacktriangleright_k \Delta_i; \varphi_i \ {}^{(i=1,2)}}{P_1 \mid P_2 \blacktriangleright_k \Delta; \bigwedge_{1 \leq i \leq 3} \varphi_i} \ \Delta_1 \sqcup \Delta_2 = \Delta; \varphi_3$$

[I-IN]

$$\frac{e : ?[\mathsf{T}]^\lambda_\tau \blacktriangleright \Delta_1; \varphi_1 \quad P \blacktriangleright_k \Delta_2, x : \mathsf{S}; \varphi_2 \quad \bot \notin |\Delta_2|}{e?(x).P \blacktriangleright_k \Delta; \bigwedge_{1 \leq i \leq 3} \varphi_i \wedge \mathsf{T} = \$^{-\lambda}_0 \mathsf{S} \wedge \lambda < |\Delta_2| \quad \Delta_1 \sqcup \Delta_2 = \Delta; \varphi_3}$$

[I-OUT]

$$\frac{e : ![\mathsf{T}]^\lambda_\tau \blacktriangleright \Delta_1; \varphi_1 \quad f : \mathsf{S} \blacktriangleright \Delta_2; \varphi_2 \quad \bot \notin |\Delta_2|}{e!f \blacktriangleright_k \Delta; \bigwedge_{1 \leq i \leq 3} \varphi_i \wedge \mathsf{T} = \$^{-\lambda}_{-k} \mathsf{S} \wedge \lambda < |\Delta_2| \quad \Delta_1 \sqcup \Delta_2 = \Delta; \varphi_3}$$

[I-NEW]

$$\frac{P \blacktriangleright_k \Delta, a : \#[\mathsf{T}]^\lambda_\tau; \varphi}{(\nu a)P \blacktriangleright_k \Delta; \varphi}$$

[I-IN*]

$$\frac{e : ?[\mathsf{T}]^* \blacktriangleright \Delta_1; \varphi_1 \quad P \blacktriangleright_k \Delta_2, x : \mathsf{S}; \varphi_2 \quad \overline{\mathtt{un}}(\Delta_2)}{*e?(x).P \blacktriangleright_k \Delta; \bigwedge_{1 \leq i \leq 3} \varphi_i \wedge \mathsf{T} = \mathsf{S} \quad \Delta_1 \sqcup \Delta_2 = \Delta; \varphi_3}$$

[I-OUT*]

$$\frac{e : ![\mathsf{T}]^* \blacktriangleright \Delta_1; \varphi_1 \quad f : \mathsf{S} \blacktriangleright \Delta_2; \varphi_2 \quad \begin{matrix} \bot \notin |\Delta_2| \\ \Delta_1 \sqcup \Delta_2 = \Delta; \varphi_3 \end{matrix}}{e!f \blacktriangleright_k \Delta; \bigwedge_{1 \leq i \leq 3} \varphi_i \wedge \mathsf{T} = \$^{-\eta}_{-k} \mathsf{S} \quad \eta \ \mathtt{fresh}}$$

[I-NEW*]

$$\frac{P \blacktriangleright_k \Delta, a : \#[\mathsf{T}]^*; \varphi}{(\nu a)P \blacktriangleright_k \Delta; \varphi}$$

In [T-IN], [T-OUT], and [T-OUT*], shifting is used for updating message levels, consuming tickets, and realizing level polymorphism. In rules [I-IN], [I-OUT], and [I-OUT*], analogous shiftings are performed on type expressions, except that they are inverted and recorded in constraints. For example, when typing the continuation P of a process $e?(x).P$ using [T-IN], if e has type $?[T]^n_m$ then the type of x is required to be $\$^n_0 T$. In the reconstruction algorithm, we record this requirement as the constraint $\mathsf{T} = \$^{-\lambda}_0 \mathsf{S}$, where S is the type synthesized for x in P. We invert the shifting because shifting is defined only on proper type expressions, and in [I-IN] (and the other rules mentioned) only S is guaranteed to be proper, while T in general is not.

Finally, note that [I-WEAK] has no correspondent rule in Table 1. This rule is necessary because the premises of [I-IN], [I-IN*], [I-NEW], and [I-NEW*] *assume* that bound names occur in their scope. Since type environments are generated by the algorithm as it works through an expression or a process, this assumption may not hold if a bound name is never used in its scope. Naturally, the type T of an unused name must be unlimited, whence the constraint $\mathsf{un}(\mathsf{T})$. We also require T to be proper, to preserve the invariant that all environments synthesized by the algorithms have proper types. In principle, [I-WEAK] makes the rule set in Table 2 not syntax directed, which is a problem if we want to consider this as an algorithm. In practice, the places where [I-WEAK] may be necessary are easy to spot (in the premises of all the aforementioned rules for the binding constructs). What we gain with [I-WEAK] is a simpler presentation of the rules.

To state the properties of the reconstruction algorithm, we need a notion of constraint satisfiability. A *variable assignment* σ is a map from type/integer variables to types/integers. We say that σ *covers* X if σ provides assignments to all the type/integer variables occurring in X, where X may be a constraint, a type/integer expression, or an environment. When σ covers X, the *application* of σ to X, written $\sigma\mathsf{X}$, substitutes all type/integer variables according to σ and evaluates all integer expressions in X. When σ covers φ, we say that σ *satisfies* φ if $\sigma \vDash \varphi$ is derivable by the rules:

$$\frac{}{\sigma \vDash \text{true}} \qquad \frac{}{\sigma \vDash \mathsf{T} = \mathsf{S}} \ \sigma\mathsf{T} = \sigma\mathsf{S} \qquad \frac{}{\sigma \vDash \varepsilon \leq \varepsilon'} \ \sigma\varepsilon \leq \sigma\varepsilon' \qquad \frac{\sigma \vDash \varphi_i}{\sigma \vDash \varphi_1 \wedge \varphi_2} \ {}^{(i=1,2)}$$

Whenever we apply an assignment σ to a set of type expressions in reference to a derivation that is parametric on k, we will implicitly assume that all integer expressions in ticket slots evaluate to non-negative integers and that, if $k = 1$, all integer expressions in level slots evaluate to non-negative integers. The value of k and the set of type expressions will always be clear from the context.

The reconstruction algorithm is *correct*, namely each derivation obtained through the algorithm such that the resulting constraint is satisfiable corresponds to a derivation in the type system:

Theorem 4.1 (Correctness). *If $P \blacktriangleright_k \Delta; \varphi$ and $\sigma \vDash \varphi$ and σ covers Δ, then $\sigma\Delta \vdash_k P$.*

The algorithm is also *complete*, meaning that if there exists a typing derivation for the judgment $\Gamma \vdash_k P$, then the algorithm is capable of synthesizing an environment Δ from which Γ can be obtained by means of a suitable variable assignment:

Theorem 4.2 (Completeness). *If $\Gamma \vdash_k P$, then $P \blacktriangleright_k \Delta; \varphi$ for some Δ, φ, and σ such that $\sigma \vDash \varphi$ and $\Gamma = \sigma\Delta$.*

Note that the above results do not give any information about how to verify whether there exists a σ such that $\sigma \vDash \varphi$ and, in this case, how to find such σ. These problems will be addressed in Section 5. We conclude this section showing the reconstruction algorithm at work on the replicated process in Example 2.1.

Example 4.1. Below is the replicated process in Example 2.1, where we have numbered and named the relevant rules used by the algorithm as it visits the process bottom-up, left-to-right:

$$\underset{(5)\ [\text{I-IN*}]}{\underbrace{*c?(x)}}.(\nu a)\overset{(4)\ [\text{I-PAR}]}{\overbrace{(\underset{(1)\ [\text{I-OUT}]}{\underbrace{\mathtt{fst}(x)!a}} \mid \underset{(3)\ [\text{I-IN}]}{\underbrace{\mathtt{snd}(x)?(y)}}.\underset{(2)\ [\text{I-OUT*}]}{\underbrace{c!(a,y)}})}}$$

Table 3. Type environment and constraints generated for the process in Example 2.1

i	c	x	a	y	Constraint
(1)		$![\alpha_1]_{\theta_1}^{\eta_1} \times \emptyset[\alpha_2]_{\theta_2}^{\eta_2}$	$?[\alpha_3]_{\theta_3}^{\eta_3}$		$\alpha_1 = \,?[\alpha_3]_{\theta_3-k}^{\eta_3-\eta_1} \wedge \eta_1 < \eta_3$
(2)	$![\alpha_4]^*$		$![\alpha_5]_{\theta_5}^{\eta_5}$	$?[\alpha_6]_{\theta_6}^{\eta_6}$	$\alpha_4 = \,![\alpha_5]_{\theta_5-k}^{\eta_5-\eta_4} \times \,?[\alpha_6]_{\theta_6-k}^{\eta_6-\eta_4}$
(3)		$\emptyset[\alpha_7]_{\theta_7}^{\eta_7} \times \,?[\alpha_8]_{\theta_8}^{\eta_8}$			$\alpha_8 = \,?[\alpha_6]_{\theta_6}^{\eta_6-\eta_8} \wedge \eta_8 < \eta_5$
(4)		$![\alpha_1]_{\theta_1+\theta_7}^{\eta_1} \times \,?[\alpha_2]_{\theta_2+\theta_8}^{\eta_2}$	$\#[\alpha_3]_{\theta_3+\theta_5}^{\eta_3}$		$\alpha_1 = \alpha_7 \wedge \alpha_2 = \alpha_8 \wedge \alpha_3 = \alpha_5$
					$\wedge\, \eta_1 = \eta_7 \wedge \eta_2 = \eta_8 \wedge \eta_3 = \eta_5$
(5)	$\#[\alpha_9]^*$				$\alpha_9 = \,![\alpha_1]_{\theta_1+\theta_7}^{\eta_1} \times \,?[\alpha_2]_{\theta_2+\theta_8}^{\eta_2}$
					$\wedge\, \alpha_9 = \alpha_4$

Table 4. Constraint entailment rules

[S-LEVEL]
$$\frac{}{\varphi \vdash_1 0 \leq \lambda} \quad p[T]_\tau^\lambda \in dom(\varphi)$$

[S-TICKET]
$$\frac{}{\varphi \vdash_k 0 \leq \tau} \quad p[T]_\tau^\lambda \in dom(\varphi)$$

[S-CONJ]
$$\frac{}{\varphi_1 \wedge \varphi_2 \vdash_k \varphi_i} \quad i \in \{1,2\}$$

[S-SYMM]
$$\frac{\varphi \vdash_k T = S}{\varphi \vdash_k S = T}$$

[S-TRANS]
$$\frac{\varphi \vdash_k T = R \quad \varphi \vdash_k R = S}{\varphi \vdash_k T = S}$$

[S-CHAN]
$$\frac{\varphi \vdash_k p[T]_{\tau_1}^{\lambda_1} = p[S]_{\tau_2}^{\lambda_2}}{\varphi \vdash_k T = S \wedge \lambda_1 = \lambda_2 \wedge \tau_1 = \tau_2}$$

[S-CHAN*]
$$\frac{\varphi \vdash_k p[T]^* = p[S]^*}{\varphi \vdash_k T = S}$$

[S-PAIR]
$$\frac{\varphi \vdash_k T_1 \times T_2 = S_1 \times S_2}{\varphi \vdash_k T_1 = S_1 \wedge T_2 = S_2}$$

Each subprocess triggers one rule of the reconstruction algorithm which synthesizes a type environment and possibly generates some constraints. Table 3 summarizes the parts of the environments and the constraints produced at each step of the reconstruction algorithm with parameter k. We have omitted the step concerning the restriction on a, which just removes a from the environment and introduces no constraints. ∎

5 Constraint Solving

We sketch an algorithm that determines whether a constraint φ is satisfiable and, in this case, computes an assignment that satisfies it. The presentation is somewhat less formal since the key steps of the algorithm are instances of well-known techniques. The algorithm is structured in three phases, *saturation*, *verification*, and *synthesis*.

The constraint φ produced by the reconstruction algorithm does not necessarily mention all the relations that must hold between integer variables. For example, the constraint $\eta_3 - \eta_1 = \eta_6 - \eta_8 \wedge \theta_3 - k = \theta_6$ is implied by those in Table 3, but it appears nowhere. Finding all the integer constraints entailed by a given φ, regardless of whether such constraints are implicit or explicit, is essential because we use an external solver for solving them. The aim of the *saturation phase* is to find all such integer constraints. Table 4 defines an inference system for deriving entailments $\varphi \vdash_k \varphi'$. The parameter k plays the same role as in the type system. Rules [S-LEVEL] and [S-TICKET] introduce nonnegativity constraints for integer expressions that occur in level and ticket slots; level expressions are required to be non-negative only for lock freedom analysis, when $k = 1$; rule [S-CONJ] decomposes conjunctions; rules [S-SYMM] and [S-TRANS] compute the symmetric and transitive closure of type equality; finally, [S-CHAN], [S-CHAN*], and [S-PAIR] state expected congruence rules. We let $\widehat{\varphi} \stackrel{\text{def}}{=} \bigwedge_{\varphi \vdash_k \varphi'} \varphi'$. Clearly $\widehat{\varphi}$ can be computed in finite time and is satisfiable by the same assignments as (*i.e.*, it is equivalent to) φ.

The *verification phase* checks whether $\widehat{\varphi}$ is satisfiable and, in this case, computes an assignment σ_{int} that satisfies the integer constraints in it. In $\widehat{\varphi}$ all the integer constraints are explicit. These are typical constraints of an integer programming problem, for which it is possible to use dedicated (complete) solvers that find a σ_{int} when it exists (our tool supports GLPK[1] and lpsolve[2]). When this is the case, the type constraints in $\widehat{\varphi}$ are satisfiable if, for each type constraint of the form $T = S$, either T or S are type variables, or T and S have the same topmost constructor, *i.e.* they are either both int, or both unlimited/linear channel types with the same polarity, or both product types.

The *synthesis phase* computes an assignment that satisfies φ. This is found by applying σ_{int} to all the type constraints in $\widehat{\varphi}$, by choosing a canonical constraint of the form $\alpha = T$ where T is proper for each $\alpha \in \text{dom}(\widehat{\varphi})$, and then by solving the resulting system $\{\alpha_i = T_i\}$ of equations. By [4, Theorem 4.2.1], this system has exactly one solution σ_{type} and now $\sigma_{int} \cup \sigma_{type} \models \varphi$. There may be type variables α for which there is no $\alpha = T$ constraint with T proper. These type variables denote values not used by the process, like a message that is received from one channel and just forwarded on another one. These variables are assigned a type that can be computed canonically.

Example 5.1. The constraints shown in Table 3 entail $0 \leq \theta_3 - k$ and $0 \leq \theta_5 - k$ and $0 \leq \theta_6 - k$ namely $k \leq \theta_3$ and $k \leq \theta_5$ and $k \leq \theta_6$ must hold. When $k = 0$, these constraints can be trivially satisfied by assigning 0 to all ticket variables. When $k = 1$, from the type of a at step (4) of the reconstruction algorithm we deduce that a must have at least 2 tickets. Indeed, a is sent in two messages. It is only considering the remaining processes $c!(e, f)$ and $c!(f, e)$ that we learn that y is instantiated with a. Then, a needs one more ticket, to account for the further and last travel in the recursive invocation $c!(a, y)$. ∎

6   Concluding Remarks

A key distinguishing feature of the type systems in [18] is the use of polymorphic recursion. Type reconstruction in presence of polymorphic recursion is notoriously undecidable [10,7]. In our case, polymorphism solely concerns levels and reconstruction turns out to be doable. A similar situation is known for *effect systems* [1], where polymorphic recursion restricted to effects does not prevent complete type reconstruction [2].

We have conducted some benchmarks on generalizations of Example 2.1 to N-dimensional hypercubes of processes using full-duplex communication. The table below reports the reconstruction times for the analysis of an hypercube of side 5 and N varying from 1 to 4. The table details the dimension, the number of processes and channels, and the times (in seconds) spent for linearity analysis [19], constraint generation (Section 4) and saturation, solution of level and ticket constraints (Section 5). The solver used for level and ticket constraints is GLPK 4.48 and times were measured on a 13" MacBook Air running a 1.8 GHz Intel Core i5 with 4 GB of 1600MHz DDR3.

---

[1] http://www.gnu.org/software/glpk/

[2] http://sourceforge.net/projects/lpsolve/

N	Processes	Channels	Linearity	Gen.+Sat.	Levels	Tickets	Overall
1	5	8	0.021	0.006	0.002	0.003	0.032
2	25	80	0.128	0.051	0.009	0.012	0.200
3	125	600	1.439	0.844	0.069	0.124	2.477
4	625	4000	33.803	26.422	1.116	3.913	65.254

Reconstruction times scale almost linearly in the number of channels as long as there is enough free main memory. With $N = 4$, however, the used memory exceeds 10GB causing severe memory (de)compression and swapping. The running time inflates consequently. We have not determined yet the precise causes of such disproportionate consumption of memory, which the algorithms do not seem to imply. We suspect that they are linked to our naive implementation of the algorithms in a lazy language (Haskell), but a more rigorous profiling analysis is left for future investigation. Integer programming problems are NP-hard in general, but the time used for integer constraint resolution appears negligible compared to the other phases. As suggested by one reviewer, the particular nature of such constraints indicates that there might be more clever way of solving them, for example by using SMT solvers.

Our work has been inspired by previous type systems ensuring (dead)lock freedom for generic π-calculus processes [11,13] and corresponding type reconstruction algorithms [12]. These type systems and ours are incomparable: [11,13] use sophisticated behavioral types that provide better accuracy with respect to unlimited channels as used for modeling mutual exclusion and concurrent objects. On the other hand, our type systems exploit level polymorphism for dealing with recursive processes in cyclic topologies, often arising in the modeling of parallel algorithms and sessions. Whether and how the strengths of both approaches can be combined together is left for future research. A more thorough comparison between these works can be found in [18].

There is a substantial methodological difference between our approach and those addressing sessions, particularly *multiparty sessions* [8,6]. Session-based approaches are *top down* and *type driven*: types/protocols come first, and are used as a guidance for developing programs that follow them. These approaches guarantee *by design* a number of properties, among which (dead)lock freedom when different sessions are not interleaved. Our approach is *bottom up* and *program driven*: programs come first, and are used for inferring types/protocols. The two approaches can integrate and complement each other. For example, type reconstruction may assist in the verification of legacy or third-party code (for which no type information is available) or for checking the impact of code changes due to refactoring and/or debugging. Also, some protocols are hard to describe *a priori*. For example, describing the essence of full-duplex communications (Example 2.1) is far from trivial [6]. In general, processes making use of channel mobility (delegation) and session interleaving, or dynamic network topologies with variable number of processes, are supported by our approach (within the limits imposed by the type systems), but are challenging to handle in top-down approaches. Inference of progress properties akin to lock freedom for session-based calculi has been studied in [17,3], although only finite types are considered in these works.

The reconstruction of *global* protocol descriptions from *local* session types has been studied in [15,16]. In this respect, our work fills the remaining gap and provides a reconstruction tool from processes to local session types. We plan to investigate the integration with [15,16] in future work.

Acknowledgments. The authors are grateful to the reviewers for their detailed comments and useful suggestions. The first two authors have been supported by Ateneo/CSP project SALT. The first author has also been supported by ICT COST Action IC1201 BETTY and MIUR project CINA.

References

1. Amtoft, T., Nielson, F., Nielson, H.: Type and effect systems: behaviours for concurrency. Imperial College Press (1999)
2. Amtoft, T., Nielson, F., Nielson, H.R.: Type and behaviour reconstruction for higher-order concurrent programs. J. Funct. Program. 7(3), 321–347 (1997)
3. Coppo, M., Dezani-Ciancaglini, M., Padovani, L., Yoshida, N.: Inference of global progress properties for dynamically interleaved multiparty sessions. In: De Nicola, R., Julien, C. (eds.) COORDINATION 2013. LNCS, vol. 7890, pp. 45–59. Springer, Heidelberg (2013)
4. Courcelle, B.: Fundamental properties of infinite trees. Theor. Comp. Sci. 25, 95–169 (1983)
5. Dardha, O., Giachino, E., Sangiorgi, D.: Session types revisited. In: PPDP 2012, pp. 139–150. ACM (2012)
6. Deniélou, P.-M., Yoshida, N.: Multiparty session types meet communicating automata. In: Seidl, H. (ed.) ESOP 2012. LNCS, vol. 7211, pp. 194–213. Springer, Heidelberg (2012)
7. Henglein, F.: Type inference with polymorphic recursion. ACM Trans. Program. Lang. Syst. 15(2), 253–289 (1993)
8. Honda, K., Yoshida, N., Carbone, M.: Multiparty asynchronous session types. In: POPL 2008, pp. 273–284. ACM (2008)
9. Igarashi, A., Kobayashi, N.: Type reconstruction for linear π-calculus with I/O subtyping. Inf. and Comp. 161(1), 1–44 (2000)
10. Kfoury, A.J., Tiuryn, J., Urzyczyn, P.: Type reconstruction in the presence of polymorphic recursion. ACM Trans. Program. Lang. Syst. 15(2), 290–311 (1993)
11. Kobayashi, N.: A type system for lock-free processes. Inf. and Comp. 177(2), 122–159 (2002)
12. Kobayashi, N.: Type-based information flow analysis for the pi-calculus. Acta Informatica 42(4-5), 291–347 (2005)
13. Kobayashi, N.: A new type system for deadlock-free processes. In: Baier, C., Hermanns, H. (eds.) CONCUR 2006. LNCS, vol. 4137, pp. 233–247. Springer, Heidelberg (2006)
14. Kobayashi, N., Pierce, B.C., Turner, D.N.: Linearity and the pi-calculus. ACM Trans. Program. Lang. Syst. 21(5), 914–947 (1999)
15. Lange, J., Tuosto, E.: Synthesising choreographies from local session types. In: Koutny, M., Ulidowski, I. (eds.) CONCUR 2012. LNCS, vol. 7454, pp. 225–239. Springer, Heidelberg (2012)
16. Lange, J., Tuosto, E., Yoshida, N.: From communicating machines to graphical choreographies. In: POPL 2015, pp. 221–232. ACM (2015)
17. Mezzina, L.G.: How to infer finite session types in a calculus of services and sessions. In: Lea, D., Zavattaro, G. (eds.) COORDINATION 2008. LNCS, vol. 5052, pp. 216–231. Springer, Heidelberg (2008)
18. Padovani, L.: Deadlock and lock freedom in the linear π-calculus. In: CSL-LICS 2014, pp. 72:1–72:10. ACM (2014), http://hal.archives-ouvertes.fr/hal-00932356v2/
19. Padovani, L.: Type reconstruction for the linear π-calculus with composite and equi-recursive types. In: Muscholl, A. (ed.) FOSSACS 2014 (ETAPS). LNCS, vol. 8412, pp. 88–102. Springer, Heidelberg (2014)

Constraints

A Fixpoint-Based Calculus
for Graph-Shaped Computational Fields

Alberto Lluch Lafuente[1](✉), Michele Loreti[2], and Ugo Montanari[3]

[1] DTU Compute, Technical University of Denmark, Kgs. Lyngby, Denmark
albl@dtu.dk
[2] University of Florence, Firenze Italy
[3] Computer Science Department, University of Pisa, Pisa, Italy

Abstract. Coordination is essential for dynamic distributed systems exhibiting autonomous behaviors. Spatially distributed, locally interacting, propagating computational fields are particularly appealing for allowing components to join and leave with little or no overhead. In our approach, the space topology is represented by a graph-shaped field, namely a network with attributes on both nodes and arcs, where arcs represent interaction capabilities between nodes. We propose a calculus where computation is strictly synchronous and corresponds to sequential computations of fixpoints in the graph-shaped field. Under some conditions, those fixpoints can be computed by synchronised iterations, where in each iteration the attributes of a node is updated based on the attributes of the neighbours in the previous iteration. Basic constructs are reminiscent of the semiring μ-calculus, a semiring-valued generalisation of the modal μ-calculus, which provides a flexible mechanism to specify the neighbourhood range (according to path formulae) and the way attributes should be combined (through semiring operators). Additional control-flow constructs allow one to conveniently structure the fixpoint computations. We illustrate our approach with a case study based on a disaster recovery scenario, implemented in a prototype simulator that we use to evaluate the performance of a disaster recovery strategy.

1 Introduction

Coordination is essential in all the activities where an ensemble of agents interacts within a distributed system. Particularly interesting is the situation where the ensemble is dynamic, with agents entering and exiting, and when the ensemble must adapt to new situations and must have in general an autonomic behavior. Several models of coordination have been proposed and developed in the last years. Following the classification of [10] we mention (i) direct coordination, (ii) connector-based coordination, (iii) shared data space, (iv) shared deductive knowledge base, and (v) spatially distributed, locally interacting, propagating computational fields. Among them, computational fields are particularly

Research supported by the European projects IP 257414 ASCENS and STReP 600708 QUANTICOL, and the Italian PRIN 2010LHT4KM CINA.

© IFIP International Federation for Information Processing 2015
T. Holvoet and M. Viroli (Eds.): COORDINATION 2015, LNCS 9037, pp. 101–116, 2015.
DOI: 10.1007/978-3-319-19282-6_7

appealing for their ability of allowing new interactions with little or no need of communication protocols for initialization. Computational fields are analogous to fields in physics: classical fields are scalars, vectors or tensors, which are functions defined by partial differential equations with initial and/or boundary conditions. Analogously, computational fields consist of suitable space dependent data structures where interaction is possible only between neighbors.

Computational fields have been proposed as models for several coordination applications, like amorphous computing, routing in mobile ad hoc and sensor networks, situated multi agent ecologies, like swarms, and finally for robotics applications, like coordination of teams of modular robots. Physical fields, though, have the advantage of a regular structure of space, e.g. the one defined by Euclidean geometry, while computational fields are sometimes based on some (logical) network of connections. The topology of such a network may have little to do with Euclidean distance, in the sense that a node can be directly connected with nodes which are far away, e.g. for achieving a logarithmic number of hops in distributed hash tables. However, for several robotics applications, and also for swarms and ad hoc networking, one can reasonably assume that an agent can interact only with peers located within a limited radius. Thus locality of interaction and propagation of effects become reasonable assumptions.

Contributions. The main contribution of the paper is the *Soft Mu-calculus for Computational fields* (SMuC) calculus, where computation is strictly synchronous and corresponds to sequential computations of fixpoints in a graph-shaped field that represents the space topology. Our graph-based fields are essentially networks with attributes on both nodes and arcs, where arcs represent interaction capabilities between nodes. In particular, fixpoints can be computed by synchronised iterations under reasonable conditions, where in each iteration the attribute of a node is updated based on the attributes of the neighbours in the previous iteration. Basic constructs are reminiscent of the semiring μ-calculus [8], a semiring-valued generalisation of the modal μ-calculus, which provides a flexible mechanism to specify the neighbourhood range (according to path formulae) and the way attributes should be combined (through semiring operators). Additional control-flow constructs allow one to conveniently structure the fixpoint computations.

An additional contribution is a novel disaster recovery coordination strategy that we use here as a case study. The goal of the coordination strategy is to direct several rescuers present in the network to help a number of victims, where each victim may need more than one rescuer. While an optimal solution is not required, each victim should be reached by its closest rescuers, so to minimise intervention time. Our proposed approach may need several iterations of a sequence of three propagations: the first to determine the distance of each rescuer from its closest victim, the second to associate to every victim v the list of rescuers having v as their closest victim, so to select the best k of them, if k helpers are needed for v; finally, the third propagation is required for notifying each selected rescuer to reach its specific victim.

We have also developed a prototype tool for our language, equipped with a graphical interface that provides useful visual feedback to users of the language. We use indeed those visual features to illustrate the application of our approach to the aforementioned case study.

Last, we discuss several aspects related to possible distributed implementation of our calculus. In particular, we sketch a simple endpoint projection that would automatically generate distributed code to be deployed on the agents of the network and we discuss the possibility of using spanning tree based techniques to efficiently implement some of the global synchronisations involved in such endpoint projection.

Structure of the Paper. The rest of the paper is structured as follows. Sect. 2 presents the SMuC calculus. Sect. 3 presents the SMuC specification of our disaster recovery case study, which is illustrated with figures obtained with our prototypical tool. Sect. 4 discusses several performance and synchronisation issues related to distributed implementations of the calculus. Sect. 5 discusses related works. Sect. 6 concludes the paper, describes our current work and identifies opportunities for future research.

2   SMuC: A Soft μ-calculus for Computations Fields

Our computational fields are essentially networks of inter-connected agents, where both agents and their connections have attributes. One key point in our proposal is that the domain of attributes and their operations have the algebraic structure of a class of semirings usually known as *absorptive semirings* or *constraint semirings*. Such class of semirings has been shown to be very flexible, expressive and convenient for a wide range of problems, in particular for optimisation and solving in problems with soft constraints and multiple criteria [4].

Definition 1 (Semiring). *An* absorptive semiring *is a set A with two operators* $+$, $\times$ *and two constants* $\bot$, $\top$ *such that*

- $+ : 2^A \to A$ *is an associative, commutative, idempotent operator to "choose" among values;*
- $\times : A \times A \to A$ *is an associative, commutative operator to "combine" values;*
- $\times$ *distributes over* $+$;
- $\top + a = a$, $\bot + a = \bot$, $\bot \times a = a$, $\top \times a = \top$ *for all $a \in A$;*
- $\leq$, *which is defined as $a \leq b$ iff $a + b = b$, provides a lattice of preferences with top $\top$ and bottom $\bot$;*

We will use the term *semiring* to refer to absorptive semirings. Typical examples are the Boolean semiring $\langle \{true, false\}, \vee, \wedge, false, true \rangle$, the tropical semiring $\langle \mathbb{R}^+ \cup \{+\infty\}, min, +, +\infty, 0 \rangle$, and the fuzzy semiring $\langle [0, 1], max, min, 0, 1 \rangle$. A useful property of semirings is that Cartesian products and power constructions yield semirings, which allows one for instance to lift techniques for single criteria to multiple criteria.

We are now ready to provide our notion of field, which is essentially a graph equipped with semiring-valued node and edge labels. The idea is that nodes play the role of agents, and (directed) edges play the role of (directional) connections. The node labels will be used as attributes of the agents, while the node labels correspond to functions associated to the connections, e.g. representing how attribute values are transformed when traversing a connection.

Definition 2 (Field). *A field is a tuple* $\langle N, E, A, L = L_N \uplus L_E, I = I_N \uplus I_E \rangle$ *formed by*

- *a set N of nodes;*
- *a relation $E \subseteq N \times N$ of edges;*
- *a set L of node labels L_N and edge labels L_E;*
- *a semiring A;*
- *an interpretation function $I_N : L_N \to N \to A$ associating a function from nodes to values to every node label in L_N;*
- *an interpretation function $I_E : L_E \to E \to A \to A$ associating a function from edges to functions from values to values to every edge label in P;*

where node, edge, and label sets are drawn from a corresponding universe, i.e. $N \subseteq \mathcal{N}$, $E \subseteq \mathcal{E}$, $L_N \subseteq \mathcal{L}$, $L_E \subseteq \mathcal{L}'$.

As usual, we may refer to the components of a field F using subscripted symbols (i.e. N_F, E_F, ...). We will denote the set of all fields by $\mathcal{F}$.

It is worth to remark that while standard notions of computational fields tend to be restricted to nodes (labels) and their mapping to values, our notion of field includes the topology of the network and the mapping of edge (labels) to functions. As a matter of fact, the topology plays a fundamental role in our field computations as it defines how agents are connected and how their attributes are combined when communicated. On the other hand, in our approach the role of node and edge labels is different. In fact, some node labels are computed as the result of a fixpoint approximation which corresponds to a propagation procedure. They thus represent the genuine computational fields. Edge labels, instead, are assigned directly in terms of the data of the problem (e.g. distances) or in terms of the results of previous propagations. They thus represent more properly equation coefficients and boundary conditions as one can have in *partial differential equations* in physical fields.

SMuC (*Soft μ-calculus for Computations fields*) is meant to specify global computations on fields. One key aspect of our calculus are atomic computations denoted with expressions reminiscent of the semiring modal μ-calculus proposed in [8], a semiring-valued generalisation of the modal μ-calculus, used to reason about quantitative properties of graph-based structures (e.g. transition systems, network topologies, etc.). In SMuC similar expressions will be used to specify the functions being calculated by global computations, to be recorded by updating the interpretation functions of the nodes. Such atomic computations can be embedded in any language. To ease the presentation we present a global calculus where atomic computations are embedded in a simple imperative language reminiscent of WHILE [12].

Table 1. Rules of the operational semantics

$$
(\mu\text{STEP}) \qquad \frac{[\![\Psi]\!]_\emptyset^{I_F} = f \quad I_F' = I_F[^f/_i]}{\langle i \leftarrow \Psi, F \rangle \to \langle \text{skip}, F[^{I_F'}/_{I_F}] \rangle}
$$

$$
(\text{SEQ}1) \qquad \frac{\langle P, F \rangle \to \langle P', F' \rangle}{\langle P;Q, F \rangle \to \langle P';Q, F' \rangle}
$$

$$
(\text{SEQ}2) \qquad \frac{\langle P, F \rangle \to \langle P', F' \rangle}{\langle \text{skip};P, F \rangle \to \langle P', F' \rangle}
$$

$$
(\text{IFT}) \qquad \frac{[\![\Psi]\!]_\emptyset^F = \lambda n.a \ \text{for some } a \in A_F}{\langle \text{if} \cdot \text{agree} \cdot \text{on } \Psi \text{ then } P \text{ else } Q, F \rangle \to \langle P, F \rangle}
$$

$$
(\text{IFF}) \qquad \frac{[\![\Psi]\!]_\emptyset^F \neq \lambda n.a \ \text{for some } a \in A_F}{\langle \text{if} \cdot \text{agree} \cdot \text{on } \Psi \text{ then } P \text{ else } Q, F \rangle \to \langle Q, F \rangle}
$$

$$
(\text{UNTILF}) \qquad \frac{[\![\Psi]\!]_\emptyset^F \neq \lambda n.a \ \text{for some } a \in A_F}{\langle \text{until} \cdot \text{agree} \cdot \text{on } \Psi \text{ do } P, F \rangle \to \langle (P \ ; \text{until} \cdot \text{agree} \cdot \text{on } \Psi \text{ do } P), F \rangle}
$$

$$
(\text{UNTILT}) \qquad \frac{[\![\Psi]\!]_\emptyset^F = \lambda n.a \ \text{for some } a \in A_F}{\langle \text{until} \cdot \text{agree} \cdot \text{on } \Psi \text{ do } P, F \rangle \to \langle \text{skip} , F \rangle}
$$

Definition 3 (SMuC Syntax). *The syntax of* SMuC *is given by the following grammar*

$$
P, Q ::= \text{skip} \mid i \leftarrow \Psi \mid P \ ; \ P' \mid \text{if} \cdot \text{agree} \cdot \text{on } \Psi \text{ then } P \text{ else } Q
$$
$$
\mid \ \text{until} \cdot \text{agree} \cdot \text{on } \Psi \text{ do } P
$$

where $i \in \mathcal{L}$, Ψ is a SMuC *formula (cf. Def 4).*

We remark that the main difference with respect to the while language are the agree · on variants of the traditional control flow constructs. We explicitly use a different syntax in order to remark the characteristic semantics of those constructs, where the global control flow depends on the existence of agreements among all agents in the field.

The semantics of the calculus is straightforward, along the lines of WHILE [12] with fields (and their interpretation functions) playing the role of memory stores. In addition we have that the right-hand side of assignments are SMuC formulas that we will introduce next.

Given a semiring A, a function $\mathcal{N} \to A$ is called a *node valuation*. Given a set $\mathcal{Z}$ of variables, a set $\mathcal{M}$ of function symbols, an environment is a function $\rho : \mathcal{Z} \to \mathcal{N} \to A$.

Definition 4 (Syntax of SMuC Formulas). *The syntax of* SMuC *formulas is as follows:*

$$\Psi ::= i \mid z \mid f(\Psi, \ldots, \Psi) \mid [a]\Psi \mid \langle a \rangle \Psi \mid [[a]]\Psi \mid \langle\langle a \rangle\rangle.\Psi \mid \mu z.\Psi \mid \nu z.\Psi$$

with $i \in \mathcal{L}$, $a \in \mathcal{L}'$, $f \in \mathcal{M}$ and $z \in \mathcal{Z}$.

We remark that the set of functions symbols may include, among others, the semiring operator symbols $+$ and $\times$ and possibly some additional ones, for which an interpretation on the semiring of interest can be given.

Definition 5 (Semantics of SMuC Formulas). *Let F be a field. The semantics of* SMuC *formulas is given by the interpretation function $[\![\cdot]\!]_\rho^F : \Psi \to N_F \to A_F$ defined by*

$$[\![i]\!]_\rho^F = I_F(i)$$
$$[\![z]\!]_\rho^F = \rho(z)$$
$$[\![f(\Psi_1, \ldots, \Psi_n)]\!]_\rho^F = [\![f]\!]_{A_F}([\![\Psi_1]\!]_\rho^F, \ldots, [\![\Psi_n]\!]_\rho^F)]\!]_\rho^F$$
$$[\![[a]\Psi]\!]_\rho^F = \lambda n. \prod_{\{n' \mid (n,n') \in E_F\}} .I_F(a)(n,n')([\![\Psi]\!]_\rho^F(n'))$$
$$[\![\langle a \rangle.\Psi]\!]_\rho^F = \lambda n. \sum_{\{n' \mid (n,n') \in E_F\}} .I_F(a)(n,n')([\![\Psi]\!]_\rho^F(n'))$$
$$[\![[[a]]\Psi]\!]_\rho^F = \lambda n. \prod_{\{n' \mid (n',n) \in E_F\}} .I_F(a)(n',n)([\![\Psi]\!]_\rho^F(n'))$$
$$[\![\langle\langle a \rangle\rangle\Psi]\!]_\rho^F = \lambda n. \sum_{\{n' \mid (n',n) \in E_F\}} .I_F(a)(n',n)([\![\Psi]\!]_\rho^F(n'))$$
$$[\![\mu z.\Psi]\!]_\rho^F = lfp \; \lambda d.[\![\Psi]\!]_{\rho[d/z]}^F$$
$$[\![\nu z.\Psi]\!]_\rho^F = gfp \; \lambda d.[\![\Psi]\!]_{\rho[d/z]}^F$$

where lfp and gfp stand for the least and greatest fixpoint, respectively.

As usual, the semantics is well defined if so are all fixpoints. A sufficient condition for fixpoints to be well-defined is for functions $\lambda d.[\![\Psi]\!]_{\rho[d/z]}^F$ to be continuous and monotone (cf. Tarski's theorem). This implies, for instance, that if a negation operation is part of the function symbols f used in a formula, as reasonable with some but not all semiring instances, then we should ensure that all fixpoint variables have positive polarity. Another desirable property is for functions to be computable by iteration. This requires the fixpoint to be equal to Ψ^n for $n \in \mathbb{N}$, where $\Psi^{i+1} = [\![\Psi]\!]_{\rho[\Psi^i/z]}^F$ and $\Psi^0 = [\![\Psi]\!]_{\rho[\alpha/z]}^F$, with $\alpha = \bot$ if we are computing a least fixpoint and $\alpha = \top$ if we are computing a greatest fixpoint. The formulae we use in our case study satisfy the above mentioned properties.

The semantics of our calculus is a transition system whose states are pairs of calculus terms and fields and whose transitions $\to \subseteq (P \times \mathcal{F})^2$ are defined by the rules of Table 1. Most rules are standard. Rule IFT and IFT are similar to the usual rules for conditional branching. However, the condition is not a Boolean value but the existence of an agreement on the same value a to be assigned on each agent n in the field F. If such agreement exists, the then branch is taken, otherwise the else branch is followed. Similarly for the until · agree · on operator (cf. rules UntilT and UNTILF). States of the form (skip, I) represent termination. Initial states must have all node and edge labels interpreted.

```
finish ← false;
until · agree · on finish do
      /* 1st Stage: */
      /* Establishing the distance to victims */
      D ← μZ.min₁(source, ⟨dist⟩Z);

      /* 2nd Stage: */
      /* Computing the rescuers paths */
      rescuers ← μZ.init ∪ ⟨⟨grad⟩⟩Z;

      /* 3rd Stage: Engaging rescuers */
      finish ← false;
      /* engaging the rescuers */
      engaged ← μZ.choose ∪ ⟨cograd⟩Z;
      /* updating victims and available rescuers */
      victim' ← victim;
      victim ← victim ∧ ¬saved;
      rescuer ← rescuer ∧ engaged ≠ ∅;
      /* determining termination */
      finish ← (victim' == victim);

/* 4th Stage: Checking success */
if · agree · on ¬victim
      /* ended with success */
else
      /* ended with failure */
```

/* Semiring types of labels */

$$source, D : N \to T \times_1 N_{\leq N}$$
$$init, rescuers : N \to 2^{T \times N^*}$$
$$choose, engaged : N \to 2^{N^*}$$
$$dist : E \to T \times_1 N_{\leq N} \to T \times_1 N_{\leq N}$$
$$grad : E \to 2^{T \times N^*} \to 2^{T \times N^*}$$
$$cograd : E \to 2^{N^*} \to 2^{N^*}$$

Fig. 1. Robot Rescue SMuC Program

3 SMuC at Work: Rescuing Victims

The left side of Fig. 2 depicts a simple instance of the considered scenario. There, victims are rendered as black circles while landmarks and rescuers are depicted via grey and black rectangles respectively. The length of an edge in the graph is proportional to the distance between the two connected nodes. The main goal is to assign rescuers to victims, where each victim may need more than one rescuer and we want to minimise the distance that rescuers need to cover to reach their assigned victims. We assume that all relevant information of the victim rescue scenario is suitably represented in field F. More details on this will follow, but for now it suffices to assume that nodes represent rescuers, victims or landmarks and edges represent some sort of direct proximity (e.g. based on visibility w.r.t. to some sensor).

It is worth to remark that in practice it is convenient to define A as a Cartesian product of semirings, e.g. for differently-valued node and edge labels. This is indeed the case of our case study. However, in order to avoid explicitly dealing with these situations (e.g. by resorting to projection functions, etc.) which would introduce a cumbersome notation, we assume that the corresponding semiring is implicit (e.g. by type/semiring inference) and that the interpretation of functions and labels are suitably specialised. For this purpose we decorate the specification in Fig. 1 with the types of all labels.

We now describe the coordination strategy specified in the algorithm of Fig. 1. The algorithm consists of a loop that is repeated until an iteration does not

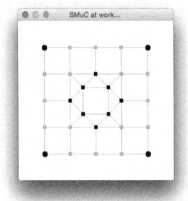 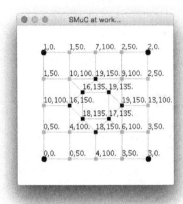

Fig. 2. Execution of Robot Rescue SMuC Program (part 1)

produce any additional matching of rescuers to victims. The body of the loop consist of different stages, each characterised by a fixpoint computation.

1st Stage: Establishing the distance to victims. In the first stage of the algorithm the robots try to establish their closest victim. Such information is saved in to D, which is valued over the total ordering semiring obtained by the lexicographical construction applied to the tropical semiring T and to the semiring $N_{\leq N}$ given by some total ordering on the nodes N. We denote such construction by $N \to T \times_1 N_{\leq N}$. In order to compute D some information is needed on nodes and arrows of the field, in particular the decorations are source and dist whose interpretation is defined as follows:

– $I(\text{source})(n) = $ if $n \in victim$ then $(0, n)$ else $(+\infty, n)$, i.e. victims point to themselves with no cost, while the rest of the nodes point to themselves with infinite cost;
– $I(\text{dist})(n, n') = \lambda(v, m).(distance(n, n') + v, n')$ where $distance(n, n')$ is the weight of (n, n'). Intuitively, dist provides a function to add the cost associated to the transition. The second component of the value encodes the direction to go for the shortest path, while the total ordering on nodes is used for solving ties.

The desired information is then computed as $D \leftarrow \mu Z.\min_1(\text{source}, \langle \text{dist} \rangle Z)$. This fix point calculation is very similar to the standard ones used to calculate reachability or shortest paths. Here $\min_1$ is the additive operation of semiring $N \to T \times_1 N_{\leq N}$, specifically for a set $B \subseteq (\mathbb{R} \cup \{+\infty\}) \times N$ the function $\min_1$ is defined as $\min_1(B) = (a, n) \in B$ such that $\forall (a', n') \in B : a \leq a'$ and if $a = a'$ then $n \leq n'$.

At the end of this stage, D associates each element with the distance to its closest victim. In the right side of Fig. 2 each node of our example is labeled with the computed distance. We do not include the second component of D (i.e.

the identity of the closest neighbour) to provide a readable figure. In any case, the closest victim is easy to infer from the depicted graph: the closest victim of the rescuer in the top-left corner of the inner box formed by the rescuers is the victim at the top-left corner of the figure, and respectively for the top-right, bottom-left and bottom-right corners.

2nd Stage: Computing the rescuers paths to the victims. In this second stage of the algorithm, the robots try to compute, for every victim v, which are the paths from every rescuer u to v — but only for those u for which v is the closest victim — and the corresponding costs, as established by D in the previous stage. Here we use the semiring $2^{T \times N^*}$ with union as additive operator, i.e. $\langle 2^{T \times N^*}, \cup, \cap, T \times N^*, \emptyset \rangle$. We use here decorations init and grad whose interpretation is defined as

- $I(\text{init})n = $ if $n \in$ rescuer then $\{(D(n), \epsilon)\}$ else $\emptyset$;
- $I(\text{grad})(n, n') = \lambda C.$ if $D(n) = (u, n')$ then $n; C$ else $\emptyset$, where operation ; is defined as $n; C = \{(cost, n; path) \mid (cost, path) \in C\}$.

The idea of label *rescuers* is to compute, for every node n, the set of rescuers whose path to their closest victim passes through n (typically a landmark). However, the name of a rescuer is meaningless outside its neighbourhood, thus a path leading to it is constructed instead. In addition, each rescuer is decorated with its distance to its closest victim. Function init associates to a rescuer its name and its distance, the empty set to all the other nodes. Function grad checks if an arc (n, n') is on the optimal path out of n. In the positive case, the rescuers in n are considered as rescuers also for n', but with an updated path; in the negative case they are discarded.

In left side of Fig. 3 the result of this stage is presented. There, the edges that are part of path from one rescuer to a victim are now marked. We can notice that some victims can be reached by more than one rescuer.

3rd Stage: Engaging the rescuers. The idea of the third stage of the algorithm is that each victim n, which needs k rescuers, will choose the k closest rescuers, if there are enough, among those that have selected n as target victim. For this computation we use the decorations choose and cograd.

- $I(\text{choose})(n) = $ if $n \in victim$ and $\text{saved}(n)$ then $opt(\text{rescuer}(n), howMany(n))$ else $\emptyset$, where:
  - $\text{saved}(n) = |\text{rescuers}(n)| \leq howMany(n)$ and $howMany(n), n \in victim$ returns the number of rescuers n needs;
  - $opt(C, k) = \{path \mid (cost, path) \in C$ and $|\{(cost', path') \mid (cost', path') < (cost, path)\}| < k\}$
    where $(cost, path) < (cost', path')$ if $cost < cost'$ or $cost = cost'$ and $path < path'$, and paths are totally ordered lexicographically;
- $I(\text{cograd}(n, n') = \lambda C.\{path \mid n; path \in C\}$.

Intuitively, choose allows a victim n that has enough rescuers to choose and to record the paths leading to them. The annotation cograd associates to each edge (n, n') a function to select in a set C of paths those of the form $n; path$.

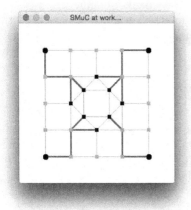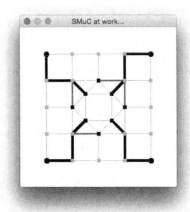

Fig. 3. Execution of Robot Rescue SMuC Program (part 2)

The computation in this step is engaged $\leftarrow \mu Z$.choose $\cup \langle$cograd$\rangle Z$, which computes the desired information: in each node n we will have the set of rescuer-to-victim paths that pass through n and that have been chosen by a victim.

The result of this stage is presented in the right side of Fig. 3. Each rescuer has a route, that is presented in the figure with black edges, that can be followed to reach the assigned victim. Again, for simplicity we just depict some relevant information to provide an appealing and intuitive representation.

Notice that this phase, and the algorithm, may fail even if there are enough rescuers to save some additional victims. For instance if there are two victims, each requiring two rescuers, and two rescuers, the algorithm fails if each rescuer is closer to a different victim.

These three stages are repeated until there is agreement on whether to finish. The termination criteria is that an iteration did not update the set of victims. In that case the loop terminates and the algorithm proceeds to the last stage.

4th Stage: Checking succes. The algorithm terminates with success when *victim'* $= \emptyset$ and with failure when *victim'* is not empty. In Fig. 4 we present the result of the computation of program of Fig. 1 on a randomly generated graph composed by 1000 landmarks, 5 victims and 10 rescuers. We can notice that, each victim can be reached by more than one rescuer and that the closer one is selected.

4   On Distributing SMuC Computations

We discuss in this section some aspects of a distributed implementation of SMuC computations. Needless to say, an obvious implementation would be based on

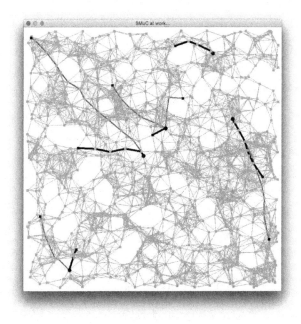

Fig. 4. Execution of Robot Rescue SMuC Program on a random graph

a *centralised* algorithm. In particular, the nodes could initially send all their information to a centralised coordinator that would construct the field, compute the SMuC computations, and distribute the results back to the nodes. This solution is easy to realise and could be based on our prototype which indeed performs a centralised, global computation, as a sequential program acting on the field. However, such a solution has several obvious drawbacks: first, it creates a bottleneck in the coordinator. Second, there are many applications in which the idea of constructing the whole field is not feasible and each agent needs to evolve independently. We discuss here some possible alternatives.

A Naïve Distributed Implementation. We start with a naïve distributed implementation based on an endpoint projection of SMuC computations on local programs on the nodes. Such projection is sketched informally in Fig. 5 where a projection function ·⌈ maps SMuC programs and formulas into local code to be executed on agents. We neglect the formal presentation of the local programming language and rely on the intuition of the reader since the main goal is to make explicit the (high) amount of synchronisation points in such an approach. Those synchronisation points are marked by underlining the corresponding statements.

Note that every occurrence of a sequential composition, every control flow construct and every fixpoint iteration involves a global synchronisation like a global barrier (e.g. sync) or a global commit (e.g. global · agree · on). Indeed,

$$\begin{aligned}
P{\upharpoonright}_F &= \parallel_{n \in N_F} n : P{\upharpoonright}_n \\
\mathsf{skip}{\upharpoonright}_n &= \mathsf{skip} \\
i \leftarrow \Psi{\upharpoonright}_n &= \mathsf{self}.i \leftarrow \Psi{\upharpoonright}_n \\
P \; ; \; P'{\upharpoonright}_n &= P{\upharpoonright}_n \; ; \; \mathsf{sync} \; ; \; P'{\upharpoonright}_n \\
\mathsf{if} \cdot \mathsf{agree} \cdot \mathsf{on} \; \Psi \; \mathsf{then} \; P \; \mathsf{else} \; Q{\upharpoonright}_n &= \nu \; \mathsf{global} \; z; \\
& \quad \overline{\mathsf{self}.z \leftarrow \Psi{\upharpoonright}_n;} \\
& \quad \mathsf{if} \cdot \mathsf{global} \cdot \mathsf{agree} \cdot \mathsf{on} \; z \; \mathsf{then} \; P{\upharpoonright}_n \; \mathsf{else} \quad Q{\upharpoonright}_n \\
\mathsf{until} \cdot \mathsf{agree} \cdot \mathsf{on} \; \Psi \; \mathsf{do} \; P{\upharpoonright}_n &= \nu \; \mathsf{global} \; z; \\
& \quad \overline{\mathsf{self}.z \leftarrow \Psi{\upharpoonright}_n;} \\
& \quad \mathsf{until} \cdot \mathsf{global} \cdot \mathsf{agree} \cdot \mathsf{on} \; z \; \mathsf{do} \\
& \qquad \overline{P{\upharpoonright}_n;} \\
& \qquad \mathsf{self}.z \leftarrow \Psi{\upharpoonright}_n; \\
i{\upharpoonright}_n &= \mathsf{self}.i \\
z{\upharpoonright}_n &= \mathsf{self}.z \\
f(\Psi_1, \ldots, \Psi_m){\upharpoonright}_n &= f(\Psi_1{\upharpoonright}_n, \ldots, \Psi_m{\upharpoonright}_n) \\
[a]\Psi{\upharpoonright}_n &= \prod_{\{n'|(n,n')\in E_F\}} .I_F(a)(n,n')(n'.\Psi{\upharpoonright}'_n) \\
\langle a \rangle \Psi{\upharpoonright}_n &= \sum_{\{n'|(n,n')\in E_F\}} .I_F(a)(n,n')(n'.\Psi{\upharpoonright}'_n) \\
[[a]]\Psi{\upharpoonright}_n &= \prod_{\{n'|(n,n')\in E_F\}} .I_F(a)(n',n)(n'.\Psi{\upharpoonright}'_n) \\
\langle\langle a \rangle\rangle.\Psi{\upharpoonright}_n &= \sum_{\{n'|(n',nn)\in E_F\}} .I_F(a)(n,n')(n'.\Psi{\upharpoonright}'_n) \\
\iota z.\Psi{\upharpoonright}_n &= \nu \; \mathsf{global} \; z; \\
& \quad \overline{\mathsf{self}.z \leftarrow \alpha(\iota);} \\
& \quad \mathsf{until} \cdot \mathsf{global} \cdot \mathsf{fixpoint}(z) \; \mathsf{do} \\
& \qquad \overline{\mathsf{self}.z \leftarrow \Psi{\upharpoonright}_n;} \\
& \quad \mathsf{sync};
\end{aligned}$$

where $\iota \in \{\mu, \nu\}$ and $\alpha(\mu) = \top$, $\alpha(\mu) = \bot$.

Fig. 5. Naïve end point projection of SMuC computations

each agent has to locally check if a step of the computation has been completely computed or if other iterations are needed to compute the correct value. This holds, in particular, when fixpoints formulas are considered. In what follows we discuss opportunities to optimise and relax those synchronisation points.

Spanning-tree Based Synchronisations. We describe now a technique that, by relying on a specific structure, can be used to perform SMuC computations in an improved way. The corner stone of the proposed algorithm is a *tree-based* infrastructure that spans the complete field. In this infrastructure each node/agent, that is identified by a unique identifier, is responsible for the coordination of the computations occurring in its sub-tree. In the rest of this section we assume that this *spanning tree* is computed in a *set-up* phase executed when the system is deployed. We also assume that each agent only interacts with its neighbours and that it knows their identities.

It should be clear from the endpoint projection in Figure 5 that when a SMuC program consists of a sequence of assignments $v_0 \leftarrow \Psi_0 \ldots v_k \leftarrow \Psi_k$, a global barrier needs to be used to ensure that all processes proceed synchronously to guarantee that the computation of v_{i+1} is started only when the computation of v_i has been globally completed. We now discuss a technique that uses a tree infrastructure to implement such global barrier in an efficient way. The optimisation regards also the possible local iterations due to the necessity to compute fixpoints.

As sketched in Fig. 5 each agent sends to (and receives from) its neighbours local values computed in Ψ_i (cf. the use of $n'\ldots$ in the projection of modal operators). Since each Ψ_i may contain several fixpoints, these values have to be computed iteratively.

An alternative to the projection in Fig. 5 would be as follows. Each value within an iteration could be sent together with the index k of the computational step and with the actual iteration. Following this approach each agent would be able to compute the values at some iteration when all the values corresponding to the previous iteration have been collected from its neighbours. When a *local* fixpoint is reached (i.e. its value did not change with respect to the previous iteration) an agent would reach a *local stability point*. An agent becomes *stable* when it is *locally stable* and all its children in the spanning tree are stable (for the leaves of the spanning tree, *local stability* and *stability* coincides). Note that an agent can be stable at a given iteration and unstable in the next one. This happens when an update of local values is propagated in the field.

The node devoted to check the global stability in the field is the root of the spanning tree. We can observe that each update in the field is propagated to the root in a number of steps that equates the height of the spanning tree. For this reason, when the root of the spanning tree is *stable* for a number of iterations that is greater than the height of the spanning tree, a global stability can be assured. After that the root informs all the nodes in the spanning tree that computation of step i is terminated and the index of the current step is updated accordingly. Each node starts the computation of step $i+1$ just after the commit for the step i has been received.

5   Related Works

In recent years, spatial computing has emerged as a promising approach to model and control systems consisting of a large number of cooperating agents that are distributed over a physical or logical space [3]. This computational model starts from the assumption that, when the density of involved computational agents increases, the underlying network topology is strongly related to the geometry of the space through which computational agents are distributed. Goals are generally defined in terms of the system's spatial structure. A main advantage of these approaches is that their computations can be seen both as working on a single node, and as computations on the distributed data structures emerging in the network (the so-called "computational fields").

One of the main examples in this area is Proto [1,2]. This language aims at providing links between local and global computations and permits the specification of the individual behaviour of a node, typically in a sensor-like network, via specific space-time operators to situate computation in the physical world. In [15] a minimal core calculus has been introduced to capture the key ingredients of languages that make use of computational fields. In [14] a typed variant of the core calculus of [15] is presented. The new proposed calculus is also equipped with a type-system ensuring self-stabilisation of any well-typed program.

The calculus proposed in this paper starts from a different perspective with respect to the ones mentioned above. In these calculi, computational fields result from (recursive) functional composition. These functions are typically used to compute a single field, which may consists of a tuple of different values. In our approach, at each step of a SMuC program a different field can be computed and then used in the rest of the computation. This is possible because in SMuC only monotone continuous functions over the appropriate semirings are considered. This guarantees the existence of fixpoints and the possibility to identify a global stability in the field computation. This is not possible in other approaches. Of course, monotonicity and continuity do not guarantee computability of the fixpoints by iteration. Other methods may be needed. Further investigations are needed to compare the expressive power of SMuC with respect to the languages and calculi previously proposed in literature.

Different middleware/platforms have been proposed to support coordination of distributed agents via computational fields [9,13,11]. In [9] the framework TOTA (*Tuples On The Air*), is introduced to provide spatial abstractions for a novel approach to distributed systems development and management, and is suitable to tackle the complexity of modern distributed computing scenarios, and promotes self-organisation and self-adaptation. In [13] a similar approach has been extended to obtain a chemical-inspired model. This extends tuple spaces with the ability of evolving tuples mimicking chemical systems and provides the machinery enabling agents coordination via spatial computing patterns of competition and gradient-based interaction. Finally, in [11] a framework for distributed agent coordination via *eco-laws* has been proposed. This kind of laws generalise the chemical-inspired ones [13] in a framework where self-organisation can be injected in pervasive service ecosystems in terms of spatial structures and algorithms for supporting the design of context-aware applications. The proposed calculus considers computational fields at a more higher level of abstraction with respect to the above mentioned frameworks. However, these frameworks could provide the means for developing a distributed implementation of SMuC.

6   Conclusion

We have presented a simple calculus, named SMuC, that can be used to program and coordinate the activities of distributed agents via computational fields. In SMuC a computation consists of a sequence of fixpoints computed in a graph-shaped field that represents the space topology modelling the underlying network. Our graph-based fields have attributes on both nodes and arcs, where the latter represent interaction capabilities between nodes. Under reasonable conditions, fixpoints can computed via synchronised iterations. At each iteration the attributes of a node are updated based according to the values of neighbours in the previous iteration. SMuC is also equipped with a set of control-flow constructs allow one to conveniently structure the fixpoint computations. We have also developed a prototype tool for our language, equipped with a graphical interface that provides useful visual feedback to users of the language. We use indeed those visual features to illustrate the application of our approach to a robot rescue case study, for which we provide a novel rescue coordination strategy, specified in SMuC.

The general aspects related to possible distributed implementation of our calculus have been also discussed. We have sketched a naïve (overly synchronised) distributed implementation and an improvement based on a spanning tree structure aimed at minimising communication and accelerating the detection of fixpoints. We are currently investigating further distribution techniques. The first one is to perform the updates in the fixpoint iterations sequentially but respecting fairness. The stable result should be the same, but efficiency should be significantly improved if causality of iteration updates is traced, e.g. using a queue as in Dijkstra's shortest path algorithm. The second idea is to update variables looking at one neighbour at a time. Under suitable conditions again the result should be the same, but the amount of asynchrony, and thus efficiency, should increase remarkably. Of course, particular instances of the fixpoint iterations (e.g. when considering associative, commutative, idempotent operations) would allow more drastic improvements by allowing agents to proceed asynchronously, synchronising to ensure a barrier between to sequential programs.

Acknowledgments. The authors wish to thank Carlo Pinciroli for interesting discussions in preliminary stages of the work.

References

1. Beal, J., Bachrach, J.: Infrastructure for engineered emergence on sensor/actuator networks. IEEE Intelligent Systems 21, 10–19 (2006)
2. Beal, J., Michel, O., Schultz, U.P.: Spatial computing: Distributed systems that take advantage of our geometric world. ACM Transactions on Autonomous and Adaptive Systems 6, 11:1–11:3 (2011)
3. Beal, J., Dulman, S., Usbeck, K., Viroli, M., Correll, N.: Organizing the aggregate: Languages for spatial computing. CoRR, abs/1202.5509 (2012)
4. Bistarelli, S., Montanari, U., Rossi, F.: Semiring-based constraint satisfaction and optimization. J. ACM 44(2), 201–236 (1997)
5. Canal, C., Villari, M. (eds.): ESOCC 2013. Communications in Computer and Information Science, vol. 393. Springer, Heidelberg (2013)
6. Kühn, E., Pugliese, R. (eds.): COORDINATION 2014. LNCS, vol. 8459. Springer, Heidelberg (2014)
7. Liò, P., Yoneki, E., Crowcroft, J., Verma, D.C. (eds.): BIOWIRE 2007. LNCS, vol. 5151. Springer, Heidelberg (2008)
8. Lluch-Lafuente, A., Montanari, U.: Quantitative mu-calculus and CTL defined over constraint semirings. Theor. Comput. Sci. 346(1), 135–160 (2005)

9. Mamei, M., Zambonelli, F.: Programming pervasive and mobile computing applications: The TOTA approach. ACM Transactions on Software Engingeering and Methodology 18, 15:1–15:56 (2009)

10. Mamei, M., Zambonelli, F.: Field-based coordination for pervasive computing applications. In: Liò et al (eds.) [7], pp. 376–386

11. Montagna, S., Viroli, M., Fernandez-Marquez, J.L., Di Marzo Serugendo, G., Zambonelli, F.: Injecting self-organisation into pervasive service ecosystems. MONET 18(3), 398–412 (2013)

12. Nielson, H.R., Nielson, F.: Semantics with Applications: An Appetizer. Undergraduate Topics in Computer Science. Springer (2007)

13. Viroli, M., Casadei, M., Montagna, S., Zambonelli, F.: Spatial coordination of pervasive services through chemical-inspired tuple spaces. TAAS 6(2), 14 (2011)

14. Viroli, M., Damiani, F.: A calculus of self-stabilising computational fields. In: Kühn, E., Pugliese (eds.) [6], pp. 163–178

15. Viroli, M., Damiani, F., Beal, J.: A calculus of computational fields. In: Canal, Villari (eds.) [5], pp. 114–128

Take Command of Your Constraints!

Sung-Shik T.Q. Jongmans[(✉)] and Farhad Arbab

Centrum Wiskunde and Informatica, Amsterdam, Netherlands
{jongmans,farhad}@cwi.nl

Abstract. Constraint automata (CA) are a coordination model based on finite automata on infinite words. Although originally introduced for compositional *modeling* of coordinators, an interesting new application of CA is actually *implementing* coordinators (i.e., compiling CA to executable code). Such an approach guarantees correctness-by-construction and can even yield code that outperforms hand-crafted code. The extent to which these two potential advantages arise depends on the smartness of CA-compilers and the existence of proofs of their correctness.

We present and prove the correctness of a critical optimization for CA-compilers: a sound and complete translation from declarative constraints in transition labels to imperative commands in a sequential language. This optimization avoids expensive calls to a constraint solver at run-time, otherwise performed each time a transition fires, and thereby significantly improves the performance of generated coordination code.

1 Introduction

Context. A promising application domain for coordination languages is programming protocols among threads in multicore applications. One reason for this is a classical software engineering advantage: coordination languages typically provide high-level constructs and abstractions that more easily compose into correct—with respect to programmers' intentions—protocol specifications than do conventional lower-level synchronization mechanisms (e.g., locks or semaphores). However, not only do coordination languages simplify programming protocols, but their high-level constructs and abstractions also leave more room for compilers to perform optimizations that conventional language compilers cannot apply. Eventually, sufficiently smart compilers for coordination languages should be capable of generating code (e.g., in Java or in C) that can compete with carefully hand-crafted code. Preliminary evidence for feasibility of this goal appears elsewhere [1,2]. A crucial step toward adoption of coordination languages for multicore programming, then, is the development of such compilers.

To study the performance advantages of using coordination languages for multicore programming, in ongoing work, we are developing compilation technology for *constraint automata* (CA) [3]. Constraint automata are a general coordination model based on finite automata on infinite words. Every CA models the behavior of a single coordinator; a product operator on CA models the synchronous composition of such coordinators (useful to construct complex coordinators out

© IFIP International Federation for Information Processing 2015
T. Holvoet and M. Viroli (Eds.): COORDINATION 2015, LNCS 9037, pp. 117–132, 2015.
DOI: 10.1007/978-3-319-19282-6_8

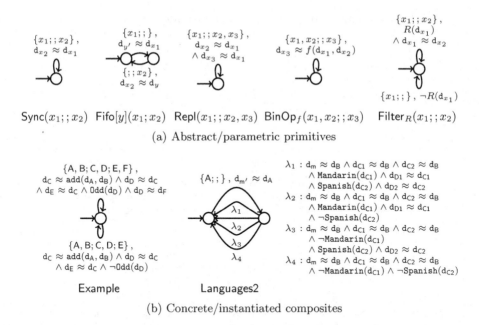

$\mathsf{Sync}(x_1;;x_2)$ $\mathsf{Fifo}[y](x_1;x_2)$ $\mathsf{Repl}(x_1;;x_2,x_3)$ $\mathsf{BinOp}_f(x_1,x_2;;x_3)$ $\mathsf{Filter}_R(x_1;;x_2)$

(a) Abstract/parametric primitives

Example   Languages2

(b) Concrete/instantiated composites

Fig. 1. Example CA. Semicolons separate input/internal/output ports.

of simpler ones). Structurally, a CA consists of a finite set of states, a finite set of transitions, a set of directed *ports*, and a set of local *memory cells*. Ports represent the boundary/interface between a coordinator and its coordinated agents (e.g., computation threads). Such agents can perform blocking I/O-operations on ports: a coordinator's input ports admit **put** operations, while its output ports admit **get** operations. Memory cells represent internal buffers in which a coordinator can temporarily store data items. Different from classical automata, transition labels of CA consist of two elements: a set of ports, called a *synchronization constraint*, and a logical formula over ports and memory cells, called a *data constraint*. A synchronization constraint specifies which ports need an I/O-operation for its transition to fire (i.e., those ports synchronize in that transition and their pending I/O-operations complete), while a data constraint specifies which particular data items those I/O-operations may involve. Figure 1 already shows some examples; details follow shortly. Essentially, a CA constrains *when* I/O-operations may complete on *which* ports. As such, CA quite literally materialize Wegner's definition of coordination as "constrained interaction" [4].

Given a library of "small" CA, each of which models a primitive coordinator with its own local behavior, programmers can compositionally construct "big" CA, each of which models a composite coordinator with arbitrarily complex global behavior, fully tailored to the needs of these programmers and their programs. Our current CA-compilers can subsequently generate Java/C code. Afterward, these compilers either automatically blend their generated code into programs' computation code or provide programmers the opportunity to do this manually. At run-time, the code generated for a big CA (i.e., a composite

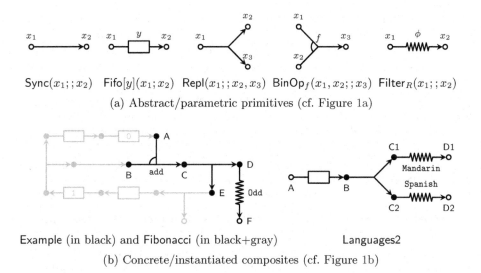

$$\mathsf{Sync}(x_1;;x_2)\quad \mathsf{Fifo}[y](x_1;x_2)\quad \mathsf{Repl}(x_1;;x_2,x_3)\quad \mathsf{BinOp}_f(x_1,x_2;;x_3)\quad \mathsf{Filter}_R(x_1;;x_2)$$

(a) Abstract/parametric primitives (cf. Figure 1a)

Example (in black) and Fibonacci (in black+gray)   Languages2

(b) Concrete/instantiated composites (cf. Figure 1b)

Fig. 2. Reo syntax for the CA in Figure 1. White vertices represent input/output ports; black vertices represent internal ports.

coordinator) executes a state machine that simulates that CA, repeatedly firing transitions as computation threads perform I/O-operations. Straightforward as this may seem, one needs to overcome a number of serious issues before this approach can yield practically useful code. Most significantly, these issues include exponential explosion of the number of states or transitions of CA, and oversequentialization or overparallelization of generated code. We have already reported our work on these issues along with promising results elsewhere [5,6,1,7].

Instead of programming with CA directly, one can adopt a more programmer-friendly syntax for which CA serve as semantics. In our work, for instance, we adopted the syntax of Reo [8,9], a graphical calculus of channels. Figure 2 already shows some examples; details follow shortly. (Other CA syntaxes beside Reo exist though [10,11,12,13], which may be at least as programmer-friendly.)

Problem. To fire a transition at run-time, code generated for a CA must evaluate the data constraint of that transition: it must ensure that the data involved in blocking I/O-operations pending on the transition's ports satisfy that constraint.

A straightforward evaluation of data constraints requires expensive calls to a constraint solver. Such calls cause high run-time overhead. In particular, because transitions fire sequentially, avoiding constraint solving to reduce this sequential bottleneck is crucial in getting good performance for the whole program.

Contribution and Organization. In this paper, we introduce a technique for statically translating a data constraint, off-line at compile-time, into a *data command*: an imperative implementation (in a sequential language with assignment and guarded failure) of a data constraint that avoids expensive calls to a constraint solver at run-time. As with our previous optimization techniques [5,1,7], we prove that the translation in this paper is sound and complete. Such correctness proofs are important, because they ensure that our compilation approach guarantees *correctness-by-construction* (e.g., model-checking results obtained for pre-optimized CA also hold for their generated, optimized implementations). We also give preliminary performance results to show our optimization's potential.

In Section 2, we discuss data constraints and CA. In Sections 3 and 4, we discuss our translation algorithm. In Section 5, we give preliminary performance results. Section 6 concludes this paper. Some relatively lengthy formal definitions and detailed proofs of Theorems 1 and 2 appear in a technical report [14].

2   Preliminaries: Data Constraints, Constraint Automata

Data constraints. Let $\mathbb{D}$ denote the finite set of all *data items*, typically ranged over by d. Let $\mathtt{nil} \notin \mathbb{D}$ denote a special object for the *empty data item*. Let $\mathbb{P}$ denote the finite set of all *places* where data items can reside, typically ranged over by x or y; every place models either a port or a memory cells. We model atomic coordination steps—the letters in the alphabet of CA—with elements from the partial function space $\mathrm{DISTR} = \mathbb{P} \rightharpoonup \mathbb{D} \cup \{\mathtt{nil}\}$, called *distributions*, typically ranged over by δ. Informally, a distribution δ associates every place x involved in the step modeled by δ with the data item $\delta(x)$ observable in x.

Let $\mathbb{F} = \bigcup \{\mathbb{D}^k \to \mathbb{D} \mid k > 0\}$ and $\mathbb{R} = \bigcup \{\wp(\mathbb{D}^k) \mid k > 0\}$ denote the sets of all *data functions* and *data relations* of finite arity. Let DATA, FUN, and REL denote the sets of all *data item symbols*, *data function symbols* and *data relation symbols*, typically ranged over by d, f, and R. Let $\mathsf{arity} : \mathrm{FUN} \cup \mathrm{REL} \to \mathbb{N}_+$ denote a function that associates every data function/relation symbol with its positive arity. Let $\mathcal{I} : \mathrm{DATA} \cup \mathrm{FUN} \cup \mathrm{REL} \to \mathbb{D} \cup \mathbb{F} \cup \mathbb{R}$ denote a bijection that associates every data item/function/relation symbol with its interpretation. A *data term* is a word t generated by the following grammar:

$$t \quad ::= \quad \mathtt{d}_x \mid \mathtt{nil} \mid d \mid f(t_1, \ldots, t_k) \text{ if } \mathsf{arity}(f) = k$$

Let TERM denote the set of all data terms. Let $\mathsf{eval} : \mathrm{DISTR} \times \mathrm{TERM} \to \mathbb{D} \cup \{\mathtt{nil}\}$ denote a function that evaluates every data term t to a data item $\mathsf{eval}_\delta(t)$ under distribution δ. For instance, $\mathsf{eval}_\delta(\mathtt{d}_x) = \delta(x)$—if δ is defined for x—and $\mathsf{eval}_\delta(d) = \mathcal{I}(d)$. If a data term t contains $\mathtt{nil}$ or $\mathtt{d}_x$ for some $x \notin \mathrm{Dom}(\delta)$, we have $\mathsf{eval}_\delta(t) = \mathtt{nil}$. This ensures that eval is a total function, even though the deltas in DISTR are partial functions. See also [14, Definition 7]. We call a term of the form $\mathtt{d}_x$ a *free variable*. Intuitively, $\mathtt{d}_x$ represents the data item residing in place x. Let $\mathsf{Free} : \mathrm{TERM} \to \wp(\mathrm{TERM})$ denote a function that maps every data term t to its set of free variables.

A *data constraint* is a word ϕ generated by the following grammar:

$$
\begin{aligned}
a \quad &::= \quad \bot \mid \top \mid t \approx t \mid t \not\approx \mathtt{nil} \mid R(t_1, \ldots, t_k) \text{ if } \mathsf{arity}(R) = k \\
\phi \quad &::= \quad a \mid \neg\phi \mid \phi \vee \phi \mid \phi \wedge \phi
\end{aligned}
$$

Let $\mathbb{DC}$ denote the set of all data constraints. We often call $t_1 \approx t_2$ atoms *equalities*. We define the semantics of data constraints over distributions. Let $\models^{\mathrm{dc}} \subseteq \mathrm{DISTR} \times \mathbb{DC}$ denote the satisfaction relation on data constraints. Its definition is standard for $\bot$ (contradiction), $\top$ (tautology), $\neg$ (negation), $\vee$ (disjunction), and $\wedge$ (conjunction). For other atoms, we have the following:

$$\delta \models^{\mathrm{dc}} t_1 \approx t_2 \quad\quad \textbf{iff} \;\; \mathsf{eval}_\delta(t_1) = \mathsf{eval}_\delta(t_2) \neq \mathsf{nil}$$
$$\delta \models^{\mathrm{dc}} t \not\approx \mathsf{nil} \quad\quad \textbf{iff} \;\; \mathsf{eval}_\delta(t) \neq \mathsf{nil} \quad\quad (\textit{i.e., notation for } \delta \models^{\mathrm{dc}} t \approx t)$$
$$\delta \models^{\mathrm{dc}} R(t_1, \dots, t_k) \;\; \textbf{iff} \;\; \mathcal{I}(R)(\mathsf{eval}_\delta(t_1), \dots, \mathsf{eval}_\delta(t_k))$$

In the second rule, if a t_i evaluates to nil, the right-hand side is undefined—hence false—because the domain of data relation $\mathcal{I}(R)$ excludes nil. If $\delta \models^{\mathrm{dc}} \phi$, we call δ a *solution* for ϕ. Let $[\![\cdot]\!] : \mathbb{DC} \to \wp(\mathrm{DISTR})$ denote a function that associates every data constraint ϕ with its meaning $[\![\phi]\!] = \{\delta \mid \delta \models^{\mathrm{dc}} \phi\}$. We write $\phi \Rightarrow \phi'$ iff $[\![\phi]\!] \subseteq [\![\phi']\!]$. We also extend function Free from data terms to data constraints.

Constraint Automata. A constraint automaton (CA) is a tuple $(Q, \mathcal{X}, \mathcal{Y}, \longrightarrow, \imath)$ with Q a set of states, $\mathcal{X} \subseteq \mathbb{P}$ a set of ports, $\mathcal{Y} \subseteq \mathbb{P}$ a set of memory cells, $\longrightarrow \subseteq Q \times (\wp(\mathcal{X}) \times \mathbb{DC}) \times Q$ a transition relation labeled with pairs (X, ϕ), and $\imath \in Q$ an initial state. For every label (X, ϕ), no ports outside X may occur in ϕ. Set $\mathcal{X}$ consists of three disjoint subsets of input ports $\mathcal{X}_{\mathrm{in}}$, *internal ports* $\mathcal{X}_{\mathrm{int}}$, and output ports $\mathcal{X}_{\mathrm{out}}$. We call a CA for which $\mathcal{X}_{\mathrm{int}} = \emptyset$ a *primitive*; otherwise, we call it a *composite*.

Although generally important, we skip the definition of the product operator on CA, because it does not matter in this paper. Every CA accepts infinite sequences of distributions [3]: $(Q, \mathcal{X}, \mathcal{Y}, \longrightarrow, \imath)$ accepts $\delta_0 \delta_1 \cdots$ if an infinite sequence of states $q_0 q_1 \cdots$ exists such that $q_0 = \imath$ and for all $i \geq 0$, a transition $(q_i, (X, \phi), q_{i+1})$ exists such that $\mathrm{Dom}(\delta_i) = X$ and $\delta_i \models^{\mathrm{dc}} \phi$.

Without loss of generality, we assume that all data constraints occur in disjunctive normal form. Moreover, because replacing a transition $(q, (X, \phi_1 \vee \phi_2), q')$ with two transitions $(q, (X, \phi_1), q')$ and $(q, (X, \phi_2), q')$ preserves behavioral congruence on CA [3], without loss of generality, we assume that the data constraint in every label is a conjunction of *literals*, typically ranged over by ℓ.

Figure 1a shows example primitives; Figure 2a shows their Reo syntax. Sync models a synchronous channel from an input x_1 to an output x_2. Fifo models an asynchronous channel with a 1-capacity buffer y from x_1 to x_2. Repl models a coordinator that, in each of its atomic coordination steps, replicates the data item on x_1 to both x_2 and x_3. BinOp models a coordinator that, in each of its atomic coordination steps, applies operation f to the data items on x_1 and x_2 and passes the result to x_3. Filter models a lossy synchronous channel from x_1 to x_2; data items pass this channel only if they satisfy predicate R.

Figure 1b shows example composites; Figure 2b shows their Reo syntax. Example—our running example in this paper—consists of instantiated primitives $\mathsf{BinOp}_{\mathsf{add}}(\mathsf{A}, \mathsf{B}; ; \mathsf{C})$, $\mathsf{Repl}(\mathsf{C}; ; \mathsf{D}, \mathsf{E})$, and $\mathsf{Filter}_{\mathsf{Odd}}(\mathsf{D}; ; \mathsf{F})$, where add and Odd have the obvious interpretation. In each of its atomic coordination steps, if the sum of the data items (supposedly integers) on its inputs A and B is odd,

Example passes this sum to its outputs E and F. Otherwise, if the sum is even, Example passes this value only to E. Figure 2b shows that Example constitutes Fibonacci. Fibonacci coordinates two consumers by generating the Fibonacci sequence. Whenever Fibonacci generates an even number, it passes that number to *only one* consumer; whenever it generates an odd number, it passes that number to *both* consumers. Finally, Languages2 consists of instantiated primitives Fifo[m](A; ; B), Repl(B; ; C1, C2), Filter$_{\text{Mandarin}}$(C1; ; D1), and Filter$_{\text{English}}$(C2; ; D2). Languages2 coordinates a producer and two consumers. If the producer puts a Mandarin (resp. English) data item on input A, Languages2 asynchronously passes this data item only to the consumer on output D1 (resp. D2). Languages2 easily generalizes to Languages$i$, for i different languages; we do so in Section 5.

3   From Data Constraints to Data Commands

At run-time, compiler-generated code executes in one or more CA-*threads*, each of which runs a state machine that simulates a CA. (We addressed the challenge of deciding the number of CA-threads elsewhere [5,6,7].) The *context* of a CA-thread is the collection of put/get operations on implementations of its input/output ports, performed by computation threads. Every time the context of a CA-thread changes, that CA-thread examines whether this change enables a transition in its current state q: for each transition $(q, (X, \phi), q')$, it checks whether every port $x \in X$ has a pending I/O-operation and if so, whether the data items involved in the pending put operations and the current content of memory cells can constitute a solution for ϕ. For the latter, the CA-thread calls a constraint solver, which searches for a distribution δ such that $\delta \models^{\text{dc}} \phi$ and $\delta_{\text{init}} \subseteq \delta$, where:

$$\delta_{\text{init}} = \{x \mapsto d \mid \text{the put pending on input port } x \text{ involves data item } d\} \atop \cup \{y \mapsto d \mid \text{memory cell } y \text{ contains data item } d\} \tag{1}$$

Constraint solving over a finite discrete domain (e.g., $\mathbb{D}$) is NP-complete [15]. Despite carefully and cleverly optimized backtracking searches, using general-purpose constraint solving techniques for solving a data constraint ϕ inflicts not only overhead proportional to ϕ's size but also a constant overhead for preparing, making, and processing the result of the call itself. Although we generally cannot escape using conventional constraint solving techniques, a practically relevant class of data constraints exists for which we can: the data constraints of many CA in practice are in fact declarative specifications of sequences of imperative instructions (including those in Figure 1). In this section, we therefore develop a technique for statically translating such a data constraint ϕ, off-line at compile-time, into a *data command*: a little imperative program that computes a distribution δ such that $\delta \models^{\text{dc}} \phi$ and $\delta_{\text{init}} \subseteq \delta$, without conventional constraint solving hassle. Essentially, we formalize and automate what a programmer would do if he/she were to write an imperative implementation of a declarative specification expressed as a data constraint. By the end of Section 4, we make the class of data constraints supported by our translation precise.

3.1   Data Commands

A data command is a word P generated by the following grammar:

$$P \quad ::= \quad \texttt{skip} \mid x := t \mid \texttt{if } \phi \texttt{ -> } P \texttt{ fi} \mid P \texttt{ ; } P$$

(We often write "value of x" instead of "the data item assigned to x".)

We adopt the following operational semantics of Apt et al. [16]. True to the idea that data commands compute solutions for data constraints, the *state* that a data command executes in is either a function from places to data items—a distribution!—or the distinguished symbol fail, which represents abnormal termination. A *configuration* is a pair of a data command and a state to execute that data command in. Let ε denote the *empty data command*, and equate $\varepsilon \texttt{ ; } P$ with P. Let $\delta[x := \mathsf{eval}_\delta(t)]$ denote an update of δ as usual. The following rules define the transition relation on configurations, denoted by $\Longrightarrow$.

$$\overline{(\texttt{skip}, \delta) \Longrightarrow (\varepsilon, \delta)} \qquad \overline{(x := t, \delta) \Longrightarrow (\varepsilon, \delta[x := \mathsf{eval}_\delta(t)])}$$

$$\frac{\delta \models^{\mathrm{dc}} \phi}{(\texttt{if } \phi \texttt{ -> } P \texttt{ fi}, \delta) \Longrightarrow (P, \delta)} \qquad \frac{\delta \not\models^{\mathrm{dc}} \phi}{(\texttt{if } \phi \texttt{ -> } P \texttt{ fi}, \delta) \Longrightarrow (\varepsilon, \mathsf{fail})}$$

$$\frac{(P, \delta) \Longrightarrow (P', \delta')}{(P \texttt{ ; } P'', \delta) \Longrightarrow (P' \texttt{ ; } P'', \delta')}$$

Note that $\texttt{if } \phi \texttt{ -> } P \texttt{ fi}$ commands are *failure* statements rather than *conditional* statements: if the current state violates the *guard* ϕ, execution abnormally terminates. The *partial correctness semantics*, which ignores abnormal termination, of a data command P in a state δ is the set of final states $\mathcal{M}(P, \{\delta\}) = \{\delta' \mid (P, \delta) \Longrightarrow^* (\varepsilon, \delta')\}$; its *total correctness semantics* is the set consisting of fail or its final states $\mathcal{M}_{\mathrm{tot}}(P, \{\delta\}) = \{\mathsf{fail} \mid (P, \{\delta\}) \Longrightarrow^* (\varepsilon, \mathsf{fail})\} \cup \mathcal{M}(P, \{\delta\})$.

Shortly, to prove the correctness of our translation from data constraints to data commands, we use Hoare logic [17], where *triples* $\{\phi\} P \{\phi'\}$ play a central role. In such triples, ϕ characterizes the set of input states, P denotes the data command to execute in those states, and ϕ' characterizes the set of output states. A triple $\{\phi\} P \{\phi'\}$ holds in the sense of partial (resp. total) correctness, if $\mathcal{M}(P, [\![\phi]\!]) \subseteq [\![\phi']\!]$ (resp. $\mathcal{M}_{\mathrm{tot}}(P, [\![\phi]\!]) \subseteq [\![\phi']\!]$). To prove properties of data commands, we use the following sound proof systems for partial (resp. total) correctness, represented by $\vdash$ (resp. $\vdash_{\mathrm{tot}}$) and adopted from Apt et al. [16].

$$\overline{\vdash \{\phi\} \texttt{ skip } \{\phi\}}$$

$$\begin{array}{c} \vdash \{\phi'\} P \{\phi''\} \\ \text{and } \phi \Rightarrow \phi' \\ \text{and } \phi'' \Rightarrow \phi''' \end{array} \qquad \begin{array}{c} \vdash \{\phi\} P \{\phi'\} \\ \text{and } \vdash \{\phi'\} P' \{\phi''\} \end{array}$$

$$\frac{}{\vdash \{\phi[\mathsf{d}_x := t]\} \; x := t \; \{\phi\}} \qquad \frac{}{\vdash \{\phi\} P \{\phi'''\}} \qquad \frac{}{\vdash \{\phi\} P \texttt{ ; } P' \{\phi''\}}$$

$$\frac{\vdash \{\phi \wedge \phi_{\mathrm{g}}\} P \{\phi'\}}{\vdash \{\phi\} \texttt{ if } \phi_{\mathrm{g}} \texttt{ -> } P \texttt{ fi } \{\phi'\}} \qquad \frac{\phi \Rightarrow \phi_{\mathrm{g}} \text{ and } \vdash_{\mathrm{tot}} \{\phi\} P \{\phi'\}}{\vdash_{\mathrm{tot}} \{\phi\} \texttt{ if } \phi_{\mathrm{g}} \texttt{ -> } P \texttt{ fi } \{\phi'\}}$$

The first four rules apply not only to $\vdash$ but also to $\vdash_{\mathrm{tot}}$. We use $\vdash$ to prove the soundness of our upcoming translation; we use $\vdash_{\mathrm{tot}}$ to prove its completeness.

3.2   Precedence

Recall the following typical data constraint over ports A, B, C, D, and E, where A and B are inputs, from Example in Figure 1b (its lower transition):

$$\phi = d_C \approx \mathsf{add}(d_A,\,d_B) \wedge d_D \approx d_C \wedge d_E \approx d_C \wedge \neg\mathsf{Odd}(d_D) \tag{2}$$

To translate data constraints to data commands, the idea is to enforce equalities, many of which occur in practice, with assignments and to check all remaining literals with failure statements. In the case of ϕ, for instance, we first assign the data items involved in their pending put operations to A and B, whose symbols are denoted by $\mathcal{I}^{-1}(\delta_{\mathrm{init}}(\mathsf{A}))$ and $\mathcal{I}^{-1}(\delta_{\mathrm{init}}(\mathsf{B}))$, with δ_{init} as defined in (1), page 122. Next, we assign the evaluation of $\mathsf{add}(d_A,\,d_B)$ to C. The order in which we subsequently assign the value of C to D and E does not matter. After the assignment to D, we check $\neg\mathsf{Odd}(d_D)$ with a failure statement. The following data command corresponds to one possible order of the last three steps.

$$P = \mathsf{A} := \mathcal{I}^{-1}(\delta_{\mathrm{init}}(\mathsf{A}))\ ;\ \mathsf{B} := \mathcal{I}^{-1}(\delta_{\mathrm{init}}(\mathsf{B}))\ ;\ \mathsf{C} := \mathsf{add}(d_A,\,d_B)\ ;$$
$$\mathsf{D} := d_C\ ;\ \mathtt{if}\ \neg\mathsf{Odd}(d_D)\ \mathtt{->}\ \mathtt{skip}\ \mathtt{fi}\ ;\ \mathsf{E} := d_C$$

If execution of P in an empty initial state successfully terminates, the resulting final state δ should satisfy ϕ (soundness). Moreover, if a δ' exists such that $\delta' \models^{\mathrm{dc}} \phi$ and $\delta_{\mathrm{init}} \subseteq \delta'$, execution of P should successfully terminate (completeness).

Soundness and completeness crucially depend on the order in which assignments and failure statements occur in P. For instance, changing the order of $\mathsf{D} := d_C$ and $\mathtt{if}\ \neg\mathsf{Odd}(d_D)\ \mathtt{->}\ \mathtt{skip}\ \mathtt{fi}$ yields a data command whose execution always fails (because D does not have a value yet on evaluating the guard of the failure statement). Such a data command is trivially sound but incomplete. Another complication is that not every equality can become an assignment. In a first class of cases, no operand matches d_x. An example is $\mathsf{add}(d_A,\,d_B) \approx \mathsf{mult}(d_A,\,d_B)$: this equality should become a failure statement, because neither of its two operands can be assigned to the other. In a second class of cases, multiple equality literals have an operand that matches d_x. An example is $\mathsf{C} \approx \mathsf{add}(d_A,\,d_B) \wedge \mathsf{C} \approx \mathsf{mult}(d_A,\,d_B)$: only one of these equalities should become an assignment, while the other should become a failure statement, to avoid conflicting assignments to C.

To deal with these complications, we define a *precedence relation* on literals that formalizes their dependencies. Recall that the data constraint in every transition label $(X,\,\phi)$ is a conjunction of literals. Let L_ϕ denote the set of literals in ϕ, and let $X_{\mathrm{in}} \subseteq X$ denote the set of *input places* (i.e., input ports and memory cells) involved in the transition. From L_ϕ and X_{in}, we construct a set of literals L to account for (i) symmetry of $\approx$ and (ii) the initial values of input places.

$$L = L_\phi \cup \{t_2 \approx t_1 \mid t_1 \approx t_2 \in L_\phi\} \cup \{d_x \approx \mathcal{I}^{-1}(\delta_{\mathrm{init}}(x)) \mid x \in X_{\mathrm{in}}\} \tag{3}$$

Obviously, $\delta \models^{\mathrm{dc}} \bigwedge L$ implies $\delta \models^{\mathrm{dc}} \phi$ for all δ (i.e., extending L_ϕ to L is sound). Now, let $\prec_L$ denote the precedence relation on L defined by the following rules:

$$\frac{d_x \approx t,\,\ell \in L\ \text{and}\ d_x \in \mathsf{Free}(\ell)}{d_x \approx t \prec_L \ell} \qquad \frac{\ell_1 \prec_L \ell_2 \prec_L \ell_3\ \text{and}\ \ell_2 \notin \{\ell_1,\,\ell_3\}}{\ell_1 \prec_L \ell_3} \tag{4}$$

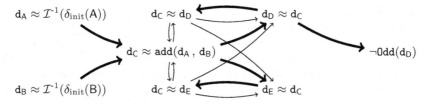

Fig. 3. Fragment of a digraph for an example precedence relation $\prec_L$ (e.g., without loops and without $\mathsf{add}(\mathsf{d_A}, \mathsf{d_B}) \approx \mathsf{d_C}$, for simplicity). An arc (ℓ, ℓ') corresponds to $\ell \prec_L \ell'$. Bold arcs represent a strict partial order extracted from $\prec_L$.

Informally, $\mathsf{d}_x \approx t \prec_L \ell$ means that assignment $x := t$ must precede ℓ (i.e., ℓ depends on x). Note also that the first rule deals with the first class of equalities-that-cannot-become-assignments; shortly, we comment on the second class.

For the sake of argument—generally, this is *not* the case—suppose that $\prec_L$ is a strict partial order on L. In that case, we can linearize $\prec_L$ to a total order $<$ on L (i.e., embedding $\prec_L$ into $<$ such that $\prec_L \subseteq <$) with a topological sort on the digraph $(L, \prec_L)$ [18,19]. Intuitively, such a linearization gives us an order in which we can translate literals in L to data commands in a sound and complete way. In Section 3.3, we give an algorithm for doing so and indeed prove its correctness. Problematically, however, $\prec_L$ is generally not a strict partial order on L: it is generally neither asymmetric nor irreflexive (i.e., graph-theoretically, it contains cycles). For instance, Figure 3 shows a fragment of the digraph $(L, \prec_L)$ for ϕ in (2), page 124, which contains cycles. For now, we defer this issue to Section 4, because it forms a concern orthogonal to our translation algorithm and its correctness. Until then, we simply assume the existence of a procedure for extracting a strict partial order from $\prec_L$, represented by bold arcs in Figure 3.

Henceforth, we assume that every $\mathsf{d}_{x_i} \approx t_i$ literal precedes all differently shaped literals in a linearization of $\prec_L$. Although this assumption is conceptually unnecessary, it simplifies some of our notation and proofs. Formally, we can enforce it by adding a third rule to the definition of $\prec_L$:

$$\frac{\mathsf{d}_x \approx t, \ell \in L \ \textbf{and} \ \left[\ell \neq \mathsf{d}_{x'} \approx t' \ \textbf{for all} \ x', t'\right]}{\mathsf{d}_x \approx t \prec_L \ell} \tag{5}$$

Proposition 1. *The rule in (5) introduces no cycles.*

(A proof appears in the technical report [14].)

3.3 Algorithm

We start by stating the precondition of our translation algorithm. Suppose that L as defined in (3), page 124, contains n $\mathsf{d}_x \approx t$ literals and m differently shaped literals. Let $\prec_L$ denote a strict partial order on L such that for every $\mathsf{d}_x \approx t \in L$ and for every $\mathsf{d}_y \in \mathsf{Free}(t)$, a $\mathsf{d}_y \approx t'$ literal precedes $\mathsf{d}_x \approx t$ according to $\prec_L$. Then, let $\ell_1 < \cdots < \ell_n < \ell_{n+1} < \cdots < \ell_{n+m}$ denote a linearization of $\prec_L$, where $\ell_i = \mathsf{d}_{x_i} \approx t_i$ for all $1 \leq i \leq n$. The three rules of $\prec_L$ in Section 3.2 induce precedence relations for which all previous conditions hold, *except* that $\prec_L$ does not necessarily denote a strict partial order; we address this issue in the next section. The previous conditions aside, we also assume $\{\mathsf{d}_{x_1}, \ldots, \mathsf{d}_{x_n}\} = \bigcup\{$ Free$(\ell_i) \mid 1 \leq i \leq n + m\}$. This extra condition means that for every free variable d_{x_i} in every literal in L, a $\mathsf{d}_{x_i} \approx t_i$ literal exists in the linearization. If this condition fails, some places can get a value only through search—exactly what we try to avoid—and not through assignment. In such cases, the data constraint is underspecified, and our translation algorithm is fundamentally inapplicable. Finally, we trivially assume that `nil` does not occur syntactically in any literal. A formal definition of this precondition appears in the technical report [14, Figure 10].

Figure 4 shows our algorithm. It first loops over the first n (according to $<$) $\mathsf{d}_x \approx t$ literals. If an assignment for x already exists in data command P, the algorithm translates $\mathsf{d}_x \approx t$ to a failure statement; if not, it translates $\mathsf{d}_x \approx t$ to an assignment. This approach resolves issues with the second class of equalities-that-cannot-become-assignments. After the first loop, the algorithm uses a second loop to translate the remaining m differently shaped literals to failure state-

```
P ← skip
i ← 1
while i ≤ n do
    if d_{x_i} ∈ {d_{x_j} | 1 ≤ j < i} then
        P ← P ; if d_{x_i} ≈ t_i -> skip fi
    else
        P ← P ; x_i := t_i
    i ← i + 1
while i ≤ n + m do
    P ← P ; if ℓ_i -> skip fi
    i ← i + 1
```

Fig. 4. Algorithm to translate data constraints to data commands

ments. The algorithm runs in time linear in $n + m$, and it clearly terminates.

The desired postcondition of the algorithm consists of its soundness and completeness. We define soundness as $\vdash \{\top\}\ P\ \{\ell_1 \wedge \cdots \wedge \ell_{n+m}\}$: after running the algorithm, execution of data command P yields a state that satisfies all literals in L on successful termination. We define completeness as $\left[\left[\delta' \stackrel{\mathrm{dc}}{\models} \ell_1 \wedge \cdots \wedge \ell_{n+m}\right.\right.$ **implies** $\vdash_{\mathrm{tot}} \{\top\}\ P\ \{\top\}\right]$ **for all** $\delta'\big]$: after running the algorithm, if a distribution δ' exists that satisfies all literals in L, data command P successfully terminated. Although soundness subsequently guarantees that the final state δ satisfies all literals in L, generally, $\delta \neq \delta'$. We use a different proof system for soundness (partial correctness, $\vdash$) than for completeness (total correctness, $\vdash_{\mathrm{tot}}$).

Theorem 1 ([14, **Theorem 3**]). *The algorithm is sound and complete.*

(A proof appears in the technical report [14].)

4   Handling Cycles

Our algorithm assumes that a precedence relation $\prec_L$ as defined in Section 3.2 is a strict partial order. However, this is generally not the case. In this section, we describe a procedure for extracting a strict partial order from $\prec_L$ without losing essential dependencies. We start by adding a distinguished symbol ★ to

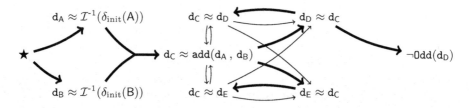

Fig. 5. Fragment of the B-graph corresponding to the digraph in Figure 3 (e.g., without looping B-arcs and without $\mathsf{add}(\mathsf{d_A}, \mathsf{d_B}) \approx \mathsf{d_C}$, for simplicity). Bold B-arcs represent an arborescence.

the domain of $\prec_L$, and we extend the definition of $\prec_L$ with the following rules:

$$\frac{\ell \in L \text{ and } \mathsf{Free}(\ell) = \emptyset}{\bigstar \prec_L \ell} \qquad \frac{\mathsf{d}_x \approx t \in L \text{ and } \mathsf{Free}(t) = \emptyset}{\bigstar \prec_L \mathsf{d}_x \approx t} \tag{6}$$

These rules state that literals without free variables (e.g., $\mathsf{d}_x \approx \mathcal{I}^{-1}(\delta_{\mathrm{init}}(x))$) do not depend on other literals. Now, $\prec_L$ is a strict partial order if the digraph $(L \cup \{\bigstar\},\ \prec_L)$ is a $\bigstar$-*arborescence*: a digraph consisting of $n-1$ arcs such that each of its n vertices is reachable from $\bigstar$ [20]. Equivalently, in a $\bigstar$-arborescence, $\bigstar$ has no incoming arcs, every other vertex has exactly one incoming arc, and the arcs form no cycles [20]. The first formulation is perhaps most intuitive here: every path from $\bigstar$ to some literal ℓ represents an order in which our algorithm should translate the literals on that path to ensure the correctness of the translation of ℓ. The second formulation simplifies observing that arborescences correspond to strict partial orders (by their cycle-freeness).

A naive approach to extract a strict partial order from $\prec_L$ is to compute a $\bigstar$-arborescence of the digraph $(L \cup \{\bigstar\},\ \prec_L)$. Unfortunately, however, this approach generally fails for $\mathsf{d}_x \approx t$ literals where t has more than one free variable. For instance, by definition, every arborescence of the digraph in Figure 3 has only one incoming arc for $\mathsf{d_C} \approx \mathsf{add}(\mathsf{d_A}, \mathsf{d_B})$, even though assignments to both A and B must precede an assignment to C. Because these dependencies exist as two separate arcs, no arborescence of a digraph can capture them. To solve this, we should somehow represent the dependencies of $\mathsf{d_C} \approx \mathsf{add}(\mathsf{d_A}, \mathsf{d_B})$ with a single incoming arc. We can do so by allowing arcs to have multiple tails (i.e., one for every free variable). In that case, we can replace the two separate incoming arcs of $\mathsf{d_C} \approx \mathsf{add}(\mathsf{d_A}, \mathsf{d_B})$ with a single two-tailed incoming arc as in Figure 5. The two tails make explicit that to evaluate an add-term, we need values for both its arguments: multiple tails represent a conjunction of dependencies of a literal.

By replacing single-tail-single-head arcs with multiple-tails-single-head arcs, we effectively transform the digraphs considered so far into B-*graphs*, a special kind of hypergraph with only B-*arcs* (i.e., *backward hyperarcs*, i.e., hyperarcs with exactly one head) [21]. Deriving a B-graph over literals from a precedence relation as defined in Section 3.2 is generally impossible though: their richer structure makes B-graphs more expressive—they give more information—than digraphs. In contrast, one can easily transform a B-graph to a precedence relation by splitting B-arcs into single-tailed arcs in the obvious way. Deriving precedence relations from more expressive B-graphs is therefore a correct way of obtaining strict partial orders that satisfy the precondition of our algorithm. Doing so just eliminates information that this algorithm does not care about anyway.

Thus, we propose the following. Instead of formalizing dependencies among literals in a set $L \cup \{\star\}$ directly as a precedence relation, we first formalize those dependencies as a B-graph. If the resulting B-graph is a $\star$-arborescence, we can directly extract a precedence relation $\prec_L$. Otherwise, we compute a $\star$-arborescence of the resulting B-graph and extract a precedence relation $\prec_L$ afterward. Either way, because $\prec_L$ is extracted from a $\star$-arborescence, it is a strict partial order whose linearization satisfies the precondition of our algorithm.

Let $\blacktriangleleft_L$ denote a set of B-arcs on $L \cup \{\star\}$ defined by the following rules, plus the straightforward B-arcs adaptation of the rules in (6), page 127:

$$
\frac{
\begin{array}{l}
\ell \in L \\
\text{and } \mathsf{Free}(\ell) = \{\mathsf{d}_{x_1}, \ldots, \mathsf{d}_{x_k}\} \\
\text{and } \mathsf{d}_{x_1} \approx t_1, \ldots, \mathsf{d}_{x_k} \approx t_k \in L
\end{array}
}{
\{\mathsf{d}_{x_1} \approx t_1, \ldots, \mathsf{d}_{x_k} \approx t_k\} \blacktriangleleft_L \ell
}
\qquad
\frac{
\begin{array}{l}
\mathsf{d}_x \approx t \in L \\
\text{and } \mathsf{Free}(t) = \{\mathsf{d}_{x_1}, \ldots, \mathsf{d}_{x_k}\} \\
\text{and } \mathsf{d}_{x_1} \approx t_1, \ldots, \mathsf{d}_{x_k} \approx t_k \in L
\end{array}
}{
\{\mathsf{d}_{x_1} \approx t_1, \ldots, \mathsf{d}_{x_k} \approx t_k\} \blacktriangleleft_L \mathsf{d}_x \approx t
}
\tag{7}
$$

The first rule generalizes the first rule in (4), page 124, by joining sets of dependencies of a literal in a single B-arc. The second rule states that $\mathsf{d}_x \approx t$ literals do not necessarily depend on d_x (as implied by the first rule) but only on the free variables in t: intuitively, a value for x can be derived from values of the free variables in t (cf. assignments). Note that literals can have multiple incoming B-arcs. Such multiple incoming B-arcs represent a disjunction of conjunctions of dependencies. Importantly, as long as all dependencies represented by *one* incoming B-arc are satisfied, the other incoming B-arcs do not matter. An arborescence, which contains one incoming B-arc for every literal, therefore preserves enough dependencies. Shortly, Theorem 2 makes this more precise. Figure 5 shows a fragment of the B-graph for data constraint ϕ in (2), page 124.

One can straightforwardly compute an arborescence of a B-graph $(L \cup \{\star\},$ $\blacktriangleleft_L)$ with a graph exploration algorithm reminiscent of breadth-first search. Let $\blacktriangleleft_L^{\text{arb}} \subseteq \blacktriangleleft_L$ denote the aborescence under computation, and let $L_{\text{done}} \subseteq L$ denote the set of vertices (i.e., literals in L) that have already been explored; initially, $\blacktriangleleft_L^{\text{arb}} = \emptyset$ and $L_{\text{done}} = \{\star\}$. Now, given some L_{done}, compute a set of vertices L_{next} that are connected only to vertices in L_{done} by a B-arc in $\blacktriangleleft_L$. Then, for every vertex in L_{next}, add an incoming B-arc to $\blacktriangleleft_L^{\text{arb}}$.[1] Afterward, add L_{next} to L_{done}. Repeat this process until L_{next} becomes empty. Once that happens, either $\blacktriangleleft_L^{\text{arb}}$ contains an arborescence (if $L_{\text{done}} = L$) or no arborescence exists. This computation runs in linear time, in the size of the B-graph. See also Footnote 1.

---

[1] If a vertex ℓ in L_{next} has multiple incoming B-arcs, the choice among them matters not: the choice is local, because every B-arc has only one head (i.e., adding an ℓ-headed B-arc to $\blacktriangleleft_L^{\text{arb}}$ cannot cause another vertex to get multiple incoming B-arcs, which would invalidate the arborescence). General hypergraphs, whose hyperarcs can have multiple heads, violate this property (i.e., the choice of which hyperarc to add is global instead of local). Computing arborescences of such hypergraphs is NP-complete [22], whereas one can compute aborescences of B-graphs in linear time.

Given $\blacktriangleleft_L^{\mathrm{arb}}$, the following rules yield a cycle-free precedence relation on $L \cup \{\bigstar\}$:

$$\frac{\{\ell_1, \ldots, \ell_k\} \blacktriangleleft_L^{\mathrm{arb}} \ell \text{ and } 1 \leq i \leq k}{\ell_i \prec_L \ell} \quad \frac{\ell_1 \prec_L \ell_2 \prec_L \ell_3 \text{ and } \ell_2 \notin \{\ell_1, \ell_3\}}{\ell_1 \prec_L \ell_3} \quad (8)$$

Theorem 2 ([14, Theorem 4]). $\prec_L$ *as defined by the rules in (5)(8), pages 125 and 129, is a strict partial order and a large enough subset of $\prec_L$ as defined by the rules in (4)(5)(6), pages 124, 125, and 127, to satisfy the precondition of our translation algorithm in Section 3.3.*

(A proof appears in the technical report [14].) For instance, the bold arcs in Figure 3 represent the precedence relation for the arborescence in Figure 5.

If a $\bigstar$-arborescence of $(L \cup \{\bigstar\}, \blacktriangleleft_L)$ does *not* exist, every $|L|$-cardinality subset of $\blacktriangleleft_L$ has at least one vertex ℓ that is unreachable from $\bigstar$. In that case, by the rules in (6), page 127, ℓ depends on at least one free variable (otherwise, $\{\bigstar\} \blacktriangleleft_L \ell$). Because no B-graph equivalent of a path [23] exists from $\bigstar$ to ℓ, the other literals in L fail to resolve at least one of ℓ's dependencies. This occurs, for instance, when ℓ depends on d_y, while L contains no $\mathsf{d}_y \approx t$ literal. Another example is a recursive literal $\mathsf{d}_x \approx t$ with $\mathsf{d}_x \in \mathsf{Free}(t)$: unless another literal $\mathsf{d}_x \approx t'$ with $t \neq t'$ exists, all its incoming B-arcs contain loops to itself, meaning that no arborescence exists. In practice, such cases inherently require constraint solving techniques to find a value for d_x. Nonexistence of a $\bigstar$-arborescence thus signals a fundamental boundary to the applicability of our translation algorithm (although more advanced techniques of translating some parts of a data constraint to a data command and leaving other parts to a constraint solver are imaginable and left for future work). Thus, the set of data constraints to which our translation algorithm is applicable contains exactly those (i) whose B-graph has a $\bigstar$-arborescence, which guarantees linearizability of the induced precedence, and (ii) that satisfy also the rest of the precondition of our algorithm in Section 3.3.

5 Preliminary Performance Results

In the work that we presented in this paper, we focused on the formal definition of our translation and its proof of correctness. A comprehensive quantitative evaluation remains future work. Indeed, constructing a set of representative examples, identifying independent variables that may influence the outcome (e.g., number of cores, memory architecture, etc.), setting up and performing the corresponding experiments, processing/analyzing the measurements, and eventually presenting the results is a whole other challenge. Still, presenting an optimization technique and not shedding any light on its performance may leave the reader with an unsatisfactory feeling. Therefore, in this section, we provide preliminary performance results to give a rough indication of our translation's merits.

We extended our most recent CA-to-Java compiler and used this compiler to generate both *constraint-based* coordination code (i.e., generated without our translation) and *command-based* coordination code (i.e., generated with our translation) for ten coordinators modeled as CA: three elementary primitives

	Constr.	Comm.	×		Constr.	Comm.	×
Sync	33119333	39800986	1.20	Language2	17278247	24646838	1.43
Fifo	33050122	41398084	1.25	Language4	4423326	11512506	2.60
Replicator	17961129	21803913	1.21	Language6	1062306	5294838	4.98
Example	10573857	12687767	1.20	Language8	194374	1746440	8.98
Fibonacci	1818671	88947751	48.91	Language10	25649	362050	14.12

Fig. 6. Preliminary performance results for ten coordinators. Column *"Constr."* shows results for constraint-based implementations (in number of coordination steps completed in four minutes); column *"Comm."* shows restults for command-based implementations; column "×" shows the ratio of the second over the first.

from Figures 1a and 2a (to see how our optimization affects such basic cases) and seven more complex composites, including those in Figures 1b and 2b. See Section 2 for a discussion of these coordinators' behavior. The constraint-based implementations use a custom constraint solver with constraint propagation [24], tailored to our setting of data constraints. The data commands in the generated command-based implementations are imperative Java code, very similar to what programmers would hand-craft (modulo style).

In total, thus, we generated twenty coordinators in Java. We ran each of those implementations ten times on a quadcore machine at 2.4 GHz (no Hyper-Threading; no Turbo Boost) and averaged our measurements. In every run, we warmed up the JVM for thirty seconds before starting to measure the number of coordination steps that an implementation could finish in the subsequent four minutes. Figure 6 shows our results. The command-based implementations outperform their constraint-based versions in all cases. The Language$i$ coordinators furthermore show that the speed-up achieved by their command-based implementations increases as i increases. This may suggest that our optimization becomes relatively more effective as the size/complexity of a coordinator increases, as also witnessed by Fibonacci. Figure 6 shows first evidence for the effectiveness of our translation in practice, although further study is necessary.

6   Discussion

In constraint programming, it is well-known that "if domain specific methods are available they should be applied *instead* [sic] of the general methods" [24, page 2]. The work presented in this paper takes this guideline to an extreme: essentially, every data command generated for a data constraint ϕ by our translation algorithm is a little constraint solver capable of solving only ϕ, with good performance. This good performance comes from the fact that the order of performing assignments and failure statements has already been determined at compile-time. Moreover, this precomputed order guarantees that backtracking is unnecessary: the data constraint for ϕ finds a solution if one exists without search (i.e., Theorem 1). In contrast, general constraint solvers need to do this work, which our approach does at compile-time, as part of the solving process at run-time.

Execution of data commands bears similarities with *constraint propagation* techniques [24], in particular with *forward checking* [25,26]. Generally, in constraint propagation, the idea is to reduce the search space of a given *constraint satisfaction problem* (CSP) by transforming it into an equivalent "simpler" CSP, where variables have smaller domains, or where constraints refer to fewer variables. With forward checking, whenever a variable x gets a value v, a constraint solver removes values from the domains of all subsequent variables that, together with v, violate a constraint. In the case of an equality $x = y$, for instance, forward checking reduces the domain of y to the singleton $\{v\}$ after an assignment of v to x. That same property of equality is implicitly used in executing our data commands (i.e., instead of representing the domain of a variable and the reduction of this domain to a singleton explicitly, we directly make an assignment).

Our translation from data constraints to data commands may also remind one of classical *Gaussian eliminination* for solving systems of linear equations over the reals [24]: there too, variables are ordered and values/expressions for some variables are substituted into other expressions. The difference is that we have functions, relations, and our data domain may include other data types, which makes solving data constraints directly via Gaussian elimination at least not obvious. However, Gaussian elimination does seem useful as a preprocessing step for translating certain data constraints to data commands that our current algorithm does not support. Future work should clarify this possibility.

Clarke et al. worked on purely constraint-based implementations of coordinators [27]. Essentially, they specify not only the transition labels of a CA as boolean constraints but also its state space and transition relation. In recent work, Proença and Clarke developed a variant of compile-time *predicate abstraction* to improve performance [28]. They used this technique also to allow a form of interaction between the constraint solver and external components during constraint solving [29]. The work of Proença and Clarke resembles ours in the sense that we all try to "simplify" constraints at compile-time. Main differences are that (i) we fully avoid constraint solving and (ii) we consider a richer language of data constraints. For instance, Proença and Clarke have only unary functions in their language, which would have cleared our need for B-graphs.

References

1. Jongmans, S.-S.T.Q., Halle, S., Arbab, F.: Automata-Based Optimization of Interaction Protocols for Scalable Multicore Platforms. In: Kühn, E., Pugliese, R. (eds.) COORDINATION 2014. LNCS, vol. 8459, pp. 65–82. Springer, Heidelberg (2014)
2. Jongmans, S.S., Halle, S., Arbab, F.: Reo: A Dataflow Inspired Language for Multicore. In: DFM, 42–50. IEEE (2013)
3. Baier, C., Sirjani, M., Arbab, F., Rutten, J.: Modeling component connectors in Reo by constraint automata. SCP 61, 75–113 (2006)
4. Wegner, P.: Coordination as Constrained Interaction (Extended Abstract). In: Hankin, C., Ciancarini, P. (eds.) COORDINATION 1996. LNCS, vol. 1061, pp. 28–33. Springer, Heidelberg (1996)
5. Jongmans, S.-S.T.Q., Arbab, F.: Global consensus through local synchronization. In: Canal, C., Villari, M. (eds.) ESOCC 2013. CCIS, vol. 393, pp. 174–188. Springer, Heidelberg (2013)

6. Jongmans, S.S., Arbab, F.: Toward Sequentializing Overparallelized Protocol Code. In: ICE. EPTCS, vol. 166. CoRR, 38–44 (2014)

7. Jongmans, S.-S., Santini, F., Arbab, F.: Partially-Distributed Coordination with Reo. In: PDP 2014, pp. 697–706. IEEE (2014)

8. Arbab, F.: Reo: a channel-based coordination model for component composition. MSCS 14(3), 329–366 (2004)

9. Arbab, F.: Puff, The Magic Protocol. In: Agha, G., Danvy, O., Meseguer, J. (eds.) Formal Modeling: Actors, Open Systems, Biological Systems. LNCS, vol. 7000, pp. 169–206. Springer, Heidelberg (2011)

10. Arbab, F., Kokash, N., Meng, S.: Towards Using Reo for Compliance-Aware Business Process Modeling. In: Margaria, T., Steffen, B. (eds.) ISoLA 2008. CCIS, vol. 17, pp. 108–123. Springer, Heidelberg (2008)

11. Changizi, B., Kokash, N., Arbab, F.: A Unified Toolset for Business Process Model Formalization. In: Buhnova, B., Happe, J. (eds.) FESCA 2010, pp. 147–156 (2010)

12. Meng, S., Arbab, F., Baier, C.: Synthesis of Reo circuits from scenario-based interaction specifications. SCP 76(8), 651–680 (2011)

13. Bliudze, S., Sifakis, J.: Causal semantics for the algebra of connectors. FMSD 36(2), 167–194 (2010)

14. Jongmans, S.S., Arbab, F.: Take Command of Your Constraints (Technical Report). Technical Report FM-1501, CWI (2015)

15. Russell, S., Norvig, P.: Artificial Intelligence, 2nd edn. Prentice-Hall (2003)

16. Apt, K., de Boer, F., Olderog, E.-R.: Verification of Sequential and Concurrent Programs, 3rd edn. Springer (2009)

17. Hoare, T.: An Axiomatic Basis for Computer Programming. CACM 12(10), 576–580 (1969)

18. Kahn, A.: Topological Sorting in Large Networks. CACM 5(11), 558–562 (1962)

19. Knuth, D.: Fundamental Algorithms, 3rd edn. The Art of Computer Programming, vol. 1. Addison-Wesley (1997)

20. Korte, B., Vygen, J.: Combinatorial Optimization: Theory and Algorithms, 4th edn. Algorithms and Combinatorics, vol. 21. Springer (2008)

21. Gallo, G., Longo, G., Pallottino, S., Nguyen, S.: Directed hypergraphs and applications. DAM 42, 177–201 (1993)

22. Woeginger, G.: The complexity of finding arborescences in hypergraphs. IPL 44, 161–164 (1992)

23. Ausiello, G., Franciosa, P.G., Frigioni, D.: Directed Hypergraphs: Problems, Algorithmic Results, and a Novel Decremental Approach. In: Restivo, A., Ronchi Della Rocca, S., Roversi, L. (eds.) ICTCS 2001. LNCS, vol. 2202, pp. 312–328. Springer, Heidelberg (2001)

24. Apt, K.: Principles of Constraint Programming. Cambridge University Press (2009)

25. Bessière, C., Meseguer, P., Freuder, E., Larrosa, J.: On forward checking for non-binary constraint satisfaction. Artificial Intelligence 141, 205–224 (2002)

26. McGregor, J.: Relational consistency algorithms and their application in finding subgraph and graph isomorphism. Information Science 19, 229–250 (1979)

27. Clarke, D., Proença, J., Lazovik, A., Arbab, F.: Channel-based coordination via constraint satisfaction. SCP 76(8), 681–710 (2011)

28. Proença, J., Clarke, D.: Data Abstraction in Coordination Constraints. In: Canal, C., Villari, M. (eds.) ESOCC 2013. CCIS, vol. 393, pp. 159–173. Springer, Heidelberg (2013)

29. Proença, J., Clarke, D.: Interactive Interaction Constraints. In: De Nicola, R., Julien, C. (eds.) COORDINATION 2013. LNCS, vol. 7890, pp. 211–225. Springer, Heidelberg (2013)

A Labelled Semantics
for Soft Concurrent Constraint Programming

Fabio Gadducci[1]([✉]), Francesco Santini[2], Luis F. Pino[3], and Frank D. Valencia[4]

[1] Dipartimento di Informatica, Università di Pisa, Pisa, Italy
fabio.gadducci@unipi.it
[2] Istituto di Informatica e Telematica, CNR, Pisa, Italy
francesco.santini@iit.cnr.it
[3] Dipartimento di Matematica e Informatica, Università di Cagliari, Cagliari, Italy
luis.pino@unica.it
[4] CNRS and LIX, École Polytechnique de Paris, Palaiseau, France
frank.valencia@lix.polytechnique.fr

Abstract. We present a labelled semantics for Soft Concurrent Constraint Programming (SCCP), a language where concurrent agents may synchronize on a shared store by either posting or checking the satisfaction of (soft) constraints. SCCP generalizes the classical formalism by parametrising the constraint system over an order-enriched monoid: the monoid operator is not required to be idempotent, thus adding the same information several times may change the store. The novel operational rules are shown to offer a sound and complete co-inductive technique to prove the original equivalence over the unlabelled semantics.

1 Introduction

Concurrent Constraint Programming (CCP) [21] is a language based on a shared-memory communication pattern: processes may interact by either posting or checking partial information, which is represented as constraints in a global store. CCP belongs to the larger family of process calculi, thus a syntax-driven operational semantics represents the computational steps. For example, the term **tell**(c) is the process that posts c in the store, and the term **ask**(c) $\rightarrow$ P is the process that executes P if c can be derived from the information in the store.

The formalism is parametric with respect to the entailment relation. Under the name of *constraint system*, the information recorded on the store is structured as a partial order (actually, a lattice) $\leq$, where $c \leq d$ means that c can be derived from d. Under a few requirements over such systems, CCP has been provided with (coincident) operational and denotational semantics. More recently, a labelled semantics has also been provided, and the associated weak bisimilarity proved to coincide with the original semantics [1].

The research has been partially supported by the MIUR PRIN 2010LHT4KM CINA and PRIN 2010XSEMLC "Security Horizons", by the ANR 12IS02001 PACE, and by the Aut. Reg. of Sardinia P.I.A. 2010 "Social Glue".

© IFIP International Federation for Information Processing 2015
T. Holvoet and M. Viroli (Eds.): COORDINATION 2015, LNCS 9037, pp. 133–149, 2015.
DOI: 10.1007/978-3-319-19282-6_9

A key aspect of CCP is the *idempotency* of the operator for composing constraints: adding the same information twice does not change the store. On the contrary, the soft variant of the formalism (Soft CCP, or just SCCP [7]) drops idempotency: constraint systems in SCCP may distinguish the number of occurrences of a piece of information. Dropping idempotency requires a complete reworking of the theory. Although an operational semantics for SCCP has been devised [7], hitherto neither the denotational nor the labelled one has been reintroduced. This is unfortunate since due to its generality, SCCP has been successfully applied as a specification formalism for negotiation of Service Level Agreements [10], or the enforcement of ACL-based access control [8].

The objective of our work is the development of a general theory for the operational as well as the denotational semantics of SCCP, via the introduction of suitable behavioral equivalences. Reaching this objective is technically challenging, since most of the simplicity of CCP is based precisely on the premise that posting an information multiple times is the same as posting it only once.

As a language, SCCP has been used as a specification formalism for agents collaborating via a shared knowledge basis, possibly with temporal features [4]. Thus, on a methodological level, the development of behavioural equivalences for SCCP may result in the improvement on the analysis techniques for agents that need to reason guided by their preferences, more so if their knowledge (e.g. of their environment) is not complete. Indeed, the paper shows that systems specified by SCCP may benefit from the feasible proof and verification methods typically associated with bisimilarity, compared with the classical analysis based on (possibly infinite) sequences of computations. This is true also whenever agents have to coordinate despite the global problem being over-constrained (i.e., admitting no solution), and *simulation* may serve as a powerful mechanism for distilling suitable approximated solutions.

Contribution. The work in [21] establishes a denotational semantics for CCP and an equational theory for infinite agents. More recently, in [1] the authors prove that the axiomatisation is underlying a specific weak bisimilarity among agents, thus providing a clear operational understanding. The key ingredients are a complete lattice as the domain of the store, with least upper bound for constraint combination, and a notion of compactness such that domain equations for the parallel composition of recursive agents would be well-defined. On the contrary, the soft version [7] drops the upper bound for combination in exchange of a more general monoidal operator. Thus, the domain is potentially just a (not necessarily complete) partial order, possibly with finite meets and a residuation operator (a kind of inverse of the monoidal one) in order to account for algorithms concerning constraint propagation. Indeed, the main use of SCCP has been in the generalisation of classical constraint satisfaction problems, hence the lack of investigation about e.g. compactness and denotational semantics.

Therefore, in this paper we connect the works on the soft [7] and the classical (also indicated in the literature as "crisp") [21,1] paradigm by investigating a labelled semantics for SCCP. In particular, the results will be a mix of those investigated in the two communities, namely, a monoid whose underlying set of elements form a complete lattice. We will recast the notion of compactness, and afterwards the SCCP semantics, thus making the work a direct extension of the proposal for the crisp language. We will then introduce a novel labelled semantics for SCCP which will allow us to give a sound and complete technique to prove the equivalence over the unlabelled semantics.

2 A Few Technical Remarks (with Some Novelty)

This section recalls the main notions we are going to need later on. First of all, we present some basic facts concerning monoids [15] enriched over complete lattices. These are used to recast the standard presentation of the soft constraints paradigm, and to generalise the classical crisp one.

2.1 Lattice-Enriched Monoids

Definition 1 (Complete Lattices). *A partial order (PO) is a pair $\langle A, \leq \rangle$ such that A is a set of values and $\leq \subseteq A \times A$ is a reflexive, transitive, and anti-symmetric relation. A complete lattice (CL) is a PO such that any subset of A has a least upper bound (LUB).*

We denote as $\bigvee X$ the necessarily unique LUB of a subset $X \subseteq A$, and explicitly $\bot$ and $\top$ if we are considering the empty set and the whole A, respectively: the former is the bottom and the latter is the top of the PO. Obviously, CLs also have the greatest lower bound (GLB) for any subset $Y \subseteq A$, denoted as $\bigwedge Y$.

In the following we fix a CL $\mathbb{C} = \langle A, \leq \rangle$.

Definition 2 (Compact Elements). *An element $a \in A$ is compact (or finite) if whenever $a \leq \bigvee Y$ there exists a finite subset $X \subseteq Y$ such that $a \leq \bigvee X$.*

Note that for complete lattices the definition of compactness given above coincides with the one using directed subsets. It will be easier to generalise it, though, to compactness with respect to the monoidal operator (see Def. 6). We let $A^C \subseteq A$ denote the set of compact elements of $\mathbb{C}$. Note that A^C might be trivial. Consider e.g. the CL $\langle [0, 1], \geq \rangle$ (the segment of the reals with the inverse of the usual order), used for probabilistic constraints [12]: only the bottom element 1 is compact. As we will see, the situation for the soft paradigm is more nuanced.

Definition 3 (Monoids). *A commutative monoid with identity (IM) is a triple $\langle A, \otimes, 1 \rangle$ where $\otimes : A \times A \rightarrow A$ is a commutative and associative function and $\forall a \in A. \otimes (a, 1) = a$.*

We will often use an infix notation, such as $a \otimes b$ for $a, b \in A$. The monoidal operator can be defined for any multi-set: it is given for a family of elements $a_i \in A$ indexed over a finite, non-empty set I, and it is denoted by $\bigotimes_{i \in I} a_i$. Whenever for an index set I all the a_i's are different, we write $\bigotimes S$ instead of $\bigotimes_{i \in I} a_i$ for the set $S = \{a_i \mid i \in I\}$. Conventionally, we also denote $\bigotimes \emptyset = \bot$. We now move our attention to the domain of values we are going to consider.

Definition 4 (CL-enriched IMs). *A CL-enriched IM (CLIM) is a triple* $\mathbb{S} = \langle A, \leq, \otimes \rangle$ *such that* $\langle A, \leq \rangle$ *is a CL,* $\langle A, \otimes, \perp \rangle$ *is an IM, and furthermore the following holds*

(distributivity) $\forall a \in A. \forall X \subseteq A. a \otimes \bigwedge X = \bigwedge \{a \otimes x \mid x \in X\}$

Remark 1. The reader who is familiar with the soft constraint literature may have noticed that we have basically rewritten the standard presentation using a CLIM instead of an absorptive semiring, recently popularized as c-semiring [6], where the $a \oplus b$ operator is replaced by the binary LUB $a \vee b$. Besides what we consider a streamlined presentation, the main advantage in the use of CLIMs is the easiness in defining the LUB of infinite sets and, as a consequence, the notion of $\otimes$-compactness given below. An alternative solution using infinite sums can be found in [14, Section 3], and a possible use is sketched in [5].

Thanks to distributivity, we can show that $\otimes$ is monotone, and since $\perp$ is the identity of the monoid, monotonicity implies that the combination of constraints is increasing, i.e., $\forall a, b \in A. a \leq a \otimes b$ holds. Finally, we recall that by definition $\bigwedge \emptyset = \top$, so that $\forall a \in A. a \otimes \top = \top$ also holds.[1]

In the following, we fix a CLIM $\mathbb{S} = \langle A, \leq, \otimes \rangle$. The next step is to provide a notion of infinite composition. Our definition is from [15] (see also [14, p. 42]).

Definition 5 (Infinite Composition). *Let I be a (countable) set of indexes. Then, composition $\bigotimes_{i \in I} a_i$ is given as $\bigvee_{J \subseteq I} \bigotimes_{j \in J} a_j$ for all finite subsets J.*

Should I be finite, the definition gives back the usual multiset composition, since $\otimes$ is monotone and increasing. Indeed, as the infinitary composition is also monotone and increasing, and by construction $\bigotimes A = \bigvee A = \top$ holds. We now provide a notion of compactness with respect to the monoidal operator.

Definition 6 ($\otimes$-compact Elements). *An element $a \in A$ is $\otimes$-compact (or $\otimes$-finite) if whenever $a \leq \bigotimes_{i \in I} a_i$ then there exists a finite subset $J \subseteq I$ such that $a \leq \bigotimes_{j \in J} a_j$.*

We let $A^{\otimes} \subseteq A$ denote the set of $\otimes$-compact elements of $\mathbb{S}$. It is easy to show that a compact element is also $\otimes$-compact, i.e. $A^C \subseteq A^{\otimes}$. Indeed, the latter notion is definitively more flexible. Consider e.g. the CLIM $\langle [0, 1], \geq, \times \rangle$ examined above, which corresponds to the segment of the reals with the inverse of the usual order and multiplication as monoidal product. Since any infinite multiplication tends to 0, then all the elements are $\otimes$-compact, except the top element itself, that is, precisely 0.

Remark 2. It is easy to show that idempotency implies that $\bigotimes$ coincides with LUBs, that is, $\bigotimes S = \bigvee S$ for all subsets $S \subseteq A$. In other words, the whole soft structure collapses to a complete distributive lattice. Indeed, requiring distributivity makes the soft paradigm not fully comparable with the crisp one. We are going to discuss it again in the concluding remarks.

---

[1] A symmetric choice $\langle A, \otimes, \top \rangle$ with distributivity with respect to $\bigvee$ (and thus $a \otimes \perp = \perp$) is possible: the monoidal operator would be decreasing, so that for example $a \otimes b \leq a$. Indeed, this is the usual order in the semiring-based approach to soft constraints [5].

2.2   Some Operators: Residuation and Cylindrification

We close this section by presenting two operators on CL-enriched IMs.

The first is a simple construction for building a weak inverse of the monoidal operator in CL-enriched monoids, known in the literature as residuation [14,13].

Definition 7 (Residuation). *Let $a, b \in A$. The residuation of a with respect to b is defined as $a \ominus b = \bigwedge \{c \in A \mid a \leq b \otimes c\}$.*

The definition conveys the intuitive meaning of a division operator: indeed, $a \leq b \otimes (a \ominus b)$, thanks to distributivity. Also, $(a \otimes b) \ominus b \leq a$ and $a \ominus (b \otimes c) = (a \ominus b) \ominus c$. Residuation is monotone on the first argument: if $a \leq b$ then $a \ominus c \leq b \ominus c$ and $a \ominus b = \bot$. For more properties of residuation we refer to [3, Tab. 4.1].

Most important for our formalism is the following result on $\otimes$-compactness.

Lemma 1. *Let $a, b \in A$. If a is $\otimes$-compact, so is $a \ominus b$.*

Proof. If $a \ominus b \leq \bigotimes_{i \in I} a_i$, then by monotonicity $a \leq \bigotimes_{i \in I \cup \{*\}} a_i$ for $a_* = b$. By $\otimes$-compactness of a there exists a finite $J \subseteq I$ such that $a \leq \bigotimes_{j \in J \cup \{*\}} a_j$, and by the definition of division $a \ominus b \leq \bigotimes_{j \in J} a_j$, hence the result holds. $\qquad\square$

Most standard soft instances (boolean, fuzzy, probabilistic, weighted, and so on) are described by CL-enriched monoids and are residuated: see e.g. [5]. For these instances the $\ominus$ operator is used to (partially) remove constraints from the store, and as such is going to be used in Section 4. In fact, in the soft literature it is required a tighter relation of (full) invertibility, also satisfied by all the previous CLIMs instances, stated in our framework by the definition below.

Definition 8. *A CLIM $\mathbb{S}$ is invertible if $b \leq a$ implies $b \otimes (a \ominus b) = a$ for all $a, b \in A^{\otimes}$.*

We now consider two families of operators for modelling the hiding of local variables and the passing of parameters in soft CCP. They can be considered as generalised notions of existential quantifier and diagonal element [21], which are expressed in terms of operators of cylindric algebras [18]. [2]

Definition 9 (Cylindrification). *Let V be a set of variables. A cylindric operator $\exists$ over $\mathbb{S}$ and V is given by a family of monotone, $\otimes$-compactness preserving functions $\exists_x : A \to A$ indexed by elements in V such that for all $a, b \in A$ and $x, y \in V$*

1. $\exists_x a \leq a$;
2. $\exists_x (a \otimes \exists_x b) = \exists_x a \otimes \exists_x b$;
3. $\exists_x \exists_y a = \exists_y \exists_x a$.

Let $a \in A$. The support of a is the set of variables $sv(a) = \{x \in V \mid \exists_x a \neq a\}$.

For a finite $X \subseteq V$ we denote by $\exists_X a$ any sequence of function applications. Also, we fix a set of variables V and a cylindric operator $\exists$ over CLIM $\mathbb{S}$ and V.

---

[2] However, since we consider monoids instead of groups, the set of axioms of diagonal operators is included in the standard one for cylindric algebras.

Definition 10 (Diagonalisation). *A diagonal operator δ for $\exists$ is given by a family of idempotent elements $\delta_{x,y} \in A$ indexed by pairs of elements in V such that $\delta_{x,y} = \delta_{y,x}$ and for all $a \in A$ and $x, y, z \in V$*

1. *$\delta_{x,x} = \bot$;*
2. *if $z \notin \{x, y\}$ then $\delta_{x,y} = \exists_z(\delta_{x,z} \otimes \delta_{z,y})$;*
3. *if $x \neq y$ then $a \leq \delta_{x,y} \otimes \exists_x(a \otimes \delta_{x,y})$.*

Axioms 1 and 2 above plus idempotency imply that $\exists_x \delta_{x,y} = \bot$, which in turn implies (again with axiom 2 and idempotency of $\exists$) that $sv(\delta_{x,y}) = \{x, y\}$ for $x \neq y$. Diagonal operators are going to be used for modelling variable substitution and parameter passing. In the following, we fix a diagonal operator δ for $\exists$.

Definition 11 (Substitution). *Let $x, y \in V$ and $a \in A$. The substitution $a[^y/_x]$ is defined as a if $x = y$ and as $\exists_x(\delta_{x,y} \otimes a)$ otherwise.*

We now rephrase some of the laws holding for the crisp case (see [1, p.140]).

Lemma 2. *Let $x, y \in V$ and $a \in A$. Then it holds*

1. *$y \notin sv(a)$ implies $(a[^y/_x])[^x/_y] = a$;*
2. *$a[^y/_x] \otimes b[^y/_x] = (a \otimes b)[^y/_x]$;*
3. *$x \notin sv(a[^y/_x])$.*

Proof. Consider e.g. the most difficult item 2. By definition $a[^y/_x] \otimes b[^y/_x] = \exists_x(\delta_{x,y} \otimes a) \otimes \exists_x(\delta_{x,y} \otimes b)$, which in turn coincides with $\exists_x(\delta_{x,y} \otimes a \otimes \exists_x(\delta_{x,y} \otimes b))$ by axiom 2 of $\exists$; by axiom 3 of $\delta_{x,y}$ we have that $(a \otimes b)[^y/_x] = \exists_x(\delta_{x,y} \otimes a \otimes b) \leq \exists_x(\delta_{x,y} \otimes a \otimes \exists_x(\delta_{x,y} \otimes b))$, while the vice versa holds by the monotonicity of $\exists_x$. $\square$

3   Deterministic Soft CCP

We now introduce our language. We fix an invertible CLIM $\mathbb{S} = \langle C, \leq, \otimes \rangle$, which is also cylindric over a set of variables V, denoting by c an element in $C^\otimes$.

$$A ::= \ \mathbf{stop} \mid \mathbf{tell}(c) \mid \mathbf{ask}(c) \to A \mid A \parallel A \mid \exists_x A \mid p(x).$$

Let $\mathcal{A}$ be the set of all agents, which is parametric with respect to a set $\mathcal{P}$ of (unary) procedure declarations $p(x) = A$ such that $fv(A) = \{x\}$.[3]

In Tab. 1 we provide a reduction semantics for SCCP: a pair $\langle \Gamma, \to \rangle$, for $\Gamma = \mathcal{A} \times C^\otimes$ the set of configurations and $\longrightarrow \ \subseteq \ \Gamma \times \Gamma$ a family of binary relations indexed over sets of variables, i.e., $\longrightarrow = \bigcup_{\Delta \subseteq V} \longrightarrow_\Delta$ and $\longrightarrow_\Delta \ \subseteq \ \Gamma \times \Gamma$.

In **R1** a constraint c is added to the store σ. **R2** checks if c is entailed by σ: if not, the computation is blocked. Rules **R3** and **R4** model the interleaving of two agents in parallel. Rule **R5** replaces a procedure identifier with the associated body, renaming the formal parameter with the actual one: $A[^y/_x]$ stands for the

---

[3] The set of free variables of an agent is defined in the expected way by structural induction, assuming that $fv(\mathbf{tell}(c)) = sv(c)$ and $fv(\mathbf{ask}(c) \to A) = sv(c) \cup fv(A)$.

Table 1. Reduction semantics for SCCP

R1 $\dfrac{sv(\sigma) \cup sv(c) \subseteq \Delta}{\langle \textbf{tell}(c), \sigma \rangle \longrightarrow_\Delta \langle \textbf{stop}, \sigma \otimes c \rangle}$ **Tell**   **R2** $\dfrac{c \leq \sigma \wedge sv(\sigma) \cup sv(c) \subseteq \Delta}{\langle \textbf{ask}(c) \to A, \sigma \rangle \longrightarrow_\Delta \langle A, \sigma \rangle}$ **Ask**

R3 $\dfrac{\langle A, \sigma \rangle \longrightarrow_\Delta \langle A', \sigma' \rangle \wedge fv(B) \subseteq \Delta}{\langle A \parallel B, \sigma \rangle \longrightarrow_\Delta \langle A' \parallel B, \sigma' \rangle}$ **Par1**   **R4** $\dfrac{\langle A, \sigma \rangle \longrightarrow_\Delta \langle A', \sigma' \rangle \wedge fv(B) \subseteq \Delta}{\langle B \parallel A, \sigma \rangle \longrightarrow_\Delta \langle B \parallel A', \sigma' \rangle}$ **Par2**

R5 $\dfrac{\{y\} \cup sv(\sigma) \subseteq \Delta \wedge p(x) = A \in \mathcal{P}}{\langle p(y), \sigma \rangle \longrightarrow_\Delta \langle A[^y/_x], \sigma \rangle}$ **Rec**   **R6** $\dfrac{fv(A) \cup sv(\sigma) \subseteq \Delta \wedge w \notin \Delta}{\langle \exists_x A, \sigma \rangle \longrightarrow_\Delta \langle A[^w/_x], \sigma \rangle}$ **Hide**

agent obtained by replacing all the occurrences of x with y.[4] Rule **R6** hides the variable x occurring in A. The variable w that replaces x is globally fresh, as ensured by requiring $w \notin \Delta$. The latter is more general than just requiring that $w \notin fv(A) \cup sv(\sigma)$, since $\langle B, \rho \rangle \longrightarrow_\Delta$ implies that $fv(B) \cup sv(\rho) \subseteq \Delta$.[5]

We denote $fv(A) \cup sv(\sigma)$ as $fv(\gamma)$ for a configuration $\gamma = \langle A, \sigma \rangle$, and by $\gamma[^z/_w]$ the component-wise application of substitution $[^z/_w]$. Clearly $\gamma \longrightarrow_\Delta \gamma'$ implies $fv(\gamma) \subseteq \Delta$, and we now further provide three lemmata on reduction.

Lemma 3 (Mono). *Let* $\langle A, \sigma \rangle \longrightarrow_\Delta \langle B, \sigma' \rangle$ *be a reduction. Then,* $\sigma \leq \sigma'$ *and* $sv(\sigma') \subseteq \Delta$.

The proof is straightforward: only rule **R1** can modify the store, and $\sigma \leq \sigma \otimes c$ as well as $sv(\sigma \otimes c) \subseteq sv(\sigma) \cup sv(c)$ hold, since as shown above $fv(\textbf{tell}(c)) \cup sv(\sigma) \subseteq \Delta$.

Lemma 4 (Operational Mono). *Let* $\langle A, \sigma \rangle \longrightarrow_\Delta \langle B, \sigma' \rangle$ *be a reduction and* $\rho \in C^\otimes$ *such that* $sv(\rho) \subseteq \Delta$. *Then, there exists a reduction* $\langle A, \sigma \otimes \rho \rangle \longrightarrow_\Delta \langle B, \sigma' \otimes \rho \rangle$.

The proof is straightforward, since as before $sv(\sigma \otimes \rho) \subseteq sv(\sigma) \cup sv(\rho)$ and moreover $\sigma, \rho \in C^\otimes$ ensure that $\sigma \otimes \rho \in C^\otimes$.

3.1 Observational Semantics

To define fair computations (Def. 12), we introduce enabled and active agents. Note that any transition is generated by an agent of the shape $\textbf{tell}(c)$ or $\textbf{ask}(c) \to A$ or $p(x)$ or $\exists_x A$ via the application of precisely one instance of one of the axioms **R1**, **R2**, **R5**, and **R6** of Tab. 1. An agent of such shape is *active* in a transition $t = \gamma \to \gamma'$ if it generates such transition, i.e. if there is a derivation of t where that agent is used in the building axiom. Moreover, an agent is *enabled* in a configuration γ if there is a transition $\gamma \to \gamma'$ such that the agent is *active* in it.

Definition 12 (Fair Computations). *Let* $\gamma_0 \to_{\Delta_1} \gamma_1 \to_{\Delta_2} \gamma_2 \to_{\Delta_3} \cdots$ *be a (possibly infinite) computation. It is fair if it is increasing (i.e.,* $\Delta_k \subseteq \Delta_{k+1}$ *for any k) and whenever an agent A is enabled in some* γ_i *then A is active in* $\gamma_j \to_{\Delta_{j+1}} \gamma_{j+1}$ *for some* $j \geq i$.

Note that fairness is well given: the format of the rules allows us to always trace the occurrence of an agent along a computation.

---

[4] With the usual conventions, so that e.g. $(\exists_y A)[^y/_x] = \exists_w((A[^w/_y])[^y/_x])$ for $w \notin sv(A) \cup \{x, y\}$ and $\textbf{tell}(c)[^y/_x] = \textbf{tell}(c[^y/_x])$, the latter defined according to Def. 11.

[5] Our rule is reminiscent of (8) in [21, p. 342].

Definition 13 (Observables). *Let* $\xi = \gamma_0 \to_{\Delta_1} \gamma_1 \to_{\Delta_2} \ldots$ *be a (possibly infinite) computation with* $\gamma_i = \langle A_i, \sigma_i \rangle$. *Result*$(\xi)$ *is* $\bigvee_i (\exists_{X_i} \sigma_i)$, *for* $X_i = (fv(\gamma_i)) \setminus (fv(\gamma_0))$.

Similarly to crisp programming [21], if a finite computation is fair then it is deadlocked and its result coincides with the store of the last configuration.

Proposition 1 (Confluence). *Let* γ *be a configuration and* ξ_1, ξ_2 *two (possibly infinite) computations of* γ. *If* ξ_1 *and* ξ_2 *are fair, then Result*$(\xi_1) = $ *Result*(ξ_2).

The proposition is an immediate consequence of the lemma below.

Lemma 5. *Let* $\gamma \to_{\Delta_i} \gamma_i$ *be reductions for* $i = 1, 2$. *Then one of the following holds*

1. $\xi_i = \gamma \to_{\Delta_i} \gamma_i[^z/_{w_i}]$ *and* $\gamma_1[^z/_{w_1}] = \gamma_2[^z/_{w_2}]$ *for* $w_i \notin \Delta_i$ *and* z *fresh;*
2. $\xi_i = \gamma \to_{\Delta_i} \gamma_i[^{z_i}/_{w_i}] \to_{\Delta_1 \cup \Delta_2 \cup \{z_i\}} \gamma_3$ *for* $w_i \notin (\Delta_1 \cap \Delta_2) \cup fv(\gamma_3)$ *and* z_i's *fresh.*

In both cases, Result$(\xi_1) = $ *Result*(ξ_2).

Proof. First of all, note that the calculus is deterministic except for the parallel and the hiding operators. Consider the latter. The problem may arise if different fresh variables are chosen, let us say w_1 and w_2. However, $\gamma_1[^z/_{w_1}] = \gamma_2[^z/_{w_2}]$ by replacing the new variables with a globally fresh one, as in item 1.

So, let us assume that the two reductions occur on the opposite sides of a parallel operator. Also, let $\gamma \to_{\Delta_1} \gamma_1$ replace a hiding operator with a variable w_1 (hence we have $w_1 \notin \Delta_1$). If $w_1 \in fv(\gamma_2)$, since $w_1 \notin \gamma$ and the only reduction enlarging the set of free variables is the replacement of a hiding operator, also $\gamma \to_{\Delta_2} \gamma_2$ must replace a hiding operator with variable w_1, and thus it suffices to replace w_1 with fresh variables z_1 and z_2 in the two reductions, in order for item 2 to be verified. If $w_1 \notin fv(\gamma_2)$, then ξ_2 is obtained by replacing in γ_2 the hiding operator with z_1 instead of w_1. As for obtaining ξ_1, the only problematic case is if $\gamma \to_{\Delta_2} \gamma_2$ also replaces a hiding operator with a variable $w_2 \in \Delta_1 \cup fv(\gamma_1)$. However, we have that $w_2 \notin fv(\gamma_1)$ since otherwise (as shown above) $w_1 = w_2$, thus ξ_1 is obtained by replacing in γ_1 the hiding operator with z_2 instead of w_2, and item 2 is then verified.

Among the remaining cases, the only relevant one is whenever both actions add different constraints to the store. So, let us assume that $\gamma = \langle A_1 \parallel A_2, \sigma \rangle$ such that $\langle A_1, \sigma \rangle \to_{\Delta_1} \langle B_1, \sigma_1 \rangle$ and $\langle A_2, \sigma \rangle \to_{\Delta_2} \langle B_2, \sigma_2 \rangle$. Note that since reduction semantics is monotone (Lemma 3) and σ is $\otimes$-compact, also σ_1 is $\otimes$-compact and furthermore we have $\sigma_1 = \sigma \otimes (\sigma_1 \ominus \sigma)$. Now, operational monotonicity (Lemma 4) ensures us that $\langle B_1 \parallel A_2, \sigma \otimes (\sigma_1 \ominus \sigma) \rangle \to_{\Delta_1 \cup \Delta_2} \langle B_1 \parallel B_2, \sigma \otimes (\sigma_1 \ominus \sigma) \otimes (\sigma_2 \ominus \sigma) \rangle$ and by symmetric reasoning the latter configuration is the one we were looking for. $\square$

The result above is a local confluence theorem, which is expected, since the calculus is essentially deterministic. The complex formulation is due to the occurrence of hiding operators: as an example, different fresh variables may be chosen for replacing $\exists_x$, such as w_1 and w_2 in the first item above, and then a globally fresh variable z has to be found for replacing them.

As a final remark, note that $\gamma \rightarrow_\Delta \gamma'$ with $z \in fv(\gamma)$ and $w \notin fv(\gamma')$ implies $\gamma[^w/_z] \rightarrow_{(\Delta \setminus \{z\}) \cup \{w\}} \gamma'[^w/_z]$. Combined with the proposition above, they ensure that fair computations originating from a configuration are either all finite or all infinite, and furthermore they have the same result. So, in the following we denote as $Result(\langle A, \sigma \rangle)$ the unique result of the fair computations originating from $\langle A, \sigma \rangle$. This fact allows to define an observation-wise equivalence.

Definition 14 (Observational Equivalence). *Let $A, B \in \mathcal{A}$ be agents. They are observationally equivalent ($A \sim_o B$) if $Result(\langle A, \sigma \rangle) = Result(\langle B, \sigma \rangle)$ for all $\sigma \in C^\otimes$.*

It is easily shown that $\sim_o$ is preserved by all contexts, i.e., it is a *congruence*.[6]

3.2 Saturated Bisimulation

As proposed in [1] for crisp languages, we define a barbed equivalence between two agents [17]. Since barbs are basic observations (predicates) on the states of a system, in this case they correspond to the compact constraints in $C^\otimes$, and we say that $\langle A, \sigma \rangle$ verifies c, or that $\langle A, \sigma \rangle \downarrow_c$ holds, if $c \le \sigma$. However, since *barbed bisimilarity* is an equivalence already for CCP, along [1] we propose the use of *saturated bisimilarity* in order to obtain a congruence: Defs. 15 and 16 respectively provide the strong and weak definition of saturated bisimilarity.

Definition 15 (Saturated Bisimilarity). *A saturated bisimulation is a symmetric relation R on configurations such that whenever $(\langle A, \sigma \rangle, \langle B, \rho \rangle) \in R$*

1. *if $\langle A, \sigma \rangle \downarrow_c$ then $\langle B, \rho \rangle \downarrow_c$;*
2. *if $\langle A, \sigma \rangle \longrightarrow \gamma_1'$ then there exists γ_2' such that $\langle B, \rho \rangle \longrightarrow \gamma_2'$ and $(\gamma_1', \gamma_2') \in R$;*
3. *$(\langle A, \sigma \otimes d \rangle, \langle B, \rho \otimes d \rangle) \in R$ for all $d \in C^\otimes$.*

We say that γ_1 and γ_2 are saturated bisimilar ($\gamma_1 \sim_s \gamma_2$) if there exists a saturated bisimulation R such that $(\gamma_1, \gamma_2) \in R$. We write $A \sim_s B$ if $\langle A, \bot \rangle \sim_s \langle B, \bot \rangle$.

We now let $\longrightarrow^*$ denote the reflexive and transitive closure of $\longrightarrow$, restricted to increasing computations. We say that $\gamma \Downarrow_c$ holds if there exists $\gamma' = \langle A, \sigma \rangle$ such that $\gamma \longrightarrow^* \gamma'$ and $c \le \exists_X \sigma$ for $X = fv(\gamma') \setminus fv(\gamma)$.

Definition 16 (Weak Saturated Bisimilarity). *Weak saturated bisimilarity ($\approx_s$) is obtained from Def. 15 by replacing $\longrightarrow$ with $\longrightarrow^*$ and $\downarrow_c$ with $\Downarrow_c$.*

Since $\sim_s$ (and $\approx_s$) is itself a saturated bisimulation, it is obvious that it is upward closed, and it is also a congruence with respect to all the contexts of SCCP (i.e., it is preserved under any context): indeed, a context $C[\bullet]$ can modify the behaviour of a configuration only by adding constraints to its store.

---

[6] Recall that a context $C[\bullet]$ is a syntactic expression with a single hole $\bullet$ such that replacing $\bullet$ with an agent A in the context produces an agent, denoted by $C[A]$. For example if $C[\bullet]$ is the context **tell**$(c) \parallel \bullet$ then $C[A] = $ **tell**$(c) \parallel A$. An equivalence $\cong$ between agents is a congruence if $A \cong B$ implies $C[A] \cong C[B]$ for every context $C[\bullet]$.

We now show that $\approx_s$, as given in Def. 16, coincides with the observational equivalence $\sim_o$ (see Def. 14). First we recall the notion of and a classic result on *cofinality*: two (possibly infinite) chains $c_0 \leq c_1 \leq \ldots$ and $d_0 \leq d_1 \leq \ldots$ are said to be *cofinal* if for all c_i there exists a d_j such that $c_i \leq d_j$ and, viceversa, for all d_i there exists a c_j such that $d_i \leq c_j$.

Lemma 6. *Let $c_0 \leq c_1 \leq \ldots$ and $d_0 \leq d_1 \leq \ldots$ be two chains. (1) If they are cofinal, then they have the same limit, i.e., $\bigvee_i c_i = \bigvee_i d_i$. (2) If the elements of the chains are $\otimes$-compact and $\bigvee_i c_i = \bigvee_i d_i$, then the two chains are cofinal.*

Proof. Let us tackle (2), and consider the sequence $e_0 = c_0$ and $e_i = c_{i+1} \ominus c_i$. Each e_i is the difference between two consecutive elements of a chain. Since the CLIM is invertible we have $c_k = \bigotimes_{i \leq k} e_i$ and thus $\bigvee_i c_i = \bigotimes_i e_i$. Since each d_j is $\otimes$-compact and $d_j \leq \bigotimes_i e_i$, there is a k such that $d_j \leq \bigotimes_{i \leq k} e_i$. The same reasoning is applied to the chain $d_0 \leq d_1 \leq \ldots$, thus the result holds. $\square$

For proving Proposition 2 we now relate weak barbs and fair computations.

Lemma 7. *Let $\xi = \gamma_0 \longrightarrow \gamma_1 \longrightarrow \gamma_2 \longrightarrow \ldots$ be a (possibly infinite) fair computation. If $\gamma_0 \Downarrow_d$ then there exists a store σ_i in ξ such that $d \leq \exists_{X_i}\sigma_i$ for $X_i = fv(\gamma_i) \setminus fv(\gamma_0)$.*

The lemma holds since the language is deterministic and computations fair.

Proposition 2. *$A \sim_o B$ if and only if $A \approx_s B$.*

Proof. The proof proceeds as follows.

From $\approx_s$ to $\sim_o$. Assume $\langle A, \perp \rangle \approx_s \langle B, \perp \rangle$ and take a $\otimes$-compact $c \in C^{\otimes}$. Let

$$\langle A, c \rangle \longrightarrow \langle A_0, \sigma_0 \rangle \longrightarrow \langle A_1, \sigma_1 \rangle \longrightarrow \ldots \longrightarrow \langle A_n, \sigma_n \rangle \ldots \longrightarrow \ldots \tag{1}$$

$$\langle B, c \rangle \longrightarrow \langle B_0, \rho_0 \rangle \longrightarrow \langle B_1, \rho_1 \rangle \longrightarrow \ldots \longrightarrow \langle B_n, \rho_n \rangle \ldots \longrightarrow \ldots \tag{2}$$

be two fair computations. Since $\approx_s$ is upward closed, $\langle A, c \rangle \approx_s \langle B, c \rangle$ and thus $\langle B, c \rangle \Downarrow_{\sigma_i}$ for all σ_i. By Lemma 7, it follows that there exists an ρ_j (in the above computation) such that $\exists_{\Gamma_i}\sigma_i \leq \sigma_i \leq \exists_{\Gamma'_j}\rho_j$, and analogously for all ρ_i. Then $\sigma_0 \leq \sigma_1 \leq \ldots$ and $\rho_0 \leq \rho_1 \leq \ldots$ are cofinal and by Lemma 6, it holds that $\bigvee_i \exists_{\Gamma_i}\sigma_i = \bigvee_i \exists_{\Gamma'_i}\rho_i$, which means $Result(\langle A, c \rangle) = Result(\langle B, c \rangle)$.

From $\sim_o$ to $\approx_s$. Assume $A \sim_o B$. First, we show that $\langle A, c \rangle$ and $\langle B, c \rangle$ satisfy the same weak barbs for all $c \in C$. Let (1) and (2) be two fair computations. Since $A \sim_o B$, then $\bigvee_i \exists_{\Gamma_i}\sigma_i = \bigvee_i \exists_{\Gamma'_i}\rho_i$. Since all (the projections of) the intermediate stores of the computations are $\otimes$-compact, then by Lemma 6, for all σ_i there exists an ρ_j such that $\exists_{\Gamma_i}\sigma_i \leq \exists_{\Gamma'_j}\rho_j$. Now suppose that $\langle A, c \rangle \Downarrow_d$. By Lemma 7, there exists a σ_i such that $d \leq \exists_{\Gamma_i}\sigma_i$. Thus $\langle B, c \rangle \Downarrow_d$. It is now easy to prove that $R = \{(\gamma_1, \gamma_2) \mid \exists c. \langle A, c \rangle \longrightarrow^* \gamma_1 \& \langle B, c \rangle \longrightarrow^* \gamma_2\}$ is a weak saturated bisimulation (Def. 16). Take $(\gamma_1, \gamma_2) \in R$. If $\gamma_1 \Downarrow_d$ then $\langle A, c \rangle \Downarrow_d$ and, by the above observation, $\langle B, c \rangle \Downarrow_d$. Since SCCP is confluent, also $\gamma_2 \Downarrow_d$. The fact that R is closed under $\longrightarrow^*$ is evident from the definition of R. While for proving that R is upward-closed take $\gamma_1 = \langle A', \sigma' \rangle$ and $\gamma_2 = \langle B', \rho' \rangle$. By Lemma 4 for all $a \in C, \langle A, c \otimes a \rangle \longrightarrow^* \langle A', \sigma' \otimes a \rangle$ and $\langle B, c \otimes a \rangle \longrightarrow^* \langle B', \rho' \otimes a \rangle$. Thus, by definition of R, $(\langle A', \sigma' \otimes a \rangle, \langle B', \rho' \otimes a \rangle) \in R$. $\square$

4   A Labelled Transition System for Soft CCP

Although $\approx_s$ is fully abstract, it is to some extent unsatisfactory because of the upward-closure, namely, the for-all quantification in condition 3 of Def. 16.

In Tab. 2 we refine the notion of transition (given in Tab. 1) by adding a label that carries additional information about the constraints that cause the reduction. Hence, we define a new labelled transition system (LTS) obtained by the family of relations $\xrightarrow{\alpha}_\Delta \subseteq \Gamma \times \Gamma$ indexed over $\langle C^\otimes, 2^V \rangle$; as a reminder, Γ is the set of configurations, $C^\otimes$ the set of $\otimes$-compact constraints, and, as for the unlabelled semantics in Section 3, transitions are indexed by sets of variables. Rules in Tab. 2 are identical to those in Tab. 1, except for a constraint α that represents the minimal information that must be added to σ in order to fire an action from $\langle A, \sigma \rangle$ to $\langle A', \sigma' \rangle$, i.e., $\langle A, \sigma \otimes \alpha \rangle \longrightarrow_\Delta \langle A', \sigma' \rangle$.

Table 2. An LTS for SCCP

$$\textbf{LR1}\ \frac{sv(\sigma) \cup sv(c) \subseteq \Delta}{\langle \textbf{tell}(c), \sigma \rangle \xrightarrow{\perp}_\Delta \langle \textbf{stop}, \sigma \otimes c \rangle}\ \textbf{Tell} \qquad \textbf{LR2}\ \frac{sv(\sigma) \cup sv(c) \subseteq \Delta}{\langle \textbf{ask}(c) \to A, \sigma \rangle \xrightarrow{c \ominus \sigma}_\Delta \langle A, \sigma \otimes (c \ominus \sigma) \rangle}\ \textbf{Ask}$$

$$\textbf{LR3}\ \frac{\langle A, \sigma \rangle \xrightarrow{\alpha}_\Delta \langle A', \sigma' \rangle \wedge fv(B) \subseteq \Delta}{\langle A \parallel B, \sigma \rangle \xrightarrow{\alpha}_\Delta \langle A' \parallel B, \sigma' \rangle}\ \textbf{Par1} \qquad \textbf{LR4}\ \frac{\langle A, \sigma \rangle \xrightarrow{\alpha}_\Delta \langle A', \sigma' \rangle \wedge fv(B) \subseteq \Delta}{\langle B \parallel A, \sigma \rangle \xrightarrow{\alpha}_\Delta \langle B \parallel A', \sigma' \rangle}\ \textbf{Par2}$$

$$\textbf{LR5}\ \frac{\{y\} \cup sv(\sigma) \subseteq \Delta \wedge p(x) = A \in \mathcal{P}}{\langle p(y), \sigma \rangle \xrightarrow{\perp}_\Delta \langle A[^y/_x], \sigma \rangle}\ \textbf{Rec} \qquad \textbf{LR6}\ \frac{fv(A) \cup sv(\sigma) \subseteq \Delta \wedge w \notin \Delta}{\langle \exists_x A, \sigma \rangle \xrightarrow{\perp}_\Delta \langle A[^w/_x], \sigma \rangle}\ \textbf{Hide}$$

Rule **LR2** says that $\langle \textbf{ask}(c) \to A, \sigma \rangle$ can evolve to $\langle A, \sigma \otimes \alpha \rangle$ if the environment provides a minimal constraint α that added to the store σ entails c, i.e., $\alpha = c \ominus \sigma$. Notice that, differently from [1], here the definition of this minimal label comes directly from a derived operator of the underlying CLIM (i.e., from $\ominus$), which by Lemma 1 preserves $\otimes$-compactness.

The LTS is sound and complete with respect to the unlabelled semantics.

Lemma 8 (Soundness). *If* $\langle A, \sigma \rangle \xrightarrow{\alpha}_\Delta \langle A', \rho \rangle$ *then* $\langle A, \sigma \otimes \alpha \rangle \longrightarrow_\Delta \langle A', \rho \rangle$.

Proof. We proceed by induction on (the depth) of the inference of $\langle A, \sigma \rangle \xrightarrow{\alpha}_\Delta$ $\langle A', \rho \rangle$. We consider **LR2**: the other cases are easier to verify.

Using **LR2** then $A = (\textbf{ask}(c) \to A')$, $\alpha = c \ominus \sigma$ and $\rho = (\sigma \otimes (c \ominus \sigma)) = (\sigma \otimes \alpha)$. We know that $c \leq (\sigma \otimes (c \ominus \sigma))$ then by using **R2** $\langle A, \sigma \otimes \alpha \rangle \longrightarrow_\Delta \langle A', \rho \rangle$. □

Lemma 9 (Completeness). *If* $\langle A, \sigma \otimes d \rangle \longrightarrow_\Delta \langle A', \rho \rangle$ *then there exist* $\alpha, a \in C^\otimes$ *such that* $\langle A, \sigma \rangle \xrightarrow{\alpha}_\Delta \langle A', \rho' \rangle$ *and* $\alpha \otimes a = d$ *and* $\rho' \otimes a = \rho$.

Proof. We proceed by induction on (the depth) of the inference of $\langle A, \sigma \otimes d \rangle \longrightarrow_\Delta$ $\langle A', \rho \rangle$. We consider **LR2**: The other cases are easier to verify.

Using **LR2** then $A = \textbf{ask}(c) \rightarrow A'$, $\rho = \sigma \otimes d$ and $c \leq \rho$. Now consider $\langle A, \sigma \rangle \xrightarrow{\alpha}_{\Delta} \langle A', \rho' \rangle$, where $\alpha = (c \ominus \sigma) \leq d$ and $\rho' = (\sigma \otimes \alpha)$. Take $a = d \ominus (c \ominus \sigma)$ then we can check that the conditions verify. First by invertibility $\alpha \otimes a = (c \ominus \sigma) \otimes (d \ominus (c \ominus \sigma)) = d$ and finally $\rho' \otimes a = \sigma \otimes \alpha \otimes a = \sigma \otimes d = \rho$. $\square$

Theorem 1. $\langle A, \sigma \rangle \xrightarrow{\perp}_{\Delta} \langle A', \sigma' \rangle$ *if and only if* $\langle A, \sigma \rangle \longrightarrow_{\Delta} \langle A', \sigma' \rangle$.

Strong and Weak Bisimilarity on the LTS. We now proceed to define an equivalence that characterises $\sim_s$ without the upward closure condition. Differently from languages such as Milner's CCS, barbs cannot be removed from the definition of bisimilarity because they cannot be inferred by the transitions.

Definition 17 (Strong Bisimilarity). *A strong bisimulation is a symmetric relation R on configurations such that whenever $(\gamma_1, \gamma_2) \in R$ with $\gamma_1 = \langle A, \sigma \rangle$ and $\gamma_2 = \langle B, \rho \rangle$*

1. *if $\gamma_1 \downarrow_c$ then $\gamma_2 \downarrow_c$,*
2. *if $\gamma_1 \xrightarrow{\alpha} \gamma_1'$ then $\exists \gamma_2'$ such that $\langle B, \rho \otimes \alpha \rangle \longrightarrow \gamma_2'$ and $(\gamma_1', \gamma_2') \in R$.*

We say that γ_1 and γ_2 are strongly bisimilar ($\gamma_1 \sim \gamma_2$) if there exists a strong bisimulation R such that $(\gamma_1, \gamma_2) \in R$.

Whenever σ and ρ are $\otimes$-compact elements, the first condition is equivalent to require $\sigma \leq \rho$. Thus $(\gamma_1, \gamma_2) \in R$ would imply that γ_1 and γ_2 have the same store. As for the second condition, we adopted a *semi-saturated* equivalence, introduced for CCP in [1]. In the bisimulation game a label can be simulated by a reduction including in the store the label itself.

Definition 18 (Weak Bisimilarity). *A weak bisimulation is a symmetric relation R on configurations such that whenever $(\gamma_1, \gamma_2) \in R$ with $\gamma_1 = \langle A, \sigma \rangle$ and $\gamma_2 = \langle B, \rho \rangle$*

1. *if $\gamma_1 \downarrow_c$ then $\gamma_2 \Downarrow_c$,*
2. *if $\gamma_1 \xrightarrow{\alpha} \gamma_1'$ then $\exists \gamma_2'$ such that $\langle B, \rho \otimes \alpha \rangle \longrightarrow^* \gamma_2'$ and $(\gamma_1', \gamma_2') \in R$.*

We say that γ_1 and γ_2 are weakly bisimilar ($\gamma_1 \approx \gamma_2$) if there exists a weak bisimulation R such that $(\gamma_1, \gamma_2) \in R$.

With respect to the weak equivalence for crisp constraints, some of its characteristic equivalences do not hold, so that e.g. $\textbf{ask}(c) \rightarrow \textbf{tell}(c) \not\approx \textbf{stop}$. As usual, this is linked to the fact that the underlying CLIM may not be idempotent.

We can now conclude by proving the equivalence between $\sim_s$ and $\sim$ and between $\approx_s$ and $\approx$ (hence, $\approx$ is further equivalent to $\sim_o$, using Proposition 2). We start by showing that $\sim$ is preserved under composition.

Lemma 10. *If $\langle A, \sigma \rangle \sim \langle B, \rho \rangle$, then $\langle A, \sigma \otimes a \rangle \sim \langle B, \rho \otimes a \rangle$ for all $a \in C^{\otimes}$.*

Proof. We need to show that $R = \{ ((\langle A, \sigma \otimes a \rangle \sim \langle B, \rho \otimes a \rangle)) \mid \langle A, \sigma \rangle \sim \langle B, \rho \rangle \}$ satisfies the two properties in Def. 17.

i) From the hypothesis $\langle A, \sigma \rangle \sim \langle B, \rho \rangle$, we have that $\rho = \sigma$, thus $\langle A, \sigma \otimes a \rangle$ and $\langle B, \rho \otimes a \rangle$ satisfy the same barbs.

ii) Supposing $\langle A, \sigma \otimes a \rangle \xrightarrow{\alpha} \langle A', \sigma' \rangle$, we need to prove the existence of B' and ρ' such that $\langle B, \rho \otimes a \otimes \alpha \rangle \to \langle B', \rho' \rangle$ and $(\langle A', \sigma' \rangle, \langle B', \rho' \rangle) \in R$. By Lemma 8 and Lemma 9 we obtain $\langle A, \sigma \rangle \xrightarrow{\alpha'} \langle A', \sigma'' \rangle$, and there exists b' such that $\alpha' \otimes b' = a \otimes \alpha$ (1) and $\sigma'' \otimes b' = \sigma'$ (2). From the labelled transition of $\langle A, \sigma \rangle$ and the hypothesis $\langle A, \sigma \rangle \sim \langle B, \rho \rangle$, we have that $\langle B, \rho \otimes \alpha' \rangle \to \langle B', \rho'' \rangle$, with $\langle A, \sigma'' \rangle \sim \langle B, \rho'' \rangle$ (3). By (1) we have $\langle B, \rho \otimes a \otimes \alpha \rangle = \langle B, \rho \otimes \alpha' \otimes b' \rangle$ and $\langle B, \rho \otimes \alpha' \otimes b' \rangle \to \langle B, \rho'' \otimes b' \rangle$ (due to operational monotonicity). Finally, by the definition of R and (3), we conclude that $(\langle A', \sigma'' \otimes b' \rangle, \langle B', \rho'' \otimes b' \rangle) \in R$, and, by (2), $\langle A', \sigma'' \otimes b' \rangle = \langle A', \sigma' \rangle$.   □

Theorem 2. $\sim_s = \sim$

Proof. The equivalence $\sim_s = \sim$ can be proved by using Lemma 10.

From $\sim$ **to** $\sim_{sb}$. We show that $R = \{(\langle A, \sigma \rangle, \langle B, \rho \rangle) \mid \langle A, \sigma \rangle \sim \langle B, \rho \rangle\}$ is a saturated bisimulation, i.e., for $(\langle A, \sigma \rangle, \langle B, \rho \rangle) \in R$ the conditions in Def. 15 are satisfied

i) If $\langle A, \sigma \rangle \downarrow_c$, then we have $\langle B, \rho \rangle \downarrow_c$ by the hypothesis $\langle A, \sigma \rangle \sim \langle B, \rho \rangle$.

ii) Suppose that $\langle A, \sigma \rangle \to \langle A', \sigma' \rangle$. By Theorem 1 we have $\langle A, \sigma \rangle \xrightarrow{\perp} \langle A', \sigma' \rangle$. Since $\langle A, \sigma \rangle \sim \langle B, \rho \rangle$, then $\langle B, \rho \otimes \perp \rangle \to \langle B', \rho' \rangle$ with $\langle A', \sigma' \rangle \sim \langle B', \rho' \rangle$. Since $\rho = \rho \otimes \perp$, we have $\langle B, \rho \rangle \to \langle B', \rho' \rangle$.

iii) By Lemma 10, $(\langle A, \sigma \otimes c' \rangle, \langle B, \rho \otimes c' \rangle) \in R$ for all $c' \in C^{\otimes}$.

From $\sim_{sb}$ **to** $\sim$. We show that $R = \{(\langle A, \sigma \rangle, \langle B, \rho \rangle) \mid \langle A, \sigma \rangle \sim_{sb} \langle B, \rho \rangle\}$ is a strong bisimulation, i.e., for $(\langle A, \sigma \rangle, \langle B, \rho \rangle) \in R$ the conditions in Def. 17 are satisfied

i) If $\langle A, \sigma \rangle \downarrow_c$, then we have $\langle B, \rho \rangle \downarrow_c$ by the hypothesis $\langle A, \sigma \rangle \sim_{sb} \langle B, \rho \rangle$.

ii) Suppose that $\langle A, \sigma \rangle \xrightarrow{\alpha} \langle A', \sigma' \rangle$. Then by Lemma 8 we have $\langle A, \sigma \otimes \alpha \rangle \to \langle A', \sigma' \rangle$. Since $\langle A, \sigma \rangle \sim_{sb} \langle B, \rho \rangle$, then $\langle A, \sigma \otimes \alpha \rangle \sim_{sb} \langle B, \rho \otimes \alpha \rangle$ and thus $\langle B, \rho \otimes \alpha \rangle \to \langle B', \rho' \rangle$ with $\langle A', \sigma' \rangle \sim_{sb} \langle B', \rho' \rangle$.   □

In order to prove the correspondence between weak bisimulations, we need a result analogous to Lemma 10. The key issue is the preservation of weak barbs by the addition of constraints to the store, which is trivial in strong bisimulation.

Lemma 11. *Let* $\langle A, \sigma \rangle \approx \langle B, \rho \rangle$ *and* $a, c \in C^{\otimes}$. *If* $\langle A, \sigma \otimes a \rangle \downarrow_c$, *then* $\langle B, \rho \otimes a \rangle \Downarrow_c$.

Proof. If $\langle A, \sigma \otimes a \rangle \downarrow_c$, then $c \leq \sigma \otimes a$. Since $\langle A, \sigma \rangle \approx \langle B, \rho \rangle$ and $\langle A, \sigma \rangle \downarrow_\sigma$, then there exists $\langle B', \rho' \rangle$ such that $\langle B, \rho \rangle \to^* \langle B', \rho' \rangle$ and $\sigma \leq \exists_\Gamma \rho'$ for $\Gamma = fv(\langle B', \rho' \rangle) \setminus fv(\langle B, \rho \rangle)$. Let us assume, without loss of generality, that $\Gamma \cap (sv(a)) = \emptyset$; since reductions are operationally monotone (Lemma 4), we have $\langle B, \rho \otimes a \rangle \to^* \langle B', \rho' \otimes a \rangle$. Finally, $c \leq \sigma \otimes a = \sigma \otimes \exists_\Gamma a \leq \exists_\Gamma \rho' \otimes \exists_\Gamma a \leq \exists_\Gamma (\rho' \otimes a)$, hence $\langle B, \rho \otimes a \rangle \Downarrow_c$.   □

The result below uses Lemma 11 and a rephrasing of the proof of Lemma 10

Lemma 12. *If* $\langle A, \sigma \rangle \approx \langle B, \rho \rangle$, *then* $\langle A, \sigma \otimes a \rangle \approx \langle B, \rho \otimes a \rangle$ *for all* $a \in C^{\otimes}$.

Theorem 3. $\approx_s = \approx$

Labelled versus Saturated Semantics. The main appeal of saturated semantics resides in always being a congruence and, in fact, the minimal congruence contained in standard bisimulation [19]. The main drawback of this approach is that it is in principle necessary to check the behaviour of a process under every context. The problem is somewhat mitigated for SCCP, since it suffices to close the store with respect to any possible compact element (item 3 of Def. 15). At the same time, checking the feasibility of a reduction may require some computational effort, either for solving the combinatorial problem associated with calculating $\sigma \otimes d$, or for verifying if $c \leq \sigma$, as with agent **ask**(c) $\rightarrow$ A.

This is the reason for searching labelled semantics and suitable notions of bisimilarity that may alleviate such a burden. The key intuition is to consider labels which somehow represent the "minimal context allowing a process to reduce", so that a bisimilarity-checking algorithm in principle needs to verify this minimal context only, instead of every one. The idea has been exploited in the simpler framework of crisp CCP [1], and it is based on [16,9].

Example 1. Let us consider the agents **ask**(c) $\rightarrow$ **stop** and **stop**. To prove that they are weakly bisimilar, it has to be proved that $\gamma \approx \gamma'$ for configurations $\gamma = \langle \text{ask}(c) \rightarrow \text{stop}, \bot \rangle$ and $\gamma' = \langle \text{stop}, \bot \rangle$. Consider the following relation

$$\mathcal{R} = \{(\langle \text{ask}(c) \rightarrow \text{stop}, \bot \rangle, \langle \text{stop}, \bot \rangle), (\langle \text{stop}, c \rangle, \langle \text{stop}, c \rangle)\}$$

It is quite easy to prove that it is a bisimulation, and in fact the smallest one identifying the two configurations. It suffices to note that by definition $c \oplus \bot = c$.

In order to prove that $\gamma \approx_s \gamma'$, instead, we surely need to consider an infinite relation. Indeed, the smallest saturated bisimulation equating the two configuration is given by the relation below

$$S = \{(\langle \text{ask}(c) \rightarrow \text{stop}, d \rangle, \langle \text{stop}, d \rangle), (\langle \text{stop}, e \rangle, \langle \text{stop}, e \rangle) \mid d, e \in C^\otimes \& c \leq e\}$$

The relation above clearly is a saturated bisimulation, but any naive automatic check for that property might involve rather complex calculations.

Another reason for the complexity of checking saturated bisimilarity is the need of considering the closure $\longrightarrow^*$ of the reduction relation, which may cause a combinatorial explosion. Think e.g. of the agents $\prod_{i \in I} \text{ask}(c_i) \rightarrow$ **stop** and **stop**. Of course, they might be proved equivalent by exploiting the fact that saturated bisimilarity is a congruence, and by verifying that **stop** $\| A \approx_s A$ for all the agents A. A direct proof would instead require a check for each store of the reductions arising from all the possible interleaving of the c_i elements.

5 Towards an Axiomatisation for Weak Bisimilarity

Once the behaviour of an agent is captured by an observational equivalence, it is natural to look for laws characterizing it. Given its correspondence with the standard equivalence via fair computations, weak bisimilarity is the preferred behavioural semantics for soft CCP. A sound and complete axiomatisation was proposed for CCP in [21]. Unfortunately, the lack of idempotence in the soft formalism makes unsound some of the axioms presented in that classical paper.

$$
\begin{array}{llll}
\mathbf{ask}(c) \rightarrow \mathbf{stop} = \mathbf{stop} & (1) & \mathbf{tell}(\bot) = \mathbf{stop} & (2) \\
\mathbf{ask}(\bot) \rightarrow A = A & (3) & A \parallel \mathbf{stop} = A & (4) \\
A \parallel B = B \parallel A & (5) & A \parallel (B \parallel C) = (A \parallel B) \parallel C & (6) \\
\mathbf{tell}(c) \parallel \mathbf{tell}(d) = \mathbf{tell}(c \otimes d) & (7) & \mathbf{ask}(c) \rightarrow (A \parallel B) = (\mathbf{ask}(c) \rightarrow A) \parallel (\mathbf{ask}(c) \rightarrow B) & (8) \\
\exists_x \mathbf{tell}(c) = \mathbf{tell}(\exists_x c) & (9) & \exists_x (\mathbf{ask}(c) \rightarrow A) = \mathbf{ask}(\forall_x c) \rightarrow \exists_x A & (10)
\end{array}
$$

$$
\exists_x (\mathbf{tell}(c) \parallel_{i \in I} \mathbf{ask}(c_i) \rightarrow \mathbf{tell}(d_i)) = \mathbf{tell}(\exists_x c) \parallel \exists_x (\parallel_{i \in I} \mathbf{ask}(c \Rightarrow_x c_i) \rightarrow \mathbf{tell}(d_i)) \tag{11}
$$

Fig. 1. Axioms for simple agents (1-8) and for agents with quantifiers (9-11)

Consider e.g. the law $\mathbf{ask}(c) \rightarrow \mathbf{ask}(d) \rightarrow \mathbf{tell}(e) = \mathbf{ask}(c \otimes d) \rightarrow \mathbf{tell}(e)$, denoted as $L3$ in [21], and let us assume that $c = d$. Since $c \neq c \otimes c$, only the agent in the left-hand side of the law is guaranteed to add e, starting from a store σ such that $c \leq \sigma$. On a similar note, most of the axioms in [21] involving the parallel composition also do not hold, since as a general remark posting a constraint twice is different from adding it just once.[7]

We now introduce a set of sound axioms for SCCP in Figure 1. As for those of CCP in [21], they rely on an additional operator which is intuitively the dual of the existential quantifier of cylindric algebras.

Definition 19 (Co-cylindrification). *Let V be a set of variables. A co-cylindric operator $\forall$ over $\mathbf{S}$ and V is given by a family of monotone, $\otimes$-compactness preserving functions $\forall_x : A \rightarrow A$ indexed by elements in V such that for all $a, b \in A$ and $x \in V$*

1. $\forall_x a \leq b$ if and only if $a \leq \exists_x b$.

If the $\forall$ operators play the role of universal quantifiers, a further family of operators had been introduced in [21] for providing the role of implication, in order to provide a complete set of axioms for CCP. In our context, such an operator can be derived by means of residuation.

Lemma 13. *Let $a, b, c \in C$, $x \in V$ and $a \Rightarrow_x b = \exists_x a \otimes \forall_x (b \ominus a)$. Then, $b \leq a \otimes \exists_x c$ if and only if $a \Rightarrow_x b \leq \exists_x a \otimes \exists_x c$.*

Clearly, $a \Rightarrow_x b \in C^\otimes$ if a and b do. These properties for $a \Rightarrow_x b$ are the immediate extensions of those holding for the crisp setting. Exploiting co-cylindrification and the latter operator we can now state Eq. 10 and Eq. 11. In Eqs. 1-3 we present the axioms related to *ask* and *tell*. Axioms on parallel composition are instead represented in Eqs. 4-6. In Eqs. 7-8 we show how adding two constraints and prefixing distributes though parallel composition.

Proposition 3. *Axioms 1-11 in Figure 1 are sound with respect to weak bisimilarity.*

As for completeness, again the lack of idempotency made it impossible to rest the proof schema adopted for the CCP case, since the normal form exploited in [21] for proving completeness cannot be lifted to SCCP agents.

---

[7] As an example, the law $L1$ of [21] states $\mathbf{ask}(c) \rightarrow \mathbf{tell}(d) = \mathbf{ask}(c) \rightarrow (\mathbf{tell}(c) \parallel \mathbf{tell}(d))$, which is false precisely for the lack of idempotence: $c \leq \sigma$ does not imply $\sigma = \sigma \otimes c$. For the sake of completeness, the other unsound axioms are $L10$, $L11$, and $L12$.

6 Conclusions and Further Work

Inspired by [1] that investigated the crisp variant of the language, in this paper we studied the behavioural semantics of the deterministic fragment of soft CCP [7], and proposed a sound axiomatisation in the spirit of [21].

Using residuation theory (as e.g. in [5] for soft constraints problems) provides an elegant way to define the minimal information that enables the firing of actions in the LTS shown in Sec. 4. This choice allowed for the study of the observational equivalence of agents in terms of weak and strong bisimilarity on such LTS, and it allowed for relating them to the corresponding barbed bisimilarities of (unlabelled) reductions and with the standard semantics via fair computations. The two kinds of equivalences, as well as the sound axiomatisation for weak bisimilarity, are presented in this paper for the first time.

For future work, we plan to provide a complete axiomatisation and a denotational semantics for soft CCP by building on the work for the crisp case in [21]. Concerning the axioms, we will try and investigate the relationship between soft CCP and a logical system whose fundamental properties are closely related to the ones we have investigated in this paper; namely *affine linear logic* [11]. This logical system *rejects contraction* but *admits weakening*, which intuitively correspond to dropping idempotence and preserving monotonicity in the soft formalism. The denotational model of CCP is based on *closure operators*: Each agent is compositionally interpreted as a monotonic, extensive and idempotent operator/function on constraints. We shall then investigate a denotational model for soft CCP processes based on *pre-closure operators* [2] (or *Čech closure operators*), i.e., closure operators that are not required to be idempotent.

Finally, we plan to consider two extensions of the language, checking how far the results given in this paper can be adapted. As evidenced by [20] a non-deterministic extension is an interesting challenge since the closure under any context for the saturated bisimilarity gets more elaborated than just closing with respect to the addition of constraints (Defs. 15 and 16, condition 3), and similarly one also needs to find the right formulation of bisimilarity for the labelled transitions systems. Also, the presence of residuation makes intuitive the definition of a retract operator for the calculus. Even if the operational semantics would be less affected, retraction would require a complete reformulation of the denotational semantics via fair computations, since monotonicity (as stated in Lemma 3) would not hold anymore [8]. Finally, we might consider languages with temporal features, such as *timed* SCCP [4], where a reduction takes a bounded period of time and it is measured by a discrete global clock. Maximal parallel steps are adopted there with a new construct that can e.g. express time-out and pre-emption, and developing suitable temporal variants of bisimilarity might reveal a worthwhile, albeit difficult task.

References

1. Aristizábal, A., Bonchi, F., Palamidessi, C., Pino, L.F., Valencia, F.D.: Deriving labels and bisimilarity for concurrent constraint programming. In: Hofmann, M. (ed.) FOSSACS 2011. LNCS, vol. 6604, pp. 138–152. Springer, Heidelberg (2011)
2. Arkhangelskii, A.V., Pontryagin, L.S.: General Topology I. Springer (1990)
3. Baccelli, F., Cohen, G., Olsder, G., Quadrat, J.P.: Synchronization and Linearity: An Algebra for Discrete Event Systems. Wiley (1992)
4. Bistarelli, S., Gabbrielli, M., Meo, M.C., Santini, F.: Timed soft concurrent constraint programs. In: Lea, D., Zavattaro, G. (eds.) COORDINATION 2008. LNCS, vol. 5052, pp. 50–66. Springer, Heidelberg (2008)
5. Bistarelli, S., Gadducci, F.: Enhancing constraints manipulation in semiring-based formalisms. In: ECAI 2006. FAIA, vol. 141, pp. 63–67. IOS Press (2006)
6. Bistarelli, S., Montanari, U., Rossi, F.: Semiring-based constraint satisfaction and optimization. Journal of ACM 44(2), 201–236 (1997)
7. Bistarelli, S., Montanari, U., Rossi, F.: Soft concurrent constraint programming. ACM Transactions on Computational Logic 7(3), 563–589 (2006)
8. Bistarelli, S., Santini, F.: A secure non-monotonic soft concurrent constraint language. Fundamamenta Informaticae 134(3-4), 261–285 (2014)
9. Bonchi, F., Gadducci, F., Monreale, G.V.: Reactive systems, barbed semantics, and the mobile ambients. In: de Alfaro, L. (ed.) FOSSACS 2009. LNCS, vol. 5504, pp. 272–287. Springer, Heidelberg (2009)
10. Buscemi, M.G., Montanari, U.: CC-pi: A constraint-based language for specifying service level agreements. In: De Nicola, R. (ed.) ESOP 2007. LNCS, vol. 4421, pp. 18–32. Springer, Heidelberg (2007)
11. Dal Lago, U., Martini, S.: Phase semantics and decidability of elementary affine logic. Theoretical Computer Science 318(3), 409–433 (2004)
12. Fargier, H., Lang, J.: Uncertainty in constraint satisfaction problems: a probabilistic approach. In: Moral, S., Kruse, R., Clarke, E. (eds.) ECSQARU 1993. LNCS, vol. 747, pp. 97–104. Springer, Heidelberg (1993)
13. Galatos, N., Jipsen, P., Kowalski, T., Ono, H.: Residuated Lattices: An Algebraic Glimpse at Substructural Logics, vol. 151. Elsevier (2007)
14. Golan, J.: Semirings and Affine Equations over Them: Theory and Applications. Kluwer (2003)
15. Karner, G.: Semiring-based constraint satisfaction and optimization. Semigroup Forum 45(XX), 148–165 (1992)
16. Leifer, J.J., Milner, R.: Deriving bisimulation congruences for reactive systems. In: Palamidessi, C. (ed.) CONCUR 2000. LNCS, vol. 1877, pp. 243–258. Springer, Heidelberg (2000)
17. Milner, R., Sangiorgi, D.: Barbed bisimulation. In: Kuich, W. (ed.) ICALP 1992. LNCS, vol. 623, pp. 685–695. Springer, Heidelberg (1992)
18. Monk, J.D.: An introduction to cylindric set algebras. Logic Journal of IGPL 8(4), 451–496 (2000)
19. Montanari, U., Sassone, V.: Dynamic congruence vs. progressing bisimulation for CCS. Fundamenta informaticae 16(2), 171–199 (1992)
20. Pino, L.F., Bonchi, F., Valencia, F.D.: A behavioral congruence for concurrent constraint programming with nondeterministic choice. In: Ciobanu, G., Méry, D. (eds.) ICTAC 2014. LNCS, vol. 8687, pp. 351–368. Springer, Heidelberg (2014)
21. Saraswat, V.A., Rinard, M.C., Panangaden, P.: Semantic foundations of concurrent constraint programming. In: Wise, D.S. (ed.) POPL 1991, pp. 333–352. ACM Press (1991)

Agent-Oriented Techniques

Parallelisation and Application of AD^3 as a Method for Solving Large Scale Combinatorial Auctions

Francisco Cruz-Mencia[1,2(✉)], Jesus Cerquides[2], Antonio Espinosa[1],
Juan Carlos Moure[1], and Juan A. Rodriguez-Aguilar[2]

[1] IIIA-CSIC, Campus de la UAB, s/n, Bellaterra, Barcelona, Spain
{fcruz,cerquide,jar}@iiia.csic.es
[2] CAOS-UAB, Campus de la UAB, s/n,Bellaterra, Barcelona, Spain
{antoniomiguel.espinosa,juancarlos.moure}@uab.cat

Abstract. Auctions, and combinatorial auctions (CAs), have been successfully employed to solve coordination problems in a wide range of application domains. However, the scale of CAs that can be optimally solved is small because of the complexity of the winner determination problem (WDP), namely of finding the bids that maximise the auctioneer's revenue. A way of approximating the solution of a WDP is to solve its linear programming relaxation. The recently proposed Alternate Direction Dual Decomposition algorithm (AD^3) has been shown to efficiently solve large-scale LP relaxations. Hence, in this paper we show how to encode the WDP so that it can be approximated by means of AD^3. Moreover, we present $PAR\text{-}AD^3$, the first parallel implementation of AD^3. $PAR\text{-}AD^3$ shows to be up to 12.4 times faster than CPLEX in a single-thread execution, and up to 23 times faster than parallel CPLEX in an 8-core architecture. Therefore $PAR\text{-}AD^3$ becomes the algorithm of choice to solve large-scale WDP LP relaxations for hard instances. Furthermore, $PAR\text{-}AD^3$ has potential when considering large-scale coordination problems that must be solved as optimisation problems.

Keywords: Combinatorial auctions · Large-scale coordination · Large-scale optimisation · Linear programming

1 Introduction

Auctions are a standard technique to solve coordination problems that has been successfully employed in a wide range of application domains [24]. Combinatorial auctions (CAs) [7] are a particular type of auctions that allow to allocate entire bundles of items in a single transaction. Although computationally very complex, auctioning bundles has the great advantage of eliminating the risk for a bidder of not being able to obtain complementary items at a reasonable price in a follow-up auction (think of a CA for a pair of shoes, as opposed to two consecutive single-item auctions for each of the individual shoes). CAs are expected to deliver more *efficient* allocations than non-combinatorial auctions complementarities between items hold.

Research supported by MICINN projects TIN2011-28689-C02-01, TIN2013-45732-C4-4-P and TIN2012-38876-C02-01.

© IFIP International Federation for Information Processing 2015
T. Holvoet and M. Viroli (Eds.): COORDINATION 2015, LNCS 9037, pp. 153–168, 2015.
DOI: 10.1007/978-3-319-19282-6_10

CAs have been also employed to solve a variety of coordination problems (e.g. transportation [31], emergency resource coordination in disaster management [26], or agent coordination in agent-driven robot navigation [32]). However, although such application domains claim to be large-scale, namely involving thousands and even millions of bids, current results indicate that the scale of the CAs that can be optimally solved is small [19,25]. For instance, CPLEX (a state-of-the-art commercial solver) requires a median of around 3 hours to solve the integer linear program encoding the Winner Determination Problem (WDP) of a hard instance of a CA with only 1000 bids and 256 goods. This fact seriously hinders the practical applicability of current solvers to large-scale CAs.

Linear Programming (LP) relaxations are a standard method for approximating combinatorial optimisation problems in computer science [5]. Yanover et al. [36] report that realistic problems with a large number of variables cannot be solved by off-the-shelf, commercial LP solvers (such as CPLEX). Instead, they propose the usage of TRBP, a message-passing, dual-decomposition algorithm, to solve LP relaxations, and show that TRBP significantly outperforms CPLEX. Since then, many other message-passing and dual decomposition algorithms have been proposed to address this very same problem [17,18,13,28]. The advantage over other approximate algorithms is that the underlying optimisation problem is well-understood and the algorithms are convergent and provide certain guarantees. Moreover, there are ways of tightening the relaxation toward the exact solution [34].

In order to solve LP relaxations, there has been a recent upsurge of interest in the Alternating Direction Method of Multipliers (ADMM), which was invented in the 1970s by Glowinski and Marroco [14] and Gabay and Mercier [12]. As discussed in [6], ADMM is specially well suited for application in a wide variety of large-scale distributed modern problems. Along this line, Martins has proposed AD^3 [22], a novel algorithm based on ADMM, which proves to outperform off-the-shelf, commercial LP solvers for problems including declarative constraints. AD^3 has the same modular architecture of previous dual decomposition algorithms, but it is faster to reach consensus, and it is suitable for embedding in a branch-and-bound procedure toward the optimal solution. Martins derives efficient procedures for handling logic factors and a general procedure for dealing with dense, large, or combinatorial factors. Notice that until [21], the handling of declarative constraints by message-passing algorithms was barely addressed, and not well understood. This hindered their application to combinatorial auction WDPs, which typically require this type of constraints. Therefore, AD^3 constitutes a promising tool to solve WDPs in CAs.

As discussed in [21] (see section 7.5), AD^3 is largely amenable to parallelisation, since AD^3 separates an optimisation problem into subproblems that can be solved in parallel. Nonetheless, to the best of our knowledge there is no parallel implementation of AD^3. Therefore, the potential speedups that AD^3 may obtain when running on multicore environments remain unexplored. And yet, this path of research is encouraged by recent experiences in parallelisation of ADMM applied to solve an unconstrained optimisation problem [23]. Indeed, Miksik et al. show that a parallel implementation of ADMM delivers large speedups for large-scale problems. Notice though that the work in [23] cannot be employed to solve the WDP for CAs because it cannot handle hard constraints.

The main purpose of this paper is to demonstrate that the optimisation and parallelisation of AD^3 can deliver enormous benefits when solving relaxations of large-scale combinatorial optimisation problems, and in particular WDPs in large-scale CAs. With this aim, we make the following contributions:

- We show how to encode the WDP for CAs so that it can be approximated by AD^3. For this endeavour we employ the computationally-efficient factors provided by AD^3 to handle hard constraints.
- We propose an optimised, parallel implementation of AD^3, the so-called $PAR\text{-}AD^3$. Our implementation is based on a mechanism for distributing the computations required by AD^3 as well as on a data structure organisation that together favor parallelism.
- We show that while AD^3 is up to 12.4 times faster than CPLEX in a single-thread execution, $PAR\text{-}AD^3$ is up to 23 times faster than parallel CPLEX in an 8-core architecture. Therefore $PAR\text{-}AD^3$ becomes the algorithm of choice to solve large-scale WDP LP relaxations.

To summarise, our results indicate that $PAR\text{-}AD^3$ obtains significant speed-ups on multi-core environments, hence increasing AD^3's scalability and showing its potential for application to large-scale combinatorial optimisation problems in particular and for large-scale coordination problems that can be cast as combinatorial optimisation problems. The rest of the paper is organised as follows. First, we introduce some background on AD^3. Next, we detail how to encode the WDP for CAs by means of AD^3. Thereafter, we thoroughly describe $PAR\text{-}AD^3$ and afterwards we present empirical results. Finally, we draw some conclusions and set paths to future research.

2 Background

Graphical models are widely used in computer vision, natural language processing and computational biology, where a fundamental problem is to find the maximum a posteriori probability (MAP) given a factor graph. Since finding the exact MAP is frequently an intractable problem, significant research has been carried out to develop algorithms that approximate the MAP.

Linear Programming (LP) relaxations have been extensively applied to approximate the MAP for graphical models since [30]. Typically, such application domains lead to sparse problems with a large number of variables and constraints (i.e beyond 10^4). As shown in [36], message passing algorithms have been proved to outperform state-of-the-art commercial LP solvers (such as e.g. CPLEX) when approximating the MAP for large-scale problems. This advantage stems from the fact that message-passing algorithms better exploit the underlying graph structure representing the problem.

Along this direction, several message passing algorithms have been proposed in the literature: ADMM [10], TRBP [35], MPLP [13], PSDD [18], Norm-Product BP [16], and more recently Alternate Direction Dual Decomposition (AD^3) [2].

As discussed in [22], the recently-proposed AD^3 has some very interesting features in front of other message passing algorithms: it reaches consensus faster than other algorithms such as ADMM, TRBP and PSDD; it does have neither the convergence problems of MPLP nor the instability problems of Norm-Product BP; and its anytime design allows to stop the optimisation process whenever a pre-specified accuracy is reached. Furthermore, as reported in [22], AD^3 has been empirically shown to outperform state-of-the-art message passing algorithms on large-scale problems.

Besides these features, AD^3 also provides a library of computationally-efficient factors that allow to handle declarative constraints within an optimisation problem. This opens the possibility of employing AD^3 to approximate constrained optimisation problems.

Algorithm 1 outlines the main operations performed by AD^3 on a factor graph G with a set of factors F, a set of variables V, and a set of edges $E \subseteq F \times V$. AD^3 receives a set of parameters θ that encode variable coefficients and a penalty constant η able to regulate the update step size. We use the function $\partial(x)$ to denote all the neighbours (i.e. connected nodes) of a given graph node. The primal variables q and p, the dual λ as well as the unary log-potentials ξ are vectors which are updated during the execution. We refer the reader to [22] for a detailed description of the algorithm. AD^3 is an iterative three-step algorithm designed to approximate an objective function encoded as a factor graph. A key aspect of AD^3 is that it separates the optimisation problem into independent subproblems that progress to reach consensus on the values to assign to primal and dual variables. Thus, during the first step, *broadcast*, the optimisation problem is split into separate subproblems, each one being distributed to a factor. Thereafter, each factor locally solves its local subproblem. In AD^3, this computations is carried on solving a quadratic problem. During the second step, *gather*, each variable gathers the subproblems' solutions of the factors it is linked to. Finally, during the third step, *Lagrange updates*, the Lagrange multipliers for each subproblem are updated.

Algorithm 1. Alternating Directions Dual Decomposition(AD^3)

---

input: factor graph G, parameters θ, penalty constant η
1: initialize p (i.e. $p_i = 0.5 \forall i \in 1 \ldots |V|$), initialize $\lambda = 0$
2: **repeat**   ▷ Broadcast
3:     **for each** factor $\alpha \in F$ **do**
4:         **for each** $i \in \partial(\alpha)$ **do**
5:             set unary log-potentials $\xi_{i\alpha} := \theta_{i\alpha} + \lambda_{i\alpha}$
6:         **end for**
7:         $\hat{q}_\alpha := \text{SolveQP}(\theta_\alpha + \xi_\alpha, (p_i)_{i \in \partial(\alpha)})$
8:     **end for**
9:     **for each** variable $i \in V$ **do**   ▷ Gather
10:        compute avg $p_i := |\partial(i)|^{-1} \sum_{\alpha \in \partial(i)} \hat{q}_{i\alpha}$
11:        **for each** $\alpha \in \partial(i)$ **do**   ▷ Lagrange updates
12:            $\lambda_{i\alpha} := \lambda_{i\alpha} - \eta(\hat{q}_{i\alpha} - p_i)$
13:        **end for**
14:    **end for**
15: **until** convergence
output: primal variables p and q, dual variable λ

A distinguishing feature of AD^3 is that both the broadcast and update steps can be safely run in parallel. Indeed, notice that, since subproblems are independent, they can be safely distributed in different factors so that each one independently computes a local solution. AD^3 provides a collection of factors for which their quadratic problems are defined. As an example we present how the quadratic problem for the XOR factor is solved in Algorithm 2, where the input of the algorithm are the potentials $Z_\alpha : z_0, \ldots, z_K$ relative to the factor α. Note that in Algorithm 1 the call to the SOLVEQP method has two parameters, the second parameter is omitted here since it is not needed to solve the XOR. Algorithm 2 proceeds as follows. Lines 11-13 are responsible of checking if the constraint XOR is already satisfied. Then, if not satisfied, the Z_α vector is transformed using the projection onto simplex method described by [9]. This method navigates through Z_α in decreasing order, to find the pivot element y_i and the value of τ. Afterwards this τ is used to perform the actual projection. To this end, two auxiliary vectors Z'_α and Y_α are used: the former will contain the algorithm output and the latter is used to contain a sorted copy of Z_α. Although there are ways to obtain the pivot without the need of sorting the vector Z_α (described in [9]), in AD^3 is preferable to have a persistent sorted vector since order of elements is commonly preserved or barely altered across the iterations. Therefore efficient sorting methods on nearly-ordered sequences can be applied. An important feature of the XOR factor is that its quadratic problem can be solved in $O(K \cdot log K)$, where K stands for the number of variables connected to the factor.

Algorithm 2. SOLVEQP for an XOR factor

input: $Z_\alpha : z_0, \ldots, z_K$, vector with α log-potentials
1: **function** FINDTAU(Y_α)
2:     $\tau = 0.0$;
3:     $sum := \sum_{y_i \in Y_\alpha} y_i$
4:     **for each** $y_i \in Y_\alpha$ **do**
5:         $\tau := \frac{sum-1}{K-i}$
6:         **if** $y_i > \tau$ **then break**
7:         update $sum := sum - y_i$
8:     **end for**
9:     return τ
10: **end function**
11: $z'_i := max(0, z_i)$, for each $z_i \in Z_\alpha$
12: $sum := \sum_{z'_i \in Z'_\alpha} z'_i$
13: **if** $sum > 1.0$ **then**   ▷ Projection onto simplex
14:     sort Z_α into Y_α: $y_0 \leq \ldots \leq y_K$
15:     $\tau :=$ FINDTAU(Y_α)
16:     $z'_i := max(z_i - \tau, 0)$, for each $z_i \in Z_\alpha$
17: **end if**
output: Z'_α

As to gather, the step in which the subproblems communicate their local results, each variable can independently (from the rest of variables) gather and aggregate the results computed by the factors it is linked to. Despite being highly prone to parallelisation, to the best of our knowledge there is only one public implementation of AD^3 and cannot run in parallel [1]. The recent contributions to the parallelisation of ADMM to solve unconstrained optimisation problems [23] are very encouraging because they show that it is possible to obtain very significant speedups by exploiting nowadays parallel hardware. This finding spurs and motivates the need for a parallel implementation of AD^3.

But before that, in the next section we show that the WDP for CAs can be solved by means of AD^3.

3 Solving Combinatorial Auctions with AD³

A Combinatorial Auction (CA) is an auction in which bidders can place bids for a combination of items instead of individual ones. In this scenario, one of the fundamental problems is the Winner Determination Problem (WDP), which consists in finding the set of bids that maximise the auctioneer's benefit. Notice that the WDP is an $\mathcal{NP}$-complete problem.

Although special-purpose algorithms have addressed the WDP (e.g. [11,29]), the state-of-the-art method for solving a WDP is to encode it as an integer linear program (ILP) and solve it using an off-the-shelf commercial solver (such as CPLEX [1] or Gurobi [15]). Nonetheless, this approach fails to scale to large CA instances. Indeed, as noticed in [31], real problems may involve up to millions of bids. Therefore, such real problems are out of reach for state-of-the-art optimal solvers, and hence the need for heuristic approaches arise.

As observed in [4], "The simplest and, perhaps most tempting approach, to an optimization-based heuristic is to round the solution to a linear programming relaxation". Furthermore, solutions to an LP relaxation can provide a very effective start to finding a good feasible solution to the non-relaxed optimisation problem. Hereafter we focus on solving the LP relaxation of the WDP by means of AD^3. Since AD^3 requires a factor graph to operate, we first show how to encode the WDP as a factor graph. Then we show how AD^3 can run on top of this factor graph. We shall start by showing such encoding by means of an example to finally derive a general procedure.

Consider an auctioneer puts on sale a pair of goods g_1, g_2. Say that the auctioneer receives the following bids: b_1 offering \$20 for g_1 ; b_2 offering \$10 for g_2; and finally b_3 offering \$35 for goods g_1 and g_2 together. The WDP for this CA can be encoded as the following ILP:

$$
\begin{aligned}
\text{maximise} \quad & 20 \cdot x_1 + 10 \cdot x_2 + 35 \cdot x_3 \\
\text{subject to} \quad & x_1 + x_3 \leq 1 && [constraint\ c_1] \\
& x_2 + x_3 \leq 1 && [constraint\ c_2] \\
& x_1, x_2, x_3 \in \{0, 1\}
\end{aligned}
$$

where x_1, x_2, and x_3 stand for binary decision variables that indicate whether each bid is selected or not; constraint c_1 expresses that good g_1 can only be allocated to either bid b_1 or bid b_3 and constraint c_2 encodes that good g_2 can only be allocated to either bid b_2 or bid b_3.

---

[1] Available at http://www.ark.cs.cmu.edu/AD3/

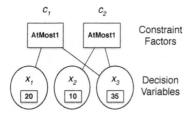

Fig. 1. Factor graph encoding of our CA example

Now we can encode the optimisation problem above into a factor graph as illustrated in Figure 1. First, we create a variable node for each bid. Each variable contains its bid's offer (indicates the value that the auctioneer obtains when the variable is active). For instance, variable x_1 for bid b_1 contains value 20. Then we create a factor node per good, connecting the bids that compete for the good, and which are therefore incompatible. For instance, factor c_1 is linked to the variables corresponding to bids b_1 and b_3.

We observe that each factor representing a constraint in the factor graph in figure 1 corresponds to the "AtMost1" function introduced by Smith and Eisner [33], which is satisfied if there is at most one active input. Although AD^3 does not directly support "AtMost1" constraints, as seen in [21], an XOR factor can be used to define it by adding a slack variable to the factor. The XOR factor complexity is $O(K \cdot logK)$, where K stands for the number of variables connected to the XOR factor. Notice that the operation of AD^3 when solving the WDP only involves computationally-efficient factors.

4   Parallel Realisation of AD^3

The AD^3 algorithm is amenable to general, architecture-level optimisation and parallelisation [21]. We propose an efficient realisation of the message-passing algorithmic pattern using shared variables and targeting multicore computer architectures. The so-called PAR-AD^3, that exploits the inherent parallelism at two dimensions: thread-level and data-level. For that, we reorganise both the data structures layout and the order of operations. The approach is generalisable to other similar graph processing algorithms. The key insights of our design are:

- An edge-centric representation of the shared variables that improves memory access performance.
- A reorganisation of the operations that promotes parallel scaling (thread parallelism) and vectorising (data parallelism).

4.1   Edge-centric Shared Data Layout

AD^3 is a message passing algorithm that iterates on three steps: *broadcast, gather* and *Lagrange multiplier update*. The message passing pattern isolates the operations applied to the different elements of the graph (factors, variables and edges), so that multiple operations can be performed concurrently on the graph data. These operations and data can then be physically distributed along different computation and storage elements.

The memory requirements of AD^3 are approximately proportional to the number of edges, and, for the problem sizes considered, they are fulfilled by most current shared-memory computer systems. In this situation, the fastest and most efficient mechanism for communication and synchronisation between processing cores is using shared variables (instead of explicit messages). The different processing cores of the computer will operate concurrently on the different elements of the graph (factors, variables or edges), both reading input data and generating new results stored in the shared memory. Execution performance is improved with a careful selection of synchronisation operations at the right point and an appropriate data structures layout.

Memory access performance is very sensitive to the data layout and data access pattern. When a loop has to iterate along a large regular data structure, the best performance is achieved when the next elements of the structure are naturally fetched from the next memory positions at each step of the iteration. Since AD^3 demands more computation work operating in edge data than in vertex or factor data, we adopt an edge-centric data representation, as reported in [27]. We want all information related to edges, such as unary log-potentials or lagrangian components, to be stored in consecutive memory positions. With this purpose, we apply a memory layout transformation that converts data structures originally designed in an Array of Structures (AOS) representation to a Structure of Arrays (SOA) representation.

Figure 2 illustrates how data was stored in memory in AD^3 and how the data layout is modified in PAR-AD^3. For the sake of clarity, we present data regarding 2 variables and 4 edges. AD^3 encodes the information following an AOS representation, where all properties related to each variable or edge are stored consecutively (see figure 2a). As the design is variable-centric, iterating on all the edges in the graph requires an indirect and scattered access to the variables (edges are accessed using the pointers associated to each variable). In contrast, the PAR-AD^3 SOA memory layout (figure 2b) stores the properties of variables and edges sequentially, thus resulting in a different array for each edge or variable property. Now, iterating on all edges of the graph requires consecutive accesses to array elements. The AOS memory representation of AD^3 benefits from memory access patterns where all the variable properties are used together, meanwhile the SOA memory representation of PAR-AD^3 benefits from the access of any property traversing all variables or edges.

To summarise, the PAR-AD^3 data representation transforms many scattered memory accesses into sequential, improving the memory access throughput. A derived advantage of the simplified edge access pattern is to foster better parallel scaling and vectorisation, but we need additional algorithmic transformations that are described in the next section.

4.2   Reordering Operations

Parallel scaling means distributing compute operations on large chunks of data along different computational units sharing the same memory space. Vectorising applies data parallelism strategies inside the same computational unit, and consists in using instructions that operate simultaneously on a small vector of consecutive data elements.

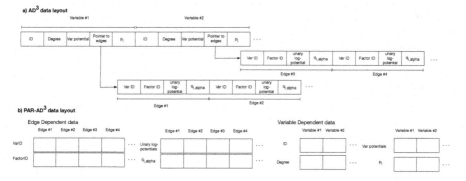

Fig. 2. a) AOS data representation of AD^3, compared to b) SOA data representation of $PAR\text{-}AD^3$

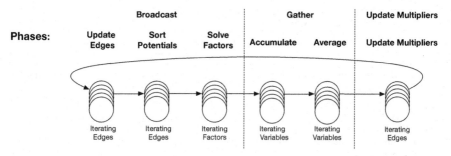

Fig. 3. Processing phases and parallelism in $PAR\text{-}AD^3$

Both parallel scaling and vectorising are usually applied to simple loop iterations with clearly separated inputs and outputs, no recurrent dependencies, and sequential accesses to vector elements.

Our proposal reshapes the way the algorithm defines the graph operations towards a new structure of many simple consecutive loops, outlined in figure 3. The original *Broadcast* step is now split in three phases: *update edge*, *sort potential* and *solve factors*. Also, the original *Gather* step is now split in two phases: *accumulate* and *average*. Note that we iterate on factors twice and also iterate on variables twice: this makes the loops simpler and provides more data locality. As a result, all phases are now parallelised for concurrent execution (thread parallelism) and four out of six are vectorised: *update edge*, *accumulate*, *average* and *update multiplier*.

Algorithm 3 shows a pseudo-code of $PAR\text{-}AD^3$ as a result of the optimizations applied. A pool of parallel threads is created outside of the main loop (line 2). Whenever a parallel loop inside the main loop is reached (lines 4, 9, 12, 19, 24, 27), the loop iterations are distributed to the threads for parallel execution. There is an implicit synchronisation after each loop, so that all threads wait for the generation of the results in one loop before starting the execution of the next.

As thoroughly described in the next section, these contributions have a significant impact in the sequential execution as well as allow good parallel scalability when an increasingly large number of threads are used. Since a clear trend in computer architecture is an increase of parallelism both at instruction and thread level, (for example,

Algorithm 3. *PAR-AD³* pseudo-code

---

input: factor graph G, parameters θ, penalty constant η
1: initialize p (i.e. $p_i = 0.5 \forall i \in 1 \ldots |V|$), initialize $\lambda = 0$
2: create threads
3: **repeat**
4:      **parallel for** $i\alpha \in E$ **do**   ▷ Update edges
5:           Update log-potentials $\xi_{i\alpha} := \theta_{i\alpha} + \lambda_{i\alpha}$
6:           compute $\hat{q}_{i\alpha} = \theta_{i\alpha} + \xi_{i\alpha}$
7:           compute $\hat{q}'_{i\alpha} = max(0, \hat{q}_{i\alpha})$
8:      **end for**
9:      **parallel for** factor $\alpha \in F$ **do**   ▷ Sort potentials
10:          $\hat{q}\_sorted_\alpha := \text{sort}(\hat{q}_\alpha)$
11:     **end for**
12:     **parallel for** factor $\alpha \in F$ **do**   ▷ Solve factors
13:          $sum = \sum_{i\in\partial(\alpha)}(\hat{q}'_{i\alpha})$
14:          **if** $sum > 1.0$ **then**
15:               $\tau := \text{FindTau}(\hat{q}\_sorted_\alpha)$
16:               $q'_{i\alpha} := \max(q_{i\alpha} - \tau, 0)$, for each $q_{i\alpha} \in q_\alpha$
17:          **end if**
18:     **end for**
19:     **parallel for** variable $i \in V$ **do**   ▷ Acummulate
20:          **for** $i \in \partial(\alpha)$ **do**
21:               $\tilde{p}_i := \tilde{p}_i + \hat{q}_{i\alpha}$
22:          **end for**
23:     **end for**
24:     **parallel for** variable $i \in V$ **do**   ▷ Average
25:          $p_i := \tilde{p}_i / |\partial(i)|$
26:     **end for**
27:     **parallel for** $i\alpha \in E$ **do**
28:          $\lambda_{i\alpha} := \lambda_{i\alpha} - \eta(\hat{q}_{i\alpha} - p_i)$ ▷ Update multipliers
29:     **end for**
30:     update η
31: **until** convergence
output: primal variables p and q, dual variable λ

---

the intel Xeon Phi accelerator operates with 512-bit vector registers and contains more than 60 execution cores) the methodology applied to *PAR-AD³* makes it ready to benefit from upcoming improvements.

5   Empirical Evaluation

In this section, we assess *PAR-AD³* performance against the state-of-the-art optimisation software CPLEX with the aim of determining the scenarios for which *PAR-AD³* is the algorithm of choice. We also quantify its current gains, both in sequential and parallel executions. To this end, we first find the data distributions and range of problems that are best suited for *PAR-AD³*. Thereafter, we briefly analyse two algorithmic key features: convergence and solution quality. Afterwards, we quantify the speedups of *PAR-AD³* with respect to CPLEX in sequential and parallel executions. From this analysis we conclude that *PAR-AD³* does obtain larger benefits from parallelisation than

CPLEX. Indeed, *PAR-AD^3* achieves a peak speedup of 23X above CPLEX barrier, the state-of-the-art solver for sparse problems.

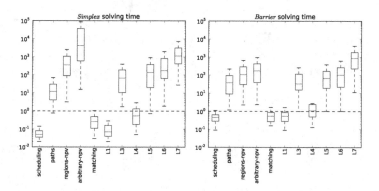

Fig. 4. Solving time for different distributions, single thread. a) Simplex b) Barrier

Experiment Setup. In order to generate CA WDP instances, we employ CATS, the CA generator suite described in [20]. Each instance is generated out of the following list of distributions thoroughly described in [19]: arbitrary, matching, paths, regions, scheduling, L1, L3, L4, L5, L6 and L7. We discarded to employ the L2 distribution, because the CATS generator is not capable of generating large instances. While the first five distributions were designed to generate realistic CA WDP instances, the latter ones generate artificial instances. The main difference between the two distribution categories is the use of dummy goods that add structure to the problem inspired in some real life scenarios. i.e. Paths models the transportation links between cities; Regions models an auction of real estate or an auction where the basis of complementarity is the two-dimensional adjacency of goods; Arbitrary extends regions by removing the two-dimensional adjacency assumption, and it can be applied to model electronic parts design or procurement; Matching models airline take-off and landing rights auctions; and Scheduling models a distributed job-shop scheduling domain. Artificial (or Legacy) distributions have been often criticised [3,20,8] mainly due to their poor applicability, specially in the economic field. However they are interesting in order to study the algorithm performance in different situations. Both *AD^3* and *PAR-AD^3* are well suited for large-scale hard problems. For this reason, we first determine which of these distributions are hard to solve, putting special attention to the realistic ones. For our experimentation, we considered a number of goods within $[10^3, 10^4]$ in steps of 10^3 goods. Furthermore, the number of bids ranged within $[10^4, 4 \cdot 10^4]$ in steps of 10^4 bids. Each problem scenario is characterised by a combination of distribution, number of goods, and number of bids. Our experiments consider 5 different instances for each problem scenario and we analyse their mean value. Experiments are executed in a computer with two four-core Intel Xeon Processors L5520 @2.27GHz with 32 GB RAM with the hyper-threading mechanism disabled.

Different Distributions Hardness. We empirically determine the hardness of the relaxation for our experimental data by solving the LP using CPLEX simplex (simplex

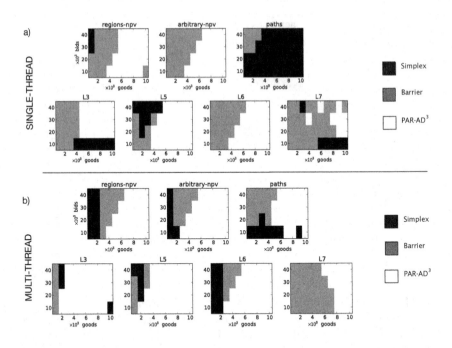

Fig. 5. Fastest algorithm solving different distributions and problem sizes. a) Single-thread, b) Multi-thread.

henceforth), CPLEX barrier (barrier henceforth), the state-of-the art algorithms. Results are plot in figures 4a and 4b. According to the results, scheduling and matching from the realistic distributions and L1, L4 from the legacy ones are very well addressed by simplex, where solving time is, in general, less than one second. Both AD^3 and PAR-AD^3 are not competitive in this scenario. Applicability of PAR-AD^3 will be shown to be effective to the rest of distributions, especially in hard instances. Barrier is also doing a good job when the problems are hard, particularly in the arbitrary and regions distributions, where the representation matrix is more sparse.

Single-thread Analysis. After comparing the publicly-available version of AD^3 against sequential PAR-AD^3, we observed that PAR-AD^3 outperformed AD^3 even in sequential execution, reaching an average speedup of 3X and a peak speedup of 12.4X. Moreover, we observed that the harder the instances, the larger the speedups of PAR-AD^3 with respect to AD^3. Since both algorithms are well suited for hard instances, this is particularly noticeable. Next, we compared the single-thread average performance of PAR-AD^3 against simplex and barrier. The results are plot in Figure 5a ,where we display the best algorithm for the different distributions and problem sizes. PAR-AD^3 is shown to be well suited for larger problems (the upper-right corner) in almost all the distributions. In general, barrier is the best algorithm in the mid-sized problems, while simplex applicability is limited to a small number of cases. Distribution paths presents a different behaviour, where adding goods increases the average bid arity and this is beneficial for simplex, which runs better in dense problems.

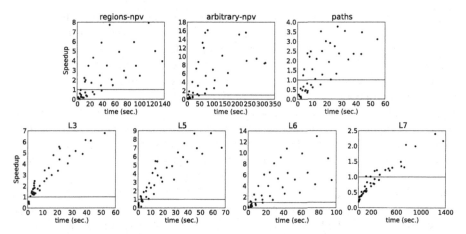

Fig. 6. Speedup of $PAR\text{-}AD^3$ for different distributions against barrier in a multi-thread execution

In general, the larger the WDP instances, the larger the $PAR\text{-}AD^3$ benefits. Single-threaded $PAR\text{-}AD^3$ reaches a peak speedup of 12.4 for the hardest distribution when compared to barrier, the best of the two state-of-the-art solvers.

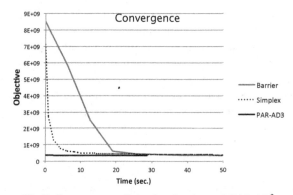

Fig. 7. Convergence of simplex, barrier and $PAR\text{-}AD^3$

Convergence and Solution Quality. Figure 7 shows a trace of an execution that illustrates the way the different solvers approximate the solution over time (using a regions distribution, 5×10^3 goods, and 10^4 bids). We chose this run because the similar performance of the three algorithms made them comparable. Note that $PAR\text{-}AD^3$ converges to the solution in 29 sec., while barrier requires 102 sec. and simplex 202 sec. (not visible in the figure). Furthermore, notice that $PAR\text{-}AD^3$ quickly reaches a high-quality bound, hence promptly guaranteeing close-to-the-solution anytime approximations. In general, our experimental data indicate that the initial solution provided by $PAR\text{-}AD^3$ is always significantly better than the one assessed by both simplex and barrier. Finally, upon convergence, there is a maximum deviation of 0.02% between $PAR\text{-}AD^3$ solutions and those assessed by CPLEX. Note that we run CPLEX with default parameters, has the feasibility tolerance set to 10^{-6}. This means that CPLEX solutions may be infeasible up to a range of 10^{-6} per variable. In the same sense, $PAR\text{-}AD^3$ feasibility tolerance is set to 10^{-12}. This good initial solution is a nice property that makes $PAR\text{-}AD^3$ suitable to be used as a method able to obtain quick bounds, either to be embedded in a MIP solver or also to provide a fast solution able to be used towards an approximate solution.

Multi-thread Analysis. We have run $PAR\text{-}AD^3$, simplex and barrier with 8 parallel threads each, hence using the full parallelism offered by our computer. The results are displayed in figure 5b. When comparing with figure 5a (corresponding to the single-thread execution), we observe that $PAR\text{-}AD^3$ outperforms simplex and barrier in many more scenarios, and in general $PAR\text{-}AD^3$ applicability grows in concert with the parallel resources in all cases. Hence, we infer that $PAR\text{-}AD^3$ better benefits from parallelisation than simplex and barrier. The case of the paths distribution is especially remarkable since simplex is faster than other algorithms when running in a single-thread scenario. Nonetheless, as $PAR\text{-}AD^3$ better exploits parallelism, it revealed to be the most suitable algorithm for hard distributions when running in multi-threaded executions, including paths. In accordance with those results, it is expected that increasing the number of computational units will widen the range of applicability of $PAR\text{-}AD^3$.

Finally, we compared $PAR\text{-}AD^3$ performance against barrier using 8 threads. We only compare $PAR\text{-}AD^3$ to barrier since it is the best suited algorithm for the selected distributions (i.e in some executions $PAR\text{-}AD^3$ can be up to three orders of magnitude faster than simplex). Figure 6 shows the average performance speedup of $PAR\text{-}AD^3$ versus barrier as a function of the total running time of the execution of barrier (shown in the X-axis). We observe a clear trend in all scenarios: the harder the problem becomes for barrier, the larger the speedups obtained by $PAR\text{-}AD^3$. Our peak speedup is 23X (16X when taking the mean execution time of the different instances). The best results are achieved in the arbitrary distribution, which in addition was significantly better solved by barrier than by simplex according to figure 4. We recall that arbitrary is a distribution that can be applied to the design of electronic parts or procurement since it removes the two-dimensional adjacency of regions. In arbitrary, larger speedups correspond to the more sparse scenario, i.e. the bottom-right corner in figure 5.

6   Conclusions

In this paper we have tried to open up a path towards solving large-scale CAs. We have proposed a novel approach to solve the LP relaxation for the WDP. Our approach encodes the optimisation problem as a factor graph and uses AD^3, a dual-decomposition message-passing algorithm, to efficiently find the solution.

In order to achieve higher efficiency, we identified some of the bottlenecks found in message-passing graph-based algorithms and proposed some techniques to achieve good performance and scalability, in particular when executing in parallel. As a result of this analysis, we rearranged the operations performed by AD^3 providing a new algorithm, the so-called $PAR\text{-}AD^3$, which is an optimised and parallel version of AD^3.

Our experimental results validate $PAR\text{-}AD^3$ efficiency gains in large scale scenarios. We have shown that $PAR\text{-}AD^3$ performs better than CPLEX for large-scale CAs in the computationally hardest distributions, both in single- and multi-threaded scenarios, with a peak speedup of 23X. Furthermore, the speedup is larger in multi-threaded scenarios, showing that *PAR-AD*^{3} scales better with hardware than CPLEX. Therefore, *PAR-AD*^{3} has much potential to solve large-scale coordination problems that can be cast as optimisation problems.

References

1. IBM ILOG CPLEX Optimizer,
   http://www-01.ibm.com/software/integration/optimization/cplex-optimizer/ (last 2010)
2. Aguiar, P., Xing, E.P., Figueiredo, M., Smith, N.A., Martins, A.: An augmented lagrangian approach to constrained map inference. In: Proceedings of the 28th International Conference on Machine Learning (ICML 2011), pp. 169–176 (2011)
3. Andersson, A., Tenhunen, M., Ygge, F.: Integer programming for combinatorial auction winner determination. In: Proceedings of the Fourth International Conference on MultiAgent Systems, pp. 39–46. IEEE (2000)
4. Ball, M.O.: Heuristics based on mathematical programming. Surveys in Operations Research and Management Science 16(1), 21–38 (2011)
5. Bertsimas, D., Tsitsiklis, J.: Introduction to Linear Optimization, 1st edn. Athena Scientific (1997)
6. Boyd, S., Parikh, N., Chu, E., Peleato, B., Eckstein, J.: Distributed optimization and statistical learning via the alternating direction method of multipliers. Foundations and Trends® in Machine Learning 3(1), 1–122 (2011)
7. Cramton, P., Shoham, Y., Steinberg, R.: Combinatorial auctions. MIT Press (2006)
8. De Vries, S., Vohra, R.V.: Combinatorial auctions: A survey. INFORMS Journal on Computing 15(3), 284–309 (2003)
9. Duchi, J., Shalev-Shwartz, S., Singer, Y., Chandra, T.: Efficient projections onto the l1-ball for learning in high dimensions. In: Proceedings of the 25th International Conference on Machine Learning, pp. 272–279. ACM (2008)
10. Eckstein, J., Bertsekas, D.P.: On the douglas?rachford splitting method and the proximal point algorithm for maximal monotone operators. Mathematical Programming 55(1-3), 293–318 (1992)
11. Fujishima, Y., Leyton-Brown, K., Shoham, Y.: Taming the computational complexity of combinatorial auctions: Optimal and approximate approaches. In: International Joint Conferences on Artificial Intelligence (IJCAI), pp. 548–553 (1999)
12. Gabay, D., Mercier, B.: A dual algorithm for the solution of nonlinear variational problems via finite element approximation. Computers & Mathematics with Applications 2(1), 17–40 (1976)
13. Globerson, A., Jaakkola, T.S.: Fixing max-product: Convergent message passing algorithms for map lp-relaxations. In: Advances in Neural Information Processing Systems, pp. 553–560 (2008)
14. Glowinski, R., Marroco, A.: Sur l'approximation, par éléments finis d'ordre un, et la résolution, par pénalisation-dualité d'une classe de problèmes de dirichlet non linéaires. ESAIM: Mathematical Modelling and Numerical Analysis-Modélisation Mathématique et Analyse Numérique 9(R2), 41–76 (1975)
15. Gu, Z., Rothberg, E., Bixby, R.: Gurobi 4.0.2. software (December 2010)
16. Hazan, T., Shashua, A.: Norm-product belief propagation: Primal-dual message-passing for approximate inference. IEEE Transactions on Information Theory 56(12), 6294–6316 (2010)
17. Kolmogorov, V.: Convergent tree-reweighted message passing for energy minimization. IEEE Transactions on Pattern Analysis and Machine Intelligence 28(10), 1568–1583 (2006)
18. Komodakis, N., Paragios, N., Tziritas, G.: Mrf optimization via dual decomposition: Message-passing revisited. In: IEEE 11th International Conference on Computer Vision, ICCV 2007, pp. 1–8. IEEE (2007)

19. Leyton-Brown, K., Nudelman, E., Shoham, Y.: Empirical hardness models: Methodology and a case study on combinatorial auctions. Journal of the ACM (JACM) 56(4), 22 (2009)

20. Leyton-Brown, K., Pearson, M., Shoham, Y.: Towards a universal test suite for combinatorial auction algorithms. In: Proceedings of the 2nd ACM Conference on Electronic Commerce, pp. 66–76. ACM (2000)

21. Martins, A.F.T.: The Geometry of Constrained Structured Prediction: Applications to Inference and Learning of Natural Language Syntax. PhD thesis, Columbia University (2012)

22. Martins, A.F.T., Figueiredo, M.A.T., Aguiar, P.M.Q., Smith, N.A., Xing, E.P.: Ad^3: Alternating directions dual decomposition for map inference in graphical models. Journal of Machine Learning Research 46 (2014) (to appear)

23. Miksik, O., Vineet, V., Perez, P., Torr, P.H.S.: Distributed non-convex admm-inference in large-scale random fields. In: British Machine Vision Conference, BMVC (2014)

24. Parsons, S., Rodriguez-Aguilar, J.A., Klein, M.: Auctions and bidding: A guide for computer scientists. ACM Comput. Surv. 43(2), 10:1–10:59 (2011)

25. Ramchurn, S.D., Mezzetti, C., Giovannucci, A., Rodriguez-Aguilar, J.A., Dash, R.K., Jennings, N.R.: Trust-based mechanisms for robust and efficient task allocation in the presence of execution uncertainty. Journal of Artificial Intelligence Research 35(1), 119 (2009)

26. Ramchurn, S.D., Rogers, A., Macarthur, K., Farinelli, A., Vytelingum, P., Vetsikas, I., Jennings, N.R.: Agent-based coordination technologies in disaster management. In: Proceedings of the 7th International Joint Conference on Autonomous Agents and Multiagent Systems: Demo Papers, pp. 1651–1652 (2008)

27. Roy, A., Mihailovic, I., Zwaenepoel, W.: X-stream: edge-centric graph processing using streaming partitions. In: Proceedings of the Twenty-Fourth ACM Symposium on Operating Systems Principles, pp. 472–488. ACM (2013)

28. Rush, A.M., Sontag, D., Collins, M., Jaakkola, T.: On dual decomposition and linear programming relaxations for natural language processing. In: Proceedings of the 2010 Conference on Empirical Methods in Natural Language Processing, pp. 1–11. Association for Computational Linguistics (2010)

29. Sandholm, T., Suri, S., Gilpin, A., Levine, D.: Cabob: A fast optimal algorithm for combinatorial auctions. In: International Joint Conference on Artificial Intelligence, vol. 17, pp. 1102–1108 (2001)

30. Santos Jr., E.: On the generation of alternative explanations with implications for belief revision. In: Proceedings of the Seventh conference on Uncertainty in Artificial Intelligence, pp. 339–347. Morgan Kaufmann Publishers Inc. (1991)

31. Sheffi, Y.: Combinatorial auctions in the procurement of transportation services. Interfaces 34(4), 245–252 (2004)

32. Sierra, C., Lopez de Mantaras, R., Busquets, D.: Multiagent bidding mechanisms for robot qualitative navigation. In: Castelfranchi, C., Lespérance, Y. (eds.) ATAL 2000. LNCS (LNAI), vol. 1986, pp. 198–212. Springer, Heidelberg (2001)

33. Smith, D., Eisner, J.: Dependency parsing by belief propagation. In: Proceedings of the Conference on Empirical Conference on Empirical Methods in Natural Language Processing, pp. 145–156 (October 2008)

34. Sontag, D., Meltzer, T., Globerson, A., Jaakkola, T.S., Weiss, Y.: Tightening lp relaxations for map using message passing. arXiv preprint arXiv:1206.3288 (2012)

35. Wainwright, M.J., Jaakkola, T.S., Willsky, A.S.: Tree-reweighted belief propagation algorithms and approximate ml estimation by pseudo-moment matching. In: Workshop on Artificial Intelligence and Statistics, vol. 21, p. 97. Society for Artificial Intelligence and Statistics (2003)

36. Yanover, C., Meltzer, T., Weiss, Y.: Linear programming relaxations and belief propagation – an empirical study. J. Mach. Learn. Res. 7, 1887–1907 (2006)

Handling Agent Perception in Heterogeneous Distributed Systems: A Policy-Based Approach

Stephen Cranefield[1]([✉]) and Surangika Ranathunga[2]

[1] Department of Information Science, University of Otago, Dunedin, New Zealand
stephen.cranefield@otago.ac.nz
[2] Department of Computer Science & Engineering, Faculty of Engineering,
University of Moratuwa, Moratuwa, Sri Lanka
surangika@cse.mrt.ac.lk

Abstract. Multi-agent systems technologies have been widely investigated as a promising approach for modelling and building distributed systems. However, the benefits of agents are not restricted to systems solely comprised of agents. This paper considers how to ease the task of developing agents that perceive information from asynchronously executing external systems, especially those producing data at a high frequency. It presents a design for a *percept buffer* that, when configured with domain-specific percept metadata and application-specific *percept management policies*, provides a generic but customisable solution. Three application case studies are presented to illustrate and evaluate the approach.

1 Introduction

Multi-agent systems (MAS) technologies have been widely investigated as a promising approach for modelling and building distributed systems. In particular, much MAS research focuses on developing theories and tools that address the requirements of autonomous distributed software components that must act, interact and coordinate with each other in complex domains. Typically, agents are conceptualised as having incomplete and changing knowledge, the ability to act proactively to satisfy explicit goals, adaptive behaviour through the selection of plans that best respond to goals in a given situation, and the ability to communicate knowledge and requests to each other.

This paper considers, in particular, agents based on the popular Belief-Desire-Intention (BDI) agent model [4], which is inspired by human practical reasoning. Agent development platforms implementing this model, such as Jason [3], allow programmers to write code in terms of a dynamic belief base that is updated as *percepts* are received from the external *environment*, and *plans* are triggered by changes in beliefs and the creation of new goals by other plans. Plans can also cause *actions* to be performed in the environment. The developer must provide an environment class that models the application state visible to the agent and/or affected by its actions. At its simplest, this is a simulation of a physical environment. However, BDI agents have proven their value beyond simple simulated systems. They have been used for implementing robots [16,15], "intelligent virtual agents" [13,7,2] that control avatars in virtual worlds and

© IFIP International Federation for Information Processing 2015
T. Holvoet and M. Viroli (Eds.): COORDINATION 2015, LNCS 9037, pp. 169–185, 2015.
DOI: 10.1007/978-3-319-19282-6_11

multi-player games, and even for real-time control of satellites [6]. As well as these situations where an agent's 'body' is controlled by software external to the agent, it may also be the case that an agent is only a component of a larger distributed system involving multiple technologies and protocols. In this case, it may be most convenient for the agent programmer to regard the external systems as part of its environment, and therefore a source of percepts and the target of actions [5].

This paper therefore considers the problem of providing an agent with a view of one or more external system components as a source of percepts, extending our previous architecture in which agent 'endpoints' act as a bridge between agents and message-based routing and mediation middleware [5][1]. There are several aspects to this problem:

1) Agents perceive the environment periodically and asynchronously from the changes occurring in the external systems. Therefore, multiple changes may occur between agent perceptions, and it is necessary to buffer these changes. **2)** BDI agents have a relatively slow execution cycle, and thus information from external systems such as virtual worlds and robot sensors may arrive much faster than the agent's perception rate. Delivering all buffered percepts to the agent on each perception may exceed its ability to trigger and execute plans. Therefore, buffered percepts should be amalgamated or summarised between perceptions. **3)** The question of whether a percept should replace an older buffered one is dependent on the domain ontology. Thus, percept buffering requires domain knowledge. **4)** The logic for summarising related buffered percepts is application-dependent. Thus, percept buffering needs application knowledge.

The first two issues above have been repeatedly encountered by researchers [6,8,12,13,10]. However, as yet, agent development tools do not provide any platform-level solution to these problems, leaving the agent programmer to implement their own application-level solutions.

This paper provides a solution to this problem, informed by the third and fourth observations above, by introducing the concepts of a *percept buffer* and configurable *percept management policies*. Together, these control the number and form of percepts provided to an agent. Given a generic percept buffer, a developer can use this in conjunction with common policies from a library or custom application-specific ones, to configure the buffer to avoid information loss and reduce the cognitive load needed for percept handling. A percept buffer therefore provides a general platform-, domain- and application-independent framework for tackling the problems of handling percepts representing information from external systems in a flexible way.

2   Related Work

The difficulty of handling high frequency percepts in BDI agent systems has been acknowledged by researchers implementing situated agents [12,13]. However, we are not aware of any implemented concrete solution to this problem.

---

[1] Our previous work also addresses interpreting actions as requests to external systems, but here we focus on percepts.

There is some research on abstracting the low-level sensor data received from an external environment before providing it to a BDI agent [13,16]. Similar to receiving low-level sensor data, it is also possible that the agent could receive a continuous data stream from the environment. In such a case, this continuous data stream should be discretized before providing it to the agent as percepts. Such an abstraction engine has been described by Dennis et al. [6] in the context of using BDI agents to control a satellite. By providing only abstract environment information and/or discretized information to an agent, the problem of cognitive overload can be minimised. However, this does not directly address the problem of high frequency perception—the abstracted environment information may still arrive at too high a frequency for a relatively slow BDI agent. Moreover, this previous work implements the sensor data abstraction components outside the BDI agent system, thus providing it with no control over the type and amount of the percepts it provides to agents.

An alternative approach to minimising the cognitive overload is actively filtering out percepts that do not fit certain criteria. Percept filtering is discussed alongside attention theories, where it is argued that given the fact that agent attention is a limited resource, the agent should be able to filter-out information that falls outside its current attention. Filtering can be of two-forms: top-down (goal-driven), or bottom-up. Top-down filtering refers to retaining only those percepts that are relevant to the currently pursued goals of the agent [14]. Bottom-up filtering refers to identifying salient information in the incoming percept stream that should catch the agent's attention. The work of van Oijen and Dignum [11] presents an example for goal-driven filtering of percepts by an intelligent virtual agent (IVA). When an agent adopts a new goal, it can specify the type of percepts required for that goal. This filtering is terminated as soon as the agent stops pursuing the current goal. Ideally, an IVA should be able to strike a balance between the two types of filtering.

The use of a cache or a buffer to keep environment information required by an agent is not new. For example, Oijen et al. [12] present the use of a cache to store a high level domain model derived from lower-level game state data. This information is kept until game state changes invalidate the cached derived data. Their ontology loosely corresponds to our percept metadata (see Sect. 5). However, although agents can filter the percepts they wish to perceive via subscriptions, there is no counterpart to our policies for summarising or aggregating multiple percepts received between perceptions.

3 Managing Agent Perception Using Policies

At the heart of our approach is the use of policies to manage the number of percepts produced for the deliberation process of an agent. Policies may be generic ones that are useful across a range of applications, and may be parameterised to configure them for specific applications. On the other hand, agent programmers may develop their own application-specific policies, which can be plugged into our framework via a simple interface. We also allow agents to dynamically change the policies used to pre-process their incoming percepts in order to change the focus of their attention—an example of this is given in Sect. 9.2.

Some useful application-independent policies are listed below.

Keep latest percept. This policy will simply *replace* the previously processed matching percepts with the new one. This might be appropriate, for example, for percepts that represent sensor readings (with the sensor identifier treated as a percept *key*). If multiple readings for the same sensor arrive between two agent perceptions, the agent may only need to perceive the latest reading.

Keep latest with history. As above, this policy will ensure that at most one percept for a given functor (predicate name), arity (number of arguments) and list of key argument values is kept in the queue of percepts waiting to be perceived. However, in case the agent wishes to inspect the full recent history of matching percepts (since the previous perception), the policy records this history in the percept as an additional argument. This policy could also be refined to associate a time stamp with each percept in the history list. This policy illustrates an important feature of the design of our percept buffer: we support the use of policies that change the structure of percepts, e.g. by changing their functors and arities.

Keep most significant. Rather than keeping only the most recent percept (e.g. from a sensor), this policy will keep the one with the most significant value. For example, for a sensor monitoring Nitrogen Dioxide concentrations at a city intersection, the agent may be interested in the highest reading since the last perception.

4   Architecture

Figure 1 shows our architecture for using percept buffers to handle percept buffering, amalgamation and summarisation. We assume that percepts relevant to the agent are received via one or more channels, shown on the left hand side of the figure. These are responsible for delivering percepts obtained from external sources, such as virtual worlds, complex event detection engines and enterprise messaging systems, to the appropriate agents' percept buffers. It is the responsibility of these channels to perform whatever data preprocessing is necessary to produce percepts in an appropriate format for the agent platform used[2].

The channels also have the role of adding specific metadata to each percept to specify how the agents' percept buffers should combine this new information with any percepts that are in the buffer waiting for the agent to perceive them. Most importantly, this metadata includes the name of a *policy* to be used to amalgamate matching percepts (if required). The notion of a matching percept is defined by indicating the *key argument indices*, i.e. the argument positions that form a (possibly compound) key for a percept with that functor and arity,

---

[2] Eventually it may be possible to use a platform-independent format for percepts, such as the "interface intermediate language" proposed by Behrens et al. [1].

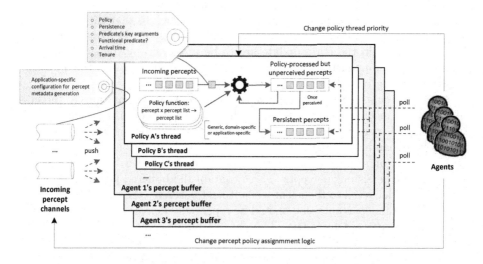

Fig. 1. The architecture and interfaces of a percept buffer

and whether or not the percept's predicate is *functional*, i.e. whether it can only have a single value at any time for given arguments at the key argument indices. Percepts are also specified as being *transient* or *persistent*. Transient percepts are only stored until the agent's next perception, whereas persistent percepts are treated as part of the environment's state, and are also perceived by the agent in subsequent perceptions (unless replaced by newer percepts, or they expire as specified by the percept's *arrival time* and *tenure*). Note that the aim of the percept buffer is not to act as the agent's memory in general. However, we see its role as providing an agent environment that encapsulates the external sources of percepts. We therefore allow an agent developer the option of using the buffer to store persistent state that may not be made available repeatedly by the external system.

The percept metadata, and the implementations of the policies used (conforming to a simple interface—see Sect. 6), provide the domain- and application-specific information used by the percept buffers. Therefore, configuring our approach for a specific application involves providing a mechanism for the channels to add the required metadata, e.g. application-specific rules. More detail on our metadata scheme is given in Sect. 5.

The architecture allows agents to dynamically control their perception by changing how channels assign policies to percepts (based on their functor and arity), and the priorities of the threads that execute policies. The mechanisms for providing this functionality will depend on the agent platform used. Our implementation, using Jason [3], provides agent "internal actions" for this purpose.

Each agent has its own percept buffer, which has percepts, along with their metadata, pushed to it from the channels. A single percept may be delivered at a time, e.g. when a stream of data is being consumed by a channel, or a set of percepts may be delivered together, with the intention that these represent a complete state update for the agent. In the latter case, we assume that there is a single channel or that the channels have been designed so that the buffer does not need to synchronise state updates from different channels. We also assume that all percepts in the state update are to be processed by the same policy[3], or that it does not matter if a single state update results in different policies' outputs being perceived by the agent at different times[4].

For each percept-processing policy in use, a percept buffer maintains a (thread-safe) queue of incoming percept sets that have been pushed on the queue by the channels. Each percept set on the queue is either a singleton set (in the case of percept streaming) or represents a state update. In addition, for each policy, there is a list of processed but unperceived percepts and a list of previously perceived but persistent percepts. These contain the buffered percepts that are waiting to be delivered to the agent when it next perceives the environment. The latter list contains percepts that should be repeatedly delivered to the agent, according to the percept metadata. The percept buffer creates a thread for each policy that repeatedly takes percept sets from the incoming queue and combines them with the buffered percepts to produce an updated list of buffered percepts.

When the agent perceives, it consumes the percepts in the unperceived percept list. It also receives percepts from the persistent percept list. At this time, the persistent percept set is updated with the newly perceived percepts that are annotated as being persistent. This may involve some instances of functional percepts being replaced with new ones. As there is a separate perceived persistent percept set for each policy, we require that functional persistent percepts with a given functor and arity are always associated with the same policy; otherwise the updating of persistent percepts cannot be guaranteed to be done correctly.

5   Percept Metadata

The following metadata scheme is used by channels when annotating percepts before delivering them to the agents' percept buffers. In this way, domain- and application-specific knowledge can be provided on how percepts should be treated.

Policy This metadata element specifies the name of the policy that should be used to combine a new percept with any 'matching' ones that have been processed by the policy but not yet perceived.

Persistent This element can be true or false, depending on whether the percept should be stored in the percept buffer persistently and repeatedly perceived by the agent until it is replaced by newer information or it expires.

KeyArgs As described above, the key arguments for a percept are those that comprise a compound key. The value of this optional element is a list of argu- ment indices. This defines which processed but unperceived percepts match a

---

[3] It is possible for a single policy to process percepts with different functors.

[4] Our current implementation adds an additional assumption: that all percepts in an incoming percept set have the same persistence (transient or persistent), but this is simpler to remove than the other assumptions.

new one: percepts match if they have the same functor, arity, and values at the key argument indices.

FuncPred This has value `true` if the percept is an instance of a predicate that is functional, i.e. only one instance of the predicate can exist for any specific values of the key arguments. Subsequent percepts with the same key arguments must replace older ones. This is only used when updating the perceived persistent percepts. This is because policies have the responsibility of deciding how to resolve the co-existence of new and old matching unperceived percepts—the developer may wish the agent to receive all percepts that have arrived since the last perception, or an aggregation or summary of them.

ArrivalTime This records the time at which the percept arrived.

Tenure This optionally specifies an interval after which the percept is no longer useful and should be deleted even if not perceived. This is most useful for persistent percepts.

```
public interface Policy {
  public List<WrappedPercept> applyPolicy(
    WrappedPercept percept,
    List<WrappedPercept> queuedPercepts);

  public List<WrappedPercept> eventToStatePercepts(WrappedPercept p);

  public WrappedPercept transformPerceptAfterPerception(WrappedPercept p);
}
```

Fig. 2. The policy interface

6 Defining and Applying Policies

A policy is defined by a class that implements the interface shown in Java in Fig. 2[5]. The key method is `applyPolicy`. This is called for each percept in the new percept set in turn. The first argument, of class `WrappedPercept`, represents a newly received percept, wrapped by another object recording its metadata. The second argument, `queuedPercepts`, should be a list of the percepts that have been previously output by this method, are not yet perceived by the agent, and which match the new percept based on the functor, arity and KeyArgs metadatum. As new percepts arrive, the `applyPolicy` method will be repeatedly called to combine newly arrived percepts with those queued for perception by the agent. For some policies this will result in reducing the number of percepts received by the agent on each perception. By providing application-specific policy classes, the developer can customise how this is done. Some example policies were outlined in Sect. 3.

The other two methods in the policy interface are optional (they can just return a null value) and are discussed in Sections 7 and 8.

Pseudocode for the `run` method of a policy thread is shown in Algorithm 1. The key line of the algorithm is line 19, which obtains the application-specific

---

[5] A separate policy factory class is used to associate names with policy classes.

Algorithm 1. The policy thread's algorithm

Data: policyName: Name of policy handled by this thread
      newPerceptQueue: Blocking queue of percept sets
      unperceivedPercepts: Concurrent map from policy names to percept list
      partitions

1 forever do
2   newPercepts ← newPerceptQueue.take ()
3   oldPercepts ← unperceivedPercepts.get (policyName)
4   if oldPercepts = null then
5 | oldPercepts ← empty percept list partition
6   end
7   applyPolicyToAllPercepts (policyName, newPercepts, oldPercepts)
8   oldValue ← unperceivedPercepts.replace (policyName, oldPercepts)
9   if oldValue = null and oldPercepts ≠ null then
         // The agent has concurrently consumed old percepts
10   oldPercepts ← empty percept list partition
11   applyPolicyToAllPercepts (newPercepts, oldPercepts)
12   unperceivedPercepts.put (policyName, oldPercepts)
13   end
14 end

15 Procedure applyPolicyToAllPercepts (policyName, newPercepts, oldPercepts)
16 foreach p ∈ newPercepts do
17   key ← partitionKey (p)
18   matchingPercepts ← oldPercepts [key]
19   processedPercepts ← getPolicyObject (policyName).
                    applyPolicy (p, matchingPercepts)
20   oldPercepts [key] ← processedPercepts
21 end

---

policy object for the given policy name and calls the `applyPolicy` method. For brevity, in the algorithm we write "percept" to mean wrapped percept (a percept with its metadata). The percepts processed by the policy but not yet perceived, as well as the perceived persistent percepts, are represented as "percept list partitions". This data structure stores a list of percepts as a set of sublists. Each sublist contains the percepts with a given *partition key*: a triple combining a functor, arity and specific tuple of values for the key arguments of the predicate with that functor and arity, e.g. $\langle sensor\_reading, 2, \langle sensor72 \rangle \rangle$. This is a special case of a map, and we write $p[k]$ for the sublist of percept list partition p with partition key k.

The algorithm runs an infinite loop that takes each (possibly singleton) set of new percepts from the new percepts queue and processes it. Line 2 retrieves a set of new percepts and line 3 looks up the percepts that have been previously processed by this thread but not yet perceived. Lines 4–6 create a new percept list partition if there are no previously processed but unperceived percepts. Line 7 calls a procedure (lines 15–21) that, for each new percept, looks up the matching percepts in the percept list partition, gets the policy object and applies it, and then updates the percept list partition with the results. The main algorithm (line 8) then checks whether the list of previously processed percepts for this policy, stored in unperceivedPercepts with the policy name as a key, has been consumed by the agent since the policy thread last retrieved it. The agent signals that this has occurred by removing the concurrent map entry for that key. In this case, the policy thread applies the policy to all new percepts starting with an empty percept partition list as the list of old percepts (lines 10–12). These policy applications cannot be skipped in case the policy is designed to change the structure of the incoming percepts, as in the "keep latest with history" policy described in Sect. 3.

The policy thread runs concurrently with the channels, which add new percept sets to newPerceptQueue, and the agent, which consumes the percepts stored in unperceivedPercepts for each policy. Therefore, the algorithm must be defined in terms of thread-safe data structures to ensure correct behaviour. In particular, we have chosen the BlockingQueue and ConcurrentMap data structures provided by Java for the implementations of newPerceptQueue and unperceivedPercepts, respectively. The take method (line 2) is used to retrieve a set of new percepts, and if the queue is empty, this method will block until a channel adds new percepts to the queue. Line 8 calls the replace operation on a concurrent map. This is an atomic operation that replaces the value for a given key in the map, and returns the previous value, or null if there was no previous value.

7 Agent Perception

Algorithm 2 presents the procedure run when the agent initiates a perception. For each policy in use, the percepts output by the policy but not yet perceived are retrieved, along with the persistent percepts, and added to the result set to be returned to the agent. In line 5, the remove method is called on the concurrent map unperceivedPercepts. This is an atomic operation to remove the map's value for the given key (the policy name in this case) and return the value retrieved, or null if there was no value. Removing the value signals to the policy thread that the percepts have been (or are in the process of being) perceived.

Lines 10–18 handle persistent percepts. In line 10 the policy's eventToState-Percepts method is invoked on the percept. This allows a single percept from a channel (e.g. an update for some element of the state) to be translated to a set of percepts representing the updated (persistent) state information. This is described further in Sect. 8. If there is a non-null result from this call, the original policy-processed but unperceived percept p is treated as a representation of a transient event and added to the set of percepts to be returned to the agent. The transformed 'state percept' is then passed to procedure updatePersistentPercepts to update the persistent state. If

---

Algorithm 2. Handling an agent request for percepts

Data: unperceivedPercepts, persistentPercepts: Concurrent maps from policy
      names to percept list partitions

1 Function perceive(): Set of percepts

2 result ← empty list

3 currTime ← current time

4 foreach policyName in keys of unperceivedPercepts do

5   newPerceptsPartition ← unperceivedPercepts.remove(policyName)

6   persPerceptsPartition ← persistentPercepts.get(policyName)

7   if newPerceptsPartition $\neq$ null then

8   foreach p $\in$ newPerceptsPartition do

9   if p.isPersistent() then

10   statePercepts ←
                getPolicyObject(policyName).eventToStatePercepts(p)

11   if statePercepts $\neq$ null then
                // There are separate event and state representations
                // The event percept goes directly to the agent

12   addUnwrappedPerceptIfNotExpired(p, result, currTime)

13   foreach statePercept $\in$ statePercepts do

14   updatePersistentPercepts(statePercept, currTime,
                    persPerceptsPartition)

15   end

16   else

17   updatePersistentPercepts(p, currTime,
                  persPerceptsPartition)

18   end

19   else

20   addUnwrappedPerceptIfNotExpired(p, result, currTime)

21   end

22   end

23   end

24   foreach p $\in$ persPerceptsPartition do

25   afterPerceptionPercept ← getPolicyObject(policyName).

26   transformPerceptAfterPerception(p)

27   if afterPerceptionPercept $\neq$ null then

28   Remove p from persPerceptsPartition

29   Add afterPerceptionPercept to persPerceptsPartition

30   end

31   addUnwrappedPerceptIfNotExpired(p, result, currTime)

32   end

33   persistentPercepts.put(policyName, persPerceptsPartition)

34 end

35 return result

---

eventToStatePercepts returned null, the unmodified percept is passed to that
procedure.

The algorithm for `updatePersistentPercepts` is not shown due to lack of space. This uses the percept's partition key (its functor, arity and key argument values) to obtain the sublist of `persPerceptsPartition` that matches the percept. If the percept's predicate is functional (according to the percept metadata), the matching percepts are removed from that sublist. If not, any expired percepts are removed from the sublist (using their `ArrivalTime` and `tenure` metadata, if present, and `currTime`). In either case, the (still wrapped) percept is added to the sublist if it has not expired.

Transient percepts are handled in line 20. They are added to the result set if not already expired.

Finally, in lines 24–32 all persistent percepts are added to the result set. There is one wrinkle here. The policy may have added extra information to the percept, as in the "keep latest with history" policy described in Sect. 3. The policy method `transformPerceptAfterPerception` gives developers the option to remove this extra information from persistent percepts if it should only be perceived once.

8   Events and States

As discussed above, Algorithm 2 calls two optional policy methods: `eventToStatePercepts` and `transformPerceptAfterPerception`. The role played by these methods has been explained above. In this section we briefly explain the motivation for these methods.

Plans in a BDI agent program can be triggered by the addition of new beliefs to the agent's belief base. The belief base can also be queried from within the context conditions or bodies of its plans. These illustrate two different uses of percepts within a BDI program: (i) to react to new information by triggering a plan, and (ii) to look up previously received information in the course of instantiating or executing a plan. We believe that in many agent programs this distinction corresponds to the difference between using percepts to encode (i) events, and (ii) state information. However, it is also the case that some percepts can represent both an event and state information. In particular, a percept may encode a change of state, and may be used in the agents' plans both to trigger a plan and for looking up the current state at a later time. Our design for percept management policies aims to support developers in achieving separation of concerns when handling event and state information in their agent plans. Specifically, the policy method `eventToStatePercepts`, shown in Fig. 2 and used in Algorithm 2, will be applied to a policy-processed persistent percept p, just before the agent perceives it. The method can return `null` if this functionality is not required. Otherwise, the result is a list of percepts, which encode the information in the original percept in a different way for storage in the persistent percept list. The original percept p is treated as transient and sent to the agent once only.

For example, a percept $approved(ag, doc, stg)$ received from a channel may indicate that agent ag has approved document doc to move to stage stg of a publishing workflow. The policy method `eventToStatePercepts` can be used to generate a persistent record of the state of the document, e.g. $doc\_state(doc, stg)$.

9   Case Studies

We have implemented a prototype percept buffer by extending our open source *camel-agent* software [5]. This provides a connection between the Jason BDI agent platform [3] and the Apache Camel message routing and mediation engine [9]. We use Camel message-processing *routes* as our channels. These routes receive information from external systems using Camel's wide range of endpoints for various networking technologies and protocols. The resulting Camel messages are transformed and filtered as required, using one of Camel's domain-specific languages. Percept metadata is added in the form of message headers, and the messages are then delivered to camel-agent's *agent percept endpoints*. These use endpoint configuration information or Camel message headers to identify the recipient agents(s), and the messages are then delivered to these agents' percept buffers.

We also provide Java implementations for Jason internal actions to dynamically control the processing of percepts within the percept buffer by altering the logic used by channels to assign policies to percepts, and by changing the priorities of policy threads.

To demonstrate and evaluate the use of percept buffers, we developed policies to handle three different sources of streaming data: two demonstration data streams on the web and a live stream of events from a Minecraft server.

9.1   Demo Data Streams

We first evaluated the utility of our approach by configuring channels to consume data from two data streams streamed live over the web by PubNub, Inc.[6]: the Game State Sync stream and the Sensor Network stream. These provide simulated data streams described as (respectively) "updated state information of clients in a sample online multiplayer role-playing game" and "sensor information from artificial sensors". For each of these data streams we used the PubNub Java client library to create a channel that subscribes to the stream and sends the data received (translated to Jason syntax), along with the required percept metadata, to the queue of incoming percepts for the single agent used in this scenario. For the Game State Sync stream, the channel produces a single percept for each data item on the stream. For the Sensor Network stream, a single data item is converted to four percepts recording different aspects of the sensor reading.

The formats of the data items in the two streams are shown below, after translation to Jason literals.

Game State Sync:

```
action(PlayerId, CoordX, CoordY,
       ActionName, ActionType, ActionValue)
```

---

[6] http://www.pubnub.com/developers/demos/

Sensor Network:

radiation(SensorUUID, Radiation)
humidity(SensorUUID, Humidity)
photosensor(SensorUUID, LightLevel)
temperature(SensorUUID, Temperature)

Consuming the Game State Stream. As the messages received from the Game State Sync stream represent events, we configured the channel connected to this stream to mark all action percepts as transient (and so the FuncPred metadata element is not relevant). As the stream uses (seemingly) randomly generated three digit numbers as identifiers in action percepts, the chance of two or more matching agent IDs occurring between consective agent perceptions is very low, so we did not specify any key arguments for the action predicate. This means that all action percepts match each other. A simple, but non-trivial, Jason agent program was used to handle the percepts received[7]. We investigated the effect of three different policies for handling these percepts. Our purpose here is not to analyse or criticise the operation of any specific agent platform (and Jason in particular), but to illustrate the problems that arise when handling streams of percepts.

First, using the policy "keep latest percept" as a baseline case confirmed (not surprisingly) that buffering is needed when percepts are being produced and consumed asynchronously. This policy stores no more than one percept between consecutive agent perceptions. During a ten minute run, 5625 messages were received from the Game State channel (9.4 messages per second). Although Jason's perception rate was significantly higher (an average of 60.2 per second), 404 percepts were lost (7.2%) due to the lack of buffering. In addition, although 5221 action percepts were delivered to the agent, there were only 5216 plan invocations[8]. The missing plan invocations were not just delayed slightly—after an additional minute the count was the same.

In another ten minute run using the default policy (to queue all percepts until they are perceived), 5369 messages (all distinct) were received on the channel and these were all delivered to the agent. However, there were only 5260 plan invocations, suggesting that Jason was unable to cope with this load. For this, and the previous policy, similar results were observed in a previous run (which used an older version of Jason).

A final run was performed using the "keep latest with history" policy. For each set of matching percepts (as determined by the KeyArgs metadata element), this policy retains only the latest percept in the unperceived percepts data structure, but stores a list of older matching percepts within an additional argument (or by using some other method provided by the agent platform for adding information

---

[7] The plan handling action percepts updates a belief counting plan invocations, checks that the player ID is not in a given five-element list (chosen to never match any player IDs), and calls a subgoal that is handled by a plan with the trivial body 'true'. Ten other trivial plans handle belief additions that never occur.

[8] All percepts were distinct, and therefore were genuinely new beliefs.

to percepts—we used a Jason *annotation*). The result is fewer percepts for the agent plans to handle, and the programmer can choose under what conditions the history of older recent percepts should be examined.

When using this policy, 5597 messages were received on the channel during a 10 minute run. Fewer percepts, 5111, were delivered to the agent when using this policy, but there were still two plan invocations missing. Similar results were observed in a second run, when three plan invocations were missing. In this case the percept buffer and choice of policy have not completely solved the problem of missing plan invocations. Jason has a configuration option to set the number of BDI reasoning cycles that are performed beween two consecutive perceptions. Setting this to 2 allowed the "keep latest with history" to further amalgamate percepts between perceptions, and 5416 percepts from the channel were amalgamated into 1096 percepts delivered to the agent. All these led to plan invocations, Two more runs produced similar results.

These results show that setting appropriate policies in a percept buffer can significantly reduce the number of percepts that a BDI plan must handle. However, it may also be necessary to control the rate of agent perception to allow the buffer time to amalgamate or summarise percepts over a longer period of time.

Consuming the Sensor Network Stream. In this section we use the sensor network stream to demonstrate how the percept buffer gives developers the flexibility to customise the delivery of percepts to the agent.

First, we consider default percept metadata settings that label all percepts as being transient and to be queued until perceived (the default policy). As the first argument of each of the sensor reading predicates is the sensor identifier, we declare this to be the key argument. However, for this setting to be useful we had to customise the channel to replace the sensor identifier with a random number from 0 to 19—the stream unrealistically uses random IDs that never appear to reoccur. For the purposes of our discussion, we assume that the agent is only interested in monitoring radiation settings, and the agent has a plan to count these percepts, as well as two more plans that handle percepts related to reporting (and which only consist of a `println` action). With these settings, during a ten minute run, 22508 percepts were delivered to the percept buffer. A quarter of these (the 5627 radiation percepts) should have triggered plan invocations, but only 5307 plan invocations were counted.

We next considered the combined use of two policies. The radiation percepts were handled by a policy that, for given key argument values, keeps a single percept with an added timestamp in the unperceived percepts list (using a Jason annotation). Also, when a new percept arrives and a matching unperceived percept is present, the policy keeps whichever of the two has the maximum radiation reading. This assumes that the agent is monitoring for peak readings and should not miss any. The other percepts were sent to a policy that ignores them by simply removing them from the incoming queue. With this combination of policies, 5622 messages on the channel resulted in 5613 percepts delivered to the agent, all of which resulted in plan invocations. This demonstrates that for this application, filtering out the unwanted percepts by using the "ignore" policy achieved a better outcome than delivering them and letting the agent code ignore them. The use of a "keep maximum" policy had little effect on reducing percept numbers, but ensured the agent would not miss the most significant events.

The final policy we consider is one that converts events to state information using the `eventToStatePercepts` method. We note that the stream does not deliver information for all sensors at once—sensor readings arrive one at a time. We assume that the developer wishes to treat the received sensor readings as state information that can be queried in plan context conditions and bodies and not just as events that trigger plans. Therefore we configured the channel to label the radiation percepts as persistent. However, the readings are time-dependent and lose their validity over time, so we set a 10 second tenure period for percepts. We specify that the first argument of the radiation predicate has no key arguments. This allows a policy to collect all unperceived percepts with this predicate into a list, wrapped in a radiation_list percept. On agent perception, this is sent as a one-off percept to the agent, while a set of persistent percepts are produced by the `eventToStatePercepts` method. The persistent percepts use a functor (radiation_state) that is different from the original percepts. This predicate is specified as functional with its first argument being the key argument, so that the persistent percepts are appropriately maintained over time. With this configuration, over a ten minute run, 5748 messages were collected into 5491 radiation_list percepts that were delivered to the agent, all of which resulted in plan invocations (although, it should be noted that the plan is very simple: it just updates a count belief). In addition, the persistent percepts accounted for another 500087 percepts. These included repeated percept deliveries, which would cause no "new percept" events to be output from Jason's belief update function, but also prevented Jason from removing these percepts from the agent's belief base.

9.2   Sensing Data from Minecraft

An additional case study involved connecting the percept buffer to a channel linked (via a web socket) to a mineflayer[9] JavaScript bot for Minecraft. Minecraft[10] is a single or multiplayer game in which players mine the environment for materials, construct buildings, and (in "survival mode") fight monsters. We investigated the impact of the percept buffer on the speed of an agent performing a specific sensory task over a stream of events from Minecraft. The events represented the position of the bot and the movements of various creatures in the simulated world, and the task was to detect ten distinct squid and then ten distinct bats within a certain range. This task can be achieved using a simple Jason program comprising two short plans, but as 100–200 events arrive per second, we endeavoured to provide a policy to ease the task. Our policy treated

---

[9] https://github.com/andrewrk/mineflayer
[10] https://minecraft.net

the percepts as transient, and ignored percepts from outside the specified range as well as percepts related to creatures other than the target species (initially squid). It also kept only the latest unperceived percept for a given individual creature. We connected two agents to the same Minecraft event stream. One used our special policy, while the other used the null policy (buffering only). The channel was configured to treat percepts recording the bot's own position as persistent for both agents. The Jason plan for the null policy agent performed range checking as well as counting and tracking which of the target creatures had already been seen (using their identifiers). The plan for the agent with the special policy did not need to perform range checking, and received a smaller number of percepts. Once the first part of the task was completed (counting 10 distinct squid), the plan used an internal action to request the channel to change the policy used for its percepts so that only bat percepts were delivered to it. This demonstrates the ability to change policies dynamically to change an agent's focus of attention.

Unfortunately the task performance times for the two agents were almost identical to within a few milliseconds for each of eight runs. This is probably due to the task needing only simple plans that can do all necessary percept filtering using plan "context conditions", for which Jason is (presumably) well optimised. However, this case study demonstrates that the use of the percept buffer allowed the agent code to be simplified and did not add any overhead for the performance of the task, even though the performance was not improved.

10   Conclusion

This paper has presented a design for an agent percept buffer to simplify the handling of percepts from external systems—especially high frequency streams. Rather than relying on programmers to build a custom agent environment encapsulating external sources of percepts, a percept buffer provides a generic solution that can be customised for a given application. This is done by (a) configuring the channels that deliver percepts to the buffer to attach domain-specific information about those percepts, and (b) providing appropriate application-specific policies. This work provides the first platform-independent and detailed proposal for addressing a problem that is often faced, but which must currently be tackled in an ad hoc application-specific manner.

We defined the architecture and algorithms for processing percepts in the percept buffer and for responding to perception requests from agents. We also defined a percept metadata scheme used for providing the buffer with domain-specific information about the percepts. Three case studies were presented to illustrate the flexibility offered by our approach for handling percept streams, and to evaluate its benefits.

Future work includes extending the metadata scheme to allow the absence of certain percepts in a stream to be considered significant, based on some form of local closed world reasoning. Further experimentation with larger and more realistic applications is also needed.

References

1. Behrens, T.M., Hindriks, K.V., Dix, J.: Towards an environment interface standard for agent platforms. Annals of Mathematics and Artificial Intelligence 61, 261–295 (2011)
2. Bogdanovych, A., Rodriguez-Aguilar, J.A., Simoff, S., Cohen, A.: Authentic interactive reenactment of cultural heritage with 3D virtual worlds and artificial intelligence. Applied Artificial Intelligence 24(6), 617–647 (2010)
3. Bordini, R.H., Hubner, J.F., Wooldridge, M.: Programming Multi-Agent Systems in AgentSpeak using Jason. Wiley (2007)
4. Bratman, M.: Intention, plans, and practical reason. Harvard University Press (1987)
5. Cranefield, S., Ranathunga, S.: Embedding agents in business processes using enterprise integration patterns. In: Winikoff, M. (ed.) EMAS 2013. LNCS, vol. 8245, pp. 97–116. Springer, Heidelberg (2013)
6. Dennis, L.A., Fisher, M., Lincoln, N.K., Lisitsa, A., Veres, S.M.: Declarative abstractions for agent based hybrid control systems. In: Omicini, A., Sardina, S., Vasconcelos, W. (eds.) DALT 2010. LNCS, vol. 6619, pp. 96–111. Springer, Heidelberg (2011)
7. Gemrot, J., Brom, C., Plch, T.: A periphery of Pogamut: From bots to agents and back again. In: Dignum, F. (ed.) Agents for Games and Simulations II. LNCS, vol. 6525, pp. 19–37. Springer, Heidelberg (2011)
8. Hindriks, K.V., van Riemsdijk, B., Behrens, T., Korstanje, R., Kraayenbrink, N., Pasman, W., de Rijk, L.: UnREAL Goal bots: Conceptual design of a reusable interface. In: Dignum, F. (ed.) Agents for Games and Simulations II. LNCS, vol. 6525, pp. 1–18. Springer, Heidelberg (2011)
9. Ibsen, C., Anstey, J.: Camel in Action. Manning Publications Co. (2010)
10. Jason-users: Update rate of Jason. Thread on Jason-users mailing list (2014), http://sourceforge.net/p/jason/mailman/message/29859084/
11. van Oijen, J., Dignum, F.: A perception framework for intelligent characters in serious games. In: Proceedings of the 10th International Conference on Autonomous Agents and Multiagent Systems, IFAAMAS, pp. 1249–1250 (2011)
12. Oijen, J., Poutré, H., Dignum, F.: Agent perception within CIGA: Performance optimizations and analysis. In: Müller, J.P., Cossentino, M. (eds.) AOSE 2012. LNCS, vol. 7852, pp. 99–117. Springer, Heidelberg (2013)
13. Ranathunga, S., Cranefield, S., Purvis, M.: Identifying events taking place in Second Life virtual environments. Applied Artificial Intelligence 26(1-2), 137–181 (2012)
14. So, R., Sonenberg, L.: The roles of active perception in intelligent agent systems. In: Lukose, D., Shi, Z. (eds.) PRIMA 2005. LNCS, vol. 4078, pp. 139–152. Springer, Heidelberg (2009)
15. Wei, C., Hindriks, K.V.: An agent-based cognitive robot architecture. In: Dastani, M., Hübner, J.F., Logan, B. (eds.) ProMAS 2012. LNCS, vol. 7837, pp. 54–71. Springer, Heidelberg (2013)
16. Ziafati, P., Dastani, M., Meyer, J.J., van der Torre, L.: Event-processing in autonomous robot programming. In: Proceedings of the 12th International Conference on Autonomous Agents and Multiagent Systems, IFAAMAS, pp. 95–102 (2013)

Blending Event-Based and Multi-Agent Systems Around Coordination Abstractions

Andrea Omicini[1(✉)], Giancarlo Fortino[2], and Stefano Mariani[1]

[1] ALMA MATER STUDIORUM–Università di Bologna, Italy
{andrea.omicini, s.mariani}@unibo.it
[2] Università della Calabria, Rende (CS), Italy
g.fortino@unical.it

Abstract. While event-based architectural style has become prevalent for large-scale distributed applications, multi-agent systems seemingly provide the most viable abstractions to deal with complex distributed systems. In this position paper we discuss the role of coordination abstractions as a basic brick for a unifying conceptual framework for agent-based and event-based systems, which could work as the foundation of a principled discipline for the engineering of complex software systems.

Keywords: Multi-agent systems · Event-based systems · Coordination models · TuCSoN

1 Introduction

In order to address some of the most common sources of *accidental complexity* – such as distributed interaction and large-scale concurrency [2] – the *event-based* architectural style has become prevalent for large-scale distributed applications in the last years [10]. At the same time, multi-agent systems (MAS) are expected to provide the most viable abstractions to deal with the modelling and engineering of complex software systems [14,15]. As a result, MAS and event-based system (EBS) stand nowadays as the two most likely candidate paradigms for modelling and engineering complex systems—the targets of many research activities on coordination models and technologies, too.

The relevance of interaction issues in both MAS and EBS suggests that coordination abstractions and mechanisms could play an essential role in making agent-based and event-based models coexist without harming conceptual integrity of systems. Starting from the essential of both paradigms, we point out the role of coordination in a unifying conceptual framework for MAS and EBS, which could work in principle as the foundation of a coherent discipline for the modelling and engineering of complex software systems.

2 MAS as Coordinated Systems

A common way to look at MAS is to interpret them according to the main first-class abstractions: agents, societies, and environment [34].

© IFIP International Federation for Information Processing 2015
T. Holvoet and M. Viroli (Eds.): COORDINATION 2015, LNCS 9037, pp. 186–193, 2015.
DOI: 10.1007/978-3-319-19282-6_12

Agents are computational entities whose defining feature is *autonomy* [24]. Agents model *activities* for the MAS, expressed through their *actions* along with their motivations—namely, the *goals* that determine and explain the agent's course of actions. When goals are explicitly represented through *mentalistic abstractions* – as in the case of BDI agent architectures [28] – *intelligent agents* [35] are involved, which set their course of actions according to their beliefs, desires, goals, intentions, available actions, and plans.

A critical issue in MAS is *handling dependencies* between agents: that is, understanding how (intelligent) agent actions mutually interfere when each agent aims at pursuing its own goal, and ruling them so as to make MAS achieve its overall system goal. Handling dependencies is first of all a *coordination* problem [16]. Through the notion of *social action* [4], MAS capture dependencies in terms of agent *societies*, built around *coordination artefacts* [23]. Societies represent then the ensembles where the collective behaviours of the MAS are coordinated towards the achievement of the overall system goals. Generally speaking, *coordination models* are the most suitable tools to harness complexity in MAS [6], as they are explicitly meant to provide the *coordination media* that "glue" agents together [12,5] by governing agent interaction in a MAS [33].

Besides agents and societies, *environment* is an essential abstraction for MAS modelling and engineering [34], to be suitably represented, and related to agents. The notion of environment captures the unpredictability of the MAS context, by modelling the external resources and features relevant for the MAS, along with their dynamics. Along with the notion of *situated action* – as the realisation that coordinated, social, intelligent action arises from strict interaction with the environment, rather than from rational practical reasoning [29] – this leads to the requirement of *situatedness* for agents and MAS, often translated into the need of being sensitive to *environment change* [9]. This basically means dependency, again: so, agent behaviour should be affected by environment change.

In all, this means that *(i)* things happen in a MAS because of either agent activity or environment change, *(ii)* complexity arises from both social and situated interaction. Also, this suggests that coordination – in charge of *managing dependencies* [16] – could be used to deal with both forms of dependency in a uniform way; so, furthermore, that coordination artefacts could be exploited to handle both social and situated interaction [17].

3   EBS as Coordinated Systems

According to [10], an EBS is "a system in which the integrated components communicate by generating and receiving *event notifications*" where an *event* is an occurrence of a happening relevant for the system – e.g., a state change in some component –, and a *notification* is the reification of an event within the system, and provides for the event description and data. Components in EBS basically act as either *producers* or *consumers* of notifications: producers *publish* notifications, and provide an *output interface* for subscription; consumers *subscribe* to notifications as specified by producers. According to the *event-based architectural style*, producers and consumers do not interact directly, since their interaction is mediated by the *event bus*, which abstracts away all the complexity of the *event notification service*.

In *distributed event-based systems* (DEBS) [19], a fundamental issue is represented by *distributed notification routing*, that is, the way in which notifications are routed to distributed consumers. Issues such as *event aggregation* and *transformation* have to be addressed by making individual event notifications meaningful for consumers. Relationships between events should be detected, and event *hierarchies* could be required to provide for different levels of abstraction.

In the overall, EBS are basically *coordinated* systems, where coordination is event-based [18]: process activities are mostly driven by event notifications generated by producers; transformed, aggregated, filtered, distributed by the event bus; and finally interpreted and used by consumers. Producer / consumer coordination is then *mediated* by the event bus, working as the system *coordinator*, which encapsulates and possibly automates most of the coordination activities in an EBS. As an aside, it should be noted that role of the event bus in EBS typically raises the well-known issues of the *inversion of control*: that is, control over the logic of program execution is somehow inverted [13].

4   EBS and MAS: Towards a Unifying Framework

Following [17], three are the steps for integrating MAS and EBS: recognising the *sources of events*, defining the *boundary artefacts* mediating the interaction with the event sources, and providing expressive *event-based coordination* models.

The first step is looking at agents and environment as event sources. MAS could then be seen as EBS where agents encapsulate *internal events*, while environment models *external events* through dedicated abstractions – environment *resources* – capturing the unpredictable dynamics of relevant external events. Dually, producers in an EBS are to be classified as either agents – if responsible for the designed, internal events – or environment resources—if used to model external, unpredictable events. This induces a higher-level of expressiveness in EBS: since agents encapsulate control along with the criteria for its management – expressed in terms of high-level, mentalistic abstractions –, articulated *events histories* can be modelled along with their *motivations*. In addition, since MAS environment is modelled as a first-class event-based abstraction, all *causes of change* and disruption in a MAS are modelled in a uniform way as *event prosumers* (producers and consumers)—thus improving conceptual integrity.

The second main step deals with the need for a *general event model*, requiring architectural abstractions mediating between event producers and the whole system, aimed at uniformly handling hugely-heterogeneous event sources—both agents and resources. Denoted as *boundary artefacts*, they make it possibile to translate every sorts of occurrences into a uniform system of notifications according to a common event model. This is, for instance, how Agent Communication Contexts [8] and Agent Coordination Contexts [21] work for agents, and how *event mediators* (or, *correlators*) work in the Cambridge Event Architecture [1].

Thus, boundary artefacts could be conceived *(i)* in EBS as the abstraction mediating between components and the event bus, accounting for the many diverse models for data in event notifications, *(ii)* in MAS as the constrainers for agent interaction, accounting for environment diversity and agent autonomy [33].

5   EBS and MAS: The Role of Coordination

If agents and environment work as event prosumers, coordination abstractions should deal with interaction of any sort – agent-agent, agent-environment, environment-environment interaction – taking care of their mutual dependencies, by coordinating the many resulting flows of events [16].

According to [10], the potential of event-based coordination is recognised both in academia and industry, and there exists a considerable amount of related related literature on event notification systems. In fact, a number of *event-based middleware* providing such services (e.g., JEDI [7]), as well as a number of *event-based coordination* models [27,31], technologies [11], and formalisms [20,32], witness the role of event-based middleware in the engineering of complex distributed systems, as well as the event-based nature of the most relevant coordination models, including tuple-based ones [20].

Along this line, the third step in the integration of MAS and EBS is the comprehension that coordination media [5] can handle multiple event flows [25] according to their mutual dependencies in both MAS and EBS. From the MAS viewpoint, this means that the role of coordination models in MAS [6] is to provide event-driven coordination media governing event coordination in MAS. From the EBS viewpoint, coordination in EBS is event-based [18], and the event bus and service work as the system coordinators. This means that coordination media could work as the core for an event-based architecture, and that EBS could be grounded in principle upon a suitably-expressive coordination middleware, designing the event bus around the coordination services [30].

As a result, since all events are uniformly represented through the same general event model, coordination artefacts can be used to deal with both social and situated dependencies, governing every sorts of interaction through the same set of coordination abstractions, languages, and mechanisms [17]—thus enforcing conceptual integrity. Then, coordination artefacts provide a specific computational model for dealing with event observation, manipulation, and coordination—which should make life easier for programmers and engineers.

In the context of EBS, coordination media provide a suitable way to automatise event handling, and to encapsulate the logic for the coordination of multiple related flows of events, thus counterfeiting the negative effects of inversion of control on the large scale for EBS.

6   Case Study: TuCSoN Coordination as Event-Based

The TuCSoN coordination model and infrastructure [26] can be used to illustrate in short the role of coordination in blending MAS and EBS, in particular pointing out the notions of boundary and coordination artefacts.

In detail, the basic TuCSoN architecture can be represented as in Figure 1, and explained in terms of the following MAS-EBS components.

Agents. A TuCSoN agent is any computational entity exploiting TuCSoN coordination services. To act within a TuCSoN-coordinated MAS, agents should obtain an ACC from the TuCSoN node. Any action from any agent towards the MAS – either social or situated – is *mediated* by its associated ACC.

ACC. *Agent coordination contexts* [21]) represent TuCSoN boundary artefacts devoted to agents. ACC both *enable* and *constraint* agents interactions, mapping every agent operation into events asynchronously dispatched to tuple centres. ACC thus *decouple* agents from MAS in control, reference, space, and time.

Probes. TuCSoN environmental resources. They are handled as sources of perceptions (*sensors*) or makers of actions (*actuators*) in a uniform way. Probes do not directly interact with the MAS, but through *mediation* of their transducer.

Transducers. The boundary artefacts devoted to probes [3]. Each probe is assigned to a transducer, specialised to handle events from that sort of probe, and to act on probes through situation operations. Transducers thus decouple probes from tuple centres in terms of control, reference, space and time.

Events. TuCSoN adopts and generalises the ReSpecT *event model* [22]. ReSpecT is the logic-based language used to program the behaviour of TuCSoN tuple centres [22]. ACC and transducers translate external events (activities and

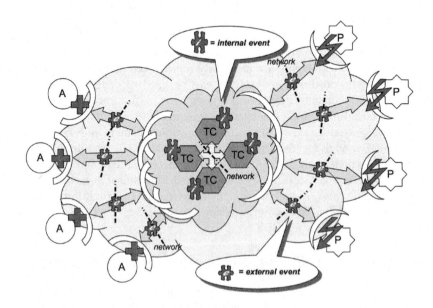

Fig. 1. TuCSoN event-based architecture

change) into internal events that tuple centres can handle to implement the policies required for MAS coordination. Thus, internal events essentially correspond to event notifications in standard EBS.

Tuple Centres. Tuple centres [22] constitute TuCSoN architectural component implementing coordination artefacts, thus in charge of managing dependencies. As such, they are meant to govern both social and situated interactions [17]. By adopting ReSpecT tuple centres, TuCSoN relies on *(i)* the ReSpecT language to program coordination laws, and *(ii)* the ReSpecT situated event model to implement events [3].

By looking at a TuCSoN-coordinated MAS with a event-based perspective,

- ACC and transducers are the boundary artefacts representing agents and environment, respectively, in the MAS, by translating activities and changes in a common event (notification) model;
- tuple centres are the coordination artefacts dealing with both social and situated dependencies by making it possible to program the coordination of events of any sorts in a clean and uniform way.

Under such a perspective, TuCSoN already provides in some way both a model and a technology to engineer coordinated MAS as EBS. Essentially, this means that when using TuCSoN for the coordination of a distributed system, either perspectives – event-based and agent-based – can be adopted by engineers according to their specific design needs, and blended together in a coherent way around the coordination abstractions provided by the TuCSoN model and middleware.[1]

7 Conclusion

Many large-scale distributed systems are nowadays designed and developed around event-based methods and technologies. At the same time, agent-based abstractions (and, in spite of their limited maturity, agent technologies, too) are more and more adopted to face the intricacies of complex systems engineering, in particular when requirements such pervasiveness, intelligence, mobility, and the like, have to be addressed. Altogether, this suggests that a conceptual framework blending together abstractions and technologies from both EBS and MAS could represent a fundamental goal for the research on complex system engineering.

In this position paper we suggest that a fundamental role in such a conceptual framework could be played by coordination models and technologies, with the focus on coordination artefacts working as both event-based and agent-based abstractions. Coordination models and middleware could then provide the technical grounding for a principled, comprehensive methodology for complex system engineering, allowing for the integration of event-based and agent-based tools and techniques without harming conceptual integrity.

---

[1] http://tucson.unibo.it

References

1. Bacon, J., Moody, K., Bates, J., Heyton, R., Ma, C., McNeil, A., Seidel, O., Spiteri, M.: Generic support for distributed applications. Computer 33(3), 68–76 (2000)
2. Brooks, F.P.: No Silver Bullet Essence and Accidents of Software Engineering. Computer 20(4), 10–19 (1987)
3. Casadei, M., Omicini, A.: Situated tuple centres in ReSpecT. In: Shin, S.Y., Ossowski, S., Menezes, R., Viroli, M. (eds.) 24th Annual ACM Symposium on Applied Computing (SAC 2009), vol. III, pp. 1361–1368. ACM, Honolulu (2009)
4. Castelfranchi, C.: Modelling social action for AI agents. Artificial Intelligence 103(1-2), 157–182 (1998)
5. Ciancarini, P.: Coordination models and languages as software integrators. ACM Computing Surveys 28(2), 300–302 (1996)
6. Ciancarini, P., Omicini, A., Zambonelli, F.: Multiagent system engineering: The coordination viewpoint. In: Jennings, N.R., Lespérance, Y. (eds.) Intelligent Agents VI. LNCS (LNAI), vol. 1757, pp. 250–259. Springer, Heidelberg (2000)
7. Cugola, G., Di Nitto, E., Fuggetta, A.: The JEDI event-based infrastructure and its application to the development of the OPSS WFMS. IEEE Transactions on Software Engineering 27(9), 827–850 (2001)
8. Di Stefano, A., Pappalardo, G., Santoro, C., Tramontana, E.: The transparent implementation of agent communication contexts. Concurrency and Computation: Practice and Experience 18(4), 387–407 (2006)
9. Ferber, J., Müller, J.P.: Influences and reaction: A model of situated multiagent systems. In: Tokoro, M. (ed.) 2nd International Conference on Multi-Agent Systems (ICMAS 1996), pp. 72–79. AAAI Press, Tokio (1996)
10. Fiege, L., Mühl, G., Gärtner, F.C.: Modular event-based systems. The Knowledge Engineering Review 17(4), 359–388 (2002)
11. Freeman, E., Hupfer, S., Arnold, K.: JavaSpaces Principles, Patterns, and Practice: Principles, Patterns and Practices. The Jini Technology Series. Addison-Wesley Longman (June 1999)
12. Gelernter, D., Carriero, N.: Coordination languages and their significance. Communications of the ACM 35(2), 97–107 (1992)
13. Haller, P., Odersky, M.: Event-based programming without inversion of control. In: Lightfoot, D.E., Ren, X.-M. (eds.) JMLC 2006. LNCS, vol. 4228, pp. 4–22. Springer, Heidelberg (2006)
14. Jennings, N.R.: On agent-based software engineering. Artificial Intelligence 117(2), 277–296 (2000)
15. Jennings, N.R.: An agent-based approach for building complex software systems. Communications of the ACM 44(4), 35–41 (2001)
16. Malone, T.W., Crowston, K.: The interdisciplinary study of coordination. ACM Computing Surveys 26(1), 87–119 (1994)
17. Mariani, S., Omicini, A.: Coordinating activities and change: An event-driven architecture for situated MAS. Engineering Applications of Artificial Intelligence 41, 298–309 (2015)
18. Milicevic, A., Jackson, D., Gligoric, M., Marinov, D.: Model-based, event-driven programming paradigm for interactive Web applications. In: 2013 ACM International Symposium on New Ideas, New Paradigms, and Reflections on Programming & Software (Onward! 2013), pp. 17–36. ACM Press, New York (2013)

19. Mühl, G., Fiege, L., Pietzuch, P.: Distributed Event-Based Systems. Springer, Heidelberg (2006)
20. Omicini, A.: On the semantics of tuple-based coordination models. In: 1999 ACM Symposium on Applied Computing (SAC 1999), pp. 175–182. ACM, New York (1999)
21. Omicini, A.: Towards a notion of agent coordination context. In: Marinescu, D.C., Lee, C. (eds.) Process Coordination and Ubiquitous Computing, chap. 12, pp. 187–200. CRC Press, Boca Raton (2002)
22. Omicini, A., Denti, E.: From tuple spaces to tuple centres. Science of Computer Programming 41(3), 277–294 (2001)
23. Omicini, A., Ricci, A., Viroli, M.: Coordination artifacts as first-class abstractions for MAS engineering: State of the research. In: Garcia, A., Choren, R., Lucena, C., Giorgini, P., Holvoet, T., Romanovsky, A. (eds.) SELMAS 2005. LNCS, vol. 3914, pp. 71–90. Springer, Heidelberg (2006)
24. Omicini, A., Ricci, A., Viroli, M.: Artifacts in the A&A meta-model for multi-agent systems. Autonomous Agents and Multi-Agent Systems 17(3), 432–456 (2008)
25. Omicini, A., Ricci, A., Zaghini, N.: Distributed workflow upon linkable coordination artifacts. In: Ciancarini, P., Wiklicky, H. (eds.) COORDINATION 2006. LNCS, vol. 4038, pp. 228–246. Springer, Heidelberg (2006)
26. Omicini, A., Zambonelli, F.: Coordination for Internet application development. Autonomous Agents and Multi-Agent Systems 2(3), 251–269 (1999)
27. Papadopoulos, G.A., Arbab, F.: Coordination models and languages. In: Zelkowitz, M.V. (ed.) The Engineering of Large Systems. Advances in Computers, vol. 46, pp. 329–400. Academic Press (1998)
28. Rao, A.S., Georgeff, M.P.: BDI agents: From theory to practice. In: Lesser, V.R., Gasser, L. (eds.) 1st International Conference on Multi Agent Systems (ICMAS 1995), pp. 312–319. The MIT Press, San Francisco (1995)
29. Suchman, L.A.: Situated actions. In: Plans and Situated Actions: The Problem of Human-Machine Communication, chap. 4, pp. 49–67. Cambridge University Press, New York (1987)
30. Viroli, M., Omicini, A.: Coordination as a service. Fundamenta Informaticae 73(4), 507–534 (2006); special issue: Best papers of FOCLASA 2002
31. Viroli, M., Omicini, A., Ricci, A.: On the expressiveness of event-based coordination media. In: Arabnia, H.R. (ed.) International Conference on Parallel and Distributed Processing Techniques and Applications (PDPTA 2002), vol. III, pp. 1414–1420. CSREA Press, Las Vegas (2002)
32. Viroli, M., Ricci, A.: Tuple-based coordination models in event-based scenarios. In: 22nd International Conference on Distributed Computing Systems, Workshop Proceedings, pp. 595–601. IEEE CS (2002)
33. Wegner, P.: Coordination as constrained interaction. In: Hankin, C., Ciancarini, P. (eds.) COORDINATION 1996. LNCS, vol. 1061, pp. 28–33. Springer, Heidelberg (1996)
34. Weyns, D., Omicini, A., Odell, J.J.: Environment as a first-class abstraction in multi-agent systems. Autonomous Agents and Multi-Agent Systems 14(1), 5–30 (2007)
35. Wooldridge, M.J., Jennings, N.R.: Intelligent agents: Theory and practice. Knowledge Engineering Review 10(2), 115–152 (1995)

Shared Spaces

Klaim-DB: A Modeling Language
for Distributed Database Applications

Xi Wu[2], Ximeng Li[1], Alberto Lluch Lafuente[1(✉)],
Flemming Nielson[1], and Hanne Riis Nielson[1]

[1] DTU Compute, Technical University of Denmark, Kgs. Lyngby, Denmark
{ximl,albl,fnie,hrni}@dtu.dk
[2] Shanghai Key Laboratory of Trustworthy Computing,
Software Engineering Institute, East China Normal University, Shanghai, China
xiwu@sei.ecnu.edu.cn

Abstract. We present the modelling language, Klaim-DB, for distributed database applications. Klaim-DB borrows the distributed nets of the coordination language Klaim but essentially re-incarnates the tuple spaces of Klaim as databases, and provides high-level language abstractions for the access and manipulation of structured data, with integrity and atomicity considerations. We present the formal semantics of Klaim-DB and illustrate the use of the language in a scenario where the sales from different branches of a chain of department stores are aggregated from their local databases. It can be seen that raising the abstraction level and encapsulating integrity checks (concerning the schema of tables, etc.) in the language primitives for database operations benefit the modelling task considerably.

1 Introduction

Today's data-intensive applications are becoming increasingly distributed. Multi-national collaborations on science, economics, military etc., require the communication and aggregation of data extracted from databases that are geographically dispersed. Distributed applications including websites frequently adopt the Model-View-Controller (MVC) design pattern in which the "model" layer is a database. Fault tolerance and recovery in databases also favors the employment of distribution and replication. The programmers of distributed database applications are faced with not only the challenge of writing good queries, but also that of dealing with the coordination of widely distributed databases. It is commonly accepted in the formal methods community that the *modelling* of complex systems in design can reduce implementation errors considerably [1,11].

Klaim [2] is a kernel language for specifying distributed and coordinated processes. In Klaim, processes and information repositories exist at different localities. The information repositories are tuple spaces, that can hold data and

---

X. Wu – Part of the work was done when Xi Wu was a visiting researcher at DTU compute.

T. Holvoet and M. Viroli (Eds.): COORDINATION 2015, LNCS 9037, pp. 197–212, 2015.
DOI: 10.1007/978-3-319-19282-6_13

code. Processes can read tuples from (resp. write tuples to) local or remote tuple spaces, or spawn other processes to be executed at certain localities. Many distributed programming paradigms can be modelled in Klaim.

While Klaim provides an ideal ground for the modelling of networked applications in general, the unstructured tuple spaces and low-level operations mostly targeting individual tuples create difficulty in the description of the data-manipulation tasks usually performed using a high-level language such as SQL. A considerable amount of meta-data needed by databases has to be maintained as particular tuples or components of tuples, the sanity checks associated with database operations have to be borne in mind and performed manually by the programmer, difficulties arise when batch operations are performed and atomicity guarantees are needed, and so on.

To support the modelling of applications operating on distributed, structured data, we propose the language Klaim-DB, which is inspired by Klaim in that it allows the distribution of *nodes*, and remote operations on data. Its succinct syntax eases the precise formulation of an operational semantics, giving rigor to high-level formal specification and reasoning of distributed database applications. The language also borrows from SQL, in that it provides structured data organized as databases and tables, and high-level actions that accomplish the data-definition and data-manipulation tasks ubiquitous in these applications.

We use a running example of database operations in the management of a large-scale chain of department stores. Each individual store in the chain has its local database containing information about the current stock and sales of each kind of product. The semantic rules for the core database operations will be illustrated by the local query and maintenance of these individual databases, and our final case study will be concerned with data aggregation across multiple local databases needed to generate statistics on the overall product sales.

This paper is structured as follows. In Section 2, the syntax of Klaim-DB is presented, which is followed by the structural operational semantics specified in Section 3, with illustration of the semantic rules for the main database operations. Our case study is then presented in Section 4. Extensions of Klaim-DB and a discussion of alternative language design choices are covered in Section 5. We conclude in Section 6 with a discussion of related works.

2   Syntax

The syntax of Klaim-DB is presented in Table 1. A net N models a database system that may contain several databases situated at different localities. As in standard Klaim [2], we distinguish between physical localities, also called sites ($s \in \mathcal{S}$), and logical localities ($\ell \in \mathcal{L}$) that are symbolic names used to reference sites. At each site s, there is an "allocation environment" $\rho : \mathcal{L} \hookrightarrow \mathcal{S}$ mapping the logical localities known at s to the sites referred to by them.

We assume for simplicity that there is only one database at each site. The syntax $s ::_\rho C$ for a node of the net captures the ensemble C of processes and tables of the database at the site s, where the allocation environment is ρ.

Table 1. The Syntax of Klaim-DB

$N ::= \text{nil} \mid N_1 \| N_2 \mid (\nu s)N \mid s ::_\rho C$

$C ::= P \mid (I, R) \mid C_1 | C_2$

$P ::= \text{nil} \mid a.P \mid A(\tilde{e}) \mid \text{foreach}_s \; T \text{ in } R : P \mid \text{foreach}_p \; T \text{ in } R : P \mid P_1; P_2$

$a ::= \text{insert}(t, tb)@\ell \mid \text{insert\_tb}(TBV, tb)@\ell \mid \text{delete}(T, \psi, tb, !TBV)@\ell \mid$
$\quad \text{sel\_ext}(T, \psi, tb, t, !TBV)@\ell \mid \text{sel\_int}(T, \psi, TBV, t, !TBV') \mid$
$\quad \text{update}(T, \psi, t, tb)@\ell \mid \text{aggr}(T, \psi, tb, f, T')@\ell \mid \text{create}(I)@\ell \mid \text{drop}(tb)@\ell$

$t ::= e \mid t_1, t_2$

$T ::= e \mid !x \mid T_1, T_2$

The parallel composition of different nodes is represented using the $\|$ operator. With the restriction operator $(\nu s)N$, the scope of s is restricted to N. Each table is represented by a pair (I, R) where I is an interface that publishes certain structural information about the table as attributes (for example, $I.id$ stands for the table identifier and $I.sk$ is a schema describing the data format of the table), and R is a multiset of tuples, in which each tuple corresponds to one row of data. The construct $C_1 | C_2$ is the parallel composition of different components.

We distinguish between tuples t and templates T. A template T can contain not only actually fields that are expressions e, but also formal fields $!x$ where x is a variable that can be bound to values.

A process P can be an inert process nil, an action prefixing $a.P$, a parameterized process invocation $A(\tilde{e})$, a looping process $\text{foreach}_s \; T$ in $R : P$, or $\text{foreach}_p \; T$ in $R : P$, or a sequential composition $P_1; P_2$, for which we require that $bv(P_1) \cap fv(P_2) = \emptyset$. Looping is introduced in addition to recursion via process invocation, to ease the task of traversing tables or data selection results in a natural way. We also allow both prefixing and sequential composition in our language, as in CSP [4]. Sequential composition is needed to facilitate the specification of possible continuation after the completion of a loop, whereas prefixing is retained and used in situations where substitutions need to be applied after receiving an input. The difference between the two variants of looping process is that the sequential loop $\text{foreach}_s \; T$ in $R : P$ goes through the different rounds sequentially, while the parallel loop $\text{foreach}_p \; T$ in $R : P$ forks one parallel process for each round.

A process can perform nine different kinds of actions. Actions $\text{insert}(t, tb)@\ell$, $\text{insert\_tb}(TBV, tb)@\ell$, $\text{delete}(T, \psi, tb, !TBV)@\ell$, $\text{sel\_ext}(T, \psi, tb, t, !TBV)@\ell$, $\text{sel\_int} (T, \psi, TBV, t, !TBV')$, $\text{update}(T, \psi, t, tb)@\ell$ and $\text{aggr}(T, \psi, tb, f, T')@\ell$ are used to access/manipulate the data inside a table; they resemble the operations performed by the "Data-Manipulation Language" in SQL. On the other hand, actions $\text{create}(I)@\ell$, and $\text{drop}(tb)@\ell$ are used for the creation and deletion of a table — they correspond to the operations performed by the "Data-Definition Language" in SQL.

The actions $\text{insert}(t, tb)@\ell$ and $\text{insert\_tb}(TBV, tb)@\ell$ are used to insert a new row t, or all the rows of a table bound to the table variable TBV, into a table

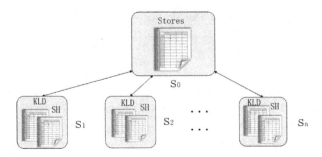

Fig. 1. Running Example

named tb inside the database at ℓ, respectively. On the other hand, the action delete($T, \psi, tb, !TBV$)@ℓ deletes all rows matching the pattern T and the predicate ψ from table tb in the database located at ℓ, and binds the deleted rows to the table variable TBV.

The language has two variants of "selection": an "external" one that selects data from tables actually existing in databases, identified by their table identifiers, and an "internal" one that selects data from temporary tables bound to table variables. The action sel_ext($T, \psi, tb, t, !TBV$)@ℓ performs the "external" selection. It picks all rows matching the pattern T as well as satisfying the predicate ψ, from the table identified by tb of the database located at ℓ, and binds the resulting table into the table variable TBV. On the other hand, sel_int($T, \psi, TBV, t, !TBV'$) performs the "internal" selection, i.e., from the content of the table variable TBV, and binds the resulting table further into the table variable TBV'. In sel_int($T, \psi, TBV, t, !TBV'$), the meanings of T, ψ, and t are the same as those in sel_ext($T, \psi, tb, t, !TBV$)@ℓ. In both variants, we require that each component of t should be a value or a bound variable of T.

The action update(T, ψ, t, tb)@ℓ replaces each row matching T yet satisfying ψ in table tb (at ℓ) with a new row t, while leaving the rest of the rows unchanged. It is required that $fv(t) \subseteq bv(T)$.

The action aggr(T, ψ, tb, f, T')@ℓ applies the aggregation function f on the multiset of all rows meeting T and ψ in table tb (at ℓ) and binds the aggregation result to the pattern T'.

The action create(I)@ℓ (resp. drop(tb)@ℓ) creates a table identified by I (resp. drops the table identified by tb) in the database at ℓ. An item is a row in a table containing sequences of values, which can be obtained from the evaluation of an expression e. Pattern-matching is used to manage the data inside a table by means of a given template T, which is a sequence of values and variables.

Setting the Scene for the Running Example. Consider the management of a large-scale chain of department stores, in which the head office can manage the sales of different imaginative brands (e.g., KLD, SH,...) in its individual branches, as shown in Figure 1.

We will use underlined symbols for logical and physical localities, as well as allocation environments, to distinguish between their uses in the example and elsewhere (e.g., in the semantics). Suppose the database of the head office is maintained on machine s_0 and the databases of its branches are maintained on machines s_1 to s_n. The site s_0 has the local environment $\rho_0 = [self \mapsto s_0][\ell_1 \mapsto s_1]...[\ell_n \mapsto s_n]$. We use $\rho_j = [self \mapsto s_j]$ as the local environment for each site s_j — this restricts database accesses across different local databases and corresponds to a centralized architecture.

City	Address	Shop_Name	Brand	Logical_Locality
CPH	ABC DEF 2, 1050	Shop1	$\{KLD, SH, ...\}$	ℓ_1
CPH	DEF HIJ 13, 2800	Shop2	$\{KLD, SH, ...\}$	ℓ_2
CPH	HIJ KLM 26, 1750	Shop3	$\{KLD, SH, ...\}$	ℓ_3
AAL	KLM NOP 3, 3570	Shop4	$\{LAM, IMK, ...\}$	ℓ_4
AAL	NOP QUW 18, 4500	Shop5	$\{LAM, IMK, ...\}$	ℓ_5
...	...	...	...	...

Fig. 2. The Table Stores

A table with identifier Stores exists in the database of the head office, and records the information of its branches, as shown in Figure 2. The header partially describes the schema I_0 of the table, and the subsequent rows, constituting the multiset R_0, contain the information of the different branches. Formally, we have $I_0.id =$ Stores, $I_0.sk =<$ "City" : $String$, "Address" : $String$, "Shop_name" : $String$, "Brand" : Set, "Logical_Locality" : $String >$.

Each database of a branch has several tables identified by the name of the brand, which record the information of the stock and sales of the corresponding brand. The table of one shoe brand, KLD, in one branch, is shown in Figure 3. The identifier of this table is KLD and the schema is $<$ "Shoe_ID" : $String$, "Shoe_name" : $String$, "Year" : $String$, "Color" : $String$, "Size" : Int, "In-stock" : Int, "Sales" : $Int >$.

Shoe_ID	Shoe_name	Year	Color	Size	In-stock	Sales
001	HighBoot	2015	red	38	5	2
001	HighBoot	2015	red	37	8	5
001	HighBoot	2015	red	36	3	1
001	HighBoot	2015	black	38	3	2
001	HighBoot	2015	black	37	5	2
002	ShortBoot	2015	green	38	2	0
002	ShortBoot	2015	brown	37	4	3
...	...	...	...	...	...	...

Fig. 3. The Table KLD in one branch

To sum up, the network of databases and operating processes can be represented by

$$s_0 ::_{\rho_0} ((I_0, R_0)|C_0') \parallel s_1 ::_{\rho_1} ((I_1, R_1)|C_1') \parallel ... \parallel s_n ::_{\rho_n} ((I_n, R_n)|C_n'),$$

where for $j \in \{1, ..., n\}$, (I_j, R_j) describes the local table for the brand KLD inside its database at s_j, and for each $k \in \{0, ..., n\}$, C_k' stands for the remaining processes and tables at the site s_k.

3   Semantics

We devise a structural operational semantics [8] for Klaim-DB, as shown in Table 3 and Table 4. The semantics is defined with the help of a structural congruence — the smallest congruence relation satisfying the rules in Table 2, where the α-equivalence of N and N' is denoted by $N \equiv_\alpha N'$.

Table 2. The Structural Congruence

$N_1 \| N_2 \equiv N_2 \| N_1$	$(\nu s_1)(\nu s_2)N \equiv (\nu s_2)(\nu s_1)N$
$(N_1 \| N_2) \| N_3 \equiv N_1 \| (N_2 \| N_3)$	$N_1 \| (\nu s)N_2 \equiv (\nu s)N_1 \| N_2 \quad \text{(if } s \notin \mathsf{fn}(N_1)\text{)}$
$N \| \mathsf{nil} \equiv N$	$s ::_\rho C \equiv s ::_\rho C \| \mathsf{nil}$
$N \equiv N' \quad \text{(if } N \equiv_\alpha N'\text{)}$	$s ::_\rho (C_1 \| C_2) \equiv s ::_\rho C_1 \; \| \; s ::_\rho C_2$

We start by explaining our notation used in the semantic rules. The evaluation function $\mathcal{E}[\![\cdot]\!]_\rho$ evaluates tuples and templates under the allocation environment ρ. The evaluation is performed pointwise on all the components of tuples t and templates T, much in the manner of standard Klaim [2]. We denote by $[a/b]$ the substitution of a for b; in particular, when a and b are tuples of the same length, point-wise substitution is represented. Pattern matching is performed with the help of the *predicate match*(eT, et) where eT is an evaluated template and et is an evaluated tuple. This *match*(eT, et) can be defined in a manner much like that of [2]. In more detail, *match*(eT, et) gives a boolean value indicating whether the pattern matching succeeded. In case it did, the substitution $\sigma = [et/eT]$ can be resulted. For example, *match*$((3, !x, !y), (3, 5, 7)) = \mathsf{true}$ and $[(3, 5, 7)/(3, !x, !y)] = [5/x, 7/y]$. We denote by $\psi\sigma$ the fact that the boolean formula ψ is satisfied after the substitution σ is applied to it. We will use $\uplus$, $\cap$ and $\setminus$ to represent the union, intersection and substraction, of multisets and the detailed definitions are given in Appendix A.

The notation $I[a \mapsto b][...]$ represents the update of the interface I that maps its attribute a to b; multiple updates are allowed. In addition, we will use $I.sk \downarrow_t^T$ to represent the projection of the schema $I.sk$ according to the template T (matching the format requirements imposed by $I.sk$) and the tuple t. When t only contains constants or the bound variables of T as its components, $I.sk \downarrow_t^T$ is a new schema that describes only the columns referred to in the variable components of t. Since we have left the schema under-specified, this projection operation is illustrated in Example 1, rather than formally defined.

Example 1. Suppose $I.sk =<$ *"Shoe_ID"* : *String*, *"Shoe_name"* : *String*, *"Year"* : *String*, *"Color"* : *String*, *"Size"* : *Int*, *"In-stock"* : *Int*, *"Sales"* : *Int* $>$, which specifies that the table having I as its interface has seven columns: *"Shoe_ID"* of type *String*, *"Shoe_name"* of type *String*, *"Year"* of type *String*, *"Color"* of type *String*, *"Size"* of type *Int*, *"In-stock"* of type *Int*, *"Sales"* of type *Int*. Suppose in addition that $T = ($ *"001"*, *"HighBoot"*, !x, !y, !z, !w, !$p)$ and $t = (y, z, p)$. Then $I.sk \downarrow_t^T =<$ *"Color"* : *String*, *"Size"* : *Int*, *"Sales"* : *Int* $>$. $\qquad\square$

Table 3. The Semantics for Actions

$$(\text{INS}) \ \frac{\rho_1(l) = s_2 \quad I.id = tb \quad t \models I.sk \quad R' = R \uplus \{\mathcal{E}[\![t]\!]_{\rho_1}\}}{s_1 ::_{\rho_1} \text{insert}(t, tb)@\ell.P \parallel s_2 ::_{\rho_2} (I, R) \to s_1 ::_{\rho_1} P \parallel s_2 ::_{\rho_2} (I, R')}$$

$$(\text{INS\_TB}) \ \frac{\rho_1(l) = s_2 \quad I.id = tb \quad I'.sk = I.sk \quad R'' = R \uplus R'}{s_1 ::_{\rho_1} \text{insert\_tb}((I', R'), tb)@\ell.P \parallel s_2 ::_{\rho_2} (I, R) \to s_1 ::_{\rho_1} P \parallel s_2 ::_{\rho_2} (I, R'')}$$

$$(\text{DEL}) \ \frac{\begin{array}{c} R' = \{t \mid t \in R \wedge \neg(match(\mathcal{E}[\![T]\!]_{\rho_1}, t) \wedge \psi[t/\mathcal{E}[\![T]\!]_{\rho_1}])\} \\ R'' = \{t \mid t \in R \wedge match(\mathcal{E}[\![T]\!]_{\rho_1}, t) \wedge \psi[t/\mathcal{E}[\![T]\!]_{\rho_1}]\} \\ \rho_1(l) = s_2 \quad I.id = tb \quad \sigma' = [(I, R'')/TBV] \end{array}}{s_1 ::_{\rho_1} \text{delete}(T, \psi, tb, !TBV)@\ell.P \parallel s_2 ::_{\rho_2} (I, R) \to s_1 ::_{\rho_1} P\sigma' \parallel s_2 ::_{\rho_2} (I, R')}$$

$$(\text{SEL\_EXT}) \ \frac{\begin{array}{c} \rho_1(l) = s_2 \quad I.id = tb \quad I' = I[id \mapsto \bot][sk \mapsto I.sk\downarrow_t^T] \quad \sigma' = [(I', R')/TBV] \\ R' = \{\mathcal{E}[\![t\sigma]\!]_{\rho_1} \mid \exists t' : t' \in R \wedge match(\mathcal{E}[\![T]\!]_{\rho_1}, t') \wedge \sigma = [t'/\mathcal{E}[\![T]\!]_{\rho_1}] \wedge \psi\sigma\} \end{array}}{s_1 ::_{\rho_1} \text{sel\_ext}(T, \psi, tb, t, !TBV)@\ell.P \parallel s_2 ::_{\rho_2} (I, R) \to s_1 ::_{\rho_1} P\sigma' \parallel s_2 ::_{\rho_2} (I, R)}$$

$$(\text{SEL\_INT}) \ \frac{\begin{array}{c} I' = I[id \mapsto \bot][sk \mapsto I.sk\downarrow_t^T] \quad \sigma' = [(I', R')/TBV] \\ R' = \{\mathcal{E}[\![t\sigma]\!]_{\rho_1} \mid \exists t' : t' \in R \wedge match(\mathcal{E}[\![T]\!]_{\rho_1}, t') \wedge \sigma = [t'/\mathcal{E}[\![T]\!]_{\rho_1}] \wedge \psi\sigma\} \end{array}}{s_1 ::_{\rho_1} \text{sel\_int}(T, \psi, (I, R), t, !TBV).P \to s_1 ::_{\rho_1} P\sigma'}$$

$$(\text{UPD}) \ \frac{\begin{array}{c} \rho_1(l) = s_2 \quad I.id = tb \\ R_1' = \{t' \mid t' \in R \wedge \neg(\exists \sigma : match(\mathcal{E}[\![T]\!]_{\rho_1}, t') \wedge \sigma = [t'/\mathcal{E}[\![T]\!]_{\rho_1}] \wedge \psi\sigma \wedge \mathcal{E}[\![t\sigma]\!]_{\rho_1} \models I.sk)\} \\ R_2' = \{\mathcal{E}[\![t\sigma]\!]_{\rho_1} \mid \exists t' : t' \in R \wedge match(\mathcal{E}[\![T]\!]_{\rho_1}, t') \wedge \sigma = [t'/\mathcal{E}[\![T]\!]_{\rho_1}] \wedge \psi\sigma \wedge \mathcal{E}[\![t\sigma]\!]_{\rho_1} \models I.sk\} \end{array}}{s_1 ::_{\rho_1} \text{update}(T, \psi, t, tb)@\ell.P \parallel s_2 ::_{\rho_2} (I, R) \to s_1 ::_{\rho_1} P \parallel s_2 ::_{\rho_2} (I, R_1' \uplus R_2')}$$

$$(\text{AGGR}) \ \frac{\begin{array}{c} t' = f(\{t \mid \exists \sigma' : t \in R \wedge match(\mathcal{E}[\![T]\!]_{\rho_1}, t) \wedge \sigma' = [t/\mathcal{E}[\![T]\!]_{\rho_1}] \wedge \psi\sigma'\}) \\ \rho(l) = s_2 \quad I.id = tb \quad match(\mathcal{E}[\![T']\!]_{\rho_1}, t') \end{array}}{\begin{array}{c} s_1 ::_{\rho_1} \text{aggr}(T, \psi, tb, f, T')@\ell.P \parallel s_2 ::_{\rho_2} (I, R) \to \\ s_1 ::_{\rho_1} P[t'/\mathcal{E}[\![T']\!]_{\rho_1}] \parallel s_2 ::_{\rho_2} (I, R) \end{array}}$$

$$(\text{CREATE}) \ \frac{\rho_1(l) = s_2}{s_1 ::_{\rho_1} \text{create}(I)@\ell.P \parallel s_2 ::_{\rho_2} \text{nil} \to s_1 ::_{\rho_1} P \parallel s_2 ::_{\rho_2} (I, \emptyset)}$$

$$(\text{DROP}) \ \frac{\rho_1(l) = s_2 \quad I.id = tb}{s_1 ::_{\rho_1} \text{drop}(tb)@\ell.P \parallel s_2 ::_{\rho_2} (I, R) \to s_1 ::_{\rho_1} P \parallel s_2 ::_{\rho_2} \text{nil}}$$

We proceed with a detailed explanation of the semantic rules in Table 3 that account for the execution of Klaim-DB actions and the ones in Table 4 that mainly describe the execution of the control flow constructs. In the explanation, we will avoid reiterating that each table resides in a database located at some ℓ, but directly state "table ... located at ℓ".

3.1   Semantics for Actions

Insertion and Deletion. The rule (INS) of Table 3 says that to insert a row t into a table tb at s_2, the logical locality ℓ needs to be evaluated to s_2 under the local environment ρ_1, the table identifier tb must agree with that of a destination table (I, R) already existing at s_2, and the tuple t needs to satisfy the requirements imposed by the schema $I.sk$. If these conditions are met, then the evaluated tuple is added into the data set R.

Example 2 (Adding new Shoes). The local action at $\underline{s_1}$ that inserts an entry for KLD high boots of a new color, white, sized "37", produced in 2015, with 6 in stock, is $\mathsf{insert}(T_0, \mathsf{KLD})@self$, where $T_0 = (\text{"001"}, \text{"}HighBoot\text{"}, \text{"2015"}, \text{"}white\text{"},$ "37", $6, 0)$. By (INS), we have

$$\underline{s_1} ::_{\underline{\rho_1}} \mathsf{insert}(T_0, \mathsf{KLD})@self.\mathsf{nil} \,\|\, \underline{s_1} ::_{\underline{\rho_1}} (I_1, R_1) \to \underline{s_1} ::_{\underline{\rho_1}} \mathsf{nil} \,\|\, \underline{s_1} ::_{\underline{\rho_1}} (I_1, R_1'),$$

where $R_1' = R_1 \uplus \{T_0\}$, since $\underline{\rho_1}(self) = \underline{s_1}$, $\mathsf{KLD} = I_1.id$ and $T_0 \models I_1.sk$. $\Box$

Deletion operations are performed according to the rule (DEL). A deletion can be performed if the logical locality ℓ refers to the physical locality s_2 under the local environment ρ_1, and the specified table identifier tb agrees with that of the table (I, R) targeted. The rows that do not match the pattern T or do not satisfy the condition ψ will constitute the resulting data set of the target.

Example 3 (Deleting Existing Shoes). The local action at $\underline{\ell_1}$, deleting all entries for white KLD high boots sized "37" produced in 2015, from the resulting table of Example 2, is $\mathsf{delete}(T_0, \mathsf{true}, \mathsf{KLD})@self$, where $T_0 = (\text{"001"}, \text{"}HighBoot\text{"},$ "2015", "$White$", "37", $!x, !y)$.

We have the transition:

$$\underline{s_1} ::_{\underline{\rho_1}} \mathsf{delete}(T_0, \mathsf{true}, \mathsf{KLD})@self.\mathsf{nil} \,\|\, \underline{s_1} ::_{\underline{\rho_1}} (I_1, R_1') \to \underline{s_1} ::_{\underline{\rho_1}} \mathsf{nil} \,\|\, \underline{s_1} ::_{\underline{\rho_1}} (I_1, R_1).$$

This reflects that the original table is recovered after the deletion. $\Box$

Selection, Update and Aggregation. The rule (SEL_EXT) describes the way the "external" selection operations are performed. It needs to be guaranteed that the logical locality ℓ is evaluated to s_2 (under the local environment ρ_1), and the identifier tb is identical to that of the table (I, R) existing at s_2. If the conditions are met, all the rows that match the pattern T and satisfy the predicate ψ, will be put into the result data set R'. The schema of the resulting table is also updated according to the pattern T and the tuple t. The resulting table (I', R') is substituted into each occurrence of the table variable TBV used in the continuation P.

Example 4 (Selection of Shoes in a Certain Color). The Klaim-DB action performed from the head office, selecting the color, size, and sales of the types of high boots that are not red, at the local database at $\underline{s_1}$, is

$$\mathsf{sel\_ext}((\text{"001"}, \text{"}HighBoot\text{"}, !x, !y, !z, !w, !p), y \neq \text{"}red\text{"}, \mathsf{KLD}, (y, z, p), !TBV)@\underline{\ell_1}.$$

According to the rule (SEL_EXT), we have the transition:

$$\underline{s_0} ::_{\underline{\rho_0}} \mathsf{sel\_ext}((\text{"001"}, \text{"}HighBoot\text{"}, !x, !y, !z, !w, !p), y \neq \text{"}red\text{"}, \mathsf{KLD}, (y, z, p), !TBV)@\underline{\ell_1}.\mathsf{nil}$$
$$\|\, \underline{s_1} ::_{\underline{\rho_1}} (I_1, R_1)$$
$$\to \underline{s_0} ::_{\underline{\rho_0}} \mathsf{nil} \,\|\, \underline{s_1} ::_{\underline{\rho_1}} (I_1, R_1).$$

The conditions $\rho_0(\ell_1) = \underline{s_1}$ and $\mathsf{KLD} = I.id$ in the premises of the rule are satisfied. The I' in (SEL_EXT) is such that $I'.id = \bot$, $I'.sk =<$ "Color" : String, "Size" : Int, "Sales" : Int $>$, and I' agrees with I on the other attributes. The table variable TBV is replaced by (I', R'), for some $R' = \{($"black", "38", "2"$), ($"black", "37", "2"$)\}$. □

"Internal" selections are performed according to the rule (SEL_INT). No constraints concerning localities/identifiers are needed. All the rows that match the pattern T and satisfy the predicate ψ are selected into the resulting data set R'. The schema of the result table is produced by using the projection operation introduced in the beginning of this section. All occurrences of the table variable TBV in the continuation P will be replaced by the resulting table (I', R') before continuing with further transitions. We use $\bot$ for $I'.id$ to indicate that (I', R') is a "temporary" table that can be thought of as existing in the query engine, rather than in the database.

The updates of data stored in tables are executed according to the rule (UPD). Again, it is checked that the specified logical locality of the table (I, R) to be updated corresponds to the site where the table actually resides, and that the specified table identifier matches the actual one. An update goes through all the elements t' of R. This t' is updated only if it matches the template T, resulting in the substitution σ that makes the predicate ψ satisfied, and $t\sigma$ is evaluated to a tuple that satisfies the schema $I.sk$. The evaluation result of $t\sigma$ will then replace t' in the original table, which is captured by R'_2 . If at least one of the above mentioned conditions is not met, then t' will be left intact (described by R'_1).

Example 5 (Update of Shoes Information). Suppose two more red KLD high boots sized 37 are sold. The following local action informs the database at $\underline{s_1}$ of this.

> update(("001", "HighBoot", "2015", "red", "37", !x, !y), true,
> ("001", "HighBoot", "2015", "red", "37", x − 2, y + 2), KLD)@self.

We have the transition:

$\underline{s_1} ::_{\rho_1}$ update(("001", "HighBoot", "2015", "red", "37", !x, !y), true, ("001", "HighBoot", "2015", "red", "37", x − 2, y + 2), KLD)@self.nil $|| \underline{s_1} ::_{\rho_1} (I, R) \rightarrow$
$\underline{s_1} ::_{\rho_1}$ nil $|| \underline{s_1} ::_{\rho_1} (I, R'_1 \uplus R'_2)$.

The multiset R'_1 consists of all the entries that are intact — shoes that are not red high boots sized 37, while R'_2 contains all the updated items. □

The rule (AGGR) describes the way aggregation operations are performed. The matching of localities and table identifiers is still required. The aggregation function f is applied to the multiset of all tuples matching the template T, as well as satisfying the predicate ψ. The aggregation result t' obtained by the application of f is bound to the specified template T' only if the evaluation of T' matches t'. In that case the substitution reflecting the binding is applied to the continuation P and the aggregation is completed.

Example 6 (Aggregation of Sales Figures).
The local aggregation returning the total sales of the shoes with ID "001", can be modelled by the Klaim-DB action $\mathsf{aggr}(T_0, \mathsf{true}, \mathsf{KLD}, sum_7, (!res))@self$, where $T_0 = (\text{"001"}, !x, !y, !z, !w, !q, !o)$, and $sum_7 = \lambda R.(sum(\{v_7|(v_1, ..., v_7) \in R\}))$, i.e., sum_7 is a function from multisets R to unary tuples containing the summation results of the 7-th components of the tuples in R.

It is not difficult to derive:

$$\underline{s_1} ::_{\rho_1} \mathsf{aggr}(T_0, \mathsf{true}, \mathsf{KLD}, sum_7, (!res))@\underline{\ell_1}.\mathsf{nil} \parallel \underline{s_1} ::_{\rho_1} (I, R)$$
$$\rightarrow \underline{s_1} ::_{\rho_1} \mathsf{nil} \parallel \underline{s_1} ::_{\rho_1} (I, R).$$

The variable $!res$ is then bound to the integer value 12 $(2 + 5 + 1 + 2 + 2)$.   □

Example 7 (Selection using Aggregation Results). Consider the query from $\underline{s_0}$ that selects all the colors, sizes and sales of the types of high boots produced in the year 2015, whose ID is "001" and whose sales figures are above average. This query can be modelled as a sequence of actions at $\underline{s_0}$, as follows.

$$\underline{s_0} ::_{\rho_0} \mathsf{aggr}(T_0, \mathsf{true}, \mathsf{KLD}, avg_7, !res)@\underline{\ell_1}.\mathsf{sel\_ext}(T_0, w \geq res, \mathsf{KLD}, (x, y, w), !TBV)@\underline{\ell_1}.\mathsf{nil}$$
$$\parallel \underline{s_1} ::_{\rho_1} (I_1, R_1),$$

where $T_0 = (\text{"001"}, \text{"}HighBoot\text{"}, \text{"2015"}, !x, !y, !z, !w)$ and
$avg_7 = \lambda R.(\frac{sum(\{v_7|(v_1, ..., v_7)\in R\})}{|R|})$ is a function from multisets R to unary tuples containing the average value of the 7-th components of the tuples in R.   □

Adding and Dropping Tables. To create a new table, the rule (CREATE) ensures that the physical site s_2 corresponding to the logical locality ℓ mentioned in the action $\mathsf{create}(I)@\ell$ does exist. Then a table with the interface I and an empty data set is created at the specified site. It remains an issue to ascertain that there are no existing tables having the same identifier $I.id$ at the target site. This is achieved with the help of the rule (PAR) in Table 4.

To drop an existing table, the rule (DROP) checks that a table with the specified identifier tb does exist at the specified site $\rho_1(l) = s_2$. Then the table is dropped by replacement of it with nil.

3.2   Semantics for Processes and Networks

Directing our attention to Table 4, the rules $(\mathrm{FOR}_\mathsf{s}^\mathsf{tt})$ and $(\mathrm{FOR}_\mathsf{s}^\mathsf{ff})$ specify when and how a loop is to be executed one more time, and has finished, respectively. The rule $(\mathrm{FOR}_\mathsf{s}^\mathsf{tt})$ says that if there are still more tuples (e.g., t_0) in the multiset R matching the pattern specified by the template T, then we first execute one round of the loop with the instantiation of variables in T by corresponding values in t_0, and then continue with the remaining rounds of the loop by removing t_0 from R. The rule $(\mathrm{FOR}_\mathsf{s}^\mathsf{ff})$ says that if there are no more tuples in R matching T, then the loop is completed. The rules $(\mathrm{FOR}_\mathsf{p}^\mathsf{tt})$ and $(\mathrm{FOR}_\mathsf{p}^\mathsf{ff})$ can be understood similarly.

Table 4. The Semantics for Processes and Nets (Continued)

$$(\text{FOR}_{\text{s}}^{\text{tt}}) \; \frac{t_0 \in R \;\; match(\mathcal{E}[\![T]\!]_\rho, t_0)}{s ::_\rho \; \textsf{foreach}_{\textsf{s}} \; T \; \textsf{in} \; R \colon P \to s ::_\rho P[t_0/\mathcal{E}[\![T]\!]_\rho]; \textsf{foreach}_{\textsf{s}} \; T \; \textsf{in} \; R \setminus \{t_0\} : P}$$

$$(\text{FOR}_{\text{p}}^{\text{tt}}) \; \frac{t_0 \in R \;\; match(\mathcal{E}[\![T]\!]_\rho, t_0)}{s ::_\rho \; \textsf{foreach}_{\textsf{p}} \; T \; \textsf{in} \; R \colon P \to s ::_\rho P[t_0/\mathcal{E}[\![T]\!]_\rho] \mid \textsf{foreach}_{\textsf{p}} \; T \; \textsf{in} \; R \setminus \{t_0\} : P}$$

$$(\text{FOR}_{\text{s}}^{\text{ff}}) \; \frac{\neg(\exists t_0 \in R : match(\mathcal{E}[\![T]\!]_\rho, t_0))}{s ::_\rho \; \textsf{foreach}_{\textsf{s}} \; T \; \textsf{in} \; R : P \to s ::_\rho \textsf{nil}} \qquad (\text{FOR}_{\text{p}}^{\text{ff}}) \; \frac{\neg(\exists t_0 \in R : match(\mathcal{E}[\![T]\!]_\rho, t_0))}{s ::_\rho \; \textsf{foreach}_{\textsf{p}} \; T \; \textsf{in} \; R : P \to s ::_\rho \textsf{nil}}$$

$$(\text{SEQ}^{\text{tt}}) \; \frac{s ::_\rho P_1 \parallel N \to s ::_\rho P_1' \parallel N'}{s ::_\rho P_1; P_2 \parallel N \to s ::_\rho P_1'; P_2 \parallel N'} \qquad (\text{SEQ}^{\text{ff}}) \; \frac{s ::_\rho P_1 \parallel N \to s ::_\rho \textsf{nil} \parallel N'}{s ::_\rho P_1; P_2 \parallel N \to s ::_\rho P_2 \parallel N'}$$

$$(\text{CALL}) \;\; s ::_\rho A(\tilde{t}) \to s ::_\rho P[\tilde{v}/\tilde{x}] \;\; \text{if} \;\; A(\tilde{x}) \triangleq P \wedge \mathcal{E}[\![\tilde{t}]\!]_\rho = \tilde{v}$$

$$(\text{PAR}) \; \frac{N_1 \to N_1'}{N_1 \| N_2 \to N_1' \| N_2} \quad \text{if} \; Lid(N_1') \cap Lid(N_2) = \emptyset$$

$$(\text{RES}) \; \frac{N \to N'}{(\nu s)N \to (\nu s)N'} \qquad (\text{EQUIV}) \; \frac{N_1 \equiv N_2 \;\; N_2 \to N_3 \;\; N_3 \equiv N_4}{N_1 \to N_4}$$

The rules (SEQ^{tt}) and (SEQ^{ff}) describe the transitions that can be performed by sequential compositions $P_1; P_2$. In particular, the rule (SEQ^{tt}) accounts for the case where P_1 cannot finish after one more step; whereas the rule (SEQ^{ff}) accounts for the opposite case. We require that no variable bound in P_1 is used in P_2, thereby avoiding the need for recording the substitutions resulting from the next step of P_1, that need to be applied on P_2.

The rule (PAR) says that if a net N_1 can make a transition, then its parallel composition with another net N_2 can also make a transition, as long as no clashes of table identifiers local to each site in $N_1 \| N_2$ are introduced. It makes use of the function $Lid(...)$ that gives the multiset of pairs of physical localities and table identifiers in networks and components. This function is overloaded on networks and components, and is defined inductively as follows.

$$\begin{aligned}
Lid(\textsf{nil}) &= \emptyset & Lid(s, P) &= \emptyset \\
Lid(N_1 \| N_2) &= Lid(N_1) \uplus Lid(N_2) & Lid(s, (I, R)) &= \{(s, I.id)\} \\
Lid((\nu s)N) &= Lid(N) & Lid(s, C_1 | C_2) &= Lid(s, C_1) \uplus Lid(s, C_2) \\
Lid(s ::_\rho C) &= Lid(s, C) &&
\end{aligned}$$

The rules (CALL), (RES) and (EQUIV) are self-explanatory.

It is a property of our semantics that no local repetition of table identifiers can be caused by a transition (including the creation of a new table). Define $no\_rep(A) = (A = \textsf{set}(A))$, which expresses that there is no repetition in the multiset A, thus A coincides with its underlying set. This property is formalized in Lemma 1 whose proof is straightforward by induction on the derivation of the transition.

Lemma 1. *For all nets N and N', if $no\_rep(Lid(N))$ and $N \to N'$, then it holds that $no\_rep(Lid(N'))$.*

Thus, imposing "non-existence of local repetition of table identifiers" as an integrity condition for the initial network will guarantee the satisfaction of this condition in all possible derivatives of the network.

Example 8 (Transition of Networks). Continuing with Example 2, we illustrate how our semantics help establish global transitions.

Suppose there is no other table at s_1 with the identifier KLD. By (PAR), and the structural congruence, we have

$$\underline{s_0}::_{\rho_0}(I_0, R_0)|C_0' \,\|\, \underline{s_1}::_{\rho_1}(I_1, R_1)|\mathsf{insert}(t_1, \mathsf{KLD})@self.\mathsf{nil}|C_1'' \,\|\, \ldots \,\|\, \underline{s_n}::_{\rho_n}(I_n, R_n)|C_n'$$
$$\to \underline{s_0}::_{\rho_0}(I_0, R_0)|C_0' \,\|\, \underline{s_1}::_{\rho_1}(I_1, R_1')|C_1'' \,\|\, \ldots \,\|\, \underline{s_n}::_{\rho_n}(I_n, R_n)|C_n',$$

where $t_1 = (\text{"001"}, \text{"}HighBoot\text{"}, \text{"2015"}, \text{"}white\text{"}, \text{"37"}, \text{"6"}, \text{"0"})$.   □

4   Case Study

Continuing with our running example, we illustrate the modelling of data aggregation over multiple databases local to different branches of the department store chain in Klaim-DB. In more detail, a manager of the head office wants statistics on the total sales of KLD high boots from the year 2015, in each branch operating in Copenhagen.

We will think of a procedure *stat* at the site s_0 of the head office, carrying out the aggregation needed. Thus the net for the database systems of the department store chain, as considered in Section 2, specializes to the following, where C_0'' is the remaining tables and processes at s_0 apart from Stores and *stat*.

$$\underline{s_0}::_{\rho_0}(stat|(I, R)|C_0'') \,\|\, \underline{s_1}::_{\rho_1}((I_1, R_1)|C_1') \,\|\, \ldots \,\|\, \underline{s_n}::_{\rho_n}((I_n, R_n)|C_n')$$

A detailed specification of the procedure *stat* is then given in Figure 4.

$stat \triangleq \mathsf{create}(I_{\mathrm{res}})@self.$
    $\mathsf{sel\_ext}((!x, !y, !z, !w, !p), \mathsf{KLD} \in w \wedge x = \text{"}CPH\text{"}, \mathsf{Stores}, (z, p), !TBV)@self.$
    $\mathsf{foreach}_p\ (!q, !u)\ \mathrm{in}\ TBV.R:$
        $\mathsf{aggr}((\text{"001"}, \text{"}HighBoot\text{"}, \text{"2015"}, !x, !y, !z, !w), \mathsf{true}, \mathsf{KLD}, sum_7, (!res))@u.$
        $\mathsf{insert}((q, \text{"}HighBoot\text{"}, res), \mathsf{result})@self;$
    ...
    $\mathsf{drop}(\mathsf{result})@self$

Fig. 4. The Procedure for Distributed Data Aggregation

First of all, a result table with the interface I_{res} is created, where $I_{\mathrm{res}}.id = $ result and $I.sk =< \text{"}Brand\text{"} : String, \text{"}City\text{"} : String, \text{"}Shop\_name\text{"} : String,$

"*Sales*" : *Int* >. Then all the logical localities of the local databases used by the branches in Copenhagen that actually sell KLD shoes are selected, together with the shop names of such branches. This result set is then processed by a parallel loop. The number of KLD high boots from 2015 that are sold is counted at each of these localities (branches), and is inserted into the resulting table together with the corresponding shop name and the information "High Boot" describing the shoe type concerned. The resulting table, displayed in Figure 5, can still be queried/manipulated before being dropped.

In the end of this case study, we would like to remark that the use of the parallel loop in carrying out all the individual remote aggregations has made the overall query more efficient. Hence some performance issues can be captured by modelling in Klaim-DB.

Shop_name	Shoe_name	Sales
Shop1	HighBoot	12
Shop2	HighBoot	53
Shop3	HighBoot	3
...	...	...

Fig. 5. The Table result

5   Extension and Discussion

Joining Tables. Our modelling language can be extended to support querying from the "join" of tables. For this extension, we make use of under-specified join expressions *je*, that can have table identifiers or table variables as parameters. The syntax of the new selection actions is shown below.

$$a ::= \dots \mid \mathsf{sel\_ext}(T, \psi, je(tb_1, \dots, tb_n), t, !TBV)@\ell_1, \dots, \ell_n$$
$$\mid \mathsf{sel\_int}(T, \psi, je(TBV_1, \dots, TBV_n), t, !TBV') \mid \dots$$

For an external selection, we allow to use a list $\ell_1, \dots, \ell_n$ of localities (abbreviated as $\bar{\ell}$), to join tables located in multiple databases. In more detail, for $i \in \{1, \dots, n\}$, tb_i is supposed to be the identifier of a table located at ℓ_i.

We use $[\![je]\!]^R$ and $[\![je]\!]^I$ to represent the interpretation of *je* in terms of how the datasets and the schemas of the joined tables should be combined. As an example, a *plain list* of table identifiers or tables (substitution of table variables) corresponds to taking the concatenation of all the schemas and selecting from the cartesian product of all the data sets.

$$[\![je]\!]^I(I_1, \dots, I_n) = \bigoplus_{j \in \{1, \dots, n\}} I_j.sk \qquad [\![je]\!]^R(R_1, \dots, R_n) = R_1 \times \dots \times R_n$$

The pattern matching against the template T and the satisfaction of the predicate ψ will be examined on tuples from $[\![je]\!]^R(R_1, \dots, R_n)$, and the predicate ψ can now impose constraints on the fields from different tables.

The adaption needed for the semantics is fairly straightforward. The semantic rules (SELJ_EXT) and (SELJ_INT) that describe selection operations from joined tables are presented in Table 5. In the rule (SELJ_EXT), although it is stipulated that the j-th table identifier specified in the list $\bar{tb}$ must be identical to the j-th table (I_j, R_j) listed as parallel components, no undesired stuck configurations are caused because of the structrual congruence.

Table 5. The Semantic Rules for Selection from Joins

$$n = |\overline{tb}| = |\overline{\ell}| \wedge \forall j \in \{1, ..., n\} : \rho_0(l_j) = s_j \wedge tb_j = I_j.id$$

$$I' = [id \mapsto \perp][sk \mapsto (\llbracket je \rrbracket^{\mathrm{I}}(\overline{I})) \downarrow_t^T] \quad \sigma' = [(I', R')/TBV]$$

(SELJ_EXT) $\dfrac{R' = \{\mathcal{E}\llbracket t\sigma \rrbracket_{\rho_1} \mid \exists t' : t' \in \llbracket je \rrbracket^{\mathrm{R}}(\overline{R}) \wedge match(\mathcal{E}\llbracket T \rrbracket_{\rho_1}, t') \wedge \sigma = (t'/\mathcal{E}\llbracket T \rrbracket_{\rho_1}) \wedge \psi\sigma\}}{\begin{array}{l} s_0 ::_{\rho_0} \mathsf{sel_ext}(T, \psi, je(\overline{tb}), t, !TBV)@\overline{\ell}.P \parallel s_1 ::_{\rho_1} (I_1, R_1) \parallel ... \parallel s_n ::_{\rho_n} (I_n, R_n) \\ \quad \to s_0 ::_{\rho_0} P\sigma' \parallel s_1 ::_{\rho_1} (I_1, R_1) \parallel ... \parallel s_n ::_{\rho_n} (I_n, R_n) \end{array}}$$

$$I' = [id \mapsto \perp][sk \mapsto (\llbracket je \rrbracket^{\mathrm{I}}(\overline{I})) \downarrow_t^T] \quad \sigma' = [(I', R')/TBV]$$

(SELJ_INT) $\dfrac{R' = \{\mathcal{E}\llbracket t\sigma \rrbracket_{\rho_1} \mid \exists t' : t' \in \llbracket je \rrbracket^{\mathrm{R}}(\overline{R}) \wedge match(\mathcal{E}\llbracket T \rrbracket_{\rho_1}, t') \wedge \sigma = (t'/\mathcal{E}\llbracket T \rrbracket_{\rho_1}) \wedge \psi\sigma\}}{s_1 ::_{\rho_1} \mathsf{sel_int}(T, \psi, je(\overline{(I, R)}), t, !TBV).P \to s_1 ::_{\rho_1} P\sigma'}$$

This extension paves the way for the general ability to operate on multiple databases by a single action, which is in line with the design philosophy of multi-database systems (e.g., [5]).

Discussion. We could have required whole tables to be received into local variables by using the standard Klaim actions $\mathsf{out}(t)@\ell$ and $\mathsf{in}(t)@\ell$, and made the selection and aggregation operations work only on table variables. In this way we could have gotten rid of "external selection". However, "external selection" on remote localities can potentially reduce the communication cost considerably, since only one tuple (for aggregation) or a part of a table (for selection) need to be returned. For selection the reduction is particularly meaningful when the resulting data set is small.

Concerning the result of selection operations, an alternative that we have not adopted is the direct placement of the result in a separate table. This table is either created automatically by the selection operation itself, with an identifier specified in the selection action, or a designated "result table" at each site. However, a problem is that the removal of the automatically created tables will need to be taken care of by the system designer making the specification, using $\mathsf{drop}(I)@\ell$ actions. And similar problems arise with the maintenance of the designated "result table" local to each site (e.g., the alteration of its schema, the cleaning of old results, etc.). To abstain from these low-level considerations, table variables are introduced and binding is used for the selection results.

The *interoperability* between database systems and ordinary applications can also be realized by bringing back the primitive Klaim actions ($\mathsf{out}(t)@\ell$, $\mathsf{in}(T)@\ell$, and $\mathsf{eval}(P)@\ell$) and allowing the co-existence of tables and plain tuples at different localities. Via the re-introduction of the eval action, we would also be able to send out mobile processes to perform complex data processing on-site.

6   Conclusion

We have proposed Klaim-DB — a modelling language that borrows insights from both the coordination language Klaim and database query languages like SQL, to support the high-level modelling and reasoning of distributed database applications. The semantics is illustrated with a running example on the query and management of the databases used by a department store chain. Data aggregation across the geographically scattered databases at the individual stores, as performed by a coordinator, is then modelled in the language. In the model, the local aggregations at the store-owned databases are performed in parallel with each other, benefiting the performance.

Our use of templates in the query actions of Klaim-DB is in line with the spirit of the QBE language (Query by Example [12]). The choice of using multiset operations for the semantics of these actions, on the other hand, has the flavor of the Domain Relational Calculus underlying QBE. The work presented in [9] discusses typical coordination issues in distributed databases in Linda, from an informal, architectural viewpoint. This work is marginally related to ours.

The specification and enforcement of security policies is an important concern in distributed database systems. A simple example is: when inserting data into a remote table, it is important to know whether the current site trusts the remote site with respect to confidentiality, and whether the remote site trusts the current site with respect to integrity. Recently, [3] and [7] address privacy and information flow issues in database applications. Another work, [10], provides an information flow analysis for locality-based security policies in Klaim. By elaborating on the language design, we provide in this paper a solid ground for any future work aiming to support security policies and mechanisms.

Another interesting line of future work is the specification of transactions (e.g., [6]). This is needed for the modelling of finer-grained coordination between database accesses.

Acknowledgments. We would like to thank the anonymous reviewers for their valuable feedback. Xi Wu is partly supported by the IDEA4CPS project, ECNU Project of Funding Overseas Short-term Studies, Domestic Academic Visit and NSFC Project (No.61361136002 and No.61321064). Ximeng Li is partly funded by SESAMO, a European Artemis project.

References

1. Abrial, J.-R.: Formal methods: Theory becoming practice. J. UCS 13(5), 619–628 (2007)
2. De Nicola, R., Ferrari, G.L., Pugliese, R.: KLAIM: A kernel language for agents interaction and mobility. IEEE Trans. Software Eng. (1998)
3. Dwork, C.: Differential privacy. In: Encyclopedia of Cryptography and Security, 2nd edn., pp. 338–340 (2011)
4. Hoare, C.A.R.: Communicating Sequential Processes. Prentice-Hall (1985)
5. Kuhn, E., Ludwig, T.: Vip-mdbs: A logic multidatabase system. In: Proceedings of the First International Symposium on Databases in Parallel and Distributed Systems, DPDS 1988, pp. 190–201. IEEE Computer Society Press (1988)
6. Kühn, E., Elmagarmid, A.K., Leu, Y., Boudriga, N.: A parallel logic language for transaction specification in multidatabase systems. Journal of Systems Integration 5(3), 219–252 (1995)

7. Lourenço, L., Caires, L.: Information flow analysis for valued-indexed data security compartments. In: Trustworthy Global Computing - 8th International Symposium, TGC 2013, pp. 180–198 (2013)
8. Plotkin, G.D.: A structural approach to operational semantics. J. Log. Algebr. Program. 60-61:17–139 (2004)
9. Thirukonda, M.M., Menezes, R.: On the use of linda as a framework for distributed database systems (2002)
10. Tolstrup, T.K., Nielson, F., Hansen, R.R.: Locality-based security policies. In: Dimitrakos, T., Martinelli, F., Ryan, P.Y.A., Schneider, S. (eds.) FAST 2006. LNCS, vol. 4691, pp. 185–201. Springer, Heidelberg (2007)
11. Woodcock, J., Larsen, P.G., Bicarregui, J., Fitzgerald, J.S.: Formal methods: Practice and experience. ACM Comput. Surv. 41(4) (2009)
12. Zloof, M.M.: Query by example. In: Proceedings of the National Computer Conference and Exposition, AFIPS 1975, pp. 431–438. ACM, New York (1975)

A   Multiset Notation

We use $\uplus$, $\cap$ and $\backslash$ to represent the union, intersection and substraction, respectively, of multisets. For a multiset S, and an element s, the application $M(S, s)$ of the multiplicity function M gives the number of repetitions of s in S. Note that for $s \notin S$, $M(S, s) = 0$. Then our notions of union, intersection and subtraction are such that

$$M(S_1 \uplus S_2, s) = M(S_1, s) + M(S_2, s)$$
$$M(S_1 \cap S_2, s) = min(M(S_1, s), M(S_2, s))$$
$$M(S_1 \backslash S_2, s) = abs(M(S_1, s) - M(S_2, s))$$

Here $abs(v)$ gives the absolute value of the integer v.

Open Transactions on Shared Memory

Marino Miculan, Marco Peressotti$^{(\boxtimes)}$, and Andrea Toneguzzo

Laboratory of Models and Applications of Distributed Systems
Department of Mathematics and Computer Science, University of Udine, Italy
{marino.miculan,marco.peressotti}@uniud.it

Abstract. *Transactional memory* has arisen as a good way for solving many of the issues of lock-based programming. However, most implementations admit *isolated* transactions only, which are not adequate when we have to coordinate *communicating* processes. To this end, in this paper we present *OCTM*, an Haskell-like language with *open* transactions over shared transactional memory: processes can *join* transactions at runtime just by accessing to shared variables. Thus a transaction can co-operate with the environment through shared variables, but if it is rolled-back, also all its effects on the environment are retracted. For proving the expressive power of *OCTM* we give an implementation of *TCCS^m*, a CCS-like calculus with open transactions.

1 Introduction

Coordination of concurrent programs is notoriously difficult. Traditional fine-grained lock-based mechanisms are deadlock-prone, inefficient, not composable and not scalable. For these reasons, *Software Transactional Memory* (STM) has been proposed as a more effective abstraction for concurrent programming [1,9,17]. The idea is to mark blocks of code as "atomic"; at runtime, these blocks are executed so that the well-known ACID properties are guaranteed. Transactions ensure deadlock freedom, no priority inversion, automatic roll-back on exceptions or timeouts, and greater parallelizability. Among other implementations, we mention *STM Haskell* [7], which allows atomic blocks to be composed into larger ones. STM Haskell adopts an *optimistic* evaluation strategy: the blocks are allowed to run concurrently, and eventually if an interference is detected a transaction is *aborted* and its effects on the memory are rolled back.

However, standard ACID transactions are still inadequate when we have to deal with *communicating* processes, i.e., which can exchange information *during* the transactions. This is very common in concurrent distributed programming, like in service-oriented architectures, where processes dynamically combine to form a transaction, and all have to either commit or abort together. In this scenario the participants cannot be enclosed in one transaction beforehand, because transactions are formed at runtime. To circumvent this issue, various forms of *open transactions* have been proposed, where the Isolation requirement is relaxed [2–4,10,12]. In particular, *TransCCS* and *TCCS^m* are two CCS-like calculi recently introduced to model communicating transactions [4,5,10]. These calculi offer methodologies for proving important properties, such as fair-testing for proving liveness and bisimulations for proving contextual equivalences.

© IFIP International Federation for Information Processing 2015
T. Holvoet and M. Viroli (Eds.): COORDINATION 2015, LNCS 9037, pp. 213–229, 2015.
DOI: 10.1007/978-3-319-19282-6_14

Now, if we try to implement cross-transaction communications *a la* $TCCS^m$ in STM Haskell or similar languages, it turns out that isolated transactions are not expressive enough. As an example, let us consider two $TCCS^m$ transactions $\langle \bar{c}.P \blacktriangleright 0 \rangle | \langle c.Q \blacktriangleright 0 \rangle$ synchronizing on a channel c. Following the standard practice, we could implement this synchronization as two parallel processes using a pair of semaphores c1,c2 (which are easily realized in STM Haskell):

$\langle \bar{c}.P \blacktriangleright 0 \rangle$ = atomic {		$\langle c.Q \blacktriangleright 0 \rangle$ = atomic {	
up c1	-- 1.1	down c1	-- 2.1
down c2	-- 1.2	up c2	-- 2.2
P		Q	
}		}	

This implementation is going to deadlock: the only possible execution order is 1.1-2.1-2.2-1.2, which is possible outside transactions but it is forbidden for ACID transactions[1]. The problem is that ordinary STM transactions are kept isolated, while in $TCCS^m$ they can merge at runtime.

In order to address this issue, in this paper we introduce software transactional memory with *open* transactions: processes can *join* transactions and transactions can *merge* at runtime, when they access to shared variables. To this end, we present $OCTM$, a higher-order language extending the concurrency model of STM Haskell with composable *open (multi-thread)* transactions interacting via *shared memory*. The key step is to separate the isolation aspect from atomicity: in $OCTM$ the atomic construct ensures "all-or-nothing" execution, but not isolation; when needed, isolated execution can be guaranteed by a new constructor isolated. An atomic block is a *participant* (possibly the only one) of a transaction. Notice that transaction merging is implicitly triggered by accessing to shared memory, without any explicit operation or *a priori* coordination. For instance, in $OCTM$ the two transactions of the example above would merge becoming two participants of the same transaction, hence the two threads can synchronize and proceed. In order to prove formally the expressivity of open memory transactions, we define an implementation of $TCCS^m$ in $OCTM$, which is proved to correctly preserve behaviours by means of a suitable notion of simulation. We have based our work on STM Haskell as a paradigmatic example, but this approach is general and can be applied to other STM implementations.

Lesani and Palsberg [12] have proposed transactions communicating through transactional message-based channels called *transactional events*. These mechanisms are closer to models like TransCCS and $TCCS^m$, but on the other hand they induce a *strict coupling* between processes, which sometimes is neither advisable nor easy to implement (e.g., when we do not know all transaction's participants beforehand). In fact, most STM implementations (including STM Haskell) adopt the shared memory model of multi-thread programming; this model is also more amenable to implementation on modern multi-core hardware architectures with transactional memory [8]. For these reasons, in $OCTM$ we have preferred to stick to *loosely coupled* interactions based on shared memory only.

---

[1] This possibility was pointed out also in [7]: "two threads can easily deadlock if each awaits some communication from the other".

Value $V ::= r \mid \lambda x.M \mid$ return $M \mid M \ggg N \mid$
newVar $M \mid$ readVar $r \mid$ writeVar $r \ M \mid$
fork $M \mid$ atomic $M \ N \mid$ isolated $M \mid$ abort $M \mid$ retry
Term $M, N ::= x \mid V \mid MN \mid \dots$

Fig. 1. Syntax of $OCTM$ values and terms

The rest of the paper is structured as follows. In Section 2 we describe the syntax and semantics of $OCTM$. The calculus $TCCS^m$, our reference model for open transactions, is recalled in Section 3. Then, in Section 4 we provide an encoding of $TCCS^m$ in $OCTM$, proving that $OCTM$ is expressive enough to cover open transactions. Conclusions and directions for future work are in Section 5. Longer proofs are in the extended version of this paper [15].

2 $OCTM$: Open Concurrent Transactional Memory

In this section we introduce the syntax and semantics of $OCTM$, a higher-order functional language with threads and open transaction on shared memory. The syntax is Haskell-like (in the wake of existing works on software transactional memories such as [7]) and the semantics is a small-step operational semantics given by two relations: $\xrightarrow{\beta}$ models transaction auxiliary operations (e.g. creation) while $\rightarrow$ models actual term evaluations. Executions proceeds by repeatedly choosing a thread and executing a single (optionally transactional) operation; transitions from different threads may be arbitrarily interleaved as long as atomicity and isolation are not violated where imposed by the program.

2.1   Syntax

The syntax can be found in Figure 1 where the meta-variables r and x range over a given countable set of locations Loc and variables Var respectively. Terms and values are inspired to Haskell and are entirely conventional[2]; they include abstractions, application, monadic operators (return and $\ggg$), memory operators (newVar, readVar, writeVar), forks, transactional execution modalities (atomic and isolated) and transaction operators (abort and retry).

Effectfull expressions such as fork or isolated are glued together by the (overloaded) monadic bind $\ggg$ e.g.:

newVar $0 \ggg \lambda x.$(fork (writeVar x 42) $\ggg \lambda y.$readVar x)

whereas values are "passed on" by the monadic unit return.

Akin to Haskell, we will use underscores in place of unused variables (e.g. $\lambda\_.0$) and $M \gg N$ as a shorthand for $M \ggg \lambda\_.N$, and the convenient do-*notation*:

$$\mathsf{do}\{x \leftarrow M; N\} \equiv M \ggg (\lambda x.\mathsf{do}\{N\})$$
$$\mathsf{do}\{M; N\} \equiv M \ggg (\lambda\_.\mathsf{do}\{N\})$$
$$\mathsf{do}\{M\} \equiv M$$

---

[2] Although we treat the application of monadic combinators (e.g. return) as values in the line of similar works [7].

possibly trading semicolons and brackets for the conventional Haskell *layout*. For instance, the above example is rendered as

```
do
      x  ←  newVar 0
      fork (writeVar x 42)
      readVar x
```

2.2 Operational Semantics

We present the operational semantics of $OCTM$ in terms of an abstract machine whose states are triples $\langle P; \Theta, \Delta \rangle$ formed by

- thread family (process) P;
- heap memory $\Theta : \mathsf{Loc} \rightharpoonup \mathsf{Term}$;
- distributed working memory $\Delta : \mathsf{Loc} \rightharpoonup \mathsf{Term} \times \mathsf{TrName}$

where Term denotes the set of $OCTM$ terms (cf. Figure 1) and TrName denotes the set of names used by the machine to identify active transactions. We shall denote the set of all possible states as State.

Threads. Threads are the smaller unit of execution the machine scheduler operates on; they execute OCTM terms and do not have any private transactional memory. Threads are given unique identifiers (ranged over by t or variations thereof) and, whenever they take part to some transaction, the transaction identifier (ranged over by k, j or variations thereof). Threads of the former case are represented by $(\![M]\!)_t$ where M is the term being evaluated and the subscript t is the thread identifier. Threads of the latter case have two forms: $(\![M \triangleright M'; N]\!)_{t,k}$, called and $(\![M \triangleright M']\!)_{t,k}$ where:

- M is the term being evaluated inside the transaction k;
- M' is the term being evaluated as *compensation* in case k is aborted;
- N is the term being evaluated as *continuation* after k commits or aborts.

Threads with a continuation are called *primary participants (to transaction k)*, while threads without continuation are the *secondary participants*. The former group includes all and only the threads that started a transaction (i.e. those evaluated in an `atomic`), while the latter group encompasses threads forked inside a transaction and threads forced to join a transaction (from outside a transactional context) because of memory interactions. While threads of both groups can force a transaction to abort or restart, only primary participants can vote for its commit and hence pass the transaction result to the continuation.

We shall present thread families using the evocative CCS-like parallel operator $\|$ (cf. Figure 2) which is commutative and associative. Notice that this operator is well-defined only on operands whose thread identifiers are distinct. The notation is extended to thread families with $\mathbf{0}$ denoting the empty family.

$$
\begin{array}{ll}
\text{Thread} & T_t ::= (\!|M|\!)_t \mid (\!|M \triangleright M'; N|\!)_{t,k} \mid (\!|M \triangleright M'|\!)_{t,k} \\
\text{Thread family} & P ::= T_{t_1} \parallel \cdots \parallel T_{t_n} \quad \forall i,j \; t_i \neq t_j \\
\text{Expressions} & \mathbb{E} ::= [-] \mid \mathbb{E} \ggg M \\
\text{Processes} & \mathbb{P}_t ::= (\!|\mathbb{E}|\!)_t \\
\text{Transactions} & \mathbb{T}_{t,k} ::= (\!|\mathbb{E} \triangleright M; N|\!)_{t,k} \mid (\!|\mathbb{E} \triangleright M|\!)_{t,k}
\end{array}
$$

Fig. 2. Threads and evaluation contexts

$$
\frac{M \not\equiv V \quad \mathcal{V}[M] = V}{M \to V} \; (\textsc{Eval}) \qquad \frac{}{\texttt{return } M \ggg N \to N M} \; (\textsc{BindReturn})
$$

$$
\frac{}{\texttt{retry} \ggg M \to \texttt{retry}} \; (\textsc{BindRetry}) \qquad \frac{}{\texttt{abort } N \ggg M \to \texttt{abort } N} \; (\textsc{BindAbort})
$$

Fig. 3. *OCTM* semantics: rules for term evaluation

Memory. The memory is divided in the heap Θ and in a distributed working memory Δ. As for traditional closed (acid) transactions (e.g. [7]), operations inside a transaction are evaluated against Δ and effects are propagated to Θ only on commits. When a thread inside a transaction k accesses a location outside Δ the location is *claimed for* k and remains claimed for the rest of k execution. Threads inside a transaction can interact only with locations claimed by their transaction. To this end, threads outside any transaction can join an existing one and different active transactions can be merged to share their claimed locations.

We shall denote the pair $\langle \Theta, \Delta \rangle$ by Σ and reference to each projected component by a subscript e.g. Σ_Θ for the heap. When describing updates to the state Σ, we adopt the convention that Σ' has to be intended as equal to Σ except if stated otherwise, i.e. by statements like $\Sigma'_\Theta = \Sigma_\Theta[r \mapsto M]$. Formally, updates to location content are defined on Θ and Δ as follows:

$$
\Theta[r \mapsto M](s) \triangleq \begin{cases} M & \text{if } r = s \\ \Theta(s) & \text{otherwise} \end{cases} \qquad \Delta[r \mapsto (M,k)](s) \triangleq \begin{cases} (M,k) & \text{if } r = s \\ \Delta(s) & \text{otherwise} \end{cases}
$$

for any $r, s \in \mathsf{Loc}$, $M \in \mathsf{Term}$ and $k \in \mathsf{TrName}$. Likewise, updates on transaction names are defined on Σ and Δ as follows:

$$
\Sigma[k \mapsto j] \triangleq (\Theta, \Delta[k \mapsto j]) \quad (\Delta[k \mapsto j])(r) \triangleq \begin{cases} \Delta(r) & \text{if } \Delta(r) = (M,l), l \neq k \\ (M,j) & \text{if } \Delta(r) = (M,k) \end{cases}
$$

for any $r \in \mathsf{Loc}$, $M \in \mathsf{Term}$ and $k, j \in \mathsf{TrName}$. Note that j may occur in Δ resulting in the fusion of the transactions denoted by k and j respectively. Finally, $\varnothing$ denotes the empty memory (i.e. the completely undefined partial function).

Behaviour. Evaluation contexts are shown in Figure 2 and the transition relations are presented in Figures 3, 4, 5. The first (cf. Figures 3) is defined on terms only and models pure computations. In particular, rule (\textsc{Eval}) allows a term M that is not a value to be evaluated by an auxiliary (partial) function, $\mathcal{V}[M]$ yielding the value V of M whereas the other three rules define the semantic of

$$\frac{M \to N}{\langle \mathbb{P}_t[M] \| P; \Sigma \rangle \to \langle \mathbb{P}_t[N] \| P; \Sigma \rangle} \text{ (TermP)} \qquad \frac{M \to N}{\langle \mathbb{T}_{t,k}[M] \| P; \Sigma \rangle \to \langle \mathbb{T}_{t,k}[N] \| P; \Sigma \rangle} \text{ (TermT)}$$

$$\frac{t' \notin \text{threads}(P) \quad t \neq t'}{\langle \mathbb{P}_t[\textbf{fork } M] \parallel P; \Sigma \rangle \to \langle \mathbb{P}_t[\textbf{return } t'] \parallel (\!(M)\!)_{t'} \parallel P; \Sigma \rangle} \text{ (ForkP)}$$

$$\frac{t' \notin \text{threads}(P) \quad t \neq t'}{\langle \mathbb{T}_{t,k}[\textbf{fork } M] \parallel P; \Sigma \rangle \to \langle \mathbb{T}_{t,k}[\textbf{return } t'] \parallel (\!(M \triangleright \textbf{return})\!)_{t',k} \parallel P; \Sigma \rangle} \text{ (ForkT)}$$

$$\text{threads}(T_{t_1} \parallel \cdots \parallel T_{t_n}) \triangleq \{t_1, \ldots, t_n\}$$

$$\frac{r \notin \text{dom}(\Sigma_\Theta) \cup \text{dom}(\Sigma_\Delta) \quad \Sigma'_\Theta = \Sigma_\Theta[r \mapsto M]}{\langle \mathbb{P}_t[\textbf{newVar } M] \parallel P; \Sigma \rangle \to \langle \mathbb{P}_t[\textbf{return } r] \parallel P; \Sigma' \rangle} \text{ (NewP)}$$

$$\frac{r \notin \text{dom}(\Sigma_\Theta) \cup \text{dom}(\Sigma_\Delta) \quad \Sigma'_\Delta = \Sigma_\Delta[r \mapsto (M,k)]}{\langle \mathbb{T}_{t,k}[\textbf{newVar } M] \parallel P; \Sigma \rangle \to \langle \mathbb{T}_{t,k}[\textbf{return } r] \parallel P; \Sigma' \rangle} \text{ (NewT)}$$

$$\frac{r \notin \text{dom}(\Sigma_\Delta) \quad \Sigma_\Theta(r) = M}{\langle \mathbb{P}_t[\textbf{readVar } r] \parallel P; \Sigma \rangle \to \langle \mathbb{P}_t[\textbf{return } M] \parallel P; \Sigma \rangle} \text{ (ReadP)}$$

$$\frac{r \notin \text{dom}(\Sigma_\Delta) \quad \Sigma_\Theta(r) = M \quad \Sigma'_\Delta = \Sigma_\Delta[r \mapsto (M,k)]}{\langle \mathbb{T}_{t,k}[\textbf{readVar } r] \parallel P; \Sigma \rangle \to \langle \mathbb{T}_{t,k}[\textbf{return } M] \parallel P; \Sigma' \rangle} \text{ (ReadT)}$$

$$\frac{M = \mathbb{E}[\textbf{readVar } r] \quad \Sigma_\Delta(r) = (M',k)}{\langle (\!(M)\!)_t \parallel P; \Sigma \rangle \to \langle (\!(\mathbb{E}[\textbf{return } M'] \triangleright \lambda\_.M)\!)_{t,k} \parallel P; \Sigma \rangle} \text{ (ReadJoin)}$$

$$\frac{\Sigma_\Delta(r) = (M,j) \quad \Sigma' = \Sigma[k \mapsto j]}{\langle \mathbb{T}_{t,k}[\textbf{readVar } r] \parallel P; \Sigma \rangle \to \langle \mathbb{T}_{t,j}[\textbf{return } M] \parallel P[k \mapsto j]; \Sigma' \rangle} \text{ (ReadMerge)}$$

$$\frac{r \notin \text{dom}(\Sigma_\Delta) \quad \Sigma_\Theta(r) = N \quad \Sigma'_\Theta = \Sigma_\Theta[r \mapsto M]}{\langle \mathbb{P}_t[\textbf{writeVar } r \ M] \parallel P; \Sigma \rangle \to \langle \mathbb{P}_t[\textbf{return } ()] \parallel P; \Sigma' \rangle} \text{ (WriteP)}$$

$$\frac{r \notin \text{dom}(\Sigma_\Delta) \quad \Sigma_\Theta(r) = N \quad \Sigma'_\Delta = \Sigma_\Delta[r \mapsto (M,k)]}{\langle \mathbb{T}_{t,k}[\textbf{writeVar } r \ M] \parallel P; \Sigma \rangle \to \langle \mathbb{T}_{t,k}[\textbf{return } ()] \parallel P; \Sigma' \rangle} \text{ (WriteT)}$$

$$\frac{M = \mathbb{E}[\textbf{writeVar } r \ M'] \quad \Sigma_\Delta(r) = (M'',k) \quad \Sigma'_\Delta = \Sigma_\Delta[r \mapsto (M',k)]}{\langle (\!(M)\!)_t \parallel P; \Sigma \rangle \to \langle (\!(\mathbb{E}[\textbf{return } ()] \triangleright \lambda\_.M)\!)_{t,k} \parallel P; \Sigma' \rangle} \text{ (WriteJoin)}$$

$$\frac{\Sigma_\Delta(r) = (N,j) \quad \Sigma' = \Sigma[k \mapsto j] \quad \Sigma'_\Delta = \Sigma_\Delta[r \mapsto (M,j)]}{\langle \mathbb{T}_{t,k}[\textbf{writeVar } r \ M] \parallel P; \Sigma \rangle \to \langle \mathbb{T}_{t,j}[\textbf{return } ()] \parallel P[k \mapsto j]; \Sigma' \rangle} \text{ (WriteMerge)}$$

Fig. 4. *OCTM* semantics: rules for $\to$

the monadic bind. The transition relation modelling pure computations can be thought as accessory to the remaining two for these model transitions between the states of the machine under definition.

Derivation rules in Figure 4 characterize the execution of pure (effect-free) terms, forks and memory operations both inside, and outside of some transaction; Derivation rules in Figure 5 characterize auxiliary operations for transaction management (e.g. creation) and their coordination (e.g distributed commits). Note that there are no derivation rules for **retry**. In fact, the meaning of **retry** is to inform the machine that choices made by the scheduler led to a state from which the program cannot proceed. From an implementation perspective this translates in the transaction being re-executed from the beginning (or a suitable check-point) following a different scheduling of its operations.

$$\frac{k \notin \mathsf{transactions}(P)}{\langle (\!|\mathbf{atomic}\ M\ N \ggg N'|\!)_t \parallel P; \Sigma \rangle \xrightarrow{new_k} \langle (\!|M \rhd N; N'|\!)_{t,k} \parallel P; \Sigma \rangle} \quad (\text{ATOMIC})$$

$$\frac{\langle (\!|M|\!)_t; \Sigma \rangle \rightarrow^* \langle (\!|\mathbf{return}\ N|\!)_t; \Sigma' \rangle}{\langle \mathbb{P}_t[\mathbf{isolated}\ M]; \Sigma \rangle \rightarrow \langle \mathbb{P}_t[\mathbf{return}\ N]; \Sigma' \rangle} \quad (\text{ISOLATEDP})$$

$$\frac{op \in \{\mathbf{abort}, \mathbf{return}\} \quad \langle (\!|M \rhd \mathbf{return}|\!)_{t,k}; \Sigma \rangle \rightarrow^* \langle (\!|op\ N \rhd \mathbf{return}|\!)_{t,k}; \Sigma' \rangle}{\langle \mathbb{T}_{t,k}[\mathbf{isolated}\ M]; \Sigma \rangle \rightarrow \langle \mathbb{T}_{t,k}[op\ N]; \Sigma' \rangle} \quad (\text{ISOLATEDT})$$

$$\frac{\Sigma'_\Delta = \mathsf{clean}(k, \Sigma_\Delta)}{\langle (\!|\mathbf{abort}\ M \rhd N; N'|\!)_{t,k}; \Sigma \rangle \xrightarrow{ab_k M} \langle (\!|N(M) \ggg N'|\!)_t; \Sigma' \rangle} \quad (\text{RAISEABORT1})$$

$$\frac{\Sigma'_\Delta = \mathsf{clean}(k, \Sigma_\Delta)}{\langle (\!|\mathbf{abort}\ M \rhd N|\!)_{t,k}; \Sigma \rangle \xrightarrow{ab_k M} \langle (\!|N(M)|\!)_t; \Sigma' \rangle} \quad (\text{RAISEABORT2})$$

$$\frac{\Sigma'_\Delta = \mathsf{clean}(k, \Sigma_\Delta)}{\langle (\!|M \rhd N; N'|\!)_{t,k}; \Sigma \rangle \xrightarrow{\widehat{ab}_k M} \langle (\!|N(M) \ggg N'|\!)_t; \Sigma' \rangle} \quad (\text{SIGABORT1})$$

$$\frac{\Sigma'_\Delta = \mathsf{clean}(k, \Sigma_\Delta)}{\langle (\!|M \rhd N|\!)_{t,k}; \Sigma \rangle \xrightarrow{\widehat{ab}_k M} \langle (\!|N(M)|\!)_t; \Sigma' \rangle} \quad (\text{SIGABORT2})$$

$$\frac{\langle P; \Sigma \rangle \xrightarrow{ab_k M} \langle P'; \Sigma' \rangle \quad \langle Q; \Sigma \rangle \xrightarrow{\widehat{ab}_k M} \langle Q'; \Sigma' \rangle}{\langle P \parallel Q; \Sigma \rangle \xrightarrow{ab_k M} \langle P' \parallel Q'; \Sigma' \rangle} \quad (\text{ABBROADCAST})$$

$$\frac{\Sigma'_\Theta = \mathsf{commit}(k, \Sigma_\Theta, \Sigma_\Delta) \quad \Sigma'_\Delta = \mathsf{clean}(k, \Sigma_\Delta)}{\langle (\!|\mathbf{return}\ M \rhd N; N'|\!)_{t,k}; \Sigma \rangle \xrightarrow{co_k} \langle (\!|\mathbf{return}\ M \ggg N'|\!)_t; \Sigma' \rangle} \quad (\text{COMMIT1})$$

$$\frac{\Sigma'_\Theta = \mathsf{commit}(k, \Sigma_\Theta, \Sigma_\Delta) \quad \Sigma'_\Delta = \mathsf{clean}(k, \Sigma_\Delta)}{\langle (\!|M \rhd N|\!)_{t,k}; \Sigma \rangle \xrightarrow{co_k} \langle (\!|M|\!)_t; \Sigma' \rangle} \quad (\text{COMMIT2})$$

$$\frac{\langle P; \Sigma \rangle \xrightarrow{co_k} \langle P'; \Sigma' \rangle \quad \langle Q; \Sigma \rangle \xrightarrow{co_k} \langle Q'; \Sigma' \rangle}{\langle P \parallel Q; \Sigma \rangle \xrightarrow{co_k} \langle P' \parallel Q'; \Sigma' \rangle} \quad (\text{COBROADCAST})$$

$$\frac{\langle P; \Sigma \rangle \xrightarrow{\beta} \langle P'; \Sigma' \rangle \quad \mathsf{transactions}(\beta) \notin \mathsf{transactions}(Q)}{\langle P \parallel Q; \Sigma \rangle \xrightarrow{\beta} \langle P' \parallel Q; \Sigma \rangle} \quad (\text{TRIGNORE})$$

$$\mathsf{transactions}(T_{t_1} \parallel \cdots \parallel T_{t_n}) \triangleq \bigcup_{1 \le i \le n} \mathsf{transactions}(T_{t_i}) \qquad \mathsf{clean}(k, \Delta)(r) \triangleq \begin{cases} \bot & \text{if } \Delta(r) = (M, k) \\ \Delta(r) & \text{otherwise} \end{cases}$$

$$\mathsf{transactions}((\!|M|\!)_t) \triangleq \emptyset$$
$$\mathsf{transactions}((\!|M \rhd M'; N|\!)_{t,k}) \triangleq \{k\} \qquad \mathsf{commit}(k, \Theta, \Delta)(r) \triangleq \begin{cases} M & \text{if } \Delta(r) = (M, k) \\ \Theta(r) & \text{otherwise} \end{cases}$$
$$\mathsf{transactions}((\!|M \rhd N|\!)_{t,k}) \triangleq \{k\}$$

Fig. 5. *OCTM* semantics: rules for $\xrightarrow{\beta}$

Due to lack of space we shall describe only a representative subset of the derivation rules from Figure 4 and Figure 5.

Reading a location falls into four cases depending on the location being claimed (i.e. occurring in Δ) and the reader being part of a transaction. The rule (READP) characterize the reading of an unclaimed location from outside any transaction; the read is performed as expected leaving it unclaimed. Rule (READT) describes the reading of an unclaimed location r by a thread belonging to some transaction k; the side effect of the reading is r being claimed for k. Rules (READMERGE) and (READJOIN) cover the cases of readings against claimed locations. In the first scenario, the reading thread belongs to a transaction resulting in the two being merged, which is expressed by renaming its transaction via a substitution. In the remaining scenario, the reading thread does not belong to any transaction and hence joins the transaction k which claimed the location. The newly created participant does not have any continuation since the whole term is set to be executed inside k; any other choice for splitting the term singling out a compensation would impose an artificial synchronization with the transaction commit. For a counter example, consider executing only the read operation inside the transaction and delaying everything after the commit; then concurrency will be clearly reduced. Because of the same reasoning, the whole term M is taken as the compensation of the participant.

Atomic transactions are created by the rule (ATOMIC); threads participating in this transaction are non-deterministically interleaved with other threads. The stronger requirement of isolation is offered by (ISOLATEDP) and (ISOLATEDT); note that their premises forbid thread or transaction creation.

Committing or aborting a transaction require a synchronization of its participants. In particular, an abort can be read as a participant vetoing the outcome of the transaction; this corresponds to (RAISEABORT1) and (RAISEABORT2). The information is then propagated by (ABBROADCAST) and (TRIGNORE) to any other participant to the transaction being aborted; these participants abort performing a transition described by either (SIGABORT1) or (SIGABORT2).

3 $TCCS^m$: CCS with Open Transactions

In order to assess the expressive power of $OCTM$, we have to compare it with a formal model for open transactions. To this end, in this section we recall $TCCS^m$ [10], a CCS-like calculus with open flat transactions: processes can synchronize even when belonging to different transactions, which in turn are joined into a distributed one. We refer to [10] for a detailed description of $TCCS^m$.

The syntax of $TCCS^m$ is defined by the following grammar

$$P ::= \sum_{i=1}^{n} \alpha_i.P_i \mid \prod_{i=0}^{m} P_i \mid P \backslash L \mid X \mid \mu X.P \mid \langle P_1 \blacktriangleright P_2 \rangle \mid \langle\!\langle P_1 \triangleright_k P_2 \rangle\!\rangle \mid \mathsf{co}.P \quad (1)$$

where $\alpha_i ::= a \mid \bar{a} \mid \tau$, a ranges over a given set of visible actions A, L over subsets of A and the bijection $(\bar{\cdot}) : A \to A$ maps every action to its *coaction* as usual. The calculus extends CCS with three constructs which represent *inactive* transactions, *active* transactions and *commit* actions respectively. Transactions such as $\langle\!\langle P_1 \triangleright_k P_2 \rangle\!\rangle$ are formed by two processes with the former being executed atomically and the latter being executed whenever the transaction is aborted, i.e. as a *compensation*. Terms denoting active transactions expose also a name (k in the previous example) which is used to track transaction fusions. For instance, consider the process denoted by $\langle\!\langle P_1 \triangleright_j P_2 \rangle\!\rangle \mid \langle\!\langle Q_1 \triangleright_k Q_2 \rangle\!\rangle$ where P_1 and Q_1 synchronize on some $a \in A$; the result of this synchronization is the fusion of the transactions j and k i.e. $\langle\!\langle P_1' \triangleright_l P_2 \rangle\!\rangle \mid \langle\!\langle Q_1' \triangleright_l Q_2 \rangle\!\rangle$. The fusion makes explicit the dependency

$$\frac{\Gamma \vdash P : \mathsf{p}}{\Gamma \vdash P : \tau} \quad \frac{\Gamma \vdash P : \mathsf{p}}{\Gamma \vdash \mathsf{co}.P : \mathsf{c}} \quad \frac{\Gamma \vdash P : \tau}{\Gamma \vdash P \backslash L : \tau}$$

$$\frac{}{\Gamma \vdash X : \Gamma(X)} \quad \frac{\Gamma[X : \mathsf{p}] \vdash P : \mathsf{p}}{\Gamma \vdash \mu X.P : \mathsf{p}} \quad \frac{\Gamma[X : \mathsf{c}] \vdash P : \mathsf{c}}{\Gamma \vdash \mu X.P : \mathsf{c}} \quad \frac{\forall i\, \Gamma \vdash P_i : \tau}{\Gamma \vdash \prod P_i : \tau}$$

$$\frac{\forall i\, \Gamma \vdash P_i : \mathsf{p}}{\Gamma \vdash \sum \alpha_i.P_i : \mathsf{p}} \quad \frac{\forall i\, \Gamma \vdash \alpha_i.P_i : \mathsf{c}}{\Gamma \vdash \sum \alpha_i.P_i : \mathsf{c}} \quad \frac{\Gamma \vdash P : \mathsf{c} \quad \Gamma \vdash Q : \mathsf{p}}{\Gamma \vdash \langle\!\langle P \triangleright_k Q \rangle\!\rangle : \mathsf{t}} \quad \frac{\Gamma \vdash P : \mathsf{c} \quad \Gamma \vdash Q : \mathsf{p}}{\Gamma \vdash \langle P \blacktriangleright Q \rangle : \mathsf{p}}$$

Fig. 6. Simple types for $TCCS^m$

between j and k introduced by the synchronization and ties them to agree on commits. In this sense, P_1' and Q_1' are participants of a *distributed transaction* [6].

As in [10] we restrict ourselves to well-formed terms. Intuitively, a term is well-formed if active transactions occur only at the top-level and commit actions occur only in a transaction (active or inactive). To this end we introduce a *type system* for $TCCS^m$, whose rules are in Figure 6. Terms that cannot occur inside a transaction have type t, terms that cannot occur outside a transaction have type c, and terms without such restrictions have type p; τ ranges over types.

Definition 1 (Well-formed $TCCS^m$ terms). *A $TCCS^m$ term P, described by the grammar in (1), is said to be* well-formed *if, and only if, $\emptyset \vdash P : \mathsf{t}$. Well-formed terms form the set* **Proc***.*

The operational semantics of well-formed $TCCS^m$ terms is given by the SOS in Figure 7 (further details can be found in [10]). The reduction semantics is given as a binary relation $\rightarrow$ defined by

$$P \rightarrow Q \iff P \xrightarrow{\triangle}_\sigma Q \vee P \xrightarrow{\beta} Q \vee P \xrightarrow{k(\tau)}_\sigma Q.$$

The first case is a synchronization between pure CCS processes. The second case corresponds to creation of new transactions and distributed commit or abort ($\beta \in \{\mathsf{new}k, \mathsf{co}k, \mathsf{ab}k\}$). The third case corresponds to synchronizations of processes inside a named (and possibly distributed) transaction. Notice that by (TSYNC) transaction fusion is *driven by communication* and that by (TSUM) any pure CCS process can join and interact with a transaction.

4 Encoding $TCCS^m$ in $OCTM$.

In this section, we prove that $OCTM$ is expressive enough to cover open transactions *a la* $TCCS^m$. To this end, we provide an encoding of $TCCS^m$ in $OCTM$. Basically, we have to implement transactions and CCS-like synchronizations using shared transactional variables and the `atomic` and `isolated` operators. The encoding is proved to be correct, in the sense that a $TCCS^m$ process presents a reduction if and only if also its encoding has the corresponding reduction.

Synchronization is implemented by means of shared transactional variables, one for each channel, that take values of type `ChState` (cf. Figure 9); this type has four constructors: one for each of the three messages of the communication protocol below plus a "nothing" one providing the default value. Let t_1 and t_2 be

$$\frac{}{\sum \alpha_i.P_i \xrightarrow{\alpha_i}_\varepsilon P_i}\ (\textsc{Sum}) \qquad \frac{P \xrightarrow{a}_\varepsilon P' \quad Q \xrightarrow{\bar{a}}_\varepsilon Q'}{P|Q \xrightarrow{\tau}_\varepsilon P'|Q'}\ (\textsc{Sync}) \qquad \frac{}{\mu X.P \xrightarrow{\tau}_\varepsilon P[\mu X.P/x]}\ (\textsc{Rec})$$

$$\frac{P \xrightarrow{\alpha}_\sigma P' \quad \mathrm{img}(\sigma) \cap \mathrm{tn}(Q) = \emptyset}{P|Q \xrightarrow{\alpha}_\sigma P'|Q[\sigma]}\ (\textsc{ParL}) \qquad \frac{\tau \neq \alpha_j}{\sum \alpha_i.P_i \xrightarrow{k(\alpha_j)}_{\varepsilon \mapsto k} \langle\!\langle P_j | \mathrm{co} \triangleright_k \sum \alpha_i.P_i \rangle\!\rangle}\ (\textsc{TSum})$$

$$\frac{P \xrightarrow{\alpha}_\varepsilon P' \quad \tau \neq \alpha \quad l \neq k}{\langle\!\langle P \triangleright_l Q \rangle\!\rangle \xrightarrow{k(\alpha)}_{l \mapsto k} \langle\!\langle P' \triangleright_k Q \rangle\!\rangle}\ (\textsc{TAct}) \qquad \frac{P \xrightarrow{k(a)}_{i \mapsto k} P' \quad Q \xrightarrow{k(\bar{a})}_{j \mapsto k} Q'}{P|Q \xrightarrow{k(\tau)}_{i,j \mapsto k} P'[j \mapsto k]|Q'[i \mapsto k]}\ (\textsc{TSync})$$

$$\frac{P \xrightarrow{\alpha}_\sigma P' \quad \alpha \notin L}{P \backslash L \xrightarrow{\alpha}_\sigma P' \backslash L}\ (\textsc{Res}) \qquad \frac{P \xrightarrow{\tau}_\varepsilon P'}{\langle\!\langle P \triangleright_k Q \rangle\!\rangle \xrightarrow{\tau}_\varepsilon \langle\!\langle P' \triangleright_k Q \rangle\!\rangle}\ (\textsc{TTau}) \qquad \frac{}{\langle\!\langle P \triangleright_k Q \rangle\!\rangle \xrightarrow{\mathrm{abk}} Q}\ (\textsc{TAb})$$

$$\frac{P \xrightarrow{\beta} P'}{P \backslash L \xrightarrow{\beta} P' \backslash L}\ (\textsc{TRes}) \qquad \frac{k \text{ fresh}}{\langle P \blacktriangleright Q \rangle \xrightarrow{\mathrm{newk}} \langle\!\langle P \triangleright_k Q \rangle\!\rangle}\ (\textsc{TNew}) \qquad \frac{\exists i \, P_i = \mathrm{co}.P_i'}{\langle\!\langle \prod P_i \triangleright_k Q \rangle\!\rangle \xrightarrow{\mathrm{cok}} \Psi_{id}(P)}\ (\textsc{TCo})$$

$$\frac{P \xrightarrow{\beta} P' \quad Q \xrightarrow{\beta} Q' \quad \beta \neq \mathrm{newk}}{P|Q \xrightarrow{\beta} P'|Q'}\ (\textsc{TB1}) \qquad \frac{P \xrightarrow{\beta} P' \quad \mathrm{tn}(\beta) \notin \mathrm{tn}(Q)}{P|Q \xrightarrow{\beta} P'|Q}\ (\textsc{TB2})$$

$$\Psi_\sigma(P) \triangleq \begin{cases} Q & \text{if } P = \mathrm{co}.Q \\ \Psi_\sigma(Q) \backslash L & \text{if } P = Q \backslash L \\ \sum \alpha_i.\Psi_\sigma(P_i) & \text{if } P = \sum \alpha_i.P_i \\ \prod \Psi_\sigma(P_i) & \text{if } P = \prod P_i \\ \mu X.\Psi_{\sigma[P/x]}(Q) & \text{if } P = \mu X.Q \\ P[\sigma] & \text{otherwise} \end{cases} \qquad \mathrm{tn}(P) \triangleq \begin{cases} \{k\} & \text{if } P = \langle\!\langle P \triangleright_k Q \rangle\!\rangle \\ \bigcup \mathrm{tn}(P_i) & \text{if } P = \prod P_i \\ \emptyset & \text{otherwise} \end{cases}$$

$$\mathrm{tn}(\beta) \triangleq \begin{cases} k & \text{if } \beta = \mathrm{newk} \\ k & \text{if } \beta = \mathrm{abk} \\ k & \text{if } \beta = \mathrm{cok} \end{cases}$$

Fig. 7. $TCCS^m$ operational semantics

the identifiers of two threads simulating $a.P$ and $\bar{a}.Q$ respectively. The protocol is composed by the following four steps:

1. t_1 checks whether the channel is free and writes on the transactional variable modelling the channel a a nonce tagged with the constructor M1;
2. t_2 reads the variable for a and accepts the synchronization offered by the challenge (M1 np) adding a fresh nonce to it and writing back (M2 np nq);
3. t_1 reads the answer to its challenge and acknowledges the synchronization writing back the nonce it read tagged with the constructor M3;
4. t_2 reads the acknowledgement and frees the channel.

Each step has to be executed in isolation with respect to the interactions with the shared transactional variable a. Nonces are meant to correlate the steps only and hence can be easily implemented in $OCTM$ by pairing thread identifiers with counter *a la* logical clock. If at any step a thread finds the channel in an unexpected state it means that the chosen scheduling has led to a state incoherent with respect to the above protocol; hence the thread executes a *retry*. This tells the scheduler to try another execution order; by fairness, we eventually find a scheduling such that the two processes do synchronize on a and these are the only executions leading to $P \mid Q$. The protocol is illustrated in Figure 8.

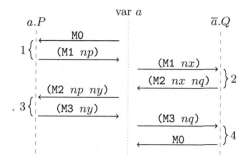

Fig. 8. Implementing $TCCS^m$ synchronization

If the synchronizing parties are involved in distinct transactions these are fused as a side effect of the interaction via the shared variable.

A choice like $\sum_{i=1}^{m} \alpha_i.P_i$ can be seen as a race of threads $t_1, \ldots, t_m$, each simulating a branch, to acquire a boolean transactional variable l (private to the group). Each t_i proceeds as follows. First, it checks l and if it is set, it returns void and terminates (another thread has already acquired it); otherwise it tries to set it while carrying out α_i, i.e. right before executing its last step of the communication protocol. If the variable is acquired by another thread while t_i is finalizing α_i then t_i issues a `retry` to retract any effect of α_i. The $OCTM$ code implementing this protocol is shown in Figure 9.

Encoding of $TCCS^m$. We can now define the encoding $\eta : \mathsf{Proc} \rightarrow \mathsf{State}$, mapping well-formed $TCCS^m$ terms to states of the $OCTM$ abstract machine. Intuitively, a process $P \equiv \prod_{i=1}^{m} P_i$ is mapped into a state with a thread for each P_i and a variable for each channel in P. Clearly, a state of this form can be easily generated by a single $OCTM$ term which allocates all variables and forks the m threads. We have preferred to map $TCCS^m$ terms to $OCTM$ states for sake of simplicity.

The map η is defined by recursion along the derivation of $\emptyset \vdash P : \mathsf{t}$ and the number m of parallel components in $P \equiv \prod_{i=1}^{m} P_i$. This is handled by the auxiliary encoding $\varsigma : \mathsf{Proc} \times \mathsf{Heap} \rightarrow \mathsf{State}$ (up to choice of fresh names) whose second argument is used to track memory allocations. The base case is given by $m = 0$ and yields a state with no threads i.e. $\langle \mathbf{0}, \Theta, \varnothing \rangle$. The recursive step is divided in three subcases depending on the structure and type of P_1 ($m > 0$).

1. If $\emptyset \vdash P_1 : \mathsf{c}$ without top-level restrictions (i.e. $P_1 \not\equiv Q \setminus \{a_1, \ldots, a_{n+1}\}$) then

$$\varsigma(\textstyle\prod_{i=1}^{m+1} P_i, \Theta) \triangleq \langle (\![\varrho(P_1)]\!)_{t_1} \parallel S; \Sigma \rangle$$

where $\langle S; \Sigma \rangle = \varsigma(\prod_{j=1}^{m-1} P_{j+1}, \Theta)$ is the translation of the rest of P and t_1 is unique w.r.t. S (i.e. $t_1 \notin \mathsf{threads}(S)$). By hypothesis P_1 does not contain any top-level active transaction or parallel composition and hence can be translated directly into a $OCTM$-term by means of the encoding ϱ (cf. Figure 10) $- \varrho(P)$ contain a free variable for each unrestricted channel occurring in P.

```
data Channel = OTVar ChState
data ChState = M1 Nonce | M2 Nonce Nonce | M3 Nonce | M0

tau l P = isolated do
    case (readVar l) of
        False → return ()
        True → chooseThis l ≫ P


chooseThis l = writeVar l False


eqOrRetry x y
    | x == y = return ()
    | otherwise = retry


bang x = fork x ≫ bang x

recv c l P = do
    nq ← newNonce
    isolated do
        case (readVar l) of
            False → return ()
            True → do
                chooseThis l
                case (readVar c) of
                    (M1 nx) → writeVar c (M2 nx nq)
                    _ → retry
    isolated do
        case (readVar c) of
            (M3 ny) → eqOrRetry ny nq ≫ writeVar c M0 ≫ P
            _ → retry

send c l P = do
    np ← newNonce
    isolated do
        case (readVar l) of
            False → return ()
            True → do
                chooseThis l
                case (readVar c) of
                    M0 → writeVar c (M1 np)
                    _ → retry
    isolated do
        case (readVar c) of
            (M2 nx ny) → eqOrRetry nx np ≫ writeVar c (M3 ny) ≫ P
            _ → retry
```

Fig. 9. Encoding channels and communication

$$\varrho(\textstyle\sum_{i=1}^{m}\alpha_i P_i) \triangleq \text{do}$$

$\quad l \leftarrow \text{newVar True}$

$\quad \forall i \in \{1, \ldots, m\}$

$\quad\quad \text{fork } \xi(\alpha_i, 1, P_i)$

$$\varrho(\textstyle\prod_{i=0}^{m} P_i) \triangleq \text{do}$$

$\quad \forall i \in \{0, \ldots, m\}$

$\quad\quad \text{fork } \varrho(P_i)$

$$\varrho(P \setminus L) \triangleq \text{do}$$

$\quad \forall c \in L$

$\quad\quad c \leftarrow \text{newVar MO}$

$\quad\quad \varrho(P)$

$$\varrho(X) \triangleq X$$

$\quad \varrho(P)$

$$\varrho(\text{co}.P) \triangleq \text{do}$$

$\quad l \leftarrow \text{newVar True}$

$\quad \text{send } co\ l\ \varrho(P)$

$$\varrho(\mu X.P) \triangleq \text{let } X = \varrho(P) \text{ in}$$

$$\varrho(\langle P \blacktriangleright Q \rangle) \triangleq \text{do}$$

$\quad co \leftarrow \text{newVar MO}$

$\quad \text{atomic p } \varrho(Q)$

$\quad \text{bang psi}$

$\quad \text{where}$

$\quad\quad \text{p = do}$

$\quad\quad\quad \varrho(P)$

$\quad\quad\quad \text{fork (abort ())}$

$\quad\quad\quad \text{psi}$

$\quad\quad \text{psi = do}$

$\quad\quad\quad l \leftarrow \text{newVar True}$

$\quad\quad\quad \text{recv } co\ l\ \text{return}$

$$\xi(\alpha_i, l, P_i) \triangleq \begin{cases} \text{recv } \alpha_i\ l\ \varrho(P_i) & \text{if } \alpha_i = c \\ \text{send } \overline{\alpha_i}\ l\ \varrho(P_i) & \text{if } \alpha_i = \overline{c} \\ \text{tau } l\ \varrho(P_i) & \text{if } \alpha_i = \tau \end{cases}$$

Fig. 10. Encoding $TCCS^m$ terms of type c

2. If P_1 has a top-level restriction (i.e. $P_1 \equiv Q \setminus \{a_1, \ldots, a_{n+1}\}$) then

$$\varsigma(\textstyle\prod_{i=1}^{m+1} P_i, \Theta) \triangleq \langle S_1[r_1/a_1, \ldots r_{n+1}/a_{n+1}] \parallel S_2; \Theta_2[r_1, \ldots, r_{n+1} \mapsto \text{MO}], \varnothing \rangle$$

where $\langle S_1; \Theta_1, \varnothing \rangle = \varsigma(Q, \Theta)$ is the translation of the unrestricted process Q, $\langle S_2; \Theta_2, \varnothing \rangle = \varsigma(\prod_{j=1}^{m-1} P_{j+1}, \Theta_1)$ is the translation of the rest of P, all threads have a unique identifier $\text{threads}(S_1) \cap \text{threads}(S_2) = \emptyset$, the heap is extended with n channel variables fresh ($r_1, \ldots, r_{n+1} \notin \text{dom}(\Theta_2)$) and known only to the translation of Q.

3. If $P_1 \equiv \langle\!\langle Q_1 \triangleright_k Q_2 \rangle\!\rangle$ is an active transaction then

$$\varsigma(\textstyle\prod_{i=1}^{m+1} P_i, \Theta) \triangleq \langle S_{co} \parallel S_{ab} \parallel S_1[r_{co}/co] \parallel S_2; \Theta_2[r_l \mapsto True, r_{co} \mapsto \text{MO}], \varnothing \rangle$$

$$S_{co} = (\!|\text{recv } r_l\ r_{co} \triangleright \varrho(Q_1); \text{bang (recv (newVar True) } r_{co})|\!)_{t_{co},k}$$

$$S_{ab} = (\!|\text{abort () } \triangleright \text{return}|\!)_{t_{ab},k}$$

where $\langle S_1; \Theta_1, \varnothing \rangle = \varsigma(Q_1, \Theta)$, $\langle S_2; \Theta_2, \varnothing \rangle = \varsigma(\prod_{j=1}^{m-1} P_{j+1}, \Theta_2)$ (like above), the thread S_{ab} is always ready to abort k as in (TAB) and S_{co} awaits on the private channel r_{co} a thread from S_1 to reach a commit and, after its commit, collects all remaining synchronizations on r_{co} to emulate the effect of Ψ (cf. Figure 7). Finally, all threads have to be uniquely identified: $\text{threads}(S_1) \cap \text{threads}(S_2) = \emptyset$ and $t_{co}, t_{ab} \notin \text{threads}(S_1) \cup \text{threads}(S_2)$

Remark 1. The third case of the definition above can be made more precise (at the cost of a longer definition) since the number of commits to be collected can be inferred from Q mimicking the definition of Ψ. This solution reduces the presence of dangling auxiliary processes and transaction fusions introduced by the cleaning process.

Like ϱ, $\varsigma(P, \Theta)$ contains a free variable for each unrestricted channel in P. Finally, the encoding η is defined on each $P \in \mathsf{Proc}$ as:

$$\eta(P) \triangleq \langle S[r_1/a_1, \dots r_n/a_n]; \Theta[r_1, \dots, r_n \mapsto \texttt{M0}], \varnothing \rangle$$

where $\langle S; \Theta, \varnothing \rangle = \varsigma(P, \varnothing)$, $\{a_1, \dots, a_n\} \subseteq A$ is the set of channels occurring in P, and $\{r_1, \dots, r_n\} \subseteq \mathsf{Loc}$.

Adequacy of translation. In order to prove that the translation η preserves the behaviour of $TCCS^m$ processes, we construct a *simulation relation* $\mathcal{S}$ between well-formed $TCCS^m$ processes and states of $OCTM$. The basic idea is that a single step of P is simulated by a sequence of reductions of $\eta(P)$, and $\eta(P)$ does not exhibit behaviours which are not exhibited by P. To this end we define an appropriate notion of *star simulation*, akin to [11]:

Definition 2 (Star simulation). *A relation* $\mathcal{S} \subseteq \mathsf{Proc} \times \mathsf{State}$ *is a* star simulation *if for all* $(P, \langle S; \Sigma \rangle) \in \mathcal{S}$:

1. *for all Q such that $P \xrightarrow{\tau}_\sigma Q$ or $P \xrightarrow{k(\tau)}_\sigma Q$, there exist S', Σ' such that $\langle S; \Sigma \rangle \to^* \langle S'; \Sigma' \rangle$ and $(Q, \langle S'; \Sigma' \rangle) \in \mathcal{S}$;*

2. *for all Q such that $P \xrightarrow{\beta} Q$, there exist S', Σ' such that $\langle S; \Sigma \rangle \xrightarrow{\beta}^* \langle S'; \Sigma' \rangle$ and $(Q, \langle S'; \Sigma' \rangle) \in \mathcal{S}$.*

3. *for all S', Σ' such that $\langle S; \Sigma \rangle \to \langle S'; \Sigma' \rangle$, there exist Q, S'', Σ'' such that $(Q, \langle S''; \Sigma'' \rangle) \in \mathcal{S}$ and one of the following holds:*

   - $P \xrightarrow{\tau}_\sigma Q$ *or* $P \xrightarrow{k(\tau)}_\sigma Q$, *and* $\langle S'; \Sigma' \rangle \to^* \langle S''; \Sigma'' \rangle$
   - $P \xrightarrow{\beta}_\epsilon Q$ *and* $\langle S'; \Sigma' \rangle \xrightarrow{\beta}^* \langle S''; \Sigma'' \rangle$.

where β-labels of the two transition relations are considered equivalent whenever are both commits or both aborts for the same transaction name. We say that P is star-simulated by $\langle S; \Sigma \rangle$ if there exists a star-simulation $\mathcal{S}$ such that $(P, \langle S; \Sigma \rangle) \in \mathcal{S}$. We denote by $\overset{*}{\approx}$ the largest star simulation.

Another technical issue is that two equivalent $TCCS^m$ processes can be translated to $OCTM$ states which differ only on non-observable aspects, like name renamings, terminated threads, etc. To this end, we need to consider $OCTM$ states up-to an equivalence relation $\cong_t \subseteq \mathsf{State} \times \mathsf{State}$, which we define next.

Definition 3. *Two $OCTM$ states are transaction-equivalent, written $\langle S_1; \Sigma_1 \rangle \cong_t \langle S_2; \Sigma_2 \rangle$, when they are equal up to:*

- *renaming of transaction and thread names;*
- *terminated threads, i.e. threads of one of the following forms:* $(\!|\texttt{return } M|\!)_t$, $(\!|\texttt{abort } M|\!)_t$, $(\!|\texttt{return} \triangleright \texttt{return}|\!)_{t,k}$, $(\!|\texttt{abort} \triangleright \texttt{return}|\!)_{t,k}$, $(\!|\texttt{psi}|\!)_t$;
- *threads blocked in synchronizations on co variables.*

Definition 4. *Let $P \in Proc$ be a well-formed process and $\langle S; \Sigma \rangle$ be a state. P is star simulated by $\langle S; \Sigma \rangle$ up to $\cong_t$ if $(P, \langle S; \Sigma \rangle) \in \overset{*}{\approx} \circ \cong_t$.*

We are now ready to state our main adequacy result, which is a direct consequence of the two next technical lemmata.

Lemma 1. *For all $P, Q \in Proc$ the following hold true:*

1. *if $P \overset{\tau}{\to}_\sigma Q$ or $P \xrightarrow{k(\tau)}_\sigma Q$, there exist S, Σ such that $\eta(P) \to^* \langle S; \Sigma \rangle$ and $\langle S; \Sigma \rangle \cong_t \eta(Q)$;*
2. *if $P \overset{\beta}{\to} Q$, there exist S, Σ such that $\eta(P) \overset{\beta}{\to}^* \langle S; \Sigma \rangle$ and $\langle S; \Sigma \rangle \cong_t \eta(Q)$.*

Proof. By induction on the syntax of P; see [15]. $\qquad\square$

Lemma 2. *For $P \in Proc$, for all S, Σ, if $\eta(P) \to \langle S; \Sigma \rangle$ then there exist Q, S', Σ' such that $\langle S'; \Sigma' \rangle \cong_t \eta(Q)$ and one of the following holds:*

- *$P \overset{\tau}{\to}_\sigma Q$ or $P \xrightarrow{k(\tau)}_\sigma Q$, and $\langle S; \Sigma \rangle \to^* \langle S'; \Sigma' \rangle$;*
- *$P \overset{\beta}{\to}_\epsilon Q$ and $\langle S; \Sigma \rangle \overset{\beta}{\to}^* \langle S'; \Sigma' \rangle$.*

Proof. By induction on the semantics of $\eta(P)$; see [15]. $\qquad\square$

Theorem 1. *For all $P \in Proc$, P is star simulated by $\eta(P)$ up to $\cong_t$.*

5   Conclusions and Future Work

In this paper we have introduced $OCTM$, a higher-order language extending the concurrency model of STM Haskell with composable *open (multi-thread)* transactions. In this language, processes can *join* transactions and transactions can *merge* at runtime. These interactions are driven only by access to shared transactional memory, and hence are implicit and loosely coupled. To this end, we have separated the isolation aspect from atomicity: the `atomic` construct ensures "all-or-nothing" execution but not isolation, while the new constructor `isolated` can be used to guarantee isolation when needed. In order to show the expressive power of $OCTM$, we have provided an adequate implementation in it of $TCCS^m$, a recently introduced model of open transactions with CCS-like communication. As a side result, we have given a simple typing system for capturing $TCCS^m$ well-formed terms.

Several directions for future work stem from the present paper. First, we plan to implement $OCTM$ along the line of STM Haskell, but clearly the basic ideas of $OCTM$ are quite general and can be applied to other STM implementations, like C/C++ LibCMT and Java Multiverse. Then, we can use $TCCS^m$ as an *exogenous orchestration language* for $OCTM$: the *behaviour* of a transactional distributed system can be described as a $TCCS^m$ term, which can be translated into a *skeleton* in $OCTM$ using the encoding provided in this paper; then, the programmer has only to "fill in the gaps". Thus, $TCCS^m$ can be seen as a kind of "global behavioural type" for $OCTM$.

In fact, defining a proper behavioural typing system for transactional languages like $OCTM$ is another interesting future work. Some preliminary experiments have shown that $TCCS^m$ is not enough expressive for modelling the dynamic creation of resources (locations, threads, etc.). We think that a good candidate could be a variant of $TCCS^m$ with local names and scope extrusions, i.e., a "transactional π-calculus".

Being based on CCS, communication in $TCCS^m$ is synchronous; however, nowadays asynchronous models play an important rôle (see e.g. actors, event-driven programming, etc.). It may be interesting to generalize the discussion so as to consider also this case, e.g. by defining an actor-based calculus with open transactions. Such a calculus can be quite useful also for modelling speculative reasoning for cooperating systems [13, 14]. A local version of actor-based open transactions can be implemented in $OCTM$ using lock-free data structures (e.g., message queues) in shared transactional memory.

Acknowledgement. We thank the anonymous referees for useful remarks and suggestions on the preliminary version of this paper. This work is partially supported by MIUR PRIN project 2010LHT4KM, *CINA*.

References

1. Abadi, M., Birrell, A., Harris, T., Isard, M.: Semantics of transactional memory and automatic mutual exclusion. ACM Trans. Program. Lang. Syst. 33(1), 2 (2011)
2. Bruni, R., Melgratti, H.C., Montanari, U.: Nested commits for mobile calculi: Extending join. In: Lévy, J., Mayr, E.W., Mitchell, J.C. (eds.) Proc. TCS. IFIP, vol. 155, pp. 563–576. Springer, Heidelberg (2004)
3. Danos, V., Krivine, J.: Transactions in RCCS. In: Abadi, M., de Alfaro, L. (eds.) CONCUR 2005. LNCS, vol. 3653, pp. 398–412. Springer, Heidelberg (2005)
4. de Vries, E., Koutavas, V., Hennessy, M.: Communicating transactions (extended abstract). In: Gastin, P., Laroussinie, F. (eds.) CONCUR 2010. LNCS, vol. 6269, pp. 569–583. Springer, Heidelberg (2010)
5. de Vries, E., Koutavas, V., Hennessy, M.: Liveness of communicating transactions (extended abstract). In: Ueda, K. (ed.) APLAS 2010. LNCS, vol. 6461, pp. 392–407. Springer, Heidelberg (2010)
6. Gray, J., Lamport, L.: Consensus on transaction commit. ACM Transactions Database Systems 31(1), 133–160 (2006)
7. Harris, T., Marlow, S., Jones, S.L.P., Herlihy, M.: Composable memory transactions. In: Proc. PPOPP, pp. 48–60 (2005)
8. Herlihy, M., Moss, J.E.B.: Transactional memory: Architectural support for lock-free data structures. In: Smith, A.J. (ed.) Proceedings of the 20th Annual International Symposium on Computer Architecture, pp. 289–300. ACM (1993)
9. Herlihy, M., Shavit, N.: Transactional memory: beyond the first two decades. SIGACT News 43(4), 101–103 (2012)
10. Koutavas, V., Spaccasassi, C., Hennessy, M.: Bisimulations for communicating transactions - (extended abstract). In: Muscholl, A. (ed.) FOSSACS 2014 (ETAPS). LNCS, vol. 8412, pp. 320–334. Springer, Heidelberg (2014)
11. Leroy, X.: A formally verified compiler back-end. Journal of Automated Reasoning 43(4), 363–446 (2009)

12. Lesani, M., Palsberg, J.: Communicating memory transactions. In: Cascaval, C., Yew, P. (eds.) Proc. PPOPP, pp. 157–168. ACM (2011)
13. Ma, J., Broda, K., Goebel, R., Hosobe, H., Russo, A., Satoh, K.: Speculative abductive reasoning for hierarchical agent systems. In: Dix, J., Leite, J., Governatori, G., Jamroga, W. (eds.) CLIMA XI. LNCS, vol. 6245, pp. 49–64. Springer, Heidelberg (2010)
14. Mansutti, A., Miculan, M., Peressotti, M.: Multi-agent systems design and prototyping with bigraphical reactive systems. In: Magoutis, K., Pietzuch, P. (eds.) DAIS 2014. LNCS, vol. 8460, pp. 201–208. Springer, Heidelberg (2014)
15. Miculan, M., Peressotti, M., Toneguzzo, A.: Open transactions on shared memory. CoRR, abs/1503.09097 (2015)
16. Milner, R.: A Calculus of Communication Systems. LNCS, vol. 92. Springer, Heidelberg (1980)
17. Shavit, N., Touitou, D.: Software transactional memory. Distributed Computing 10(2), 99–116 (1997)

VISIRI - Distributed Complex Event Processing System for Handling Large Number of Queries

Malinda Kumarasinghe, Geeth Tharanga, Lasitha Weerasinghe[✉],
Ujitha Wickramarathna, and Surangika Ranathunga

Department of Computer Science and Engineering, Faculty of Engineering,
University of Moratuwa, Katubedda, Sri Lanka

Abstract. Complex event processing (CEP) systems are used to process event data from multiple sources to infer events corresponding to more complicated situations. Traditional CEP systems with central processing engines have failed to cater to the requirement of processing large number of events generated from a large number of geographically distributed sources. Distributed CEP systems have been identified as the best alternative for this. However, designing an optimal distributed CEP system is a non-trivial task, and many factors have to be considered when designing the same. This paper presents the VISIRI distributed CEP system, which focuses on the problem of optimally processing a large number of different type of event streams using a large number of CEP queries in a distributed manner. The CEP query distribution algorithm in VISIRI is able to distribute a large number of queries among a set of CEP nodes in such a way that the event duplication in the network is minimized while not compromising the overall throughput of the system.

Keywords: Complex Event Processing,Distributed systems,Algorithms

1 Introduction

Complex event processing (CEP) systems are used to process event data from multiple sources to infer events corresponding to more complicated situations. Traditional CEP systems with central processing engines have failed to cater to the requirement of processing large number of events generated from a large number of geographically distributed sources [2,4]. Distributed CEP systems have been identified as the best alternative for this.

The middleware of complex event processing systems can be internally built around several distributed complex event processors. These processors cooperate in processing and routing events sent from event sources, and finally in delivering results to the required event sinks [1]. A processor makes use of a CEP engine internally to process the incoming events. This is done using CEP queries. Query is a mechanism for extracting events that satisfy a rule or a pattern, from incoming events. A query may contain operators such as filter, window, join, pattern and sequence.

However, simply having a middleware is not sufficient to have a distributed CEP system. Crucial decisions have to be taken on how to distribute the load

© IFIP International Federation for Information Processing 2015
T. Holvoet and M. Viroli (Eds.): COORDINATION 2015, LNCS 9037, pp. 230–245, 2015.
DOI: 10.1007/978-3-319-19282-6_15

among the complex event processing nodes in the system. There are two approaches in distributing the processing load among nodes : operator distribution and query distribution [1,4]. Operator distribution refers to the approach of dividing a query into a distinct sequence of steps to handle complex queries. Each step is allocated to a node in the system. Query distribution allocates a set of queries among the nodes of the distributed system. There are several application scenarios in distributing complex event processing as well: (1) handling large number of CEP queries and event streams, (2) handling event streams that have high event frequencies and/or large events, and (3) handling complex resource intensive queries.

VISIRI is a distributed complex event processing system for handling large number of queries and large number of different types of event streams. It presents a lightweight middleware for a distributed CEP system, and the communication among the nodes in the system is achieved via Hazelcast [3].

Its approach on distributing the processing load is by query distribution. Distributing queries in an optimal manner is a NP-Hard problem [8]. When distributing a large number of queries among a set of CEP nodes, many concerns have to be addressed. These include the throughput of the overall system, network latency in transmitting events from event sources to CEP nodes, balancing resource utilization at processing nodes, and reducing event duplication when transmitting events from sources to nodes. Existing research on query distribution focused on optimizing a subset of these concerns. For example, the COSMOS project [8] focused on reducing network latency and reducing communication between the nodes. The SCTXPF system [4] focused only on reducing the event duplication network traffic within the system.

The most important aspect of the VISIRI system is its query distribution algorithm. It focuses on reducing the event duplication network traffic within the system while making sure that the processing load is evenly distributed among the nodes. Load on a node is calculated by considering the cost of the CEP queries. The cost of queries is calculated by the cost model, which is based on the empirical studies done by Mendes et al. [5] and Schilling et al. [6]. With this query distribution algorithm, VISIRI balances the resource utilization of the CEP nodes, so that no node gets overloaded (given that there is no sudden change in the incoming event streams) and adversely affects the throughput of the overall system.

The rest of the paper is organized as follows. Section 2 discusses literature related to query distribution in distributed CEP systems, and empirical studies on the cost of CEP queries. Section 3 presents the design and implementation of the VISIRI distributed CEP system, along with detailed descriptions of its query distribution algorithm and the cost model. Section 4 presents evaluation results and finally section 5 concludes the paper.

2   Related Work

SCTXPF [4] and COSMOS [8] are examples of distributed CEP systems based on query distribution.

The query distribution algorithm in the SCTXPF system is optimized for large number of complex event processing queries and for very high events rates. It parallelizes the event processors (EPs) and then allocates certain number of CEP queries to each of them. In this algorithm, queries with common sets of attributes are assigned to the same node. This minimizes the number of EPs that need the same event streams and thus minimizes the number of multicasts. Therefore the system is able to reduce the event duplication network traffic within it. However, this algorithm assumes that all the queries require the same processing power, which is not the case most of the times. Even if two queries consume the same set of attributes, their computational intensiveness (i.e. the amount of computer resources it requires) could have very large differences. This is because the computational intensiveness of a query heavily depends on its operators. However, when the set of queries are simply divided among the nodes by the SCTXPF algorithm, each node has the same number of queries, and some nodes that have lot of high cost queries could easily get overloaded.

In contrast to the SCTXPF algorithm, VISIRI query distribution algorithm considers the cost of each query when distributing the queries among the processing nodes. This is the main difference between the two algorithms.

The COSMOS distributed CEP system employs a heuristic based graph mapping algorithm to distribute the load among CEP nodes. In this approach, processors are represented by vertices and communication latency is represented by the weight of the edges. When distributing queries, this network latency is considered. Furthermore this algorithm filters out the events from the initial nodes so that network traffic of the internal system is reduced. This model suits a problem where a particular set of queries are interested in the output of another set of queries. However, this algorithm also does not consider the cost of individual queries when distributing them among CEP nodes.

Schilling et al. [6] have studied about the cost of executing different query operators in their empirical study. According to their study, filter rules have the lowest latency and logical rules have much higher latency. Temporal windows have the highest latency. Therefore such temporal windows should be given the highest weight when considering the latency and computational intensiveness. When considering the cost versus size of the history of the temporal windows, this study suggests an exponential growth in cost. Cost versus the number of attributes has no such growth and it is almost the same for any number of attributes. However, when the number of queries in a CEP node increases, the cost increases linearly.

Furthermore Marcelo et al. [5] have studied about different engine types and how they perform on different query types. They have identified that sliding windows and jumping windows have huge differences in performance, where sliding windows take much computational power.

3   VISIRI Distributed CEP System

Figure 1 shows the VISIRI high level architecture. It consists of event sources, dispatchers, CEP nodes and event sinks. Here, event sources generate the low-level events, and the complex events identified by the CEP nodes are received by the event sources.

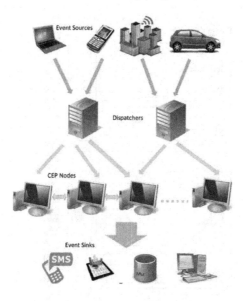

Fig. 1. VISIRI high level architecture

VISIRI CEP system assumes nearly homogeneous CEP nodes. User can freely select one CEP node and deploy the queries. After deploying the queries, that particular CEP node plays the role as the main node, which executes the query distribution algorithm (discussed later in this section). This query distribution algorithm distributes the queries among all the active CEP nodes in the system. Then the allocated queries are automatically deployed in the CEP nodes and the dispatcher is notified about the query allocation.

Dispatcher creates the forwarding table according to query allocation. Forwarding table is a map of event stream ID to the list of CEP node IPs. Job of the dispatcher is to forward the relevant event streams only to the relevant CEP nodes. Thus in contrast to directly sending events from sources to CEP nodes, employing a dispatcher reduces network traffic. Event sources send event streams to the dispatcher and using its forwarding table dispatcher forwards these event streams to relevant CEP nodes where event processing happens according to the deployed queries in CEP nodes. After processing the event streams, the resulted event streams from the CEP nodes are sent to the event sink.

3.1   Low Level Architecture

Figure 2 shows how the low-level architectural components are integrated within the system. Arrows show the flow of the event streams among different components.

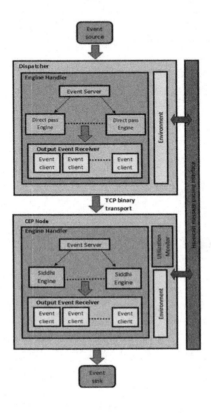

Fig. 2. VISIRI low level architecture

– Siddhi CEP engine [7] - In a CEP node, the light-weight Siddhi CEP engine is used as the processing engine. As shown in Figure 2, there is a Siddhi engine per one query in one CEP node. Siddhi engine processes the input event streams and results the output event stream. This architecture allows our system to extend to make dynamic adjustments on query distribution in runtime.
– Event client/Server - Uses TCP binary communication protocol to transport event streams.
– Environment - Each node in the system(processing node/dispatcher node) includes a its own Environment component and all data sharing tasks and message passing tasks between nodes are achieved via this component. It uses hazelcast as an intermediate interface for this communication.

3.2 Query Distribution Algorithm

The VISIRI query distribution algorithm considers the SCTXPF algorithm as its starting point. As described earlier, the SCTXPF algorithm aims at minimizing the number of event processors that need the same event streams and also reducing the difference between the numbers of queries deployed in the event processing nodes. The major improvement of the VISIRI algorithm over the SCTXPF algorithm is that it considers the cost of individual queries to make sure that queries with higher costs are not deployed in the same node. This prevents one node getting overloaded while some other nodes of the system are under-utilized.

VISIRI algorithm takes following inputs when distributing queries[1].

- Set of queries to be distributed
- Set of processing nodes and dispatchers
- Queries currently allocated for each node

The algorithm considers the following important factors:

- Costs of the queries (depending on the complexity of query operators)
- Number of existing queries in each node
- Number of common event types required for the query

A suitable cost model calculator is required to measure the complexity and costs of the queries. These costs may also depend on the underlying implementation of the complex event processing engine. However, this aspect is not considered in the VISIRI cost model. The cost model is discussed in the next section.

Algorithm 1 gives the pseudo code of our query distribution algorithm.

Line 3 finds the minimum number of queries currently assigned to a single node.

Lines 5-9 remove all nodes that have queries above a certain threshold. This is to balance the overhead of having large number of queries in the same node.

Lines 11-18 refer to the procedure to find the minimum total cost of a node. Here the total cost of a node is calculated by taking the sum of the costs of the queries deployed in that node.

In lines 20-24, all nodes having costs more than a certain threshold value are removed from the candidate list to balance the cost distribution among the nodes.

Lines 26-38 finds the nodes having maximum number of input streams in common with the given query. For example, if the query has input streams s1, s2 and s3, and queries already deployed in a Node A have s2, s3 and s4 as input streams, then node A and the query has 2 common input streams (s2 and s3). Here the input streams of a node are the union of all input streams of deployed queries. In this code segment, nodes with maximum number of common input streams are selected so that the number of new events that need to be sent over the network as inputs is minimized. This reduces event duplication and preserves network bandwidth. Here we assume all event types arrive in same frequency.

---

[1] The algorithm iteratively distributes queries, with one iteration per query.

Algorithm 1. Query distribution algorithm

Require: Query q, Node[] nodes
1: candidates = nodes;
2: //find minimum queries
3: min-queries = min(nodes[0].queryCount,nodes[1].queryCount,...)
4: //filter nodes with too many queries
5: **for** node in candidates **do**
6:     **if** node.queryCount >minQueries + QueryVariability **then**
7:         candidates.remove(node)
8:     **end if**
9: **end for**
10: //find minimum total cost
11: minCost = infinity
12: **for** node in candidates **do**
13:     cost = sum(node.queries[0].cost,node.queries[1].cost, ...)
14:     node.cost = cost
15:     **if** minCost >cost **then**
16:         minCost = cost
17:     **end if**
18: **end for**
19: //filter nodes with too much cost
20: **for** node in candidates **do**
21:     **if** node.cost >minCost + CostVariability **then**
22:         candidates.remove(node)
23:     **end if**
24: **end for**
25: //find maximum common event types
26: qInputs = q.inputStreams
27: maxCommonNodes =[]
28: maxCommonInputs = 0
29: **for** node in candidates **do**
30:     node.allInputs = union(node.queries[0].inputStreams,node.queries[1].inputStreams.)
31:     commons = count(intersect(qInputs,node.allInputs))
32:     **if** maxCommonInputs == commons **then**
33:         maxCommonNodes.add(node)
34:     **else if** maxCommonInputs >commons **then**
35:         maxCommonNodes.clear()
36:         maxCommonNodes.add(node)
37:         maxCommonInputs = commons
38:     **end if**
39: **end for**
40: candidates = maxCommonNodes
41: //select one randomly from the candidates
42: target = random.select(candidates)
43: **return** target

3.3 Cost Model

In order to calculate the cost of a given query, we have developed a cost model that gives a numeric value for a query based on the empirical studies done by Schilling et al. [6] and Marcelo et al. [5].

The cost model first identifies the queries that have filtering parts and assigns them cost values depending on the number of filtering attributes. Furthermore, a cost value is assigned to the number of attributes in the input stream definitions and the output stream definitions. This is because the literature [6] suggests that when the number of attributes in the event streams for a particular query increases the resource requirement for that query increases. Apart from that, the number of input streams and the output streams count is also added to the cost value. These values are expected to give an indication of the impact of handling large number of event streams in a query.

The cost model gives a much higher priority to queries with windows. Depending on the window length, an exponential cost is added to the query so that windows with higher length will get a higher number. Our cost model can support window queries of time or length with the expiration mode of sliding or batch.

Finally the logarithmic value of the total cost value is obtained so that the cost value can be restricted to a more meaningful range. Our cost model still does not give exact accurate values for pattern queries and join queries, but a simple numerical value depending on the aforementioned factors is given to them. In order to obtain a more accurate number, a good performance analysis has to be done on those types of queries.

Table 1 shows how the cost value changes for three different sample queries with different time windows[1].

Table 1. Sample queries and their costs generated by the cost model

	Query	Cost Value
1	from cseEventStream[price==foo.price and foo.try <5 in foo] select symbol, avg(price) as avgPrice	3.1986731175506815
2	from car [Id >=10]#window.length(10000) select brand,Id insert into filterCar;	13.815633550400394
3	from StockExchangeStream[symbol == IBM]#window.time(1 year) select max(price) as maxPrice, avg(price) as avgPrice, min(price) as minPrice insert into IBMStockQuote for all-events	31.664045840884167

4   Evaluation

4.1   Event and Query Model

Since our target is to handle large number of queries, we used randomly generated events and randomly generated queries to evaluate our system. Our system is capable of configuring the number of input event streams and the number of output

---

[1] Queries are expressed in Siddhi event processing language.

stream definitions. For evaluation purposes, we used 1000 event stream definitions and 500 output stream definitions. When generating the random queries
we use those input stream definitions and produce results to the output stream
definitions.

In our query model we initially generated a set of simple queries with around
two maximum filtering conditions and with only the length batch windows. But
later we increased the complexities of the queries to get the proper advantage
from our cost estimation model.

In our random query generator, several types of queries such as filter queries,
window queries and windows with filter queries can be created. A query may
contain either one filtering condition or two filtering conditions. In the window
queries scenario, the random query generator gives either length windows or
length batch windows and it outputs the aggregated result like maximum, sum
or average value within the window. The window length is also given by a random
value.

Below given are some of the sample Siddhi queries that were generated by the
random query generator.

```
from  stream2
   [ attr3 < 45.18  and  attr1 > 71.6  and  attr5 > 63.37
    and  attr4 > 35.71  and  attr1 > 83.35  and  attr2 > 89.95
    and  attr3 < 50.0  and  attr2 < 15.83]
   select  attr1  insert  into  stream46

from  stream2
   [ attr4 < 94.05  and  attr1 > 83.05  and  attr5 > 46.27
    and  attr2 < 34.01  and  attr2 < 32.74  and  attr3 > 59.25
    and  attr5 > 94.62  and  attr1 > 4.06]#window.lengthBatch(104)
   select   max( attr1 )  as  attr1 ,  max( attr2 )  as  attr2
   insert  into  stream3

from  stream2 # window.lengthBatch(210)
   select   max( attr1 )  as  attr1 ,  max( attr2 )  as  attr2
   insert  into  stream14
```

The queries were generated with the same seed value for the random generator
therefore the same set of queries is obtained all the time for the same number of
queries, input definitions and output definitions. Having exact queries and events
was important have a fair comparison when evaluating different algorithms and
over different configurations. Event sources were configured to generate events
in maximum rate possible.

4.2   Query Distribution Algorithm Comparison

To evaluate our algorithm we compared it with the SCTXPF algorithm and a
random query distribution algorithm. When comparing the algorithms, mainly
two factors were considered: total query execution cost variance and event duplication. As the execution cost variance we measured how much variance the
processing nodes have when the queries are distributed with respect to the es-

timated cost values. Cost threshold value (highest total cost of the queries deployed in a CEP node) for our algorithm was kept at 400 while keeping query count threshold (highest number of queries deployed in a CEP node) at 80 for both our and SCTXPF algorithm. Those values were selected to get maximum performance from the machines we used for the performance evaluation later in the evaluation process.

Multicasting of events from dispatcher to CEP nodes is a critical factor for network overhead of the system. Our algorithm focuses on minimizing the number of CEP nodes that needs same type of events by placing similar type of queries in a single node. Figure 3, Figure 4 and Figure 5 show how the event duplication changes in the system for the three different algorithms for 1000, 5000 and 10000 queries.

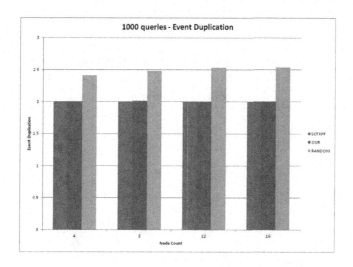

Fig. 3. Event stream duplication for 1000 queries

As can be seen in the figures, our algorithm and SCTXPF algorithm have given similar results for the event duplication as expected. Random algorithm shows clear difference in event duplication, which suggests that randomly distributing queries leads to network traffic increase within the system. Furthermore when the number of queries increases, the event duplication almost remains same for our algorithm and SCTXPF algorithm but in the random query distribution algorithm it increases drastically.

When the cost variance among the processing nodes is considered, our algorithm was able to gain a considerable advantage over the other two algorithms when the number of queries increases. Figure 6, Figure 7 and Figure 8 show how the cost variance behaves when the number of nodes increases for 1000, 5000 and 10000 queries.

According to these results we can conclude that when the number of queries increases, our algorithm is able to deploy the queries among the processing nodes

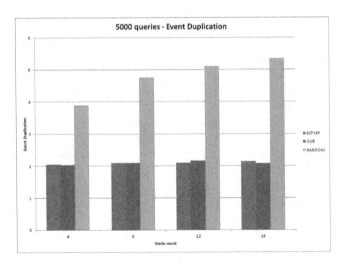

Fig. 4. Event stream duplication for 5000 queries

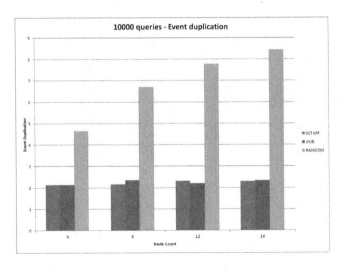

Fig. 5. Event stream duplication for 10000 queries

with minimum cost variance. Therefore all the processing nodes will receive queries with relatively equal estimated processing cost according to our cost model.

4.3 Performance Evaluation

For this performance evaluation we used the same event and query model that we used for the algorithm evaluation described above in the section 4.1.

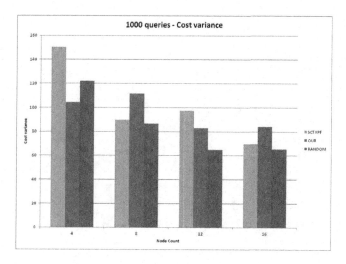

Fig. 6. Total cost variance for 1000 queries

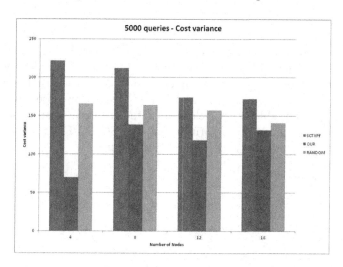

Fig. 7. Total cost variance for 5000 queries

System Configurations: For this evaluation we have used a computer lab that has Core i3 machines of 3.2 GHz. The operating system was Ubuntu 12.04 32 bit version. Each machine had 2GB RAM and the machines were connected using a 100Mbps Ethernet connection.

Results: For the performance analysis we have sent 15 sets of 1,000,000 events through the system and evaluated the throughput by averaging the total time taken for processing those sets of events.

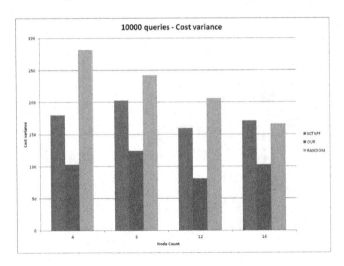

Fig. 8. Total cost variance for 10000 queries

Initially we evaluated the system for 5000 simple queries, which had around two filtering conditions and smaller length batch windows. Figure 9 shows results for this set of queries. For this set of queries, our algorithm and the SCTXPF algorithm performed in a similar manner. This is because for those simple queries our algorithm was not able to get a clear advantage from the cost model we have generated. However, both our algorithm and the SCTXPF algorithm perform better than the random query distribution algorithm.

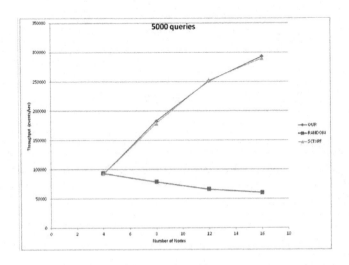

Fig. 9. Throughput for simple 5000 queries

As shown in Figure 10, the throughput changes according to the number of nodes for 2500 queries. There is a clear improvement of throughput in our algorithm for this case.

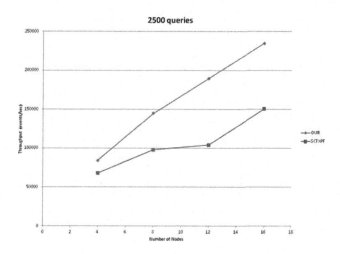

Fig. 10. Throughput for 2500 queries

Figure 11 shows how our system behaves in the case of 5000 queries and both the algorithms show less improvement when moving from 8 nodes to 12 nodes.

Figure 12 is from the results that were taken for 10000 queries. We were not able to run the case of four nodes due to the low memory capacities of the machines. And we observed a slight decrement of throughput from nodes 8 to 12.

Results Evaluation: According to the results, it can be said that our algorithm is able to deploy queries among the set of processing nodes with minimum cost variation while keeping event duplication at a low level when compared with the SCTXPF and random algorithms.

Furthermore when system throughput is considered, our algorithm has a clear advantage over the SCTXPF for all three cases- 2500 queries, 5000 queries and 10000 queries. Also we can observe that in that evaluation scenario, almost in all the cases when the number of nodes increases the throughput of the system with our algorithm increases. Therefore with higher number of nodes our algorithm is able to provide much higher throughput. However bottleneck situations with respect to network bandwidth at event sinks may arise when the number of nodes increases due to large number of queries being processed and all of them producing outputs. In the case of 10000 queries when increasing nodes 8 to 12 we can observe this kind of scenario.

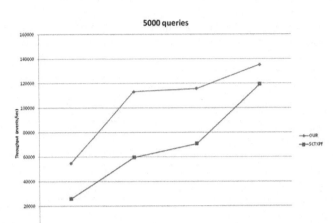

Fig. 11. Throughput for 5000 queries

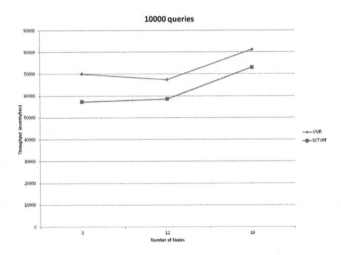

Fig. 12. Throughput for 10000 queries

5   Conclusion

This paper discussed the architecture of the VISIRI distributed CEP system, which aims at handling large number of queries and large number of different types of event streams. It includes a query distribution algorithm that takes event stream duplication and the estimated query execution cost into consideration when allocating queries among a set of processing nodes.

With that query distribution algorithm, VISIRI system is able to keep the event stream duplication below a certain level while the total cost variance among the processing nodes is kept low when compared to some other algorithms for distributing number of CEP queries. Furthermore we evaluated our system for the performance by considering the throughput as the measuring factor and our algorithm had a clear advantage over the existing algorithms.

As a future enhancement, VISIRI can be improved to support query rewriting at the dispatcher level so that unnecessary events can be filtered from the dispatcher thus reducing the internal network traffic further. Apart from that, the VISIRI system architecture can also be extended to support heterogeneous event processing engines so that different types of queries can be processed by different processing engines according to the types of queries they are best at processing. Furthermore our query distribution algorithm can also be extended to support factors such as network latency. However, we once again emphasize that coming up with an optimal query distribution algorithm that considers all these factors is a NP-hard problem.

References

1. Cugola, G., Margara, A.: Deployment strategies for distributed complex event processing. Computing 95(2), 129–156 (2013)
2. Etzion, O., Niblett, P.: Event processing in action. Manning Publications Co. (2010)
3. Hazelcast.com. Hazelcast - leading in-memory data grid IMDG (January 2015)
4. Isoyama, K., Kobayashi, Y., Sato, T., Kida, K., Yoshida, M., Tagato, H.: A scalable complex event processing system and evaluations of its performance. In: Proceedings of the 6th ACM International Conference on Distributed Event-Based Systems, pp. 123–126. ACM (2012)
5. Mendes, M.R.N., Bizarro, P., Marques, P.: A performance study of event processing systems. In: Nambiar, R., Poess, M. (eds.) TPCTC 2009. LNCS, vol. 5895, pp. 221–236. Springer, Heidelberg (2009)
6. Schilling, B., Koldehofe, B., Pletat, U., Rothermel, K.: Distributed heterogeneous event processing. DEBS (2012)
7. Suhothayan, S., Gajasinghe, K., Narangoda, I.L., Chaturanga, S., Perera, S., Nanayakkara, V.: Siddhi: A second look at complex event processing architectures. In: Proceedings of the 2011 ACM Workshop on Gateway Computing Environments, pp. 43–50. ACM (2011)
8. Zhou, Y., Aberer, K., Tan, K.-L.: Toward massive query optimization in large-scale distributed stream systems. In: Proceedings of the 9th ACM/IFIP/USENIX International Conference on Middleware, pp. 326–345. Springer-Verlag New York, Inc. (2008)

Author Index

Printed in the United States
By Bookmasters